The Right to Difference

The Right to Difference

French Universalism and the Jews

MAURICE SAMUELS

The University of Chicago Press
Chicago and London

The University of Chicago Press, Chicago 60637
The University of Chicago Press, Ltd., London
© 2016 by The University of Chicago
All rights reserved. No part of this book may be used or reproduced in any
manner whatsoever without written permission, except in the case of
brief quotations in critical articles and reviews. For more information, contact
the University of Chicago Press, 1427 E. 60th St., Chicago, IL 60637.
Published 2016
Paperback edition 2019

The University of Chicago Press gratefully acknowledges the generous support of
the Judaic Studies Program at Yale University toward the publication of this book.

28 27 26 25 24 23 22 21 20 19   1 2 3 4 5

ISBN-13: 978-0-226-39705-4 (cloth)
ISBN-13: 978-0-226-67732-3 (paper)
ISBN-13: 978-0-226-39932-4 (e-book)
DOI: https://doi.org/10.7208/chicago/9780226399324.001.0001

Library of Congress Cataloging-in-Publication Data

Names: Samuels, Maurice, author.
Title: The right to difference : French universalism and the Jews / Maurice Samuels.
Description: Chicago ; London : The University of Chicago Press, 2016. |
   Includes bibliographical references and index.
Identifiers: LCCN 2016011295 | ISBN 9780226397054 (cloth : alk. paper) |
   ISBN 9780226399324 (e-book)
Subjects: LCSH: Jews—France—Social conditions. | Antisemitism—France. |
   Jews in literature.
Classification: LCC DS135.F83 S25 2016 | DDC 305.892/4044—dc23
LC record available at http://lccn.loc.gov/2016011295

for my teachers

Contents

Acknowledgments ix

Introduction 1
1 The Revolution Reconsidered 17
2 France's Jewish Star 50
3 Universalism in Algeria 73
4 Zola and the Dreyfus Affair 95
5 The Jew in Renoir's *La grande illusion* 117
6 Sartre's "Jewish Question" 139
7 Finkielkraut, Badiou, and the "New Antisemitism" 162
Conclusion: "Je suis juif" 186

Notes 197
Index 229

Acknowledgments

I could not have completed this book without the aid of many friends and colleagues, as well as the support of a number of institutions. It is a pleasure to have the chance to thank them here.

My thanks go first to the John Simon Guggenheim Foundation for enabling me to take a year away from teaching to complete this book. I am extremely grateful to Yale University for believing in humanities research and providing the resources to make it possible. Yale's Program in Judaic Studies generously offered a publication subvention. Librarians in France and the United States, especially at the Bibliothèque nationale de France and Yale University, have been extraordinarily helpful. I also thank all the institutions at which I had the opportunity to present this material; feedback from colleagues and students at these talks has proven invaluable.

Alan Thomas at the University of Chicago Press has been an inspiring and judicious editor. Two extremely knowledgeable anonymous readers gave detailed feedback on the manuscript, and the book is far better for their effort. Randolph Petilos, Perry Cartwright, and the rest of the staff at the Press shepherded the book through production with skill and care. India Cooper did a superb job copyediting the manuscript.

I have dedicated this book to my teachers, and these include Naomi Schor, who was working on French universalism when she died and whose insights have shaped my thinking in profound ways. Susan Suleiman has been an intellectual role model since I was an undergraduate. She contributed to this project all along the way but was never more helpful than at the last minute, when she convinced me that I needed a better title. Jann Matlock has been a generous mentor, a salient critic, and a valued friend for two decades.

I am extremely fortunate to work with colleagues I not only esteem but genuinely like. Alice Kaplan introduced me to her editor and gave copious feedback on numerous drafts of this book. She has been ingeniously supportive on a daily basis and has made work a pleasure. Francesca Trivellato read large sections of the manuscript and has been generous with her insight and friendship. Howard Bloch and David Sorkin provided valuable feedback on individual chapters. Carolyn Dean has been an especially cherished interlocutor. I'm also very grateful to current and former colleagues at Yale who have contributed to this project in different ways: Bruno Cabanes, Steven Fraade, Tamar Gendler, Hannan Hever, Amy Hungerford, Paula Hyman, Kathryn Lofton, Ivan Marcus, Maria Menocal, John Merriman, Christopher Miller, Mary Miller, Hindy Najman, James Ponet, Steven Smith, and Elli Stern. I have taught this material in several undergraduate seminars and learned much from my students. Clémentine Fauré-Bellaïche and Colin Foss were always willing to lend research assistance. Agnes Bolton, Inessa Laskova, and Renee Reed provided expert administrative support.

As someone who works on the border between French and Jewish studies, I am very lucky to have met smart and generous colleagues in both disciplines. I extend my thanks to Phyllis Albert, Emily Apter, Lia Brozgal, David F. Bell, Dorian Bell, Pierre Birnbaum, Marc Caplan, Vincent Debaene, David Feldman, Jonathan Hess, Deborah Jenson, Jonathan Judaken, Ethan Katz, Sara Kippur, Elisabeth Ladenson, Lisa Leff, Bettina Lerner, Maud Mandel, Rachel Mesch, Philippe Met, Sven-Erik Rose, Alvin Rosenfeld, Henry Rousso, Debarati Sanyal, Ronald Schechter, Alyssa Sepinwall, Andrew Sobanet, Jonathan Strauss, Patrick Weil, Nicolas Weill, Liliane Weissberg, Nicholas White, and Robert Wistrich. Rachel Brownstein, Bruno Chaouat, Dan Edelstein, Steven Englund, and Julie Kalman provided smart comments on different parts of the manuscript. Peter Brooks, Françoise Lionnet, and Aron Rodrigue lent incredibly valuable support. Elisabeth Hodges, Jennifer Siegel, Jacob Soll, and Caroline Weber have shared the ups and downs of this project over the years, and I'm very thankful for their friendship. Olga Borovaya and Lawrence Kritzman also went above and beyond the call of duty.

Ghita Schwarz and Elliot Thomson are not only the best of friends but also the best of editors, and I can never thank them enough for all their help. My other nonacademic friends have been constantly supportive, and while I can't thank all of them here, I do want to single out a few who helped this project along in specific ways: Elisabeth Franck, David Geller, Ethan Herschenfeld, Valerie Steiker, Laura van Straaten, and Gillian Thomas. My family, especially Richard and Barbara Samuels, continue to make everything possible.

ACKNOWLEDGMENTS

✶

A portion of chapter 3 appeared in an earlier form as "Philosemitism and the *mission civilisatrice* in Gautier's *La Juive de Constantine*" in *French Forum* 38, nos. 1–2 (2013): 19–34. A portion of chapter 4 appeared in an earlier form as "Zola's Philosemitism: From *L'Argent* to *Vérité*" in *Romanic Review* 102, nos. 3–4 (January 2013): 503–19, copyright by the Trustees of Columbia University in the City of New York. A portion of chapter 5 appeared in an earlier form as "Renoir's *La Grande Illusion* and the 'Jewish Question'" in *Historical Reflections/Réflexions Historiques* 32, no. 1 (Spring 2006): 165–92, reprinted with permission. A portion of chapter 7 appeared in an earlier form as "Alain Badiou and Antisemitism" in *Being Contemporary*, edited by Lia Brozgal and Sarah Kippur (Liverpool: Liverpool University Press, 2016). A revised version of chapter 1 will appear in *Revisioning French Culture*, edited by Andrew Sobanet (Liverpool: University of Liverpool Press, 2017). I thank the editors for allowing me to use the revised material here.

Introduction

On January, 7, 2015, two gunmen forced their way into an editorial meeting of the French satirical journal *Charlie Hebdo* and opened fire, killing eleven and wounding eleven more. Among the dead that Wednesday morning were some of France's most celebrated cartoonists, political commentators who had made irreverence toward organized religion their trademark. The gunmen were brothers, French citizens of Algerian descent with ties to al-Qaeda in Yemen, enraged by the journal's mocking depictions of the prophet Muhammad. The shooting lasted for ten minutes, the gunmen executing their targets one by one. As they made their getaway, shouting to passersby that they had avenged Islam, they also killed a police officer who happened to be Muslim.

Two days later, while French police scoured the Paris region looking for the killers, another scene of carnage played out in the northeast corner of the capital, at the Hypercacher kosher supermarket, filled with Friday shoppers preparing for the Sabbath. Bursting into the store with multiple weapons, a French Muslim of Malian descent killed four Jewish customers and took many more hostage. Over the next several hours, as a store employee—who happened to be not only Muslim but Malian—helped several shoppers hide in a basement storage locker, the gunman gave an interview to a local TV station, proclaiming his affiliation with the so-called Islamic State and declaring his intention to target Jews. He also demanded safe passage for the *Charlie Hebdo* killers, whom he had befriended in prison, and who were now engaged in a police stand-off of their own at a signage factory to the northeast of Paris. By the end of the day, the police had put an end to both sieges, killing all three gunmen.[1]

France has witnessed more than its share of terrorism over the years, and these attacks would not be the last. But the *Charlie Hebdo* and Hypercacher attacks, along with the demonstrations that followed, raised special questions about the relation of minorities to the French republic. Immediately after the attacks, signs declaring "Je suis Charlie" (I am Charlie) could be seen in France and throughout the world, a spontaneous gesture of solidarity with the victims. But even as two million people gathered in Paris for a "national unity march," discordant voices began to sound. Some objected to the way that President François Hollande seemed to turn the rally into a photo opportunity, others to the presence at the march of the Israeli prime minister, still others to the Socialist government's exclusion of Marine Le Pen, leader of the far-right National Front party. Struggling to make sense of the violence, some observers questioned whether *Charlie Hebdo* had gone too far by ridiculing the religious beliefs of Muslims, an oppressed minority in France, while others expressed outrage that a number of Muslim students had reportedly protested the mandatory minute of silence in honor of the victims. And certain French Jews lamented that, amid all the discussion of the murdered cartoonists, little regard was being paid to the Hypercacher shoppers, victims of an increasingly banalized antisemitism.

France is clearly in the grip of a minority crisis. Home to the largest populations of both Muslims and Jews in Europe, the country has seen tensions between these groups rise since the new millennium.[2] The supermarket attack was only the latest in a series of violent incidents in which French Jews were targeted by young, disaffected men with ties to radical Islamist groups. Increasing numbers of French Jews say they are considering immigration to Israel because they don't feel safe in France. And the National Front party, which stigmatizes Arab and other immigrants, has gained popularity in recent years, further exacerbating Muslim feelings of alienation from French society caused by various forms of discrimination and everyday racism.[3] While other European countries face similar difficulties integrating their immigrant minorities, and have also experienced terrorism,[4] the situation in France has reached a crisis level not only because of the magnitude of the problem but also because of the challenge that religious and ethnic tensions pose to the French model of universalism, the underlying ideology of the republican state.[5]

Historicizing Universalism

On a basic level, universalism refers to the notion that one law applies equally to all people. Catholicism—from the Greek *katholikos*, which means universal—was the original universalism: it sought to supersede the particularism of Judaism, the laws of which supposedly apply to Jews alone, by making salvation available to all through Christ. The kind of universalism that defines French republican ideology is secular rather than religious, but it borrows its ambition from the Catholic tradition. It too aims at spreading its message to the world. French universalism emerged from the Enlightenment's belief that all people share certain fundamental qualities and thus possess certain natural, or universal, rights. The Enlightenment notion of universalism would be enshrined in the founding document of the French Revolution, the *Declaration of the Rights of Man and the Citizen* (1789), which proclaimed in its first article that all men are born and remain equal. The Revolution's commitment to universalism led to the enfranchisement not only of the masses, the Third Estate, but also of religious minorities, such as Protestants and Jews, who had been denied equality under the Old Regime.[6] While universalism in France today is seen as coextensive with a republican form of government, it is not exclusive to it. Even the nonrepublican regimes in the nineteenth century—the First Empire, Restoration Monarchy, July Monarchy, and Second Empire—continued to subscribe to certain universalist ideas, including equality before the law.

Other Western countries, such as the United States, also consider themselves universalist, but one major feature makes French universalism unique. Whereas in other countries, universalism connotes one law applying to all people equally, in France, universalism has also come to mean that the state accords rights only to individuals, not ethnic or religious groups, and that the individual must be shorn of all particularities in order to access those rights.[7] It is this divorcing of the citizen from group affiliations that defines the singularity of the French case, the "exception française" to the liberal pluralism that prevails in the Anglo-American context. If in the United States freedom is found in robust communal life, and minority groups advocate for their collective interests, in France the state does not officially recognize the religious, ethnic, racial, or (in most cases) gender identity of its citizens. Unlike in the United States, the census in France does not ask about race or religion. From the French state's point of view, the individual rights-bearing citizen is identical to every other citizen. The corollary of French universalism is a form of secularism known as *laïcité*, which has come to mean that the state must maintain absolute religious neutrality and that the public sphere must be kept free of religion.[8] Once again the contrast with the American model is instructive, for whereas the United States also guarantees freedom of religion and the separation of churches and the state, it allows a certain religiosity to pervade the public sphere. In France, *laïcité* implies freedom *from* religion as much as freedom *of* religion.

The French have rightfully vaunted the benefits of their brand of universalism. The state's rigorous policy of equality and neutrality has meant that Jews in France penetrated the highest levels of the educational and political establishments much sooner than Jews in any other country, including the United States. But in recent years, the rise of religious fundamentalism has increasingly led to a perception that the old model of French universalism has broken down. The fiercest criticism has come from critics on the far left who view universalism as the cause of, not the solution to, France's minority problems. The French brand of universalism, these critics assert, may grant individuals equality in theory, but in reality it forces minorities to assimilate to a norm that is white, Catholic, and male or risk social and economic exclusion. These critics point out that although minorities are discriminated against as a group, French universalism offers them no possibility for collective redress or political action. In another sign of the breakdown of universalism as an ideology, politicians on the far right, who traditionally opposed universalism on the grounds that it undermines France's Catholic roots, have begun couching their calls to restrict immigration in universalist language, arguing that Muslim immigrants and their children do not sufficiently respect the French tradition of *laïcité*.[9]

In response to these assaults on their ideology, partisans of universalism from the center of the French political spectrum have doubled down. They have rejected calls for a Gallic form of American affirmative action (which they refer to dismissively as "positive discrimination") on the grounds that it violates the principle of equality before the law. They have also sought measures to enforce an ever more militant *laïcité*, such as banning signs of religious affiliation in public schools, most controversially the Muslim headscarf, but also the Jewish *kippa* and large crucifixes.[10] To proponents of universalism, only a neutral and secular state can prevent France from collapsing into sectarian conflict. Their principal target is minority *communautarisme*, or what might be translated as "communalism," the elevation of religious and ethnic affiliation above national affiliation, which the universalists see as the inevitable outcome of identity politics and the main threat to republican harmony.[11]

All sides in this debate seem to agree on one basic thing: that French universalism is fundamentally opposed to minority difference, at least when this difference is expressed in public or political ways. This is the view held by the centrist defenders of universalism, who deny the very existence of religious or ethnic "communities" in France, insisting that the nation is composed only of individuals.[12] It is also the view of the critics on the right who are hostile to minorities, and of critics on the left who fault universalism for denying minorities a voice. The debate over universalism in France has been framed in such a way that defending universalist values always seems to entail opposing the greater participation of minority groups in public life, and asserting the importance of national pride and patriotism always seems to come at the expense of more particular ties.

In this book, I offer a different perspective on French universalism by arguing three interrelated things. First, I advance the idea that the notion of universalism predicated on the abstraction of the political subject from all communal ties, which the French associate with the Jacobin revolutionary tradition, is not the only form that French universalism has taken since 1789.[13] I argue that universalism has been subject to debate and negotiation throughout modern French history and has meant very different things to different people in different periods. In other words, *universalism has a history*, and recovering this history in all its complexity is essential to understanding the pitfalls, as well as the possibilities, of French universalism today.[14]

The second argument I make in this book is that French universalism has evolved in the modern period largely as a discourse on Jews. Despite representing a tiny minority of the French population, Jews have played an outsized role in the French political imagination since 1789, shaping the ways in which universalism has been theorized and implemented.[15] Tracing the development of universalist discourse through key moments in French-Jewish history, from debates over granting Jews civil rights during the Revolution, through the Dreyfus Affair and Vichy, and up to the rise of the "new antisemitism" since 2000, I show how Jewish difference has always been essential to the elaboration of French universalism, whether as its dialectical opposite or as proof of universalism's reach. As France's paradigmatic minority, Jews have provided French thinkers with a forum for debating the nature of citizenship and the state, as well as the meaning of Frenchness itself.[16]

The third argument I make is that the universal and the particular have not always been as opposed as they now appear to be. The idea that French universalism demands the elimination of public manifestations of religious, cultural, and (what we now call) ethnic difference has roots in the Revolutionary period but did not become dominant until the Dreyfus Affair in the 1890s. During most of the nineteenth century, and at various moments in the twentieth century as well, the universal and the particular were often seen to go hand in hand, one reinforcing the other. One of my goals in this book is to call attention to these earlier models of understanding the place of Jews within the French nation in order to recover a sense of what it might mean to conceive of the universal in particular terms, to see the particular not as an obstacle to universalism but as a conduit to it.

This is a book, ultimately, about how the relation of the French universal to the Jewish particular has unfolded over time. I will examine the major periods in French history when this relation was most fraught with tension (such as the Revolution, the Dreyfus Affair, and Vichy), but I will also look at moments of relative calm (such as the mid-nineteenth century), which fostered alternative modes of conceiving of the nation and of the place of minorities within it. I will show how and why a hardline version of universalism, hostile to difference, came to dominate the French political imagination in the twentieth century, as well as how more open models have surfaced time and again.

Unlike some critics, I am not against universalism as an ideal. I am fully aware of the extent to which French universalism has made it possible for individual members of minority groups—especially Jews—to attain unprecedented levels of social integration. I appreciate the goal of absolute equality that lies at French universalism's heart, and I am sensitive to the historical factors that created the opposition to the particular that characterizes French universalism today. My intention is not to graft the Anglo-American model of liberal pluralism onto the French context. On the contrary, this book shows how various models—*French* models—for integrating minority difference within a universalist framework have existed within French political culture since the time of the Revolution even as a more rigid notion of universalism came to prevail for specific historical reasons. It is my hope that recovering some of the different ways French universalism has been theorized over the past two hundred years might offer new possibilities for thinking through France's current social and political dilemmas—and perhaps some American ones as well.

Good for the Jews

For the last several years, I have directed a program devoted to the study of antisemitism. As I worked to organize lectures and conferences on the subject of anti-Jewish violence in the contemporary world, I often found myself troubled when France was under discussion. Disturbed as I was by the rising tide of violence against Jews, I was often also disturbed by the response to these attacks by many audience members at the lectures and conferences I organized. What bothered me was their assumption—reinforced by articles in the American press—that France was a fundamentally, even inherently, antisemitic country. Not only does such an assumption tend to collapse different kinds of antisemitism into one unchanging, eternal entity that frustrates analysis, but it also happens not to be true. France may have witnessed its share of antisemitism, but it is not inherently antisemitic. If it were, how then to explain the fact that France was the first European country to grant the Jews full civil rights in the eighteenth century? Or that in the nineteenth century, French Jews achieved far greater social and economic integration than their coreligionists anywhere else in the world? Or that in the twentieth century, France had no fewer than five prime ministers of Jewish origin? Moreover, if France were inherently antisemitic, why did French intellectuals like Émile Zola and Jean-Paul Sartre produce some of the most forceful condemnations of antisemitism ever written?

In order to set the record straight, I originally set out to write a book about French *philosemitism*—the defense, love, or admiration of Jews that I saw as equally present in France as antisemitism, if not more so. I quickly realized, however, that only one type of philosemitism was really unique to France: universalism. It was the radical emphasis on political equality, the determination to treat all people as individuals with the same fundamental rights, that made the unique success of Jews in French national life possible and that motivated intellectuals like Zola to rush to their defense. This kind of philosemitism was arguably not philosemitism at all. It may have been good for the Jews, but only because it insisted on not recognizing the Jews as such. I became intrigued by this paradox—that the political ideology that allowed the Jews the most freedom did so by abstracting or erasing their specificity, their difference, as Jews. Looked at from the perspective of someone interested in fostering Jewish identity, this kind of philosemitism could seem oddly similar to antisemitism.

At the center of this debate over French universalism lies the question of assimilation. To what extent does the French commitment to absolute equality for its minorities come with the expectation—either explicit or implicit—that they shed all or part of what makes them different? This question has preoccupied not only Jewish nationalist historians, concerned about the disappearance of Jewish identity in liberal Western nations, but also a certain strain of French historiography hostile to the Jacobin tradition. Both groups have seen the Revolution's offer of citizenship to the Jews as demanding assimilation as a quid pro quo. Shmuel Trigano, for instance, calls French Jews "hostages of the universal" and claims that during the Revolution, "the abstract Jew, the universal Jewish citizen, takes shape at the same time that the concrete Jew, the paragon of retrograde and obscurantist particularism, disappears."[17] Jewish emancipation, according to this view, becomes one more example of the totalitarian impulse within the French universalist tradition, aimed at the eradication of all forms of difference.

Much leftist criticism of French universalism today continues to echo these assumptions about emancipation and assimilation.[18] According to

Wendy Brown, "Jews [in France] could be and were enfranchised on the condition of assimilation, on the condition that they shed identifying and constitutive Jewish practices, or at least on the condition that these practices became completely private."[19] Brown is interested in exposing the hypocrisy of liberal regimes of tolerance in the West, which offer rights to minorities in order to control and subjugate them, and the treatment of the Jews under French universalism constitutes one of her primary case studies. She writes that Jewish emancipation in France was "tacitly or expressly dependent on assimilation, which is to say on transformation of the Jew" and that to cohabit with Frenchness, "Jewishness could no longer consist in belonging to a distinct community bound by religious law, ritualized practices, and generational continuity; rather, it would consist at most in privately held and conducted belief."[20] For Brown, French universalism is little short of a ruse designed to eliminate minorities under the guise of welcoming them.

Over the past several decades, however, certain scholars have begun to question the basis of this leftist critique by showing that French Jews did not view their emancipation as a call to assimilate.[21] While French Jews did relinquish the legal autonomy of their communities, as required by the terms of the emancipation decrees that granted them citizenship, and while they adopted the French language and French customs, they did not cease their communal existence as Jews.[22] And French Jews emphatically did not confine their Jewish identity solely to the private sphere after the Revolution. As other scholars have noted, and as I will detail in chapter 2, the middle decades of the nineteenth century saw very public—even flamboyant—performances of Jewish identity in France.[23] Nor did French Jews abandon their solidarity with other Jews, as Brown and others allege.[24] On the contrary, the creation in 1860 of the Alliance israélite universelle, the first international Jewish aid organization, indicates the extent to which French Jews saw their Jewishness as integrally linked to helping their less fortunate coreligionists abroad.[25] The twentieth century saw even more opportunities for Jews to expressing their Jewishness in public ways, through a range of associations as well as through literature and art.[26]

Brown and other critics of Jewish emancipation are largely interested in theory, not in practice. They are less concerned with how actual Jews interpreted the conditions of their emancipation than with the terms by which this emancipation was offered in the first place. As I will show, however, even these terms are far more complex than most scholars have presumed. Beginning during the Revolution itself, French thinkers have repeatedly produced challenges to the hard-line version of universalism that demands assimilation in exchange for inclusion in the nation. A strong countertradition has always existed, one that rejects the rigid opposition of the universal to the particular and seeks ways to incorporate Jewish difference into the French national framework. At the heart of this book lies the proposition that French universalism is not a fixed doctrine, with an ideologically coherent set of rules and practices, but rather a way of thinking about the state and its relation to minorities that is continually being negotiated. Indeed, as I will show, even individual theorists vacillate or reverse themselves within the course of a single essay as they try to explain the relation of the universal to the particular.

Rather than debate whether French universalism is or is not assimilationist, therefore, I argue that most theories of French universalism fall somewhere on a continuum between an *assimilationist* pole and a *pluralist* pole. Although these two terms have been the subject of critical debate, and are anachronistic when applied to the eighteenth and nineteenth centuries, I use them as heuristic tools for understanding what is at stake in discussions of minority difference in France.[27] At the far end of the assimilationist side of the spectrum lies the expectation that a minority group will completely shed its political, economic, cultural, and religious practices in order to join the majority culture. At the far end of the pluralist side lies the total acceptance and recognition of minority difference by society and the state. All the theories I discuss in the chapters that follow fall somewhere between these two poles. A large part of this book will be devoted to explaining how various models of French universalism have attempted to balance assimilation and pluralism, and to determining where they fit on the continuum. No single one of these theories of universalism, I emphasize, should be taken as constituting the true incarnation or essence of the ideology.

On the one hand, then, this book is a response to the critics who maintain that French universalism is inherently hostile to difference. These include not just Americans like Brown or Joan Wallach Scott[28] but also French theorists like Étienne Balibar, who denounce the way proponents of republican universalism use the rhetoric of equality to mask colonialist and neocolonialist forms of domination. Balibar describes the hypocrisy of "the country of human rights" attempting to educate the human race while simultaneously "assimilating dominated populations" and "differentiating individuals or groups according to a hierarchy based on their aptitude for or resistance to assimilation."[29] While I agree with this analysis of how French universalism often functions in racist and exploitative ways, I take issue with the idea that universalism is *inherently* racist and exploitative. What I object to in this critique is the tendency to reify and dehistoricize universalism, taking its worst manifestations as illustrations of a fundamental tendency and ignoring various forms of resistance to this dominant model. I believe it is important to call attention to more pluralist articulations of French universalism, not because these visions have often prevailed but because they offer the possibility of saving what is good about universalism, of separating out universalism's contradictions in order to retain the ideal of justice at its core.[30]

On the other hand, this book is a response to those hard-line universalists, such as Alain Finkielkraut, who see the French republic as imperiled by assertions of the right to difference, *le droit à la différence*, particularly when such assertions come from groups who are different from them. In his recent *L'identité malheureuse* (Unfortunate Identity, 2013), Finkielkraut defends the ban on wearing the Muslim veil in French public schools by distinguishing between the French republican model of citizenship and the pluralist model that obtains in most other Western countries.[31] French identity, according to Finkielkraut, relies on a form of universalism that others—and by others, he mainly means Americans—just cannot understand.[32] He looks back nostalgically to his own experience in French public schools in the postwar era, in which the rigorous refusal to discuss difference allowed him to succeed, in spite of the fact that his parents were Polish Jewish immigrants.[33] As he would have it, the current effort to coddle minorities by emphasizing difference in public schools has undermined this once-robust vector of equality, condemning these groups to a permanent state of inferiority and turning the nation itself into a battleground between minority "communities" competing for recognition.[34] Finkielkraut's perspective overlooks the fact that the secular schoolroom is itself a relatively recent invention and that other models for inculcating Frenchness, and managing interethnic conflict, thrived before the end of the nineteenth century.[35]

Defenders of a hard-line model of French universalism, such as Finkielkraut, often complain about Americans telling the French how to solve their minority problems. Not only is America's treatment of its minorities hardly a source of inspiration, they point out, but Americans never seem to grasp how and why French universalism and *laïcité* evolved as they did, in large measure as a way to free France from the grip of the Catholic Church. This book responds to that second criticism by paying attention to the specific history that led to the hard-line model of republican universalism that prevails today while at the same time pointing to the various ways this dominant model has been contested from within the French tradition itself.

It is my hope that the result will have something to offer the French, but also that it will have something to offer Americans, for whom the French model of universalism represents a vital point of comparison to our own. Since our twin revolutions, France has always served as a kind of mirror for the United States, one that reflects very different solutions to a similar set of problems concerning the place of minorities within a universalist framework. Whereas members of religious, racial, and ethnic minorities in the United States have had a great deal of freedom to express their difference in the public sphere, they have not always or everywhere had equality of opportunity. In France, the situation has tended to be the reverse. Better understanding how the French developed their unique form of universalism, but also how this form has been contested, may thus help Americans understand the benefits and shortcomings of their own model.

My attempt to complicate our understanding of the relation of French universalism to religious and ethnic difference has several precedents. It has much in common with Jean-François Chanet's study of the French education system and its relation to regional difference, or what Chanet terms the *petite patrie*.[36] Whereas we have long thought of the Third Republic (1870–1940) schoolmaster as the vehicle of a kind of universalizing *déracinement* or uprooting from local traditions and languages, Chanet reveals that in fact, even during the heyday of the Third Republic, the schoolroom served as a site for the celebration of regional pride and the preservation of local customs. According to Chanet, the universal and the particular were thus not as opposed as we might think.[37] Mona Ozouf, the great historian of the Revolution, has contributed to this debate by describing the conflicts in her own childhood, marked both by the lure of the universal and by her family's efforts to preserve Breton language and culture. She invites us to reconsider the opposition between the universal and the particular not just in regard to regional difference but with reference to ethnic and religious difference as well.[38]

My effort to historicize French universalism also has much in common with Jean Baubérot's work on the history of *laïcité* as a juridical concept. Baubérot distinguishes between what he calls the "new *laïcité*," developed in response to the resurgence in Muslim religiosity over the past few decades, which sees all public manifestations of religion as a threat to republican values, and a "historical *laïcité*," which was far more open to religion in public life.[39] Indeed, as Baubérot has demonstrated, in the nineteenth century, *laïcité* meant that France's three major religions (Catholicism, Protestantism, and Judaism) should be treated equally, not that religion must be evacuated from the public sphere. In his recent *La laïcité falsifiée*, Baubérot shows that not even the law of 1905 separating churches and the state decreed the banishment of religion to the private realm. On the contrary, the law proclaimed "freedom of religion and the possibility of 'its exterior manifestations in the public arena.'"[40] Although *laïcité* as such is not the subject of this book, I will return to Baubérot's arguments frequently because the question of religious difference, and its public manifestation, has been integral to debates over the place of Jews in French national life.

Jews and Other Minorities

Jews have played a major role in the construction of the French political imagination since 1789, shaping the way that universalism has been theorized and implemented. This is certainly not because of their numbers. At the time of the Revolution, there were only about 40,000 Jews in France (out of a total population of 28 million), divided among several distinct communities: around 5,000 Sephardic Jews in the southwest; about 30,000 Ashkenazic Jews in the eastern provinces of Alsace and Lorraine; and a few thousand Jews in the former papal states in and around Avignon. Additionally, between 500 and 800 Jews of varying backgrounds lived in Paris. Thanks to high fertility rates and immigration from Central Europe, the Jewish population of France grew to 96,000 by 1861.[41] This number would fall to 68,000 in 1889, following the loss of Alsace and Lorraine to Germany. By this point, the Jews constituted only about 0.17 percent of the population of France. But since 60 percent of the Jewish population resided in Paris, where they concentrated in certain neighborhoods, they constituted a visible presence in the capital by the end of the nineteenth century.

The twentieth century saw the Jewish population of France grow much larger. Roughly 40,000 Eastern European Jews settled in Paris between the 1890s and the 1920s, a tiny number compared to the several million who immigrated to the United States during this period, but still enough to change the face of the French Jewish population. Many more arrived during the 1930s, fleeing Nazi persecution, so that the Jewish population of France grew from 150,000 in 1919 to 300,000 on the eve of World War II. This represented still only 0.75 percent of the national population, but a much larger percentage of the population of Paris, where over 200,000 of these Jews lived. Another 110,000 Jews lived in colonial Algeria. During World War II, the Nazis and their French accomplices deported 76,000 Jews from metropolitan France to concentration camps in the east, only 2,500 of whom returned. But between 1956 and 1967, during the period of decolonization, France gained roughly 235,000 Jews from North Africa, making it the only country in Europe to have a larger Jewish population today than before the war. France currently has by far the largest population of Jews in Europe (around 500,000 by most estimates) and the third largest in the world, after the United States and Israel. Today about 1 percent of the French population is Jewish.

INTRODUCTION 13

Given such small numbers, how to account for the fact that so many French thinkers and writers have taken up the so-called Jewish Question over the years? David Nirenberg asks a version of this question about the West in general: "Why did so many diverse cultures—even many cultures with no Jews living among them—think so much about Judaism?" he asks in *Anti-Judaism: The Western Tradition*.[42] Nirenberg argues that the "Jewish Question" "is as much about the basic tools and concepts through which individuals in a society relate to the world and to each other, as it is about the presence of 'real' Judaism and living Jews in that society."[43] In the premodern period, Judaism played a significant role in Christian theology, both as the religion from which Christianity sprang and the religion it was destined to replace. Saint Paul explicitly associated the Jews with the antiuniversal, with tribalism, which the coming of Christ allowed mankind to overcome. Catholicism, as I have shown, would establish itself as a universal church by purporting to supersede Jewish particularity.

Partly as a result of the Catholic Church's ban on money lending, in the modern period the Jew became associated with capitalism, which for Karl Marx and others needed to be theorized, understood, and resisted. Structurally, this role is not dissimilar to that played by Jews in Christian theology: in the anticapitalist mindset, the Jew still represents that which must be overcome in order for the reign of universal harmony to take hold.[44] "'Judaism,'" Nirenberg reminds us, "is not only the religion of specific people with specific beliefs, but also a category, a set of ideas and attributes with which non-Jews can make sense of and criticize their world."[45] In other words, the Jews have offered Western thinkers a way to think through what they are not.

Prior to the modern period, this thinking often took the form of universalist theorizing: the Jew's difference, whether religious, tribal, or economic, was seen as an obstacle to universal harmony. During the Enlightenment, however, the Jew began to play a new role in the Western imagination. Rather than embodying only what must be overcome or resisted for the universal to take hold, the Jew began also (and sometimes simultaneously) to be seen as someone whose change or transformation could help bring universal harmony about. The Jew became the very symbol of universalism's power and reach. Indeed, as Ronald Schechter has pointed out, the Jews were "good to think" during the Enlightenment because they offered philosophes a test case for the powers of reason: if even a group as different as the Jews could be transformed by treating them fairly, and opening to them the world of philosophy, then anybody could.[46] It was the Jews' perceived backwardness, and their vilification by Western society, that made them the ideal recipients of the "regeneration" that the philosophes hoped to extend first to all French people and then to the entire human race. From obstacles to universalism, the Jews became its poster children.

If the Jews became the ideal objects of French universalism, it was in part because of the nature of their difference. Unlike the Protestants, the Jews of France were different enough to serve as a test case for Enlightenment principles, but not so different as to challenge the conceptual categories of the philosophes. The Jews spoke a different language, followed obscure customs, and practiced an ancient religion. To the Abbé Grégoire and others, their difference was manifest in every aspect of their physical appearance, from their putatively deformed bodies to their supposedly unpleasant odor, which Grégoire attributed to their unhealthy dietary habits. In many ways, they had farther to go on the path toward regeneration than the peasants of the French countryside, although the peasants too were seen as deviating intellectually and culturally from the universal ideal. But the Jews were not seen to be as different as the two other categories of minorities that posed a problem to the Revolutionary reformers: blacks[47] and women.[48] The difference of these two groups was seen as so fundamental that arguing about the degree to which they could be made to assimilate to a white, male model was deemed pointless.[49] Jews served as the ideal object for universalist theorizing during the Revolution; they led to such debate about the possibilities of "regeneration," I want to suggest, because their difference was perceived as contingent and mutable.

In many ways, one could argue that Muslims have become France's new Jews, its new paradigmatic minority, except that the problem of Jewish difference still continues to trouble the French universalist imagination. My point in comparing the Jews to these other minorities is not to maintain that the Jews are somehow more important as a minority—they very clearly are not—but rather that they have continually spurred some of the most significant theorizing about the place of minorities within the French nation over the past two and a half centuries.[50] To be sure, blacks and women also gave rise to significant theorizing, as have Muslims more recently. But the fact that Jews were seen as worthy of inclusion within the French universal during the French Revolution, and the fact that their presence at the very heart of the nation gave rise to continual debate through the nineteenth and twentieth centuries, sets the Jewish case apart. This is the story that I want to tell in the pages that follow.

Method

This is not a work of intellectual history in the conventional sense. While I do trace the way that thinking about the relation of universalism to the Jews has changed through time, my main interest lies in probing individual articulations of that relation. Although I indicate how and why a hard-line discourse of French universalism prevailed in the twentieth century, my goal is to uncover the moments when different possibilities for thinking about minority identity—moments of counterdiscourse—have been possible. The book is therefore organized as a series of close readings of texts. I will ask readers to follow me as I delve into the twists and turns of a novel's plot and as I look closely at camera angles in a film. Unlike conventional works of intellectual history that extract the argument of a work from its textual incarnation, this book rests on the belief that form and content cannot be split, that meaning inheres in the way things are said rather than just in the fact of the saying, and that historical analysis should also involve the kinds of in-depth interpretive investigations that are normally seen as the province of the literary scholar. While I bring the skills of close reading to bear on these texts, I do so with one eye always fixed on the historical horizon. I am interested as much in how these authors speak to each other across historical periods as in how they respond to their own historical moments. What emerges from this book is a conversation about universalism and the Jews that has preoccupied France and the French throughout the modern period.

The texts I discuss do not fall neatly into any one genre or category. My corpus includes political speeches, newspaper articles, administrative reports, philosophical treatises, plays, novels, and films. One of the main methodological assumptions I make is that all of these texts contribute to the construction of French universalism, that what some might call political or social theory is not confined to texts that announce themselves as such. However, readers intent on finding policy prescriptions in my analysis, or discussions of specific laws and practices, will no doubt be disappointed. This is not an anthropological or sociological study. Although some of the eighteenth-century texts I examine do delve into specifics about precisely which Jewish religious, cultural, economic, and political practices they would like to change and which they would permit to be maintained, most of the later texts I study do not. These texts very often operate at a high level of abstraction. They nonetheless offer models for thinking about the relation of the universal to the particular that might guide those attempting to negotiate these issues in practice.

Although I will touch at various points on the contribution by Jewish thinkers and writers to debates about French universalism, which has been considerable, this book is mainly about how non-Jewish writers think about the relationship of universalism to the Jews.[51] Some of the writers I discuss here, like Zola or Sartre, had a wide audience in their time and are among the most celebrated figures in the French literary canon today. Others had a more limited reach, and some are almost forgotten. The criterion for inclusion in my corpus was not impact but interest. My goal is not to offer a comprehensive view of the way that universalism has been understood in France over the last two hundred and fifty years but rather to look at some of the most profound or innovative articulations of universalism in different periods, even if these voices failed, until now, to have a lasting effect.

The book is structured chronologically. Chapter 1 begins in the eighteenth century, in the years leading up to the French Revolution, when a new way of thinking about the place of the Jews in the nation took shape, and offers a new interpretation of the debates over Jewish emancipation during the Revolution itself. Chapter 2 looks at some very public displays of Jewish identity during the July Monarchy (1830–48), focusing on the case of Rachel Félix, the greatest actress of her era, who challenged prevailing notions of the place of Jews in French culture. In chapter 3, I examine the dilemma that colonialism posed for French universalism, focusing specifically on the case of Algeria, which was home to large populations of indigenous Muslims and Jews. In chapter 4, I take up the case of Émile Zola, whose writing about Jews before, during, and after the Dreyfus Affair in the 1890s helped to implant the hard-line version of universalism, hostile to difference, that we know today. In chapter 5, I show how one of the most important films of the interwar period, Jean Renoir's *La grande illusion* (1937), offers a more open approach to minority difference, a resistance to Zola's brand of universalism that was also contested in Jean-Paul Sartre's *Réflexions sur la question juive* (1945), the subject of chapter 6. The final chapter looks at the return of a form of universalism that is hostile to difference in current debates about the "new antisemitism," focusing on the controversial philosophers Alain Finkielkraut and Alain Badiou. I conclude by examining the "national unity" rallies that followed the shootings at *Charlie Hebdo* and the kosher supermarket, and a speech by Prime Minister Manuel Valls, to reflect on the future of the relation between the French republic and its minorities, both Jewish and Muslim. To what extent, I ask, can France look to its own past for new models of reconciling the universal and the particular, at a time when such models are needed more than ever?

1

The Revolution Reconsidered

The French Revolution granted the Jews full civil rights. But what did it ask of them in return? According to generations of historians, the answer is simple: assimilation, the disappearance of some or all of what made the Jews distinct as a people.[1] When Count Stanislas de Clermont-Tonnerre famously declared to his fellow Revolutionaries, "To the Jews as a nation, nothing; to the Jews as individuals, everything," he seemed to describe a bargain by which Jews would surrender their traditional identity, defined by membership in a semiautonomous community, in order to be treated like every other citizen of France. And for the Revolutionaries, it has long been assumed, equality meant homogeneity. Like the drive to eliminate the privileges of the nobles and clergy, and the effort to suppress local languages, the emancipation of the Jews seemed to serve the Revolution's aim to create a nation of abstract and identical individuals, loyal to nobody but the state.

In the century following emancipation, this bargain appeared only natural. It went without saying that the Jews should shed the trappings of their former ghettoized existence in order to embrace the equality that France had been the first European nation to offer them. By the beginning of the twentieth century, Jewish nationalist historians began to believe the bargain had been a bad one, but they did not doubt that the Revolution had required the Jews to assimilate. They merely faulted the Revolution's emancipation decree for entailing the loss of Jewish identity, and for leaving France's Jews woefully unprepared to cope with the rise of antisemitism as a result.[2] During the bicentennial commemoration of the French Revolution in 1989, as historians such as François Furet began to criticize the Jacobin tradition for its supposedly totalitarian tendencies,[3] Jewish emancipation was viewed as one more example of the Revolution's eradication of the right to difference.[4] Even the Revolution's defenders, however, assumed that emancipation entailed assimilation.[5]

But did the Revolution really demand assimilation of the Jews as a quid pro quo? In this chapter, I will show that the Jews' defenders at the end of the eighteenth century argued for emancipation with a range of results in mind. Their answers to what would later come to be known as the "Jewish Question," which asked whether Jews belonged in the modern nation-state and if so on what terms, can be plotted on the continuum between the opposing poles of assimilation and pluralism that I described in the introduction. Some advocates of emancipation, especially before the Revolution broke out, did indeed want the Jews to change in a variety of ways—politically, economically, culturally, and religiously—in exchange for citizenship. Others, however—including some of the main architects of Jewish emancipation, such as Clermont-Tonnerre and even the future Jacobin leader Maximilien Robespierre himself—were far more accepting of what they referred to as Jewish "difference." It will be my contention here that if the pre-Revolutionary defenders of the Jews were largely assimilationist, the Revolution itself was closer to the pluralist pole than has previously been assumed.

From the start, Enlightenment debates over the "Jewish Question" were about more than just Jews. Building on Ronald Schechter's insight that the Jews became "good to think" in the eighteenth century, that they served as a proxy for a variety of Enlightenment concerns, I will argue that it was in debating how to incorporate the Jews into French society that the philosophes and Revolutionaries formulated some of the basic tenets of universalism as a political ideology. As the case of the Jews made apparent, there was a wide gulf between contemplating the equality of all men in theory and confronting the often recalcitrant nature of their difference in practice. For some, this difference needed to be dissipated before equality could be extended. For others, however, difference offered proof of universalism's reach. To return to these eighteenth-century debates, therefore, is to understand the origin of French universalism not as the revelation of a definitive doctrine but rather as the site of a conflict, one in which a range of options for dealing with difference were imagined.

Let Us Force Them to Change

I begin this chapter in the years leading up to the Revolution, when the question of what to do with France's Jews took on an increasing urgency. On the surface, this urgency surprises since the Jews represented such a tiny minority of the French population at the end of the eighteenth century—less than

0.2 percent. Moreover, the bulk of the period's theorizing focused on a subset of this minority—not on the relatively acculturated Sephardic Jews of the southwest, or the old community in the Papal States, but on the Ashkenazic Jews of Alsace-Lorraine, a mere 30,000 souls in a nation of 28 million. It was to these largely poor, semirural, traditionally orthodox, Yiddish-speaking Jews that the philosophes turned their attention. At a time when France consisted of a patchwork of vastly different regions, each with its own distinctive culture and patois, the Jews of France's eastern provinces could reasonably claim to be the most different of France's different peoples. And it was this difference that made the Jews so interesting to think about, as the philosophes began to outline the contours of a future society that would be formulated on more egalitarian terms.

One of the first proposals for extending something like equality to the Jews was made in 1775, when the Jews of Metz began to fight back against the laws restricting their occupations and brought suit against the town of Thionville, in Lorraine, and against its merchant guild (corp des marchands), for denying them the right to set up a printing business. To help make their case that a royal decree of August 20, 1767, which allowed both foreign nationals and French subjects the freedom to set up certain businesses, should apply to them as well, the Jews turned to a young, non-Jewish lawyer named Pierre-Louis Lacretelle.[6] Lacretelle's argument on the Jews' behalf is worth examining in detail because it is here that we first see the Jews defended in universalist terms, and first see calls for their assimilation as an extension of this universalism.

Lacretelle argued that since the decree did not specifically exempt the Jews but rather applied to all men—foreign and French—it should necessarily include the Jews irrespective of the more difficult question of whether the Jews should be considered French. "The real question at issue here is to determine whether Jews are men," Lacretelle declared.[7] This represents a significant departure from the mercantilist defenses of the Jews that had been the norm since the sixteenth century. These earlier apologies had stressed that Jews were different from other men but useful because of their unique economic talents. In his petition on behalf of the Jews of Metz, Lacretelle seeks to defend the Jews less because they possess special abilities that might stimulate the economy (although he would make this claim as well) than because they are fundamentally the same as everyone else and deserve to be treated equally. His case for allowing the Jews to set up business in Thionville ultimately rests not on exceptional utility but on the abstract, universalist principle of equality.

Lacretelle's plea reached beyond the deceptively simple reading of a royal decree to take on the larger arguments launched against the Jews by their modern critics. While his argument still emphasizes on the whole that the Jews would help the economy, it also acknowledges the question of Jewish economic "vices," including predatory moneylending and financial chicanery, which were increasingly cited by the Jews' many opponents as reasons to banish them from the kingdom or severely restrict their freedom. These tendencies toward chicanery represent, Lacretelle admits, "a lamentable truth" (29). To make his claim that the Jews deserve to be integrated despite their vices, therefore, Lacretelle latches onto a new kind of logic, one that later defenders of the Jews would adopt and expand.

Following two earlier Jewish apologists for the Jews, Isaac de Pinto and Bernard de Valabrègue, Lacretelle lays the blame for the Jews' defects on the way Christians have treated them through the centuries, on the persecutions that forced them to resort to ruse.[8] The opposite point of view, that their economic vices "are inherent to the Jews' very nature; that they are inseparable from their manners, from their beliefs, even from their religion" (29), Lacretelle calls barbaric and ridiculous. And like later defenders of the Jews, Lacretelle marshals history to make his point, tracing the long, sad saga of persecutions that left Jews with no choice but to turn to moneylending. This history, he admits, shows the Jews "always in the same occupations, with the same character, in the same state from the time of their decadence" (29), but this he explains by the fact that their history is one of continual disgrace and unhappiness.

The solution to the Jewish problem, for Lacretelle, lies in granting the Jews the freedom to become better. "Let us open our cities to them; let us permit them to spread throughout our land; let us treat them if not as compatriots, then at least as men" (34). This call for liberty would be taken up by many of the Jews' defenders in the following decade. But it was not without limitations: if Lacretelle advocates ending the multiple restrictions preventing the Jews from engaging in honorable trades, he also suggests special laws to prevent Jews from resorting to usury: "But let us also surround them with the vigilance of our Laws; *let us force them to change* [forçons-les à changer], just as we change their condition; let our rigor on the one point not recede before our kindness on the other" (34, emphasis added). That the Jews can be compelled to improve their economic practices, and their general moral state, represents the foundation of the ideology of "regeneration" that would come to define the approach of the Jews' main defender, the Abbé Grégoire, a few years later. Lacretelle even uses the term "regeneration," a decade before Grégoire, although Alyssa Goldstein Sepinwall argues that he does so in a limited, religious sense, rather than as a synonym for assimilation.[9]

Lacretelle's clear goal is to reform the commercial practices of the Jews, or in other words, to assimilate them economically: "Let that lowly greediness for profit, that cowardly insensibility, that cruel caution, that black penchant for deceit and usury be thrust from their heart" (35; Que cette basse âpreté du gain ... sortent de leur coeur), he proclaims in a subjunctive imperative, typical of the advocates of regeneration. And while he mainly confines his vision of Jewish regeneration to the economic plane, Lacretelle also raises the possibility of a more complete cultural transformation: he foresees a day when the Jews will "adopt our manners and our laws, and willingly place themselves beneath their happy yoke" and envisions "in the justice we will have finally rendered to them, the fulfillment of the hopes that still separate them from our religion" (35). Conversion, however, remains a distant goal, not subject to the coercion that Lacretelle sees as a necessity when it comes to the Jews' economic practices.

In Lacretelle's plea on behalf of the Jews of Metz, we find the essence of the regeneration ideology that offers Jews rights but demands, or expects, assimilation in return. We must, however, distinguish among types of assimilation in order to understand precisely where he fits on the continuum between assimilation and pluralism. Lacretelle *requires* economic assimilation of the Jews and recommends legal measures to "force" the Jews to change their business practices. He *expects* cultural assimilation (that the Jews will adopt French "*moeurs*") and political assimilation (that the Jews will adopt French "laws") but does not require them. Finally, he *hopes for* religious assimilation—that the Jews will one day become Christian—but puts this possibility off into a more distant future and sees it as entirely voluntary on the Jews' part: the Jews might eventually convert out of gratitude for kind treatment. Lacretelle, therefore, is more of an assimilationist than a pluralist, but he stops short of demanding that the Jews change completely as a precondition for gaining rights.

Lacretelle's innovations in arguing for the Jews would inspire two of the most famous defenders of the Jews in the following decade, the Abbé Grégoire and Christian Wilhelm Dohm.[10] Though Dohm wrote in German, and specifically addressed the condition of the Jews in Germany, the motivation for his treatise once again came from eastern France: in 1777, a scandal erupted in Alsace when a local judge named François Hell brazenly admitted to printing false receipts so that peasants could claim they had repaid the Jews to whom they owed money. Despite being the obvious victims of a conspiracy, the Alsatian Jews found themselves on the defensive. Led by the wealthy merchant Cerf Berr, they turned for help to Moses Mendelssohn, their coreligionist who had made a name for himself in philosophical circles in Berlin. Judging that a non-Jew would be better situated to defend the Alsatian Jews, however, Mendelssohn in turn asked Dohm, a Prussian official, to respond to Hell. Dohm's *On the Civic Improvement of the Jews* (1781) appeared in French translation in 1782.

Like Lacretelle, Dohm would stress the Jews' negative qualities, their economic backwardness and social isolation. As Jonathan Karp has shown, Dohm viewed the Jews as an economic liability because they produced nothing.[11] He characterized the Jews as a nation of middlemen whose usurious practices sapped wealth from honest farmers and artisans. This economic backwardness, moreover, had a negative effect on their moral character and prevented the Jews from feeling a sense of civic duty. Like Pinto, Valabrègue, and Lacretelle, however, Dohm blames Christian oppression through the centuries for the Jews' degraded state, and he describes this history of oppression in detail, emphasizing how Jews had been forced to play the roles of moneylender and middleman because of their exclusion from other, more productive professions.

Dohm displays the influence of the physiocrats, a group of economists opposed to mercantilism, who denounced commerce as a nonproductive form of labor. But unlike the physiocrats, who saw agriculture alone as valuable, Dohm believed that artisans and even merchants could contribute usefully to the economy. Only he did not believe that Jews should play this role. Here we see a complete turn against the precepts of the earlier, mercantilist mode of defending the Jews: instead of advocating the inclusion of the Jews in the nation because of their commercial skills, Dohm advocates forcibly preventing the Jews from engaging in commerce and encouraging them to take up agriculture and artisanal crafts instead. Previously forbidden areas of economic endeavor must now be open to Jews: they should be allowed to own land and join guilds. This new freedom, he hoped, would improve the Jews' morality and foster a sense of solidarity with non-Jews. His goal was "civic improvement," which is another way of saying regeneration. But unlike many others who debated the "Jewish Question" at the time, Dohm favored granting the Jews citizenship as a way to hasten their regeneration rather than requiring them first to regenerate in order to prove their worthiness for citizenship.

Significantly, Dohm did not think it necessary for the Jews to abandon their communal autonomy, their separate legal system and governance structures, as part of this bargain. He thus favored economic assimilation but not political assimilation. Nevertheless, as Jonathan Hess has shown, Dohm's project for improving the Jews formed part of a larger project of political modernization for Prussia. Arguing that the Jews could become citizens (even while maintaining separate institutions) allowed him to lay out his plans for a radically new conception of what the state should be, which is to say secular and universalist. In the new society he imagined, "the nobleman, the peasant, the scholar, the artisan, the Christian and the Jew" would all conceive of themselves as Prussians rather than as members of different estates with different privileges.[12] If Dohm's project of reforming the Jews would have the greatest impact on the Abbé Grégoire, his new conception of citizenship would influence the French Revolutionaries, although, as we will see, they would require the kind of political assimilation he deemed unnecessary.[13]

Dohm's ideas would gain exposure in France thanks to Honoré-Gabriel de Riqueti, comte de Mirabeau, who summarized them eloquently in *Sur Moses Mendelssohn, sur la réforme politique des juifs* (1787).[14] Mirabeau devotes the first part of his work to Mendelssohn, who had asked Dohm to write his essay and who laid out his own ideas about Judaism, first in a preface to a new German translation of Menasseh ben Israel's apology for the Jews and then in his own treatise, *Jerusalem*. In the latter, Mendelssohn argued forcefully for the separation of churches and state, specifically denying to rabbis any kind of temporal power, including that of excommunication. He also included a defense of Judaism as a rational religion, indeed more rational than Christianity, he argued, and hence more capable of serving as a basis for modern civil society. The implication here is that the Jews are less in need of regeneration, at least in religious matters, than others had supposed.

Mirabeau takes a cautious line in his discussion of the religious question. Although he dismisses the Talmud and Jewish thought as a "mire" out of which Mendelssohn had climbed in order to produce "the most sound philosophy" (4), he also takes pains to defend Judaism against such slanders as that it encourages its adherents to cheat non-Jews. Judaism, he concludes, is moral and rational at its core even if it has been burdened with superstition by centuries of Talmudic obscurantism. The true Mosaic basis of the religion, he maintains, "most certainly does not contain anti-social principles" (62) and enjoins no beliefs that contradict the demands of citizenship. For Mirabeau, then, as for Mendelssohn, the Jews do not require full-scale religious assimilation in order to merit emancipation, even if he thinks a little housecleaning to clear away the Talmudic cobwebs is in order.

The second section of the work presents Mirabeau's thoughts on the political reformation of the Jews through a laudatory description of Dohm's essay. Mirabeau rehearses Dohm's theory that the Jews' moral decline has resulted from their persecution by Christians: "All the honest means of subsistence are forbidden to the Jew; how can he not descend into bad faith?" he asks (70). Christians are thus doubly guilty for forcing the Jews to become usurers and then hating them for it. To blame the Jews for not being better, he reasons, is to blame the victim, to take the effect for the cause, to justify "an oppressive policy by the very evil that it engenders" (70). The way to make the Jews better is thus to cease all forms of oppression, to lift all the obstacles to their full participation in the economic life of the nation. "Banish from society every distinction that degrades them; open to them all the means of subsistence and acquisition" (88), he proclaims in what seems to be a plea for total equality.

Mirabeau has been held up by recent scholars as exemplifying a more pluralist approach to solving the "Jewish Question" than the other defenders of the Jews at the time; he seems to advocate granting rights without calling for the dissolution of Jewish identity.[15] It is true that, like Dohm, he advocates allowing Jews to retain their communal autonomy even after they become French citizens: "Let the Jews live and be judged according to their own laws" (89), he proclaims. But it is also true that he calls for a fundamental transformation of the Jewish economy, and of the Jewish moral character, which he labels "regeneration." He even goes so far as to justify, like Lacretelle, the use of force to compel the Jews to regenerate: "And even if the political reformation of the Jews were to necessitate some inconvenient measures," he asks, "even if their physical and moral regeneration were to demand a certain amount of police vigilance, a certain amount of paternalistic care, was not government created for this very purpose?" (129). He leaves vague what this "paternalistic care" might entail, but one may surmise that it involves restrictive legislation barring Jews from certain forms of commerce, like moneylending. There can be little doubt that the Jewish identity that Mirabeau imagined for the future would be very different from the one he described in his essay.

Making the Jews Happy

The desire to do something about France's Jewish minority came to a kind of climax in 1787. Along with the publication of Mirabeau's book, that year also saw an essay contest sponsored by the Academy of Metz on the subject "Is there a way of making the Jews more useful and happier in France?" The terms in which the Metz Academy formulated its question come straight out of Dohm's essay on the "civic improvement of the Jews" and clearly implied the necessity of a positive answer. Accordingly, the Academy excluded two of the nine entries, which maintained the Jews could not improve.[16] Two of the remaining entrants—Grégoire and a lawyer from Nancy, Claude-Antoine Thiéry, who both formulated positive answers—were asked to rewrite their submissions. The following year, they were selected as winners along with a new entry by a Polish Jew who had settled in Paris and who would shortly go to work at the Bibliothèque du Roi, Zalkind Hourwitz.

Sepinwall describes how the submissions to the competition fall into three broad categories.[17] She labels the rejected entries, which maintained that the Jews could not improve and could not therefore enter society, "impossibilist." On the other end of the spectrum, Hourwitz represented the "unconditionalist" position, which maintained that the Jews could integrate into Christian society immediately, without first undergoing reform. Thiéry and Grégoire fell somewhere in the middle—what Sepinwall labels the "conditionalist" position, which maintained that the Jews could eventually become productive members of society but first needed to undergo regeneration. I would argue that other differences divide the three winners as well, including the nature of the assimilation they demand of the Jews in return for allowing them to integrate into the national body. Nevertheless, as we will now see, the three winning submissions share most of the same basic assumptions about the nature and cause of Jewish economic "vices" and the way to correct them.

Grégoire's *Essay on the Physical, Moral, and Political Regeneration of the Jews* might surprise modern readers expecting it to be more clearly philosemitic. On the contrary, it seems almost *antisemitic* in its relentless detailing of Jewish moral and physical degradation. Beginning with a survey of Jewish history since the Roman era, Grégoire maintains that the only way the Jews have changed since their dispersion is in "their obstinate attachment to their belief, which they abandoned with so much facility in ancient times, and that spirit of avarice which seems to be their ruling passion."[18] Although he exculpates the Jews from certain of the worst charges leveled against them—such as poisoning wells—he emphasizes their guilt in engaging in unsavory monetary practices, especially usury. These moral failings, moreover, go hand in hand with their physical degeneration. Citing Lavater, he describes their sallow complexions, hooked noses, hollow eyes, prominent chins, frizzled hair, and overly constricted muscles of the mouth. The women, he says, have weak eyesight. The men have reddish beards—the sign of an effeminate temperament—and are given to a certain solitary vice. They are dirty and prone to diseases of the skin (55–57).

In proper Enlightenment fashion, however, Grégoire does not see these negative characteristics as signs of God's punishment for killing Christ. Nor does he see them, as later race theorists would, as innate and immutable biological characteristics. On the contrary, he traces the Jews' defects to behaviors that can be corrected. Many of the Jews' physical deformities, he explains, derive from inadequate nourishment (partly the result of kosher dietary laws) and poor living conditions. Likewise, many of their moral failings result from their outdated customs and religious prohibitions, which can be altered once the Jews renounce the Talmud, which Grégoire considers pernicious.

However, the main charge against the Jews and the main obstacle to their incorporation into Christian society—their unsavory business practices, or usury—he explains as the result of oppression: by denying the Jews the right to own land and to farm, by barring them from most honorable trades and professions, Christian society left them no choice but to make money from money, which leads inevitably to fraud and deceit. Grégoire follows Lacretelle and Dohm in placing blame for Jewish sins not on the Jews but on the Christians: "The Jews have produced the effects. You have been the causes. Who then is most culpable?" he asks his enlightened readers (54). The key to improving the Jews, he argues, lies in removing the restrictions that hang over them, in opening to the Jews the full range of economic activities. Once they have more options, he reasons, they will renounce their unsavory practices and choose the path of virtue.

According to Sepinwall, it was the possibility of regeneration that allowed Grégoire to contemplate awarding rights to a group he considered so debased.[19] It is important to recognize, moreover, that in his essay for the Metz competition, Grégoire did not support complete freedom for the Jews. While he advocated removing the restrictions that prevented the Jews from owning land and joining guilds, he also advocated imposing new ones designed to curb their usury and rectify their commerce. In addition to very specific measures designed to limit Jewish moneylending, he supports barring Jews from occupations that would offer the temptation to chicanery. "Let us exclude them also from being tax gatherers, custom-house officers, cashiers, attorneys, and from every employment which would give them too many opportunities of being guilty of extortion, of smuggling, and of receiving bribes; for we must never lose sight of the character of the people whom we wish to reform" (182), Grégoire writes. The ultimate goal of this combined carrot-and-stick approach is to transform the Jews into peasants: after a short period of retraining, they will "soon find themselves happy in draining a marsh, or improving and fertilizing waste land" (147). And once they have become farmers, he asks, what is to stop the Jews from becoming soldiers, as citizenship in the modern nation-state would demand of them?

Grégoire recommends doing away with all the special taxes that the Jewish communities had paid for centuries in Alsace and Lorraine and abolishing their communal debts. Indeed, Grégoire would have the Jews surrender their independent communal government altogether, including their religious courts. "Let there be, therefore, no syndic for managing the affairs of these people, and no Jewish communities—let them be all members of ours" (199). The future warrior against local dialects and regional languages hopes for the elimination of Yiddish, that "Tudesco-Haebraico-rabbinical jargon" (199–200), but does not propose an outright ban on it.[20] Neither does Grégoire seek to restrict the Jews' religious liberty: to do so, he writes, would only bind them to their religion more strongly. However, he is not above requiring them to receive instruction in Catholicism and to listen to sermons in church. The ultimate goal, it is clear, is for the Jews to cease to be Jews: "Complete religious liberty granted to the Jews will be a grand step towards their reformation; and, I will venture to affirm, towards their conversion; for truth is never persuasive, but when it appears in the garb of mildness" (165). Conversion, however, is only one element of a much larger assimilatory project: "By encouraging the Jews, they will insensibly adopt our manner of thinking and acting, our laws, our customs, and our manners" (173). The Jews, in other words, can be compelled to shed their difference.

The two other winners of the contest, Thiéry and Hourwitz, both employ very similar arguments about the Jews' economic vices and, like Grégoire, attribute them to a history of oppression and restriction rather than to any fundamental defect in the Jewish character. All three writers marshal the same basic historical facts in service of their demonstration, as had their predecessors, Lacretelle and Dohm. And all of them then argue that the Jews will turn to more productive economic pursuits once they have more freedom. The transformation of the Jewish character is the clear goal of all these writers, although they differ with regard to what this means, when it should take place, and what specific policies are deemed necessary to bring it about.

Thiéry advocates opening all occupations to the Jews. Unlike Grégoire, he rejects the idea of barring them from commerce: "It would be difficult and dangerous to forbid them to engage in it."[21] But he does not refrain from recommending special laws designed to make sure Jews become as productive as possible, conceding that it would be "fitting to compel all the Jews to take up some occupation or other" (86). He even floats the idea of tax incentives designed to encourage Jews to become farmers. He clearly stops short of the prospect of full equality: "I have reminded you that the Jews are men; I think I have proven that we can make them citizens, even if it is impossible to elevate them to the first rank of society" (83–84). Thiéry maintains that the Jews can never become dignitaries or exercise power in the state on account of their religion, because the state must remain firmly Christian.[22] Unlike Dohm, and unlike those who would argue for Jewish emancipation during the Revolution, Thiéry does not advocate redefining the state in secular terms. And unlike Grégoire, Thiéry has no problem allowing the Jews to maintain their communal autonomy and according to the rabbis their own sphere of influence.

In general, Thiéry is more gentle in his recommendations for how to bring about the regeneration of the Jews than Grégoire and much more concerned to avoid hurting Jewish feelings. The Jews, for Thiéry, are a group that must be coaxed toward improvement. He favors the carrot over the stick: "It is very important, I believe, to require nothing, and always to employ in their regard a confidence that invites rather than an authority that commands" (73). He argues forcefully that all signs that stigmatize the Jews and mark their abasement must be abolished so that they can eventually come to resemble everyone else. Instead of being forced to dress and act differently, they should be *encouraged* to do so; otherwise they will reject these recommendations and fall back on the strict observance of their religious laws. The same holds for education: schools must be opened to the Jews, and they should be encouraged, rather than forced, to attend. Cultural assimilation is clearly the goal for Thiéry even if he does not favor the more coercive means to bring it about advocated by Grégoire.

Hourwitz, on the other hand, makes a point of denying that the Jews need regeneration at all. As numerous scholars have argued, the only Jewish writer to enter the competition is much more positive about Jewish difference than either Grégoire or Thiéry.[23] He defends, for example, the Jews' right to Saturday repose even if this means they are ineligible for army service. At the same time, he denies that the Jews look different from non-Jews or that their bodies display any inferiorities that need correcting. The same holds for their religion, and he learnedly reveals how antisemites have misread the Talmud to argue that the Jews must cheat non-Jews. "As long as it has not been proven that the Jews are actually degenerate, I do not see the necessity, nor even the possibility, of regenerating them," he maintains. He repeats the argument about Christian responsibility for the supposed defects in the Jewish character but takes it one step further: "It is not therefore the Jews but the Christians who must be regenerated and rendered just and humane toward the former."[24]

However, even while denying the necessity of regeneration, Hourwitz provides a blueprint for its accomplishment. Many of the recommendations he makes contradict his bold, pluralistic rhetoric. For example, although he proclaims that the Jews should enjoy total and immediate economic liberty, he recommends enacting special laws to keep the Jews from usury: "In order to compel them to renounce their illicit trafficking, it is necessary to forbid them all money lending and to nullify their claims on soldiers or any other person . . . unless these claims have been properly notarized" (39). Napoleon would enact a very similar discriminatory policy designed to eliminate Jewish moneylending in Alsace in what angry Jews would call the "infamous decree" of 1808.[25] Hourwitz likewise proposes forbidding the use of Yiddish and Hebrew in commercial transactions and limiting the power of rabbis even when it comes to punishing those who break Jewish religious laws. Clearly, Hourwitz believed the Jews should assimilate politically to the rest of France. Moreover, schools should be open to the Jews in order to encourage a "conformity of language and customs" (37) that sounds suspiciously like cultural assimilation. As Frances Malino notes, however, his call for religious assimilation in the conclusion to his essay is most likely facetious: he argues that "granting the Jews liberty is the best way to convert them to Christianity" (72) because once their temporal situation has improved, the Jews will be forced to admit that the messiah has in fact already arrived.[26]

What is striking here is just how similar all these defenses of the Jews in the years leading up to the Revolution turn out to be. In addition to their structural and stylistic similarities, the three winners of the Metz essay contest—like, for that matter, Lacretelle, Dohm, and Mirabeau—all advocate integrating the Jews into the national body not in order to derive some benefit from them but in order to improve them. Departing from earlier mercantilist forms of philosemitism, they all defend the Jews not because they are good and useful but because they are bad and unproductive. All these writers set "regeneration" as their implicit or explicit goal even if they deny it (like Hourwitz) and if the ways they propose to bring it about differ slightly. All the writers seek, first and foremost, economic assimilation for the Jews: all of them want to correct the Jews' economic vices and either suggest explicit laws designed to bring this about or hint at the advisability of such laws. And all of them suggest that cultural (and possibly even religious) assimilation would be desirable and propose specific measures designed to bring this about as well. If they differ over whether the Jews should receive citizenship before or after they have regenerated, they are clear in what they expect the Jews to do in exchange for their integration. After reading these defenses of the Jews, it's not hard to see why certain critics of Jewish emancipation in France fault it for leading to assimilation, since this was indeed the expectation of the Jews' defenders in the years immediately preceding the French Revolution.

Scholars have asked why these French intellectuals in the late eighteenth century bothered at all with the Jews, who represented such a tiny minority of the French population. Ronald Schechter gives the most compelling answer: the Jews were "good to think."[27] They provided the philosophes with a forum for debating various Enlightenment ideas. And as Schechter points out, these ideas were multiple. For some, the Jews provided the perfect test case for the powers of regeneration: if even this most backward of minority groups could be transformed by reason, then surely anybody could. The Jews thus became a kind of stand-in for the larger project of transforming the entire French nation that the Revolution would attempt to put into practice. For others, however, the Jews "increasingly became 'good to think' about what a citizen was, what a nation was, and under what conditions such entities might come into existence."[28] For Schechter, this is what explains why the Revolutionary Constituent Assembly would debate the question of Jewish emancipation on more than thirty separate occasions even though they had much more pressing concerns to contemplate, like famine, the Civil Constitution of the Clergy, and war.[29]

I want to argue that the outbreak of the Revolution in 1789 marks a dividing line between the two different constellations of values the Jews symbolized. As we have seen, in the decade leading up to the Revolution, the dominant approach to defending the Jews was "regenerative" and sought to transform the Jews into productive citizens through assimilation. This mode of defending the Jews demanded that they transform their economic practices but also required varying degrees of political and cultural assimilation, while often requiring religious assimilation as well. The survey of these various proposals for reform I have provided will now allow us to appreciate how radically different were the arguments for Jewish emancipation put forward after 1789. These later proposals did not prioritize regeneration, or advocate assimilation, but rather used the Jews to define a new type of nation.[30] This new model of defending the Jews was intimately bound up with the priorities of the Revolution in its early phase, before the radicalization of the Terror. The Jews remained "good to think," but what they provoked the Revolutionaries to think about had changed radically. This change has profound implications for understanding the relation of French universalism to minority difference.

Jews, Actors, Executioners

Robert Badinter writes that there is such a thing as a logic of liberty.[31] This logic was gaining ground in France even before the Revolution. In 1787, the same year that saw so many defenses of the Jews, the king gave rights to "all those who do not profess the Catholic religion," which ostensibly meant the Protestants, but raised the possibility of Jewish rights as well.[32] Across the Atlantic, the new Constitution of the United States, also from 1787, implicitly gave rights to Jews since it made no distinctions based on religion, and the American example helped inspire the growing movement for reform in

Europe. Thus, when the French Revolution broke out in the summer of 1789, the Ashkenazic Jews of Alsace and Lorraine cautiously expected some improvement in their situation. Whereas the Sephardic Jews of the southwest were permitted to participate in elections to the Estates General (one of their members was almost elected), the crown did not allow the Jewish communities of eastern France to vote or to prepare a *cahier* with their grievances as other royal subjects were permitted to do. Furthermore, many of the *cahiers* from Alsace and Lorraine complained about Jewish lending practices, increasing the likelihood that the authorities would see the need to maintain or increase restrictions on the Jews.[33]

When the *Declaration of the Rights of Man and the Citizen* proclaimed the equality of all men before the law in August, 1789, the Jews may once again have believed this included them, particularly since the *Declaration* stipulated in article 10 that "no man may be disturbed for his opinions, even religious ones" and (over objections from conservatives) made no mention of Catholicism as the dominant religion of the nation. But it quickly became clear that the language of universalism allowed for ambiguities. As Marcel Gauchet explains, the Revolutionaries proclaimed universal equality as a way of making the case that commoners, the Third Estate, deserved to be treated as the equals of the nobles and clergy. Their goal was to define a new kind of nation unified by a sovereign will—not to enfranchise marginalized ethnic and religious minorities. The Revolutionaries were thus surprised to find themselves suddenly besieged by petitions from a wide variety of minority groups across France claiming the rights they thought had been offered them.[34]

The Jews wasted little time in submitting their own requests. On August 26, 1789, the small community of Jews in Paris submitted a formal petition for civil rights to the Constituent Assembly. At the behest of the Abbé Grégoire, a committee was established to examine the question. In October 1789, the Constituent Assembly admitted a delegation of Jews from Alsace and Lorraine led by Berr Isaac Berr, who spoke eloquently in favor of including the Jews among those eligible to become active citizens: "Let that veil of opprobrium that has so long covered us be torn from our heads," he intoned (again in the subjunctive imperative); "let men regard us as their brothers."[35] The Sephardic Jews of the southwest, meanwhile, viewed these developments with alarm. They already enjoyed near-total equality and did not want the struggles of their less acculturated coreligionists in the east to jeopardize their status by provoking new laws limiting the rights of the Jews. They thus petitioned separately for citizenship, which they argued to be a mere confirmation of the existing rights granted to them by *lettres patentes* during the Old Regime.

At first, the Abbé Grégoire led the campaign for Jewish rights, submitting to the Assembly, of which he was a member, a *Motion in Favor of the Jews*, which laid out the case for emancipation for all Jews, the Sephardim of the southwest as well as the Ashkenazim in the east. It is instructive to compare the *Motion* with Grégoire's *Essay* published two years before. For while on the surface they bear a certain similarity, so that most commentators have lumped them together, in fact they betray key differences that indicate that a radical change had taken place in the way Jews were being defended during this first phase of the Revolution.

As in his earlier *Essay*, in the *Motion* Grégoire makes the case that the Jews deserve rights in spite of their economic vices and argues that the fault for the Jews' many failings lies not with them but with the Christians who have oppressed them for centuries.[36] But whereas he still describes the necessity to regenerate the Jews economically—"to direct the character of that people in a direction other than commerce, to give them a different tendency, to show them that fortune also lies along honorable paths" (30)—he now appears much more forgiving of other forms of Jewish "difference." The fact that Jews do not want to marry Christians should not disqualify them for citizenship, he now reasons, or else Christians who don't want to marry Jews should not be citizens either. And whereas in the *Essay* he had blamed all sorts of ills, including the supposed weakness and deformity of the Jewish body, on kosher food, he now dismisses kosher dietary regulations as irrelevant to the question of whether or not Jews deserve rights: "And moreover what does this dietary difference matter to political tranquility?" (19; Et qu'importe d'ailleurs à la tranquillité politique cette différence diététique?), he asks in the *Motion*.[37] Moreover, he now seems much more willing to admit that Jews possess good qualities, including a basic morality, and even "also present reasons for us to praise them" (22–23). In other words, the call for regeneration has become much less pressing in the *Motion*; it is no longer what drives his call for equal rights.

The methods Grégoire proposes for reforming the Jews have also become much less punitive. Whereas in the *Essay* Grégoire had advocated instituting a variety of restrictions on Jewish commerce and banning Jews from certain occupations in order to push them toward regeneration, in the *Motion* he refers only vaguely to the possibility of restricting the Jews from holding public office for a period of time. Otherwise, he advocates opening to them "all the trades and professions" (46) and treating them with complete equality. And crucially, he makes this recommendation not just in the spirit of justice and in the hope of improving the Jews but also out of a desire to unify France under one law applied universally: "There is a great advantage in being able to apply the same principles of reform to the whole nation, because its character is singular" (41).

What we see here is a shift in the logic underpinning the argument for including the Jews. Whereas before the Revolution almost every one of the Jews' defenders had based his case around the need to transform the Jews, and recommended explicit laws designed to bring this assimilation about, such as barring the Jews from money lending, after 1789 the Jews' defenders argued for treating the Jews *equally*. Special laws prohibiting Jewish commerce became anathema in the new Revolutionary context. The Jews must become citizens because all men must become citizens, or such at least was the theory. (In practice, the Revolutionaries deemed certain men, such as black slaves, not to mention all women, less equal than others.) To a certain extent, the notion of equality before the law proclaimed in the *Declaration of the Rights of Man and the Citizen*, even if it was not proclaimed with Jews in mind, made the special laws designed to bring about Jewish assimilation difficult to justify, indeed contrary to the new spirit of universality driving the Revolution.

The change between Grégoire's two interventions on behalf of the Jews epitomizes this transformation: the Jews must now be made citizens to show that the laws are the same for everyone, to prove that the character of the law is, in Grégoire's words, "identical." To a certain extent, Grégoire seems uncomfortable with this shift. He seems to vacillate between arguing that the Jews can become better and arguing that everyone must be treated equally, unable to decide which is the focus of his case. And I don't think it's a coincidence that as the logic for defending the Jews changed, once regeneration ceased to be the main motivation and assimilation its sine qua non, the abbé began to play a much smaller role in defending the Jews.

Not all the Revolutionaries, of course, agreed that the Jews deserved to become citizens in the first place. The main opponents of Jewish emancipation among the members of the Constituent Assembly came from the eastern provinces where the Ashkenazic Jews resided. Their objections, as we shall see, had less to do with principle than with prejudice and practicality. These were revolutionaries, after all, men who had come together to create a radically new type of government. They had formed part of the body that proclaimed the equality of all men before the law. Nor did they oppose Jewish emancipation on religious grounds. But they represented districts that had filled *cahiers* with complaints about Jewish usury and where the local peasantry harbored long-standing resentments toward the Jews, who often provided them with the only credit they could obtain. Their arguments against extending citizenship to the Jews focused on the threat they posed to the local economy as well as on their supposed unassimilability.

The most extended debate over Jewish emancipation occurred in late December 1789, in the context of a discussion about admitting non-Catholics to all functions of citizenship. The discussion centered ostensibly on Protestants, the most numerous of the non-Catholic groups, but also touched on other dissenters, whose actions or beliefs kept them outside the Church, including actors, executioners, and Jews. These groups had been excluded from elections in certain districts and denied appointments to governmental positions on account of Old Regime laws. Complaints and confusion ensued. The Assembly now realized that it needed to make explicit exactly which men were in fact equal before the law. And it soon became clear that Jews offered the real sticking point.

Several important orators participated in the December debate—including Robespierre, the future Jacobin leader.[38] Grégoire, notably, remained on the sidelines. The most famous intervention, and the most rhetorically astute, came from Stanislas Marie Adélaïde, comte de Clermont-Tonnerre, deputy from Paris, in what would later be known as the "Speech on Religious Minorities and Questionable Professions." Along with George Washington's letter to the Jews of Newport, written eight months later, in August 1790, this speech represents one of the clearest formulations of the logic for granting Jewish equality that the West has produced.[39] It is also one of the most misunderstood. Far from implying that the Jews must change in order to merit citizenship, as many have taken it to mean, it relegates regeneration to the realm of an irrelevant side effect of the main proposition of proving the reach of Revolutionary universalism.

Clermont-Tonnerre begins by denying the need for such a speech at all. The language of equality enshrined in the *Declaration* should make it clear that all men deserve equal rights: "It would seem, gentlemen, that there was nothing more to be done and that prejudices must be silent before the language of the law."[40] But as we have seen, Revolutionary universalism was still a new enough concept that equality for all did not go without saying. And given the persistence of old prejudices, Clermont-Tonnerre agrees to spell out the principle that "professions and religions can never be criteria for ineligibility" (66), which is to say ineligibility to vote or hold office. He dispenses with the question of the "questionable" professions relatively quickly. The law cannot allow for executions and then punish the executioner for carrying them out. Similarly, the nation cannot permit theatrical spectacles and then punish those who perform them. In both cases, Clermont-Tonnerre reasons, excluding a certain category of men for performing a task that is sanctioned by the law violates the spirit of that law.

The same principle, he then argues, applies to religious minorities. The nation has the right to establish a national religion and to ban those who do not practice it. But a nation that allows for religious liberty and does not have an established religion cannot then subject religious minorities to discrimination, even if this discrimination takes the milder form of toleration. "There is no middle ground possible: either establish a national religion and submit to it all your laws; arm it with temporal power, banish from your society men who profess another religion; and erase the article from your declaration of rights, or allow everyone to have his own religious opinion, and not exclude from public functions those who take advantage of that permission" (69). Clermont-Tonnerre knew, of course, that the Revolutionaries had already refused to establish a state religion. The choice he offered was thus a false one, designed to help his colleagues realize the implications of the new kind of nation they had already created.

For Clermont-Tonnerre, including the Jews without restriction among the citizens of France was essential to defining the nature of this nation. It would be secular, but it would also be unified: there would be no "middle ground," no special laws applying to certain categories of citizens. This concern for unity responded to the need for the state to assert its sovereignty and autonomy.[41] According to Lisa Moses Leff, Clermont-Tonnerre was following Rousseau's postulate that the "general will" of the nation was sovereign only if it was universal: it must transcend individual religious beliefs.[42] As we've seen, this had also been a concern for Grégoire, who had emphasized the desirability of an "identical" law for all in his *Motion*. Clermont-Tonnerre now makes this principle essential to the new nation's legal identity, the core truth from which all other laws flow.

For Clermont-Tonnerre, the only reason for excluding members of a given religion would be if following that religion leads to immorality and thereby threatens the public good: "A religion has only one thing to prove in relation to the social body; the only test it has to take is that of morality" (69). Here, he was on less firm ground, for the deputies from Alsace and Lorraine had already in prior debates expressed reservations precisely about the supposed immorality of Jewish usury. Grégoire himself had conceded that Jewish business practices were immoral even if he blamed the Christians for leaving the Jews no other choice. Clermont-Tonnerre follows Grégoire, Dohm, Lacretelle, and all the others in exculpating the Jews by blaming the Christians: "That justly faulted usury is the effect of our own laws. Men who possess only money can only profit from money: there is the evil" (70). And like the other defenders of the Jews, he sees lifting restrictions as the solution: "Let them have land and a homeland and they will no longer lend: there is the remedy" (70). Restrictions on the Jews should not be maintained because the Jews are immoral if these restrictions are themselves the cause of that immorality.

Clermont-Tonnerre goes on to address the other series of objections raised by the critics of the Jews: that they form a nation apart, that they possess their own autonomous communal institutions, and that their religious laws and customs prevent them from mixing with other Frenchmen. As for the last of these objections, Clermont-Tonnerre points out that French laws do not require people to share the same table. Nor do they compel one person to marry another. The state therefore cannot punish the Jews for following customs that are not prohibited and that do not infringe on the national welfare. We may hope that the Jews will cease to follow these customs once they become citizens, he says, but they are not "offenses that the law can or must reach" (70; des délits que la loi puisse et doive atteindre), and they are not therefore obstacles to citizenship. This phrase is crucial to my argument that the Revolutionaries were more pluralist than has previously been recognized: Jewish cultural and religious practices, for Clermont-Tonnerre, have nothing to do with whether Jews should become citizens. Like Grégoire in his *Motion*, Clermont-Tonnerre holds out Jewish assimilation as a possible goal, but he does not make it a precondition for granting citizenship.

The question of Jewish communal autonomy is another matter, however. Here, Clermont-Tonnerre is categorical. The Jews must give up their separate laws and judges before they can become citizens: "To the Jews as a nation, nothing; to the Jews as individuals, everything" (70). This often quoted dictum has also very often been misunderstood. As David Sorkin has shown, it did not mean, as many later interpreters would suggest, that Jews must cease to identify with other Jews, that they must assimilate, or that their religion must become a purely private, individual affair.[43] It simply meant that the state will not recognize the Jews as a corporate entity, just as the state will not recognize other corporations, including guilds or the Catholic Church.[44] Supplying the sentence that followed it helps clarify the parameters of Clermont-Tonnerre's proclamation: "Their judges should not be recognized, they should only have ours; no legal protection must be given to the maintenance of the so-called laws of their Judaic corporation; there must not be any political body or order within the state; they must be citizens individually." The liberal deputy insisted that in exchange for citizenship, the Jews must recognize only the laws of the French government, or in other words, they must assimilate politically. Notably, he does not deny the Jews a group or communal identity, but he does maintain that the kind of group identity that had previously defined them—which was at once religious, cultural, *and* legal—must change. From now on, it must be *only* religious and cultural: there would no longer be a legal definition of the Jew in France.[45]

Note the imperative nature of Clermont-Tonnerre's speech, all the times he uses constructions like "there must" and "they should." And note that he is not speaking of a hypothetical future but rather using the present tense. He is not only laying down the principles for the fair and equitable treatment of minorities; he is conjuring a new nation into existence through the very force of his logic, through his performative speech act.[46] Other defenders of the Jews in this debate would similarly couch their arguments in both moral and practical terms. For Robespierre, the Jews must become citizens because to keep them apart would violate the laws of justice and compromise the long-range goals of maintaining national harmony: "I think that we cannot deprive any individual . . . of the sacred rights that the title of man bestows upon him."[47] For Clermont-Tonnerre, likewise, the justification for enfranchising the Jews was a question of instituting the most rational social formation: "It is repugnant that there should be within the state a society of non-citizens and a nation within the nation" (70). The continued existence of the Jews as a separate entity subject to different laws is less a moral outrage than an offense against his legal sensibilities.

David A. Bell has described how the Revolutionaries forged a new type of nation. They created the idea of a nation defined by ideology rather than by blood or ancestry. "In short, the meaning of 'nation' itself was changing," Bell writes, "from a fact of nature to a product of political will."[48] The efforts to regenerate "backward" groups like the Jews formed part of a much larger plan to remake the entire nation along Revolutionary lines, to inculcate in the entire population a devotion to common national ideals and to instill in them a common national culture that would transcend (or really supplant) regional differences. Belief in this vision of the *patrie* became the criterion for citizenship. Along with the United States, Revolutionary France would thus provide the model for this new type of nation based on voluntary identification rather than ancestral belonging. "From this perspective," writes Bell, "what ultimately defines the nation is less history, or race, or language, or a particular territory, although these remain important, but the common desire to join together as a nation, accepting common laws, values, institutions, and perhaps a common culture and language as well." This new vision allowed for religious and ethnic differences to persist as long as they could be subsumed to a higher ideological commonality: "The status of citizen versus foreigner is defined less by birth or mother tongue than by political stance and cultural sympathies," Bell explains; "the revolutionaries pushed these arguments to an extreme."[49]

I would like to suggest that the debate over the Jews was one of the key moments in which this new idea of the nation took shape.[50] We have already seen how Clermont-Tonnerre conjured a new idea of the nation in arguing for Jewish equality: his plea on behalf of the Jews functions as a performative speech act, describing what kind of nation France must be and now is because he proclaims the necessity of it being so. It is a nation with a single law for everyone—although there would still be restrictions, based on property, for voting and holding office. Perhaps more importantly, though, his speech also describes a nation based on ideological affiliation. This becomes plain when he answers the objections of those opponents of Jewish emancipation who claim that the Jews don't want to surrender their communal autonomy, that they constitute a nation apart, that they long for a return to Jerusalem rather than to be part of France. "Well then!" Clermont-Tonnerre says, "If they don't want to be [citizens], let them say so and then let us banish them" (70). One might easily overlook this line in Clermont-Tonnerre's long speech, particularly since it seems on the surface to contradict the generous and inclusive terms of the rest of his discussion. Actually, though, it represents the speech's essence: the liberal deputy is proclaiming that Frenchness will now be defined by voluntary affiliation, by adherence to an idea and an ideology of what the nation should be. Those who don't want to participate can leave. Mirabeau would argue something similar in the debate over the Jews the next day: "In a government like the one you are building, it is necessary that all men be men; it is necessary to banish from your breast those who are not, or who refuse to become so."[51]

Jews—but by implication, everyone—must *choose* whether to become French. Frenchness is a shared idea. And in this sense, it is a universal right, available to all who claim it—at least in theory. In practice, as we know, the Constituent Assembly at first made active citizenship available only to white men of a certain economic status. Nevertheless, the implications of this new definition of the nation were profound. It included the Jews—or those Jews who wanted to be included (and it turned out that nearly all of them did). But it excluded those who did not accept the new parameters of nationhood, such as aristocrats opposed to the Revolution, whose ancestors had defined Frenchness for centuries but who would soon find themselves forced to flee the country. Jews, moreover, served as the limit case for conceiving of the nation along these new ideological lines. Because of their very strangeness, their cultural and religious difference, their position on the literal and figurative margins of the nation, they became the symbol of what it would mean to conceive the nation as a primarily ideological entity. This, I believe, was why Revolutionaries like Clermont-Tonnerre bothered to defend them in the first place. And this was why the Jews' difference became actually valuable to the Revolution: rather than trying to assimilate it away through regeneration, they needed it to prove how inclusive, how *universal* they could be.

Other scholars, as I've said, have argued that the Jews offered the Revolutionaries a test case for the powers of regeneration. According to this view, the Jews offered the model for what the Revolution expected of all Frenchmen: transformation into a new kind of enlightened, rational citizen. And here too the Jew's initial distance from this ideal made him the perfect symbol. The Jew's retrograde customs and obstinate obscurantism made regeneration a challenge but also showed its potential powers: if the Jew could transform, then anybody could. I am arguing, however, that once the Revolution got under way, this imperative faded before a new one. The Jew now offered Revolutionaries like Clermont-Tonnerre a way to describe what France itself should be. The debate over Jewish emancipation allowed the Revolutionaries to outline the contours of a new kind of nation. This nation needed regenerated citizens to populate it. But I think it's important to note that the formation of the nation envisioned by Clermont-Tonnerre did not require regeneration to succeed. Unregenerated Jews could still be part of the nation he imagined, provided they agreed to abide by French law.

Clermont-Tonnerre pays lip service to the idea that the Jews will one day move toward regeneration by ceasing to follow their outdated customs, what he calls their "religious oddities" (travers religieux). But he notably does not insist that the Jews cease to follow customs that do not conflict with French law: "Certainly these religious oddities will disappear; and even if they would withstand both philosophy and the pleasure of finally becoming real citizens and sociable beings, they are not offenses that the law can or must reach" (70; Certes ces travers religieux disparaîtront; et quand ils survivraient et à la philosophie, et au plaisir d'être enfin de vrais citoyens et des hommes sociables, ils ne sont pas des délits que la loi puisse et doive atteindre). In contrast to the imperative present tense he uses in the rest of the speech when describing the new nation, he employs here the more hypothetical future tense (will disappear) to indicate the probability that the Jews will change—a probability that requires the qualifier "certainly" to render it more likely—and then the conditional (would withstand) to indicate the possibility that they might not. I want to insist on this conditional because it indicates the extent to which the entire process of regeneration had become secondary to that of redefining the nation.

It is surely significant that Clermont-Tonnerre's logic for emancipating the

Jews still holds even if the Jews fail to change their manners and customs. Of course, they must agree to legal assimilation, to abide by French law, and, as I discuss in the coda to this chapter, Napoleon's Grand Sanhedrin would affirm the principle that civil law takes precedence over religious law. But the various "religious oddities" that constitute the bulk of the Jews' difference—including their linguistic, dietary, and vestimentary peculiarities, which the Abbé Grégoire had tried to modify—become irrelevant for Clermont-Tonnerre. Not only is economic, cultural, and religious assimilation *not* a prerequisite for participation in the new national body for Clermont-Tonnerre; I would argue that it is not even really a goal at all despite the (conditional) lip service he pays to it. This is because the Jews' difference had once again become desirable, as it had been for the mercantilists. Only it was now desirable not because of the tangible financial advantages it could bring but because this difference allowed the Revolutionaries to articulate their universalist vision: theirs was a nation that would include a group even as different as the Jews. This was regeneration of a different, almost opposite kind. France might or might not transform the Jews, Clermont-Tonnerre's speech proclaims, but the Jews most certainly would transform France by helping to redefine what it means to be a citizen and what it means to be a nation.

Emancipation and Its Aftermath

Clermont-Tonnerre's speech has long been misinterpreted as demanding that the Jews abandon their religious and cultural identity in exchange for French citizenship. Even a defender of republican universalism like Badinter subscribes to this view: "It is the whole doctrine of assimilation that is expressed there by Clermont-Tonnerre."[52] A notable exception to this historical consensus is Phyllis Cohen Albert, who has argued persuasively that assimilation was not only not required of the Jews but was not really pursued by the majority of them either: nineteenth-century French Jews retained a high degree of ethnic identity, with a low rate of conversion and intermarriage.[53] My own prior work has described how nineteenth-century French Jews sought out new ways of expressing their Jewish identity, including through literary publication, once the Revolution had redefined the nature of Jewishness.[54] Actually, the political basis of Jewishness was restructured rather than eliminated: Napoleon would create the Jewish consistory, a governmental body that centralized Jewish religious practice and bound it closely to the state. In some ways, Jewish life in France had more of a political character after the Revolution (or after the Empire) than before.

But if French Jews did not see their emancipation as entailing an obligation to assimilate, I am also arguing that many of those most responsible for granting them citizenship imposed no obligation of this kind either. Even the arguments made on behalf of Jewish emancipation by Robespierre, the future Jacobin leader, make no reference to economic, cultural, or religious assimilation.[55] Instead, the version of universalism invoked by Robespierre in his defense of the Jews is one that implicitly contains the possibility of including difference: "All citizens who have fulfilled the conditions of eligibility that you have prescribed have the right to exercise public functions," he tells his fellow members of the Constituent Assembly.[56] What he means is that there cannot be separate laws for separate categories of individuals. Difference cannot disqualify someone from citizenship. Or to be more precise, since "eligibility" to vote or hold office was in fact dependent on economic status, he means that only economic differences must be allowed to count, and the cultural and religious difference of the Jews is not disqualifying if a Jew has met the financial requirements for active citizenship.

Robespierre reveals his familiarity with the arguments made on behalf of the Jews immediately prior to the Revolution by invoking Christian responsibility for Jewish economic vices: "How can we hold against them the persecutions that they have suffered among different peoples?" he asks. "On the contrary, these are national crimes for which we should atone by restoring to them the imprescriptible rights of man that no human power can take from them."

According to Robespierre, then, the Jews possess rights in spite of their vices. They do not need to earn these rights or prove themselves worthy of them through regeneration. The Jacobin leader appeals only to abstract principles, not to any quid pro quo: "How can the social interest be founded on the violation of the eternal principles of justice and reason that are the basis of all human societies?" he asks rhetorically, implicitly associating Jewish emancipation with the very basis of the state's new authority.

Most of those who contributed to the debate over emancipation in December 1789, however, opposed granting Jews rights. The Abbé Maury opposed emancipation on the grounds that the Jews were not capable of regeneration and were thus incapable of becoming citizens.[57] François Hell, who had stirred up controversy over the Affair of the False Receipts in the prior decade and who was now a deputy from Alsace, allowed that Jews could perhaps change to become better and proposed a series of draconian regulations designed to effect their transformation, including not permitting them to marry unless they could prove they had an honorable profession. The duc de Broglie, for his part, paid lip service to the humanitarian ideals of Clermont-Tonnerre and the other liberal deputies: "I am far from wanting to erect an obstacle to the kindness that you are seeking to bestow upon the individuals of that unfortunate nation," he maintained, before going on to propose a "severe regulation" designed to curb Jewish usury.[58] He also seemed willing to believe that the Jews could change eventually but advocated a gradual movement toward emancipation, "a wise reserve, even a sort of slowness in the desire to do good." Like several of the other deputies, he warned that moving too quickly might prove dangerous for the Jews since the local populations in the east could attack them violently if they received rights. All of these deputies opposed to emancipation were implicitly responding to the regenerative model of emancipation, epitomized by Grégoire's *Essay*, rather than to the new, nonassimilationist arguments put forth by Clermont-Tonnerre and Robespierre.

Perhaps because its participants were arguing such different points, the debate in December 1789 did not resolve the issue of Jewish equality. The Constituent Assembly voted to lift restrictions on all non-Catholics *with the exception of the Jews*, about whom they reserved judgment. Nevertheless, the deputies had crossed a major threshold. The liberal deputies in favor of emancipation, but especially Clermont-Tonnerre, had turned the question of Jewish emancipation into a referendum on the basic question of the universality of rights. Their arguments made the Jews into a symbol for a new type of nation, one governed by a single law and one based on ideological affiliation rather than ancestral ties. I'd like to suggest that as the debate continued in the following years, during which time the Revolution became increasingly radical as it moved toward a republic, it became apparent that emancipation must take place, that the Jews must become citizens, because the logic of universalism demanded it. To oppose Jewish emancipation, or to make it conditional on assimilation, became tantamount to opposing the Revolution itself.

In this context, as in so many others, supporting the Jews really had very little to do with the Jews themselves. As we've seen, one could defend the Jews passionately and still hold extremely negative views of them. The Abbé Grégoire criticized their unsavory business practices and their physical ugliness. Their religion he considered a source of superstition and often immorality. Clermont-Tonnerre and the others hardly had nicer things to say. But the defenses of Clermont-Tonnerre and Robespierre were of a very particular type: they did not value the Jews as anything other than a symbol for the work of national reconstruction they were endeavoring to bring about. As a symbol for the process of revolution, however, the Jews elicited eloquent declarations of support.

Meanwhile, different factions within France's divided Jewish communities plunged into the world of parliamentary politics to advance their own interests. In January of 1790, the Sephardic Jews presented an address to the Constituent Assembly proclaiming their preexisting claims to citizenship based on the *lettres patentes* given to them under the Old Regime. They thereby divorced their claim from that of the Ashkenazic Jews of the east. Whatever the moral implications of this lack of solidarity with their eastern coreligionists, it proved a smart maneuver for several reasons. First, it invalidated much of the criticism launched against the Jews by the deputies from Alsace and Lorraine and undermined their authority to pronounce on the question. The Sephardic Jews had already displayed their "usefulness" to France and did not suffer from the same perceived signs of moral and physical degeneration as the Ashkenazim. And why should the deputies from Alsace and Lorraine have the right to condemn the Sephardic Jews on account of their eastern coreligionists? Second, since the Sephardic Jews could claim that they had previously enjoyed the rights of citizenship under the Old Regime, it framed the question as whether or not to remove preexisting rights rather than to award new ones.

The hostile deputies perceived a danger here. Jean-François Rewbell, the deputy from Colmar and one of the Jews' fiercest opponents, argued that if the Sephardic Jews could become citizens, the Ashkenazic Jews would have to follow, because both groups in fact had a similar legal status. Isaac-René-Guy Le Chapelier rejected this line of reasoning, arguing that the Bordeaux Jews should not have to depend on the Jews of Alsace to continue enjoying the rights they already enjoyed. The debate continued along these lines for some time, with an extremely vocal minority attempting to disrupt the proceedings every time the secretary tried to call a vote. Finally, on January 28, 1790, by a vote of 374 to 224, the Assembly declared that the "Portuguese, Spanish, and Avignonnais Jews . . . will continue to enjoy the rights that they have enjoyed up to the present time . . . and as a result, they will moreover enjoy the rights of active citizens when they satisfy the conditions required by the decrees of the Assembly."[59] The inclusion of the Jews of Comtat Venaissin in this decree, even though the Comtat was not yet officially a part of France, further underscored the extent to which emancipation for other Jewish groups would likely follow that of the Sephardim.

Although the Sephardim may have intended to help themselves at the expense of the Ashkenazim, in the end, their maneuver served the latter group, as well as the Jews of Paris. Later interventions in the debate over emancipation, both for and against, would cite the emancipation of the Sephardim as a precedent. On January 18, 1791, for example, Louis-Simon Martineau demanded "that we extend to the Jews of all nations, naturalized in France, the rights of active citizens" that had been accorded to the Sephardim.[60] Broglie continued to argue against adding "a great extension to the rights previously accorded to some Jews" on the grounds that it would incite violence in Alsace and Lorraine.[61] But the horses had clearly left the barn. Although the question of Jewish emancipation would continue to surface regularly in the debates of the Assembly, it became increasingly difficult to argue that some Jews should have citizenship while others should not.

The final decree emancipating the Ashkenazim came rather suddenly on September 27, 1791, as the Constituent Assembly prepared to dissolve. The fact that the deputies returned to the question before their business could conclude indicates the extent to which certain members of the Assembly felt that something consequential for the nation rested on the fate of the Jews in France's eastern provinces. With only three days left before the Constituent Assembly would disband, the moderate deputy Adrien Duport approached the podium.[62] "I have a very short observation to make to the Assembly, which appears to me to be of the utmost importance and to demand its full attention," he declared. They had already stipulated who could become an "active citizen," he told them. They had already lifted the restrictions facing certain professions. They had already granted citizenship to non-Catholics, which largely meant Protestants, but in theory included other religious groups as well. "But there is a decree of adjournment that seems to constitute a kind of infringement of these general rights; I am speaking of the Jews."[63] For Duport the way forward was clear: since they had already declared that every man could in theory become a citizen, they had to lift the restriction on the Jews. "I believe that the freedom of religion no longer allows for distinctions to be made in the rights of citizens on account of their beliefs and I also believe that the Jews alone cannot be excepted from the enjoyment of these rights." If even pagans, Turks, Muslims, and Chinese can become citizens, he reasoned, then surely the Jews can also.

After the applause died down, one of the deputies from Alsace—Rewbell, a main opponent of Jewish emancipation—tried to take the podium, but he was prevented from doing so by Michel Regnault de Saint-Jean D'Angély, an ally of Duport.[64] "I demand that we proceed to a vote without listening to those who want to speak against this proposition," Regnault declared, "because to combat it is to combat the Constitution itself."[65] This last speech was decisive: the measure passed before any of the opponents could speak out against it. After years of debate, the Constituent Assembly finally made the Jews of Alsace and Lorraine citizens by force of logic—and by forcing a vote. One of the most monumental events in modern Jewish history occurred through a parliamentary sleight of hand. The final argument made on behalf of the Jews should not go unremarked, however: the fate of the Constitution itself, which is to say the fate of the Revolution and its radical reorganization of the state, was described as contingent on the emancipation of the Jews.[66]

As I have argued, this was because the Jews provided the Revolutionaries with a means to articulate what the new state would be, which is to say, secular and ideological rather than religious and corporate, based on voluntary affiliation with an idea rather than ancestral ties of blood. This is not to say that all those who sought to emancipate the Jews acted out of a democratic impulse. As Schechter has shown, many of them were quite undemocratic in their willingness to restrict active citizenship to the wealthy, and they may have used their generosity toward the Jews as cover for their elitism, for their unwillingness to extend the franchise to the poor masses. It is not a coincidence, Schechter points out, that the grand gestures of inclusion made by the Constituent Assembly to minority groups, including Jews, Protestants, actors, and executioners, were toward groups with very few members.[67] Emancipating the Jews ultimately changed very little in practical terms, especially since a vanishingly small number of Jews would have been wealthy enough to qualify immediately for active citizenship.[68] But if the practical import was slight, the symbolic import was great. And not just as a cover or alibi: the Revolutionaries really did redefine the nature of the nation by including the Jews within it.

The only demands placed on the Jews as a condition of their emancipation were that they renounce the privileges and exceptions that had formerly pertained to them, that they take a civil oath of allegiance to the state, and that they promise to fulfill all the duties imposed on them by the constitution. This amounted to a renunciation of their former autonomous status, and the duc de Broglie insisted that such a renunciation be made explicit.[69] But if political assimilation was therefore required, no mention was made of economic or cultural assimilation, much less of religious assimilation or conversion. Regeneration was not even raised as a desirable outcome in this final debate over emancipation. To be sure, some of the members of the Constituent Assembly may have continued to believe that the Jews must change and perhaps voted for emancipation based on that belief. And it's also true that certain Jews would interpret their emancipation as a mandate, or as a pretext, for change and would pursue a course of assimilation in the centuries that followed. But it is important to note that the terms of their emancipation did not require them to do so.

An anecdote recounted by Gary Kates illustrates the extent to which at least some of the Jews who received citizenship understood it in these nonrestrictive terms.[70] When, in the following year, the Jews of Nancy swore allegiance to the regime at a public ceremony, Berr Isaac Berr, the lay leader of the community, made certain to profess his loyalty to France but also to declare his loyalty to Judaism: "Each of us will naturally follow the religion of his father," he stated. "Thus we can be loyally attached to the Jewish religion and be at the same time good French citizens." This Jewish leader saw no compromise as necessary.[71] In the nearby village of Bischheim, however, the Jews were told by local leaders to cross themselves when they took the oath. They refused and appealed to the departmental Directory, which sided with the Jews. When they next attempted to take the oath, the crowd demanded that they remove their hats. They refused to do so. Once again both sides appealed to the departmental Directory, and once again the freedom of the Jews to follow their own religious laws if these did not conflict with their civic duties were upheld. The Jews of Bischheim succeeded in swearing allegiance explicitly to France, and implicitly to Judaism, on April 30, 1792.

Napoleonic Coda

My point in this chapter has not been to deny that some Revolutionaries believed that the Jews should give up their manners, practices, and customs in exchange for citizenship but rather to insist that the actual emancipation decrees did not require them to do so. This was because a certain strain of universalist theorizing did not object to Jewish difference but, on the contrary, valued it as a way to show just how universal the new form of government they were creating could be. Indeed, it was the feeling that the Revolution had required so little of the Jews in exchange for emancipation, and that the Jews as a result had hardly changed at all after becoming citizens, that motivated Napoleon to take up the "Jewish Question" fifteen years after the emancipation decrees.

During these intervening fifteen years, as republic gave way to empire, the Jews' critics were vocal in denouncing the way that the emancipation decrees had failed to reform Jewish economic practices. Antisemitic pamphleteers continued to call for harsh restrictions on Alsatian moneylenders, and some, such as the Catholic monarchist Louis de Bonald, even demanded the revocation of Jewish citizenship.[72] Napoleon was sensitive to these complaints, but he was even more sensitive to the charge that the newly enfranchised Jews had not sufficiently integrated into French society, that they still constituted a "nation within the nation."[73] Although Napoleon brought the Revolution to an end, he remained its heir in many ways, especially in his universalist ambition to consolidate the country under a single law. The promulgation of the Napoleonic or Civil Code in 1804 represents the culmination of his effort in this regard. But Napoleon was less motivated by the ideal of liberty than the Revolutionaries had been, and his brand of universalism was more homogenizing, less pluralist. He was even more concerned than the Jacobins about the existence of mediating bodies between the state and the individual and saw religious life as one of the prime threats to imperial authority. After the Catholic Concordat of 1801, which allowed the Church to return to France but under a tight form of state control, and the creation of Protestant consistories in 1802, Napoleon next turned his attention to Judaism.

Napoleon eventually created the Jewish consistory, but first he convened the Assembly of Jewish Notables in 1806, and then in 1807 a more official body that he grandiosely dubbed the Grand Sanhedrin after the supreme council of ancient Israel, in order to set down the limits of Jewish religious law in France.[74] The emperor gave the notables a list of twelve questions about how the Jews saw their place in the French nation, along with an implicit set of answers that the he believed would foster integration. Some of the questions, such as whether the Jews felt loyalty to France and its people, did not pose a problem. Neither did the questions about family law or whether Jews applied different standards in their business dealings with non-Jews.[75] As Paula Hyman notes, the Jewish leaders affirmed the rabbinic principle that the law of the land is the law (dina d'malkhuta dina), and whereas traditional applications of this concept had applied only to financial dealings, the Sanhedrin extended it to matters of family law that had traditionally been regulated by Jewish courts. However, the notables were also asked to condone intermarriage, which represented a far more difficult matter. While admitting that a Jew could marry a Christian and still remain a Jew, they refused to accord rabbinic sanction to such a marriage. Despite this (rare) resistance to imperial authority, Napoleon ratified their rulings.[76]

According to Hyman, the decisions of the Grand Sanhedrin constitute nothing less than "a new definition of Jewish identity in the modern world." The notables made clear that their primary identification was with France, not with other Jews, and that Judaism was solely a religion, not also a nationality. "By validating only the ritual aspects of Jewish law," Hyman writes, "they admitted their Jewishness to be partial and theoretically limited to voluntary membership in a religious community alone."[77] The Napoleonic Empire might thus might be seen as marking a decisive moment in the evolution of French universalism, when the effort to unify the country under imperial authority led to the relegation of religion to the private sphere, and to Jewish acquiescence to a policy designed to eliminate public manifestations of their difference.[78] Moreover, the Jewish consistories that were created in the Napoleonic period would work to refashion French Judaism in ways that many consider assimilatory, making its external features much more similar to Catholicism.[79]

But this was not how the members of the Grand Sanhedrin saw their mission. For one thing, their resistance to Napoleon on the question of intermarriage reflects a clear refusal to sanction assimilation. As Phoebe Maltz Bovy has recently shown, Napoleon viewed intermarriage as key to Jewish integration and instrumental in incorporating the Jews into the French nation: it seems likely that his ultimate goal was the complete dissolution of Jewish specificity by breeding it out of the population.[80] This would remain a goal even for well-meaning reformers in the decades to come: as we shall see in chapter 4, intermarriage in the hope of dissolving the Jews as a people forms part of Zola's plea on behalf of the Jews shortly before the Dreyfus Affair. The Sanhedrin's refusal of this radical form of assimilation, and Napoleon's ratification of the refusal, indicates that there was room for maneuver even within the more hard-line, imperial version of universalism.

Just as significantly, the notables used their response to Napoleon's leading questions to articulate a theory of Judaism as a universalist religion. As Leff has shown, they prefaced their responses to Napoleon's questions with a discussion of general principles that emphasized Judaism's resonance with universalist values.[81] Whereas Christian religious thinkers since Saint Paul had stigmatized Judaism as the particularist religion par excellence because of the way that it supposedly erects different laws for Jews and non-Jews, the Napoleonic notables emphasized Judaism's basic morality—a morality that it shares with Christianity—emerging from Hillel's "golden rule." This was in line with a principle articulated by Napoleon's minister Jean-Étienne-Marie Portalis in the Civil Code of 1804: "The principal articles of natural morality constitute the basis of all positive religions."[82] The doctrine of Portalis, ratified by the Sanhedrin, reflected the belief that Judaism, like France's two other "positive religions," preached moral lessons that could help shape good citizens. According to the members of the Sanhedrin, Judaism thus did not need to change in order to be brought in line with French universalism, because Judaism was already universalist in its teachings.

The members of the Sanhedrin thus did not see themselves as sacrificing Jewish specificity on the altar of French universalism. While they agreed to defer to the French Civil Code when it came to matters of business and family law, they did not evacuate Judaism of its specifically Jewish content but rather repackaged this content in such a way that it came to seem just as universalist as Christianity. True, Judaism ceased to represent a "national" identity for the members of the Sanhedrin, but this had few actual consequences in an age when a Jewish state was not yet even a thought, much less a reality. In other words, the Sanhedrin did not lead to the dissolution of Jewish identity but rather allowed for its redefinition. As I will show in the next chapter, the middle decades of the nineteenth century, a period of economic expansion and peace on the international stage, were a particularly fertile period for such redefinition in France. This period saw individual French Jews experiment with their identity in innovative ways, attempting to discover new possibilities for being both French and Jewish, at once universal and particular.

2

France's Jewish Star

> Et sur l'antique scène, autrefois rebutée,
> Où Racine soupire avec sa voix flutée,
> Où Corneille rugit ses larges vers romains,
> Leur Rachel s'éléctrise au fracas de nos mains.[1]
> BARTHÉLEMY, *"Le Peuple juif"* (1847)

On February 28, 1839, anxious crowds thronged the box office of the Comédie-Française, hoping to score a seat for that night's performance, the hottest ticket in town. This in itself was a surprising event, something inconceivable a mere six months earlier, before the new leading lady, Rachel Félix, though still a teenager, had raised the struggling national theater's ticket sales tenfold virtually overnight. That she scored her triumphs in the seventeenth-century tragedies of Racine and Corneille was more surprising still, since these classics had fallen out of favor for a decade, displaced by the free verse and freer passions of the Romantic drama. Observers could barely believe the awe with which the staid old warhorses of the Comédie's repertoire were greeted once Rachel breathed new life into them. "The days on which it announces to its public MADEMOISELLE RACHEL!," wrote the famous critic Jules Janin, "the Théâtre-Français takes on the appearance of a celebration, a serious and solemn celebration."[2]

But perhaps the most surprising thing about that evening in February 1839 was that the play Parisians were lining up to see—Racine's *Esther* (1689) —had been staged in honor of the holiday of Purim, in homage to the star's Jewish heritage. If the Comédie took on the air of a "serious celebration" that night, it was thus because of an actual celebration. The unlikelihood of this scenario deserves pause. In a country in which Jews represented a tiny minority (roughly 0.2 percent, a mere 70,000 out of a total of 33 million),[3] where they had been subjected to humiliating discrimination just fifty years before, suddenly the Comédie-Française, the repository of all that was most venerable in the French cultural tradition, had decided to celebrate a Jewish holiday of which most theatergoers had doubtless never heard. "The whole city was given over to an immense celebration," wrote Janin, "a unanimous praise, a torrent of emotion the likes of which we will never see again in our lifetimes, such that to honor this miraculous child, a Jewess, the Théâtre-Français wanted to put on the most elaborate celebration and to recount the anniversary of the deliverance of the Jewish people by Esther."[4] Like the biblical heroine she played, whose charms won the king's favor for her people, Rachel seemed to have scored a triumph not just for herself but for all of France's Jews.[5]

Not everyone, however, was prepared to follow this script. If Rachel's performances at the Comédie-Française occasioned an outpouring of philosemitism on a scale never seen before, or possibly since, they also provoked one of the first public campaigns of antisemitism in modern French history. From the beginning of her career, Rachel was denounced as an interloper, a foreigner, a Jew. And for certain critics, a Jew like Rachel could never truly understand the characters that Racine and Corneille had created — even when these characters, like Esther (or Bérénice), were supposed to be Jews.[6] Indeed, in 1839, even Janin thought that Rachel was quite simply too Jewish for the role of the Jewish queen as imagined by the Catholic Racine. "But what would Mme de Maintenon have thought," he asked in a snide review, "if she had been told that the masterpiece she commissioned from Racine would one day be treated like a synagogue canticle?"[7] If after the actress's death he would remember her performance as Esther a triumph, in 1839 he denounced it as a sacrilege.

As we saw in the last chapter, the French Revolution's emancipation of the Jews raised profound questions about the relationship of political universalism to minority difference. What did it mean for the Jews to become French? Did citizenship require them to give up some or all of what made them distinct as a people? Or was there a way for the Jews to retain their difference while also participating fully in the life of the nation? Could Jewish and French identities be reconciled? These questions were asked with increasing urgency in the 1830s and '40s, as France headed toward another revolution, and as a new generation of Jews, born as French citizens, began to enter the mainstream of French national life. Nowhere, however, were these questions asked more urgently than at France's national theater, where Rachel was attempting something completely unprecedented — to embody the heroines of Racine and Corneille, the epitome of neoclassical French culture, while also, and very publicly, performing her Jewishness.[8] This chapter reads Rachel's career through the eyes of her critics to see how new ideas about Frenchness, about French culture, and about the Frenchness of French culture took shape on the stage of the Comédie-Française during the July Monarchy.

Jews Come Center Stage

During the decade of the 1830s, French Jews became more prominent, more conspicuous, than they ever had been before. The Jewish population of Paris was swelling: from roughly 500 Jews at the time of the Revolution of 1789, there were 10,000 by 1840, an increase of almost 2,000 percent at a time when the population of the city as a whole less than doubled.[9] This increased visibility of Jews in the capital magnified their significance since Paris was in the nineteenth century, as it remains today, the center of French political, economic, and cultural life.

But the perception of an increased Jewish presence, beginning in the 1830s, had more than mere demographic causes. In the first forty years following their emancipation in 1790–91, French Jews had kept a relatively low profile. The generation that gained civil rights during the Revolutionary period had come of age during the repressive Old Regime and remained marked by it. At the time of the Revolution of 1789, most of the Ashkenazic Jews of France, who represented a large majority of the French Jewish population, lived in rural villages in Alsace and Lorraine, spoke French only as a second language if at all, and had not received a secular education.[10] Although some newly emancipated Jews began to take advantage of the opportunities the Revolution had made possible by moving to large towns and cities, and giving up traditional forms of economic activity (peddling, etc.) for more "modern" occupations, it was really their children who reaped the benefits of emancipation.

Born as French citizens, no longer encumbered by memories of state-sanctioned discrimination or by any legal obstacles to their advancement, this new generation made a significant mark beginning in the 1830s. The middle decades of the nineteenth century, often referred to as the "golden age" of Franco-Judaism, saw French Jews begin their remarkable social and economic ascent.[11] Along with prominent bankers like James de Rothschild and business leaders like Émile and Isaac Péreire, this generation produced celebrated lawyers such as Adolphe Crémieux, as well as army officers, professors, and politicians. Three Jewish deputies to the National Assembly had been elected by the 1840s.[12] Judaism itself increased in status in this period: in 1831, Louis-Philippe made Judaism an official state religion in France, putting it on a par with Catholicism and Protestantism. The government would henceforth pay the salaries of rabbis and help fund the construction of synagogues, a policy that lasted until the law of 1905 separating churches and the state.[13] This gesture of inclusion reflected the way that *laïcité* was understood in France during this period—not as the rigid separation of religion and government but as the equal treatment of France's three main religions by the state.[14]

That Jews had risen to the highest levels of banking and business, and even politics, could not have surprised many. Jews, after all, had been known for their connection to money long before their emancipation, and court Jews had maintained a privileged access to power since the time of Joseph and Pharaoh. What proved more amazing and more disturbing to observers at the time was the truly new prominence of Jews in the *cultural* life of the French nation beginning in the 1830s. Rachel was hardly the only Jewish artist of the period to capture the public's attention. Indeed, two of the most prominent cultural figures in France in the 1830s were Jews. Giacomo Meyerbeer, originally from Berlin, made his name as the composer of *Robert le Diable*, which premiered in Paris in 1831 and helped popularize the new style of French "grand opera." Fromental Halévy, the Paris-born son of a cantor, scored an equally big triumph with his own grand opera, *La juive*, which premiered in 1835. Rachel would take her stage name from the heroine of this spectacle.[15]

Jewish women were also making their mark on French culture in the period. The two most celebrated singers of the era, the sopranos Giuditta Pasta and Cornélie Falcon, the latter of whom starred both in *La juive* and in Meyerbeer's *Les Huguenots* (1836), were both thought to be Jewish.[16] "Everyone knows that M. Halévy, her coreligionist, wrote the role of Rachel, in *La juive*, for that famous singer," commented a journalist about Falcon in the Jewish newspaper *Les Archives Israélites*.[17] The article also discussed several other famous Jewish singers of the era, including Mme Nathan-Treilhet, Mlle Julian, and Mme Auguste Iffla. The influx of Jews to the French stage would only increase in the following decades. Rachel was followed into the theater by her five younger siblings, as well as by a childhood friend, Mlle Judith, another Jewish woman who became her rival at the Comédie and who would lend her name to a scurrilous, antisemitic biography of her after her death.[18]

Rachel's fame far surpassed that of all her Jewish contemporaries. It would hardly be an exaggeration to say that within a few years of her debut at the Comédie in 1838, she was the most famous Jewish artist—and one of the most famous Jewish people—in the world, on a par with the Rothschilds. This fame made her into a kind of lightning rod for the phenomenon she epitomized: her presence onstage forced the public to grapple with the sudden appearance of Jews at the center of French economic, political, and now cultural life. This was the allegorical meaning observers attached to all her performances, but especially to her performance as Esther, the Persian queen, whose public declaration of her Jewishness before her husband saved her people from destruction. "By introducing into the current repertory a play in which the Jewish nation plays such a major role," wrote a critic in *Le Corsaire* of Rachel's *Esther* in 1839, "the Comédie-Française showed its gratitude to the actress who enriched it and its appreciation for a people who had given to the theater Mlles Falcon and Rachel; to music Mssrs. Meyerbeer and Halévy, to the railroads M. Péreire and M. Rotschild [*sic*] to finance."[19] As this critic makes plain, Rachel became a stand-in for all her successful coreligionists. She performed the Jew's rise.

It is important to note that this was a role that Rachel very consciously chose to play. Like Queen Esther, she very publicly proclaimed her Jewishness. Some would say she flaunted it.[20] While we today are more accustomed to actors changing their names to sound less Jewish—Issur Danielovitch became Kirk Douglas; Judith Tuvim became Judy Holliday; Emmanuel Goldenberg became Edward G. Robinson, etc.—Rachel changed hers from the blandly unsemitic Élisa to sound *more Jewish*. As Rachel Brownstein says of her choice of name: "In mid-nineteenth-century Paris . . . 'Rachel' signified legendary, literary, tragic Jewish Woman."[21] Her younger siblings, Sarah, Dina, Lia, Raphaël, and Rébecca, along with her rival Judith, also took on explicitly Jewish stage names.[22] Clearly Jewishness was part of a carefully orchestrated marketing strategy to make these stars stand out. It lent them a hint of mystery, an exotic allure.

Rachel's self-conscious performance of her Judaism even as she ascended to ever greater heights of celebrity stood out in a period that saw several highly publicized conversions of prominent Jews to Catholicism. In the 1820s, the son and son-in-law of the grand rabbi of France converted. So too did the wife and children of Adolphe Crémieux, the president of the Jewish consistory, in the 1840s, causing no little scandal.[23] Other young, educated Jews sought a form of assimilation in the new Saint-Simonian "church," many of whose leaders were of Jewish origin. Much to the relief of the Jewish press, however, Rachel refused to convert, even as she became the consort of princes and bore Napoleon's grandchild. Articles in the *Archives Israélites* would constantly praise her devotion to her ancestral religion, rejoicing at each of the actress's many public manifestations of her Jewishness.[24] Janin concludes his posthumous biography of the actress with a detailed description of her funeral in 1858, in which thousands of fans descended on the Jewish section of Père Lachaise cemetery to listen to Grand Rabbi Isidor recite Hebrew prayers. The critic recounts how the rabbi switched to French to point out that his presence "gave the lie" to rumors that Rachel had converted on her deathbed. "To be sure, she had too much intelligence not to die in the religion of her fathers," Janin quotes the rabbi as saying.[25]

Rachel and Her Critics

For French audiences in 1839, Rachel's performance as Esther provided a particularly apt allegory for understanding the dramatic changes experienced by France's Jews since emancipation. Both the biblical Book of Esther and Racine's adaptation of it depict the rise of the Jews in Persia from an abased, endangered condition to one of prosperity, thanks to Esther's brave resolution to appear before her husband, the king Ahasuerus, and publicly proclaim her Jewishness. The play allowed non-Jewish audience members the opportunity to identify with Ahasuerus, the benevolent king who saves the Jews, and to vilify his henchman Haman, their persecutor. And it offered up Rachel as an obvious stand-in for Esther, the Jewish woman willing to be looked at, to perform her Jewish identity in public, and thus secure her people's triumph. Why, then, did so many French critics choose to identify not with Ahasuerus but with Haman? Why did certain observers at the time vilify Rachel?

To answer this question, I turn now to the hostile commentary that Rachel solicited throughout her career. We find in these rage-filled reviews a kind of antisemitism that was rare in France in this period—a violent racism and xenophobia that foreshadows the much more virulent Jew-hatred of the fin de siècle. The July Monarchy has long been recognized as the era in which a new kind of economic antisemitism was taking shape on the left of the political spectrum in France.[26] In the critical response to Rachel, however, we see that the threat of a Jewish *cultural* takeover of the nation was perceived as every bit as menacing as the economic one.

Perhaps no critic was more dogged in his denunciations of Rachel than Charles Maurice (pseud. Charles-Maurice Descombes). The founder and editor of the *Courrier des Théâtres*, a "petit journal" dedicated to theatrical gossip, Maurice hounded Rachel from the very beginning of her career, attacking her in nearly every issue of his newspaper in the late 1830s and '40s. To be sure, Maurice had it in for other Jewish performers and theater directors as well,[27] but he saves his nastiest barbs for Rachel and her family, whom he depicts as a bunch of scoundrels out to bleed the Comédie-Française dry with their excessive greed.

In one particularly mean-spirited article about Rachel's contract negotiations at the Comédie-Française in 1840, he mocks the Yiddish accents of

Rachel's parents in a manner akin to Balzac's phonetic transcription of the Jewish banker Nucingen's mangled French in his novel from the same period, *Splendeurs et misères des courtisanes* (A Harlot High and Low):[28]

> The famous ve vant more money [chai pesoin d'archent] of Papa Félix, which we were talking about the day before last has just been bettered by an even more amazing quip from Mama Rachel, for Mama and Papa equally look out for their interest in the earnings of their dear daughter. The Board tried to make the Israelite couple understand that the three month break they were demanding should be deducted from her wages . Mama Félix pretended not to understand: "Vell zen, she said, forget about ze break; ve von't ask you to pay for it. . . . Ve vill take it and zat is zat!" Oh! The Jews! How Christian they are! ["Eh! pien, dit-elle, qu'il ne soit plus question de ce gonché; nous ne te-mantons rien pour ça. . . . Nous le brenons et que tout soit tite!" Oh! les juifs!! sont-ils chrétiens!][29]

Note the way Maurice alternates between using the term "Israelite," considered polite, with the more pejorative term "Jew," viewed by nineteenth-century Jews as an insult because of its associations in the popular lexicon with usury.[30] Maurice ironizes his politeness with this juxtaposition, as well as with the sarcastic attribution of the supposedly Christian virtue of charity to the Félix family for refusing to give up their demand of paid vacations—"Oh! les juifs!! Sont-ils chrétiens!" The clear conclusion of Maurice's article is that the Jews have placed a stranglehold on the Comédie and that there is nothing the native-born Catholics can do about it. The result, he predicts, of allowing Jews onstage will be nothing short of disaster for the Comédie and for French culture more generally.

Maurice seems torn between decrying Rachel's success, which he finds inexplicable, and denying it altogether, in what clearly was a futile exercise in wishful thinking. He overcomes this dilemma, in true paranoid fashion, by attributing Rachel's popularity to a Jewish conspiracy. For not only does Maurice see Jews running the theaters and grabbing all the leading roles, he also imagines them filling the audience of the Comédie. Panning Rachel's performance as Émilie in Corneille's *Cinna*, he recounts how she was on the verge of being booed off the stage before her coreligionists in the audience came to her defense. "But all Judea had erupted in applause; it well understood the necessity of restoring their half-fallen idol to her pedestal. Thus she scored a triumph! We nevertheless found Mlle Rachel weak, uncertain, strained."[31] Here Maurice depicts the Jews as a horde of foreign invaders determined to hijack the French theater. Note that the term he uses—"Judea"—is a clear denial of the Jews' claim to Frenchness, implying either that the Jews have remained a "nation within the nation," thus violating the terms of French universalism with their continued ethnic solidarity, or that the French nation is not actually universalist and should never have included them in the first place.

Maurice would return to this image of the Jews as a horde of foreign invaders frequently, both in the *Courrier des Théâtres* as well as in the ominously titled *The Truth about Rachel* (La vérité Rachel), a book he consecrated to unmasking the actress as a hoax, which contained a chapter entitled "The Jews." Unsurprisingly, it was Rachel's performance as Esther in 1839 that occasioned Maurice's most vituperative insults and most dire prognostications. "Yesterday, the Théâtre-Français gave a performance that it wanted to render solemn," he writes in the *Courrier des Théâtres* after the Purim premiere of *Esther*, which he describes as a disgusting pandering to the star and her Jewish supporters.[32] "Mlle Rachel, in her quality as director of the theater, let it be known that she would play Esther in order to celebrate the anniversary of the day when the Israelites were saved from the massacre ordered by Haman." According to Maurice, the actual director of the Comédie, Védel, "too weak and too ineffectual to resist that order, that clucking of its golden-egg laying hen," agreed to his star's demand and let it be known that February 28 was also Rachel's birthday, hoping this would encourage some Christians to attend the performance as well.

But according to Maurice, the Jews didn't even let the Christians near the box office that night. "The whole of the Théâtre-Français was filled up with Israelites, from the pit to the rafters. . . . All you could hear was German, Swiss and all the idioms of countries where that dispersed nation had found more constant asylum." One can just imagine the suffering of the poor critic as he found himself surrounded by all those "Swiss"-speaking Jews! How, he leads us to wonder, could such a crowd understand a single word of Racine? No matter; understanding the play is not the point. Rachel's *Esther*, he declares on March 1, is merely a plot concocted to flatter the pride of the star and her rich supporters. It is, he declares, a "religious success [un succès de religion]." The next day he improves upon his bon mot: "The success of Mlle Rachel was a Jewish success [un succès de juifs]," he announces on March 2. "Let them hang a ham from the door of the Théâtre-Français and nobody would enter."[33]

Jews have invaded France, Maurice tells us. They have laid their hands on its most precious institutions, but they can never really comprehend its mysteries. "The production of *Esther* is the most bloody injury that Racine has sustained since an insolent fool once called him a scamp," he declares on March 3, in yet another round of what amounted to a week-long attack on the production. He deplores the costumes, the sets, every aspect of the play. Most of all he deplores Rachel's performance as the Jewish queen: "Mlle Rachel cannot, can never play Esther. Everything about her is wrong for the role, from the harshness of her voice to the mocking expression of her face, down to her angular body and her lack of intelligence, for she has instinct but without knowing why or how." For Maurice, Rachel is too strong, too aggressive, too haughty—far from the passive *belle juive* of stereotype, whom antisemites often found so alluring. "The role of Esther demands an entirely different kind of simplicity from that which the young actress displayed as Hermione [in Racine's *Andromaque*]," Maurice opines. "It requires a simplicity that is sweet, timid, reserved, full of candor, of submission, of modesty, and most of all endowed with a profound religious feeling."[34] This religious feeling is above all Catholic. Paradoxically, a Jew like Rachel can never understand the Christian virtues of the Jewish heroine as conceived by Racine.

The critical controversy over Rachel's performance as Esther turned on the question of race and religion. Here lay the heart of the matter, the central question that pursued Rachel throughout her career: Could a Jew, especially a Jew who boldly proclaimed her Jewishness like Rachel, interpret the roles of the French neoclassical tradition? Was French culture actually universal and hence open to everyone? Or was it Catholic in the narrow, parochial sense? To put it in yet another way, on what terms had the Jews become French? Was their entry ticket to French culture limited and conditional? Did it require them to shed their Jewish difference? Or could an actress like Rachel play one of Racine's heroines while still *acting Jewish*?

Janin's hostile review of Rachel's Esther from 1839, which I quoted at the beginning of the chapter, brings the controversy into focus. Writing in the mainstream *Journal des Débats*, which had a much higher circulation than the *Courrier des Théâtres* and a much greater claim to cultural authority, Janin nevertheless echoes the line that Maurice had been taking for months.[35] Janin begins his review by marveling at the audacity of the Comédie's celebration of Purim: "The Théâtre-Français celebrated last Thursday a strange anniversary that we thought had been abolished 1839 years ago by the coming of the Messiah; we are speaking of the anniversary of the deliverance of the Jewish people by Esther."[36] Like Maurice, Janin sees this celebration as a cynical abasement of the French national theater before the power of the Jews and a sign of incredible Jewish arrogance: "They thus revived Racine's tragedy expressly to celebrate that Israelite anniversary, expressly to celebrate the birthday of Mlle Rachel, who is Jewish, expressly to flatter the pretentions, which nothing can shake, of contemporary Israelites." Clearly, Rachel's performance as Esther was meant to pay tribute to the success of Jews in French national life. This was stating the obvious. But if Janin at first seems to stay just shy of overt hostility to the Jews, he quickly crosses the line.

The remainder of his review stigmatizes Rachel's performance as an insult to the French cultural tradition, incarnated in the seventeenth-century neoclassicism of Racine:

> But what would Mme de Maintenon have thought if she had been told that the masterpiece she commissioned from Racine would one day be treated like a synagogue canticle? What would Louis XIV have thought, who recognized himself in that oriental king Ahasuerus, charged with so much glory and so many crimes? What would Racine himself have said, that Christian inspired by the Bible, that great Catholic poet, if he could have known what they would one day make of his work which was destined for the young Christian girls of Saint-Cyr? Surely Racine would have exclaimed: God of the Jews, you have won!

According to Janin, Rachel has treated this noble piece of Christian poetry like something to be performed in a synagogue. She has turned *Esther* into a Purim *spiel*. Rachel's performance is worse than a travesty; it is an insult to the fundamentally Catholic nature of France, a sin akin to blasphemy:

> However, we Christians shouldn't feel too sorry for ourselves since we were allowed to attend that Israelite celebration; and by the God of Abraham, Isaac and Jacob! It's a good thing that we don't have to take upon ourselves the responsibility for such a performance. How they spoke those beautiful verses! How they disfigured that lovely poetry!

The Jews, Janin implies, have not just failed to assimilate to French culture; they have done something much worse: they have made French culture Jewish.

The antisemitism in the critical response to Rachel gave voice to a set of anxieties about French culture. It brought front and center a debate about who had a right to this culture, who could interpret it, and who could produce it at a time in which increasing numbers of Jews were making names for themselves in the arts. The 1830s and '40s, however, were also a time in which the notion of culture itself was taking on a new meaning. Jonathan Freedman recalls how the modern idea of culture was invented by German Romantic philosophers—Fichte, Hegel, Herder, Humboldt—at the beginning of the nineteenth century.[37] Their theorization of culture as the expression of the genius of a particular people, Freedman emphasizes, formed part of an attempt to promote German unification, to provide a rationale for the creation of a state that would group together the various territories in which German was spoken. But present in these territories, the Romantic philosophers could not help but notice, was a supposedly alien group—the Jews. The ideal of German culture that emerged in this period often explicitly defined itself against this group and in order to exclude it. Jews represented for certain German ideologues the antithesis of art and culture. They were purely mercantile beings, dedicated to crass material gain. They corrupted culture by monetizing it. According to one of the main theorists of this ideology, the composer Richard Wagner, "Our whole European art and civilization have remained to the Jew a foreign tongue."[38]

Like their German counterparts, certain French Romantics conceived of culture in narrow, deterministic terms. Rejecting the universalizing aesthetics of neoclassicism, the Greek and Roman styles favored during the Revolutionary period, the conservative strain of Romanticism looked for a specifically French aesthetic, one that would express the essence of the French national character and give form to a *volkish* model of French identity. Some found it in the Gothic architecture of the French Middle Ages. Chateaubriand's *Le génie du christianisme* (1802) helped inaugurate a trend that would culminate in Victor Hugo's novel *Notre-Dame de Paris* (1831), which takes a French Gothic cathedral as its backdrop. After Hugo's declaration in the preface to his historical drama *Hernani* (1830) that Romanticism was "liberalism in literature," the cultural politics would realign somewhat, and many Romantic writers would begin to adopt a progressive social agenda and a more open, universalist model of Frenchness.[39] But other Romantics remained tied to the more conservative model.

One of these was Pétrus Borel, who penned one of the most hostile reviews of Rachel.[40] Borel was known as the Wolfman (Le Lycanthrope) for his antisocial behavior as well as for the extravagance of his writings. Even so, the viciousness of his hostility toward Rachel is startling. The pretext for his screed against the Jewish actress was an 1844 production of Racine's *Phèdre*, starring Rachel as the tragic heroine who falls in love with her stepson. Like the 1839 Purim production of *Esther*, the 1844 *Phèdre* had a Jewish pretext: it was staged as a benefit performance in support of the Jews of Damascus who had been accused of blood libel, a Jewish cause célèbre of the period.[41] No doubt in an effort to boost ticket sales by adding a whiff of scandal to Racine's most scandalous play, the Comédie cast Rachel's younger brother, Raphaël Félix, as Hippolyte, her love interest. Rachel's younger sister Rébecca would also have a role in the production.

In his review, subtitled "*Phèdre* preyed upon by the Synagogue, Racine's fresh tears," Borel deplores the immorality of the production ("incest in the verse, incest in the troupe"), which he declares to be the kind only a Jew would devise and sure, therefore, to be a smash hit in the corrupt context of nineteenth-century Paris.[42] "Jerusalem can shake under its date palms, break free of its chains, and rejoice at the box office success of these young Hebrews, its children." But the Jews' gain is France's loss. Borel describes how the repellent production causes the statue of *Phèdre*'s creator in the lobby of the theater to weep: "But the great Racine must have shuddered sadly on his pedestal when he saw his verses given over to that rabble and his Phèdre burned by the synagogue like the Eucharist. . . . The poet seemed to beg Israel for mercy.—Useless prayer! Superfluous mourning? Israel has guts only for gold! Israel is without pity!" Borel's accusation of Jewish mercantilism destroying the soul of French classical art might have seemed a bit out of place in *Le Journal du Commerce*, the business-oriented newspaper where he published this review. But the Romantic poet seems oblivious to such ironies, so intent is he to demonize the Jews as the corruptors of everything that is noble in French culture.

For Borel, the fault lies not only with Rachel and her family, who after all are merely following a Jewish imperative to corrupt and destroy. The real fault lies with those to whom the French patrimony has been entrusted, namely the directors of the Comédie, who have failed in their mission to guard against such vile invaders: "Have we become so inept as to lend ourselves wholeheartedly to the despicable fantasy of a horde of bohemians who seem determined to sully the French stage with the mud out of which they crawled?" The reprehensible production of *Phèdre* represents merely the tip of the iceberg for Borel, the latest in a series of Jewish attacks on the French cultural tradition but only the start of much worse to come:

> The Jew is increasingly invasive in art as he is in commerce. The time is not far off when that race, formerly banned and burned, will have so decimated and subjugated us that our cities will no longer have but a little corner of their slums reserved for the last Christians, relegated there in misery and shame, just as in the Middle Ages they had a Jewish ghetto where the last dregs of Judea rotted.

Borel's hyperbolic fantasy of Jewish domination, published a year before Toussenel's *Les juifs, rois de l'époque*, explicitly links fears of a Jewish financial takeover of the nation to fears of a Jewish *cultural* takeover. It comes as no surprise that Édouard Drumont, who united these economic and cultural forms of antisemitism in his *La France juive* (1886), would cast Borel as one of the great precursors and martyrs of the cause.[43]

Rachel and Universalism

The attacks on Rachel by Maurice, Janin, and Borel are antiuniversalist. For these critics, Rachel can never truly embody one of Racine's heroines because French culture is fundamentally closed to Jews and other foreigners. Rachel may speak the lines Racine wrote, but she will do so as a Jew, and it will therefore sound false—to those who know the difference, which is to say to true French people like themselves, if any true French people are able to get into the theater once the Jews have bought up all the tickets. This attitude, I am arguing, was typical of a certain wing of the Romantic movement, which sought to police the borders of culture as a way to solidify French national identity in a time of flux. These Romantics declared not only certain performers but also certain genres and certain styles of literature "French" and hence pure, and others cosmopolitan, foreign, and hence corrupt.

However, some Romantic writers, like Théophile Gautier, had a more complex view of the relation of Jews to culture. A novelist, playwright, and poet as well as one of the era's most important journalists and critics, Gautier (whom I will discuss in greater detail in the next chapter) was more central to the Romantic movement than any other writer. Like certain of his fellow Romantics, Gautier heaped scorn on contemporary Jews throughout his career. Martine Lavaud describes how Gautier's poem "Money Changers in the Temple" (Vendeurs au temple) portrays modern Jews as a degraded race, corrupted by their base concern for financial gain, who in turn have corrupted and polluted France. According to Lavaud, the modern Jew represented for Gautier the anti-Christ in the Romantic religion of art. Worse even than the bourgeois, who was merely philistine, the Jew incarnated a kind of materialistic degradation of artistic ideals.[44]

As Lavaud also points out, however, Gautier did not include all Jews in his denunciations. He exempted classical or biblical Jews from scorn, as well as certain contemporary Jewish artists. Indeed, Gautier made an exception precisely for Rachel. In a moving tribute to the actress published in *Le Moniteur Universel* after the actress's death, Gautier describes her as successfully transcending the crass materialism he elsewhere sees as the realm of the Jews: "No actress has better rendered the synthetic human passion personified by tragedy in the form of gods, heroes, kings, princes and princesses, as if to distance them from vulgar reality and the prosaic detail."[45] Rather than lamenting Rachel's racial and religious origin, as so many of his colleagues had done, he insists instead on her noble qualities: "She was simple, beautiful, grand and male like the Greek art that she represented through French tragedy." It is almost as if the debasement from which Rachel had sprung made her all the more pure and virtuous, all the more similar to her ancient, biblical ancestors.

It is telling, though, that Gautier does not explicitly name Rachel as a Jew. This represents a departure from the general critical tendency—epitomized by Janin, Maurice, and Borel—to harp on Rachel's Jewishness obsessively, which Rachel herself in many ways encouraged by cultivating a distinctly Jewish public persona. It also departs from Gautier's own rather obsessive fascination with Jewishness in his other writings. I would like to suggest that Gautier's praise for Rachel's artistry, which he sees as embodying the austere principles of ancient Greece, provides the model for a kind of universalist political discourse that abstracts the individual from particular or local ties, including race and religion. On the spectrum between assimilation and pluralism, this type of universalism falls on the assimilationist end. This is the type of universalist discourse that sees no value in the particular, that seeks to erase minority difference. Gautier, of course, is not concerned with debating which specific aspects of their identity the Jews must renounce in order to become French. He would erase Jewish difference altogether in order to elevate the individual to the status of the universal. This was the meaning of Rachel's triumph for Gautier: her great artistry made him forget that she was a (modern) Jew.

For Rachel's antisemitic critics, French culture must exclude the Jew or risk a horrifying degradation—a ham hanging from the theater, Racine in tears. For more favorably disposed critics, like Gautier, Rachel managed to become a great artist, but only by rising above her Jewishness. She thus became the model for the kind of assimilation that a certain stripe of universalist expected not just of the artist but of all French Jews. For this type of critic, the Jew could be accepted into the hallowed halls of the Comédie-Française, and by extension into the French nation, but only abstractly, not as a Jew.

Rachel and Pluralism

There was, however, another side of the debate over Rachel. Along with the antiuniversalists (Maurice, Borel) and the assimilationist universalists (Gautier), we also find in the critical response to Rachel a more pluralist vision, one that sees Jews as eminently, perhaps even uniquely, capable of contributing to French culture. For a certain stripe of critic, Rachel's Jewishness was not an obstacle to her success but rather its precondition. We detect this tendency to ascribe miraculous powers to Rachel's heritage in the many biographies that exaggerate the extent of her foreignness and her lack of training. Indeed, most of Rachel's early biographers portray the Félix family as more traditionally Jewish than they really were. As Brownstein points out, they did not strictly keep kosher and spoke and read French and German along with Yiddish. Yet most of the early biographers refer to Rachel's parents by Jewish names—Jacob and Esther-Haya—rather than the French ones that they used in daily life.[46] These biographers likewise tend to describe the Félix family as immigrants to France, even though Jacques Félix was born in Metz, making him and his children French citizens.[47] And although many of her biographers would emphasize her lack of study, Rachel in fact spent several years at the Conservatoire—the most prestigious theatrical school in France.

The tendency to portray the Félix family as ignorant, foreign, traditional, and very Jewish Jews—a tendency to which Rachel and her family lent credence, for publicity purposes—made Rachel's triumph at the Comédie-Française while still a teenager seem nothing short of miraculous. Listen to Janin—who, we have seen, adopted an antiuniversalist, xenophobic attitude in his review of Rachel's Esther in 1839—marvel at the paradox, the very impossibility of Rachel's abrupt transition from poor Jewish immigrant to grand French tragedienne, in the hagiographic biography he wrote after her death: "That child, destined to speak to an appreciative world the most beautiful and the most educated poetic language, an Athenian language, the very language of Racine and Corneille, and all the enchantment of the *grand siècle*, was born outside of France, at its border, in Switzerland."[48] Janin cannot quite get over the fact that someone born outside France, although near it, could speak the pure French of the seventeenth century, of Racine and Corneille—a French so pure it is Greek.

Clearly this fantasy of a poor foreign girl able to speak the pure poetry of Racine without having studied made for good copy. It was a phenomenon, a curiosity, a "miracle"—the kind of sensation that would sell papers along with theater tickets and help make the reputation not only of the actress but also of the critic who discovered her. Janin's motivations in vaunting Rachel's miraculous gifts may have been self-promoting, but they nevertheless reveal an interesting set of ideas about the nature of artistic genius. "She has something better than science," Janin says of Rachel; "she has the divine spark, she has the passion, she has an inner glow that she projects all around her." Rachel's talent, according to Janin, was innate rather than acquired. Was it then the result of divine gifts or the product of historical circumstances? Janin plays on this ambiguity: "She was born in the higher realm of poetry; she already knew all its detours, she revealed all its mysteries."[49] Rachel was born an actress, Janin tells us. She was a native to the land of poetry. But she was also born a foreigner, poor, and a Jew. The implication is that there might be a connection.[50]

Other critics from the time made the link between Rachel's talent and her Jewishness explicit. Writing in the highbrow *Revue de Paris* in December 1838, a few months after Janin's initial articles "discovering" the Jewish star, Antoine de Latour includes in his long article praising Rachel's talent the by now commonplace descriptions of her humble origins: "Mlle Rachel was born in the poorhouse and her childhood was sad and pitiful."[51] But whereas Janin merely marvels that such talent could spring from poverty, de Latour argues that it was the very experience of poverty that endowed Rachel with her tragic gifts. "We conceive nevertheless that the contrast of the poverty of her home and the luxury displayed outside it vividly struck an imagination given to melancholy and . . . prepared her, without her knowing it, for the harsh emotions of the tragic muse." The school of hard knocks apparently taught the young actress far more than any actual school, even the Conservatoire, which, like Janin, he neglects to mention that she attended.

For de Latour, however, Rachel's talent for tragedy also sprang from an even deeper well. "Mlle Rachel is a Jewess," he tells us. "It is thus natural that she acquired, from their habits that remain the same even in a world that is constantly in flux, those bitter impressions of exile that never die among that people." Ascribing to the Jews an unchanging sense of dislocation, a bitterness born of thousands of years of exile that even French citizenship could not temper, de Latour draws a connection to the sufferings of the heroines of tragedy. Like Andromaque, the captive destined to pine for her native Troy, a Jew like Rachel "must have seen herself as a stranger [étrangère] among men." Jewishness thus provides Rachel with the insights into suffering, the tragic bona fides, that enable her to speak the lines of Racine with an authority belying her young age. In the surprisingly pure diction of this frail teenager, the critic hears the sorrow not just of a poor girl but of an entire people: "It would be correct to say that the first tragedy in which she debuted was the lament of the Wandering Jew."

Here we see the other side of the Romantic coin: whereas some Romantics saw the Jews as crude debasers of art, others saw them as adding an exotic leavening agent that allowed French culture to rise. The 1830s and '40s, the period of the July Monarchy, were a unique moment in French history in which Jewishness took on positive connotations for a certain progressive segment of French society. An ancient people whom the French had redeemed once again, the Jews reflected back to the French the glory of their Revolution. This was the identity that Rachel and her siblings claimed when they took on their Jewish stage names, an identity that Lisa Moses Leff calls "decidedly exotic and oriental, ancient and strong, yet French and modern as well."[52] It was also an identity that Rachel and other Jews—especially Jewish women—embodied physically. The fascination with the Jewish physical "type" that we find in the art of this period—in the images of Moroccan Jewish women by Eugène Delacroix from the 1830s or in Jean-Dominique Ingres's portrait of the baronne de Rothschild from 1848—testifies to a sense that, in the years before Arthur de Gobineau's *Essay on the Inequality of the Human Races* (1852), Jewish "racial" features could have positive connotations. As Wendy Brown puts it, "Jewish blood coursing through France was conceived as strengthening French society and improving the overall stock of a nation already at the forefront of world history."[53]

This is the lens through which the critic who signed his articles in the *Courrier Français* with the initials M. A. viewed Rachel. He begins his review of Rachel's *débuts* from October 29, 1838, with the question "Has tragedy finally found its actress?"[54] The answer is clearly yes. What remains in doubt is why this young girl—"who seems barely sixteen years old"—is able to sustain the ponderous weight of the tragic tradition. The answer has to do once again with her Jewishness, but not in the same way as for de Latour. Whereas de Latour had forged a link between Jewish suffering and tragic insight, this critic sees the connection in explicitly racial terms. "Although endowed with a frail and weak constitution, her face does not lack dignity. Her pale and elongated physiognomy bears the character of the Jewish race from which she comes." Written before the pseudo-scientific theorizing about racial hierarchies that would mark the second half of the nineteenth century in France, this racial typology of the Jew draws on Romantic stereotypes employed by Delacroix, Ingres, and so many others—the oval face, the pale skin framed by dark hair, etc. This, we learn, is the face of tragedy.

Whereas later racial theorizing would inevitably see Jewish characteristics as negative, as signs of the Jew's physical and moral degradation, certain critics in the July Monarchy saw them, when attributed to women at least, as more or less positive—as marks if not of beauty, then of distinction. Or in the case of Rachel, of tragic authenticity: "That physiognomy no doubt has nothing gracious about it," the critic for the *Courrier Français* acknowledges. "But it has the expression that is appropriate to tragedy." The critic's portrait of Rachel's distinctive facial features marks her as inferior to a certain aristocratic, French ideal of beauty but at the same time peculiarly suited to the task at hand, portraying the heroines of Racine and Corneille: "She lacks nobility, but not energy; she is quick, ardent, passionate; her eye, a bit shaded by her protruding brow, casts from the depth of its socket a tragic flash and her muscles represent emotion on that thin face." Caricaturists would frequently emphasize these same facial features—the protuberant forehead, the thin face, the penetrating gaze—but would often do so in a mocking, hostile manner.⁵⁵ Here Rachel's peculiar Jewish physiognomy becomes a mark of distinction, her greatest asset.

These critics cast aside assumptions about the "degeneration" of the Jewish people that had formed part of the platform even of liberal reformers, such as the Abbé Grégoire, since the eighteenth century. As we saw in the last chapter, those advocates of Jewish emancipation had argued that the "degeneration," both physical and moral, of the Jewish people was not innate but rather the product of centuries of persecution. By treating the Jews justly and with compassion, they hoped to "regenerate" a backward race. Jews would grow strong, healthy, and more attractive once they had equal rights. Rachel's philosemitic critics, on the other hand, value many of the same Jewish features that reformers hoped to cure. Rachel's physical weakness, her pallor and intensity, serve no longer as the stigmata of Jewish decline but rather as marks of sensibility and moral elevation.

Unencumbered by conventional beauty, Rachel's large forehead seemed to signal her intelligence and directed viewers to the powerful gaze that lay beneath it, a gaze that projected a "tragic flash." Jewishness offered these critics a way of explaining Rachel's surprising greatness. It allowed them to understand what made this poor teenage girl able to recite the lines of Racine and Corneille with such power and skill, for they saw her Jewishness as a kind of certificate of authenticity. The history of the Jewish people, the suffering and exile that left their traces on the Jewish body, seemed no longer like an obstacle to be overcome but rather like a great resource for portraying the tragic heroines of France's neoclassical repertoire.

There was more, however, to the philosemitism of these critics than a desire to redeem Jewish history and defend the Jews from the antisemites. Inherent in their praise for Rachel's theatrical genius lay a new conceptualization of French culture itself—who could interpret it and who could produce it. Rachel's critics were entering into a debate over the nature of French universalism. Praising Rachel's miraculous talent became for her defenders a way to oppose a narrow, deterministic conceptualization of Frenchness based on ancestral affiliation. To say that Rachel had the face of tragedy, that she was endowed with the ability to speak the lines of Racine because of her Jewish heritage and not in spite of it, was equivalent to saying that Jews, even very Jewish Jews, had as much right to French culture as Catholics.

This model of Frenchness derived its legitimacy not from *la terre et les morts*, from blood and soil, as the antisemitic Maurice Barrès would later put it.⁵⁶ It derived instead from the more open attitude toward Jewish difference epitomized during the Revolutionary period by Clermont-Tonnerre and Robespierre. As we saw in the last chapter, these Revolutionaries believed the nation was composed of all those who chose to be part of it, of all those who believed in France's Revolutionary mission. It was defined by an idea, not by race or religion.[57] Jewish difference thus did not need to be suppressed as a precondition for this universalism: on the contrary, the difference of the Jews confirmed universalism's reach.

Behind the praise for Rachel that calls attention to her Jewishness, therefore, lies a struggle over the values and legacy of the Revolution, and over a certain model of French universalism. By proclaiming Rachel the ideal embodiment of the French theatrical tradition, by welcoming her into the hallowed halls of the Comédie-Française not in spite of her Jewishness but because of it, these critics sent a message that anyone could join the club that is France. They carved out a place for Jewishness at the very center of French culture. To be sure, their inclusiveness was largely abstract—it didn't descend into specifics about which Jewish customs and laws should be retained or discarded as Jews became French. And also to be sure, it didn't necessarily extend from Jews to other minorities—it is no doubt the case, for these critics, that the Jews qualify for inclusion within the universal because of their specific history. But in the context of July Monarchy France, when the Jews were the main minority group struggling for acceptance, the positive portrayal of Jewishness signals a general allegiance to a more pluralist form of universalism. This was the battle that Rachel's critics were fighting, a battle that had begun during the Revolution and that continued to rage throughout the nineteenth century, as a new generation of revolutionaries attempted to return France to its republican roots.

Rachel's Revolution

We can now better understand why the vehicle for Rachel's triumph, and for the triumph of the notion of culture she represents, would be those worn out old workhorses of the Comédie's repertoire, the neoclassical tragedies of Racine and Corneille. Some observers at the time, as well as some of Rachel's later biographers, saw her preference for seventeenth-century tragedy over Romantic drama as politically conservative, but the opposite was in fact the case.[58] Neoclassicism had, after all, been the favored artistic style of the French Revolution, best exemplified in the paintings of Jacques-Louis David. To retrieve the Revolution's political legacy in the 1830s, Rachel and her promoters endeavored to revive its aesthetic legacy. That this required a rejection of Romanticism was very much the point (at least at the beginning—later, Rachel would take on a few Romantic roles, but without much success). For despite Hugo's turn leftward in the 1830s, Romanticism, as we have seen, remained associated with certain conservative notions about culture and the nation. Rachel, in other words, was acting out a republican ideal when she performed Racine and Corneille. She was affirming her allegiance to the Revolutionary tradition and to a form of universalism that the Revolutionaries had found in the ancient models of Greece and Rome.

This is not to say, however, that political divisions mapped neatly onto aesthetic ones in the nineteenth century. When antisemitic critics like Maurice and Borel bemoaned the insult that Rachel's Jewishness inflicted on the memory of Racine, they were trying to enlist the prestige of neoclassicism in support of their own reactionary, racist views. Certain cultural nationalists and xenophobes tried to claim *le grand siècle* for their cause as much as those on the left felt that the Greek and Roman style of the seventeenth century epitomized their own more democratic values.[59] This was what lay behind the insistence by Maurice and Janin that Racine's heroine Esther was really Catholic rather than Jewish. They were trying to reclaim neoclassicism from the Revolutionaries and their political descendants.

If the reactionary critics, including at times Janin, seem to be protesting too much, if the images of Louis XIV begging the Jews for mercy and Racine in tears seem over the top, it is because the seventeenth century had become such contested terrain, yet another battleground in the war over Frenchness would come to be known in the twentieth century as *la guerre franco-française* (the Franco-French war). That a critic like Janin seemed to go both ways, to be torn between opposing ideas about both the quality of Rachel's performance and her significance for French culture, can be traced, I think, to his position at the center, or *juste milieu* as it was pejoratively known, of the political spectrum in the July Monarchy. Janin's critical schizophrenia in regard to Rachel is a symptom of his ambivalent stance on French politics more generally during this period of political transition between the restoration of the Bourbon monarchy (1814–30) and the Second Republic (1848–52).

It is in the context of this political battle that we must understand what became perhaps Rachel's most celebrated performance of all, her declaiming of the "Marseillaise" during the Revolution of 1848 (see figure 1). For months, beginning immediately after the Revolution's outbreak in February, Rachel would rise from the stage after concluding a performance as a tragic heroine and chant the rousing anthem by Rouget de Lisle to wild popular acclamation. "And suddenly Mademoiselle Rachel, bearing the flag in her glorious arms, her head held high, and her eyes burning with a somber fire, began to declaim," writes Janin in his posthumous biography. "She was a Muse . . . a Fury. She was superb and terrible. We shivered and trembled, and the heroic fever took hold of every soul. How beautiful and valiant she was then

FIGURE 1. Anon., "Rachel Singing the 'Marseillaise'" (1848). Photograph courtesy of the Bibliothèque nationale de France.

in her inflexible mission, and how dangerous!"[60] Significantly, although the *juste milieu* critic might have felt that Rachel had gone too far, and no doubt feared the political forces she unleashed, he did not question her right to hold the flag.

A foreign-born Jewish woman had thus become the incarnation not just of Racine and Corneille but of the spirit of the French Revolution itself.[61] But this was only fitting. For it was the French Revolution that first gave civil rights to the Jews and that spread (temporarily) this hope of freedom to the Jews in the lands the Revolutionary army conquered. And like its predecessor, the Revolution of 1848 gave (alas, also temporary) hope to those struggling for democracy throughout Europe, including the many Jews who were still locked in ghettos in central and eastern Europe and even in nearby Italy. Significantly, the 1848 Revolution also saw Jews serve as top ministers in France's interim Revolutionary government (Adolphe Crémieux at Justice—Crémieux was a close friend of Rachel from the beginning of her career[62]—and Michel Goudchaux at Finance). Like the actress, these Jewish political leaders had taken on a symbolic role as the embodiment of French universalism, not in spite of their Judaism but because of it.[63] In Rachel, and in France, people thus saw a vision of a different type of nation, one that did not just tolerate the other but that allowed the other to become itself, to achieve its highest honors, to serve as its ideal representative.

Rachel herself eventually tired of her command performance, repeated nightly. Janin attributes her death from tuberculosis in 1858, at the age of thirty-six, to her revolutionary exertions.[64] Indeed, the extent to which Rachel's own politics were as revolutionary as those of her admirers remains in doubt. Certainly, she didn't always live up to her revolutionary role: her romantic liaisons would seem to imply Bonapartist tendencies.[65] But her intentions are beside the point. In the highly charged political atmosphere of the July Monarchy, when the battle over universalism and the legacy of the Revolution was being fiercely fought, Rachel's performances became one of the prime arenas of the conflict. Rachel's bid to embody the highest and most prestigious form of the French cultural tradition, and to do so while boldly proclaiming her Jewishness, staked out a bold vision of France as a universalist republic that welcomed Jewish difference on its own terms.

Rachel's brazen performance of Jewish identity, even while playing the Greek queens of the French theatrical repertoire, was nothing if not a provocation. That certain critics found much to hate in these performances thus comes as little surprise. Unfortunately, the recourse to racist, xenophobic, deterministic models of the nation has always been the default position not just in France but in European political and cultural life more generally.

Ultimately, the attitude toward the Jews that we find in Maurice or Borel is not so different from that found during the Dreyfus Affair at the end of the nineteenth century in France, or in Nazi Germany during the 1930s and '40s, even if some of their metaphors—the ham hanging from the door of the theater, the statue of Racine crying—stand out as memorable contributions to this ignoble tradition.

What really does stand out in the Rachel story, I have tried to show, is the existence of a countertradition. The strong strain of philosemitism that took shape in the critical response to Rachel was indeed something new—and something, I think, that in the mid-nineteenth century could only have been found in France. It's hard to imagine the national theater of any other country in the 1830s (or for that matter today) staging a play in honor of Purim, or a poor immigrant Jew like Rachel coming to embody the most sacred elements of the nation's cultural and political heritage. This is because the brand of universalism that took shape in nineteenth-century France was not a priori hostile to, or incompatible with, overt expressions of Jewish identity. While some certainly sought to exclude the Jews or push them toward assimilation, others attempted to make a place for Jewish particularity even within the space of the French universal. The example of Rachel reveals the existence in the nineteenth century of an important current of French thought that saw the Jewish particular as fully compatible with, and even as a conduit to, universalism.

3
Universalism in Algeria

Charles X invaded Algeria just one month before being ousted by the July Revolution of 1830, bequeathing to his more liberal successor, Louis-Philippe, a new colony and a host of questions about how to govern it. Foremost among these was the problem of what to do with the large numbers of Muslims and Jews who lived there. Unlike in France's plantation colonies in the Caribbean, the indigenous people of Algeria would not be made slaves. But neither could they become citizens, at least as long as they practiced religious customs—such as polygamy and divorce—that conflicted with French law. Should they thus be compelled to give up their religious traditions? Or would it better serve French interests for them to become subjects but not citizens? What would this mean in practice? And what would it mean for the legacy of political universalism, the idea that all men are born and remain equal in rights, which retained its hold over the French political imagination even after the Empire and a return to monarchy?

That the colonization of Algeria caused the French to rethink their political ideals seems self-evident, and yet historians of French political culture long acted as if the colonies could be cordoned off from the metropole. The story of France's fitful march toward democracy in the nineteenth century was told without confronting the paradox that some of the same men who fought for liberty at home implemented a system of exploitation based on racist hierarchies abroad. Recently, however, historians have begun to reexamine French republican ideology in the light of colonialism, providing a better understanding of the process by which, in the words of Alice Conklin, "the nation of the 'rights of man' deprived so many people of their freedom."[1] In what follows, I contribute to this ongoing project by examining how the policies developed to manage the indigenous populations of Algerian Jews changed the way that the French thought about the nature and reach of universalism.²

The Crémieux Decree of 1870, which extended the universal rights of citizenship to Algeria's Jews, seems at first glance to parallel the Revolution's emancipation of metropolitan Jews in 1790 and '91. But unlike the Jews of metropolitan France, who gained civil rights without having first "regenerated," the Algerian Jews experienced forty years of concerted efforts — spurred both by French military authorities and by metropolitan Jewish reformers — to transform their cultural, economic, religious, and juridical lives before they were granted citizenship.³ In Algeria, I will argue, the brand of universalism that eventually included the Jews was predicated on assimilation, the erasure of difference. It thus would seem to constitute a departure from the more pluralistic models of universalism that I have investigated in the previous chapters.

However, looked at from the perspective of the metropolitan Jews, a different picture emerges. French Jewish reformers saw their mission not as pushing the Algerian Jews toward assimilation but rather as encouraging them to acculturate. They wanted the Algerian Jews to emulate not some abstract ideal of Christianity but their own brand of Franco-Judaism, the "universalized" form of Jewish identity they had developed in the decades since their emancipation. Moreover, it was through advocacy on behalf of their Algerian coreligionists that French Jews pioneered a new and very public role for Judaism on the domestic political stage. Their effort to minimize Jewish difference in Algeria paradoxically led to the assertion of Jewish difference in metropolitan France, as they carved out a place for Jewish advocacy at the heart of the French universalist tradition.⁴ That this new model of universalism could work simultaneously to include Algeria's Jews and exclude Algeria's Muslims constitutes not the least of the contradictions I will explore in this chapter.

An Indigenous Population

Jews had lived in the area that became Algeria since the first century of the Common Era, long before the arrival of Islam. The Jewish population in the nineteenth century was a diverse one. Made up mostly of Arabic-speaking Mizrahim, it welcomed waves of Jewish migrants, including Ladino-speaking Sephardic refugees from the Inquisition and traders from Livorno. Under Ottoman rule, the Jews had second-class status: like Christians, they were considered "dhimmis," a term that derives from an Arabic word meaning "protected." As a "people of the book," Jews enjoyed certain rights but not equality with Muslims.⁵ Most lived in special Jewish quarters in northern cities like Algiers, Oran, Constantine, and Tlemcen, although there were also significant Jewish communities in the Southern Saharan regions of the Mzab. As in medieval Europe, the Jews faced restrictions on their manner of dress and occupations. Most Jews worked as small-scale artisans, shopkeepers, and peddlers. Although French invaders would later portray their condition under Ottoman domination as uniformly isolated and degraded, some Algerian Jews prospered. The Livornese elite participated in international trading networks and had significant contact with Jews in Europe.

While the overall size of the Jewish population of Algeria was smaller than that of France, Jews constituted a much bigger percentage of the total Algerian population, particularly in cities.[6] In Algiers in 1840, they represented 18.5 percent of the total population and fully one-third of the indigenous population. In Oran, they represented nearly 17 percent of the total population and 21 percent of the indigenous population. By comparison, Jews constituted less than 1 percent of the Parisian population in the 1840s.[7] Jews also constituted a sizable minority in the Saharan Mzab region, which would not come under French rule until 1882. The large communities of Jews in neighboring Morocco and Tunisia maintained close ties with the Algerian Jews and augmented their numbers throughout the nineteenth century, particularly once Algerian Jews began to benefit from preferential treatment at the hands of the French authorities.

When the French invaded Algeria in 1830, they faced the question of how to govern the indigenous population of Muslims and Jews while encouraging the immigration of Christians from France and other European countries to the colony. This was a new kind of colonial situation for the French. With the exception of Louisiana and the trading posts in West Africa, most of France's earlier colonies were islands with plantation-based economies that relied on imported slave labor. Either they did not have indigenous populations or the French drove off or killed the natives. The population of France's Caribbean colonies fell into three basic legal categories: white citizens, black slaves, and a category in between—"free men of color," which included people of mixed race. The status of this last category vacillated. In 1791, the Revolutionaries granted equal rights to freeborn men of color and then extended rights to all freemen in 1792. They eventually abolished slavery two years later, in 1794. Freemen of color lost their rights under Napoleon, who also reinstated slavery. But the July Monarchy then restored citizenship to freemen of color in 1833, not long after it began to administer Algeria. And when the Revolution of 1848 abolished slavery for good, the freed slaves in France's colonies became full French citizens.[8]

Slavery fundamentally contradicted the universalist principle that "all men were born and remain free and equal in rights," but once the slaves were freed, they became citizens with equal rights. In Algeria, on the other hand, the French divorced freedom from citizenship. Although the French killed many Muslims and contemplated expelling the Jews from the colony altogether, they eventually opted to grant the indigenous populations limited autonomy while proceeding to expropriate their land and resources.[9] Immediately after invasion, the French authorities promised to respect the religious freedom of all indigenous subjects, but this offer of liberty did not come with anything resembling the legal equality, or legal protections, of citizenship.[10] In Algeria, as Emmanuelle Saada has noted, the French invented a new category of person: the native subject as distinct from the citizen. Other French colonies would adopt this citizen-subject distinction after 1880. Algeria thus became what Saada calls a "laboratory" for France's later settler colonies in Indochina and elsewhere.[11]

The new category of "native subject" constituted less a total rejection of universalism than a kind of compromise. Through a process known as the "civilizing mission," the French came to conceive of the native subject as potentially able to attain citizenship once he (and it was always a "he" since women, even in France, did not have the rights of citizenship until 1944) had proven himself worthy by conforming to the standards of French civilization. And as Joshua Schreier has shown, the Algerian Jews would serve as the test case for this process of earning inclusion within the French universal through assimilation.[12] At the beginning of the occupation, however, the French did not yet hold this out as a possibility: their initial policy was to treat indigenous populations of Muslims and Jews as separate and unequal.

Their primary justification for not extending rights to the indigenous population of Algeria was legal. As Patrick Weil explains, the French maintained that Algerians could not become French citizens because certain elements of Muslim and Jewish religious law conflicted with the French Civil Code. Family law posed the greatest conflict since both the Koran and the Talmud permitted divorce—outlawed in France between 1816 and 1884—and, even more problematically, polygamy.[13] The occupying authorities thus initially determined that Muslims and Jews would be governed by their own "personal status" laws and would be permitted to retain their own religious courts. To a great extent, the indigenous communities of both Muslims and Jews in Algeria were treated much as the Jews in France had been treated during the Old Regime—which is to say, they were corporate entities, relatively autonomous but inferior. In Algeria, therefore, there would again be nations within the nation, and separate laws for separate people, a blatant contradiction of France's universalist principles. And, significantly, the Algerian Jews were at first treated in the same manner as Muslims by the colonizing authorities.

Regenerating the Algerian Jews

This situation did not sit well with the leaders of the Jewish community in metropolitan France, who saw the fate of the Algerian Jews as inextricably linked to their own. From the start of the occupation in the 1830s, French Jews took a special interest in their Algerian coreligionists. As Aron Rodrigue has noted, although there had been some individual commercial contacts made in the eighteenth century, this was really the first time an emancipated Jewish community in the West came in direct contact with a traditional community of Eastern Jews.[14] As the first European Jews to gain full emancipation, and at a time when the English and German Jews were still fighting for full equality in their countries, the French Jews saw it as their mission to guide their oriental coreligionists on the path toward modernization by eliminating their outdated customs and pernicious "vices."[15] Anticipating France's "civilizing mission," their ultimate aim was to make the Algerian Jews worthy of becoming French citizens.

To be sure, the French Jews saw much in the Algerians that needed correcting. Articles in French Jewish periodicals scrutinized their manners and customs for signs of backwardness. In its first year of publication in 1840, the *Archives Israélites* published articles lamenting the sorry state of Algerian Jewry in almost every issue. One report by a Jewish doctor in the French army declares the Algerian Jews "an execrable race" because of their stubborn attachment to religious superstitions and "outrageous fanaticism."[16] But while he maintains that most of the Algerian Jews oppose French colonization, he detects certain signs of hope, including a tendency to send their children to France for schooling. In a similar manner, a letter "On the State of the Jews of Algeria and on the Means of Lifting Them from Abjection," also published in 1840, focuses on the filth and poverty of Algerian Jewish homes. This observer also denounces the immoral economic practices of the Algerian Jews, who are marked by a "calculating mindset."[17] He concludes with a series of suggestions to improve them, including reforming their religious and educational institutions and mandating service in the French army.[18]

In addition to advocating cultural, economic, and legal assimilation for the Algerian Jews, metropolitan Jewish reformers would constantly call for religious reform. The Algerian rabbis were repeatedly condemned by the French Jews as "fanatic" and castigated for fostering superstition, as well as "religious decadence and moral laxity."[19] The home became the site of particular pressure: "immoral" practices, such as divorce and polygamy, were denounced as reformers tried to remodel the Algerian Jewish family according to the increasingly bourgeois standards of the metropolitan Jews. It is important to note that while the French Jews did not pull punches in criticizing the "abjection" of the Algerian Jews, they consistently held out the possibility that they were capable of change. And the transformation that the metropolitan Jews themselves had undergone in the fifty years since their emancipation was consistently cited as a model.

As Schreier shows, Adolphe Crémieux and other French Jewish leaders decided that the metropolitan Jewish consistory should take the lead in transforming the Algerian Jews. Crémieux tried to sell this plan to the French authorities by touting the benefits that would accrue to the military occupation if the Algerian Jews could be made French. In an 1833 letter to the minister of the interior, Crémieux argued that the modernization of the Algerian Jews under the guidance of the French Jewish consistory could eventually help further France's "political goals" in the region. The Algerian Jews were seen as potential middlemen, able to interpret both linguistically and culturally between the French and the Muslims. Both the metropolitan Jews and the French military authorities believed that the French Jews would gladly aid the colonizers in order to improve their status vis-à-vis the Muslims who had long subjugated them. Another appeal by metropolitan Jewish leaders in 1836 mentioned the "advantage for the government could result from a Jewish consistory at Algiers."[20] The French Jews sought to play the Algerian Jews against the Muslims, casting the former as potential allies against the latter in the service of colonization.

It was in this context that two French Jews, Jacques-Isaac Altaras and Joseph Cohen, undertook a journey to Algeria with the support of the War Ministry in 1842. Altaras, a wealthy naval outfitter and president of the Marseille Consistory, was born in Syria and spoke Arabic. Cohen, a young lawyer who would go on to edit the scholarly journal *La Vérité Israélite*, had an interest in Jewish history. Together they spent two months visiting the cities in both the eastern and western French-occupied regions of the country. They had already published an article in the *Archives Israélites* arguing that the Algerian Jews had benefited from the overthrow of Muslim rule and that this should render them more likely to support French imperial aims in the region. They also pointed out that the community suffered from a variety of vices that could be cured by bringing them more in line with French cultural norms.[21]

Their report begins by invoking the problems that plague the Algerian Jewish population, which they ascribe to centuries of oppression at the hands of Muslims, to poverty, and to the brusque transition to French rule, which caused a general relaxing of moral standards: "There is moral turpitude among the lower classes; there is also poverty."[22] All the purported idealism and all the political calculation that historians like Conklin have found in the ideology of the "civilizing mission" can be found in the Altaras and Cohen report: after invoking the high-minded goal of bestowing upon this degraded people the gift of French civilization, what they refer to as "that noble and grand mission to morally improve a population that has wallowed for eighteen centuries in a degrading servitude" (68), they highlight the various benefits that France would gain from winning the Jews to their cause. The Jews speak the local language, they are accustomed to the harsh climate, and they are a naturally industrious group. Moreover, they possess "an eager and deep sympathy for the nation that gave them liberty and offered them their share of the benefits of civil equality" (67). Here, Altaras and Cohen jump the gun a bit, since no civil equality had yet been granted, but their clear goal is to move the French authorities in this direction as quickly as possible.

They provide a number of specific recommendations for transforming the Algerian Jews into useful servants of the French regime. These include, first and foremost, forcing them to assimilate politically by giving up their communal autonomy, including their religious court (Beit Din) and communal leader (Mekdam), who traditionally negotiated with the authorities on behalf of the Jewish community. Algerian Jews must submit to French civil law, which means abandoning polygamy and divorce. They should likewise assimilate culturally by giving up traditional dress and furnishing their homes in the French style. Furthermore, they must be sent to French schools, which should guide them toward economic assimilation: Algerian Jews should be made to engage in "productive" occupations, especially farming for the lower classes, rather than petty commerce. "Professional and agricultural instruction is indispensible to those families that the conquest placed in a position of lowly fortune" (172). Training the poor Algerian Jews in manual and agricultural trades "would assure them a profession that is at once honorable and useful to the colony" (172–73). Jews should also be welcomed into the armed forces.

If one hears echoes of the Enlightenment discourse of "regeneration" in the Altaras and Cohen report, it is not by accident. As I showed in chapter 1, the Abbé Grégoire complained about many of the same "vices" in the Jews of Alsace and Lorraine at the end of the eighteenth century and offered almost exactly the same prescription for making the Jews of France's Eastern provinces "happier" and "more useful" to France, including forcing them to surrender their communal autonomy and directing the poor to adopt manual and agricultural occupations.

Altaras and Cohen view the Algerian Jews as being like Alsatian Jews at an earlier stage of their development.[23] And just as the French Jews had been "regenerated" through exposure to French civilization, so too could the Algerian Jews be transformed. Like Grégoire, Altaras and Cohen imply that the benefits of French citizenship must be accorded only to those who already share French values and customs. Ultimately, as we saw in chapter 1, the French Revolutionaries would depart from Grégoire's approach by emancipating the French Jews without demanding assimilation as either a precondition or a quid pro quo. This is not the case for Altaras and Cohen: their version of universalism is one that insists on the renunciation of difference before rights can be given.

Crucially, however, the Algerian Jews are depicted by Altaras and Cohen as not only desiring regeneration but as having already begun the process of assimilation to French cultural norms: "If one penetrates into the more intimate secrets of their existence, one finds in them an admirable aptitude to assimilate the principles of civilization that we bring them" (67). Unlike the many contemporary descriptions published in the *Archives Israélites* that detail the backward customs and fanaticism of the Algerian Jews, Altaras and Cohen give numerous examples of the ways that Algerian Jews, in the twelve years since the arrival of the French (less in some parts of the country), had already started to make the changes deemed necessary for meriting citizenship. These include attending French schools, adopting Western styles of dress, reading French newspapers, and most significantly, according to this head of the Marseille Consistory, learning to speak French "with a purity of accent that often puts to shame the defective pronunciation of Southerners." Altaras and Cohen present "assimilation" as not just inevitable but in fact already apparent: "The Israelites have indeed drawn nearer to us and have joined our society with a tireless energy. . . . The work of assimilation is evident," they declare (83–84).

Altaras and Cohen take special pains to demonstrate the ways in which the Algerian Jews display a greater aptitude for assimilation to French culture than their Muslim neighbors. Whereas Jewish men frequent cafés and business circles, "the other indigenous people scornfully keep away" from these arenas of French sociability. Whereas Jewish women can be seen on the street, Muslim women remain at home and heavily veiled. "Besides which, the interior of the Israelite family is more expansive and more open than the domestic interior of the Muslim" (84). The relative opacity of the Muslim home compared to that of the Jew also reflects the Muslim's resistance to adopting the norms of French family law and sexual conduct (such as the renunciation of polygamy and divorce). The Jews are seen as more intelligent than the

Muslims, and this in turn makes them more open to French influence: "The intelligence of the Israelite population is sufficiently developed to understand the generous ideas and the duties of our civilization and is also sufficiently malleable and supple that it responds to our efforts and recognizes their utility" (99). Finally, the Jews have no problem accepting the essential principle that the law of the land takes precedence over Jewish religious law, and they have a long history of submitting to various forms of temporal authority. This makes them far more willing than the Muslims to accept French domination.

As Schreier has argued, the construction of the Jews as eager assimilators and the Muslims as obstinately hostile to French civilization became key to the French mode of colonial domination in Algeria. "The logic of French-Jewish emancipation," Schreier writes, "was paradoxically the same as that which justified Muslims' exclusion."[24] In other words, the French (including metropolitan French Jews) played the Algerian Jews against the Muslims, drawing the former into their cultural orbit, while pushing the latter away. This permitted the French to pay lip service to universalism and the "civilizing mission" with a minimum of obligation. By treating the Jews with deference and eventually offering them citizenship, they showed that equality was in theory possible for those native subjects who accepted French cultural norms. At the same time, the French could feel justified in excluding the large majority of Muslims because of their perceived unwillingness to assimilate as the Jews had done. Altaras and Cohen lay the ideological groundwork for this policy in their report.

Following Crémieux, they conclude with a call to create consistories in Algeria with real power to coerce the Jews into regeneration: "A Consistory in Algeria cannot be created to represent Israelite society, but rather to direct it and to hasten its assimilation with France" (181). The French government proved at least partially open to this recommendation. An *ordonnance* of November 5, 1845, created consistories in Algeria but placed them under the control of the French military authority rather than the metropolitan Jewish consistory. Nevertheless, the Algerian consistory would include a number of metropolitan Jews among its members, as well as local Jews with Westernizing sympathies, and rabbis would be imported from the metropole with the explicit aim of compelling the Algerian Jews to send their children to French schools and to adopt French manners and comportments.[25] This was a clear first step toward the eventual goal called for by Crémieux of granting French citizenship to the Algerian Jews. And despite what was perceived by the metropolitan Jews as a setback when the Algerian Jews were once again treated the same as Muslims by an 1865 decree allowing members of both indigenous groups to petition for French citizenship on an individual basis, the Crémieux Decree of 1870 followed the differential logic established by the Altaras and Cohen report by enfranchising the Jews but not the Muslims.

As Sarah Stein has recently shown, there was one exception to this policy: the Saharan Jews. When France eventually took control of the southern region of the Mzab in 1882, the authorities decide to exclude the Jews living there from the Crémieux Decree and to treat them in the same manner as the Muslim indigenous population. Like the Muslims, the Saharan Jews remained subject to military authority and were permitted to retain their rabbinical courts and traditional legal customs (including polygamy and divorce). They were not to be the object of France's "civilizing mission" and were declared outside the reach of French universalism. Stein underscores how the designation of the Saharan Jews as administratively different from the Jews of the north—even though the boundaries between the two groups were porous—reflects the "invented" nature of French colonial categories and the way that "difference is legislated into reality."[26] I would add that it also demonstrates the degree to which the special status the French accorded to the Jews in the north resulted from specific strategic considerations rather than from any deep belief in the innate worthiness of the Jews as a people. The arbitrary nature of French designations was made manifest, moreover, in 1961 when, on the eve of the French departure from Algeria, the French government abruptly reversed this policy, turning the Saharan Jews into French citizens overnight so that they could be moved en masse to France before Algeria became independent.

Gautier's *La juive de Constantine*

Colonization involved real physical violence: the French struggled to put down revolts in Algeria for decades after the conquest of 1830. But the French also fought a war of ideology. The mission to bring "civilization" to colonized peoples allowed the French to justify their domination, perhaps especially to critics and skeptics of colonialism at home. Literature was a major weapon in this war. In this section, I examine how a play by the leading Romantic writer and critic, Théophile Gautier, coauthored with the popular dramatist Noël Parfait, depicted the French occupation of Algeria in 1846.[27] *La juive de Constantine* (The Jewess of Constantine), I will argue, attempts to answer the all-important question of what to do with the indigenous population of Jews and Muslims. In the process, it advances a changing view of universalism in line with the new colonialist ideology.

La juive de Constantine was not a success. Inspired by a trip to Algeria, in which Gautier and Parfait were struck by the exotic customs of the indigenous Jews and Muslims, the play opened at the Porte-Saint-Martin theater in Paris on November 12, 1846, and closed after a mere twenty performances.[28] Critics seemed to take a perverse pleasure in attacking Gautier, one of their own, devoting uncharacteristically long articles to skewering the play after lamenting how sorry they were to do so: "Of course I would have liked to recount the success . . . of this evening," wrote Jules Janin in the *Journal des Débats*, "but given all the boos, the catcalls, and the boredom . . . given that flat, murky, talentless production . . . we must be honest with our two colleagues if we want to conserve the ability to be fair and sincere with everyone else."[29] So awful did the critic for *Le Constitutionnel* find the play that he sarcastically suggested it must have been written not by Gautier at all but rather by the Algerian rebel Abd El-Kader in order to discourage the French from further colonization by boring them to tears.[30]

It is tempting to follow these critics in dismissing the play as a badly constructed compendium of cultural clichés and threadbare theatrical conventions. In what follows, however, I want to suggest that despite its dramatic shortcomings, *La juive de Constantine* merits closer attention for the insights it provides into the ideology of the French colonial endeavor at a key historical moment. For we find here, amid the clichés and conventions, a road map to what would become France's strategy in managing the indigenous population of Muslims and Jews in Algeria. Twenty-five years before the Crémieux Decree would enfranchise Algeria's Jews while continuing to consign Muslims to second-class status, the play articulates a rationale for this hierarchy based on the relative capacity of these groups to assimilate French legal and cultural norms. In the process, it advances a view of French universalism as beneficent but conditional, predicated on the perceived willingness of the colonized subject to assimilate to French cultural norms.

First, a short summary of the rather complicated action of the play. The curtain opens on the eastern Algerian city of Constantine "in the first two years of the French occupation."[31] At the start of the play, Dominique, a French soldier, is keeping watch on the shop of a Jewish merchant for his superior officer, Maurice d'Harvières, who is in love with the Jew's beautiful daughter, Léa. Maurice and Léa plot to run off to France to get married, but their plans are foiled when a Muslim woman, Kadidja, who is in love with Maurice, betrays their intentions to Léa's father, Nathan. When Nathan confronts his daughter about her illicit love for the Frenchman, she reveals that she has already converted to Christianity. A rabbinical scholar in addition to being a merchant, Nathan knows that the Talmud commands him to treat his apostate daughter as if she has died or face the censure of the Jewish community. But the wily Jew concocts a plan: he will give Léa a sleeping draught in order to fake her death, allowing her to escape with Maurice and save his honor.³²

At the start of the third act, Maurice has been captured by Ben Aïssa, the brother of Kadidjah, who is also in love with Léa. The jealous Ben Aïssa wants to kill Maurice but then hears that the *belle juive* they both love is dead. Kadidjah arranges for Maurice to escape. Act 4 takes place at the Jewish cemetery as Nathan frees his daughter from her fake tomb and bids her farewell, refusing her entreaties to join her and her Christian lover in France. Both Maurice and Ben Aïssa come to the cemetery to see Léa's grave for themselves, and discover she is in fact still alive. Ben Aïssa then attempts to kill Maurice, but Nathan stabs the Arab and flees. Maurice is arrested for attempted murder. Nathan considers turning himself in for the crime, despite the fact that this will free Maurice to elope with his daughter, but he is prevented from doing so by Ben Aïssa, who reveals that he has kidnapped Léa and will throw her off a cliff if Nathan tries to free the Frenchman. Moreover, if Nathan admits that he stabbed Ben Aïssa in order to protect his daughter, his fellow Jews will learn that he tricked them by faking her death. Nathan struggles over this dilemma, and Ben Aïssa throws a sack containing a woman off the cliff. In the final scene, we learn that the sack contained Kadidjah, who substituted herself for the Jewess. The play ends with Nathan braving communal shame and forgiving his daughter.

Without a doubt, *La juive de Constantine* trades in ethnic and cultural stereotypes. And yet, to a reader familiar with Romantic-era representations of Jews in France, the play surprises with its relative philosemitism—its positive, almost idealized, portrait of its Jewish characters. This is evident in the representation of the eponymous heroine, who bears all the trappings of the Romantic topos of the *belle juive*. While such a representation may idealize, it does so with prurient, fetishistic aims. As in the template for the type, Walter Scott's best-selling novel *Ivanhoe* (1819), Léa possesses a physical beauty "that she derives from the nobility of her race."³³ Like Scott's Rebecca, Léa possesses moral beauty as well and is instructed in the healing arts. Gautier seems to echo not just Scott but dozens of other contemporary representations featuring beautiful Jewish women who become romantically involved with Christian men.³⁴ Contemporary Jewish authors like Eugénie Foa also reproduced this scenario: indeed, many aspects of Gautier's play seem borrowed from Foa's work.³⁵ Altaras and Cohen, it should be noted, also mention in their report how the beautiful Jewish women of Algeria attract the attentions of French army officers.³⁶

However, Romantic lust for the *belle juive* usually goes hand in hand with an extremely negative portrayal of male Jews. The topos of the hideous, grasping Jewish father and his beautiful daughter stretches back at least to Shakespeare's *The Merchant of Venice*, and it reappears in a variety of Romantic texts, including some by Gautier himself.[37] It is all the more surprising, then, that Gautier diverges from cliché in his portrayal of the Jewish father in *La juive de Constantine*. Gautier does not describe Nathan as physically ugly or dirty. And for a merchant, Nathan seems surprisingly unconcerned with business affairs. The play starts with Dominique, sent to spy on Léa for Maurice, complaining that the Jew's shop rarely seems to open. We don't see Nathan scheming to defraud Christians or hoarding his ill-gotten gains. On the contrary, he seems totally absorbed with his daughter and the Talmud, and worried principally about his standing within Constantine's Jewish community. At the end of the play, when he must choose between his daughter's death and exposure for having violated the law, his dilemma has none of the baseness of Shylock's weighing of his daughter and his ducats. The struggles of Gautier's Jew may reflect his misguided allegiance to outmoded beliefs, but they do not render him crass or abject.

Jewish audiences in France seem to have registered this difference, reacting to the play with guarded appreciation for its avoidance of the kind of overt hostility that had become so common in representations of Jews on the French stage. Deriding the fashion for dropping the "obligatory Jew" into every play needing a bit of "local color," the critic for *Les Archives Israélites* wittily complains, "For such a long time they massacred us for real, that before cutting us to pieces ["avant de nous mettre en pièces," a pun also meaning "to put us in plays"], it would be nice first to let us catch our breath."[38] But even while gently mocking Gautier's play—"the least of its faults being that it is totally lacking in interest"—the critic acknowledges that at least Gautier avoids depicting his Jews as dirty, money-grubbing scoundrels: "We are happy to find two eminent litterati . . . attempt to put Jews onstage while ennobling their thoughts, elevating their sentiments, and giving them a different aspect from that ignoble mask that the theater up to now always fixes on their faces." According to the French Jewish critic, even if Gautier missed an opportunity to depict the austere beauty of genuine Jewish customs in *La juive de Constantine*, he nevertheless avoided the worst slanders that many of his contemporaries found it only too easy to reproduce.

Why then has Gautier borrowed so many Romantic conventions of representing Jews only to depart from them? The answer can be found in the play's attempt to grapple with the social and political difficulties of the colonial situation in Algeria. Gautier's relative philosemitism makes sense when we view it as a response to the question of whether or not to extend citizenship to the indigenous Muslim and Jewish populations, and how to reconcile

French civil law with Muslim and Jewish religious laws, issues that the French faced with increasing urgency in the 1840s. Indeed, many strange features of the play—including the constant references to conflicting legal codes—only make sense when viewed in this specific context.

In the opening scenes, Dominique, the French soldier sent to spy on Nathan and his daughter, bridles at the limits placed on his authority over the local Muslim population by French law. "If it weren't for the Court-Martial that compels me to moderation, I would have given you a lesson in politeness!" he says to Ben Aïssa, after the Muslim rebel refuses his offer to share some tobacco and coffee. Then, when paying his bill at the café, Dominique comments: "The [army] high command recommends that we pay for all our drinks on the pretext that we are in a conquered country and that we mustn't antagonize the vanquished . . . so let's be generous" (3). Right from the start, therefore, Gautier depicts French law as moderate and just, attentive to the differences between groups but designed to facilitate commerce among them. The "generosity" incumbent on the occupying soldier reflects a conception of French law as capable of providing the basis for a harmonious colonial society in which different groups would interact in the spirit of friendship and cooperation.

Muslim law, on the other hand, is depicted as keeping its adherents rigidly separated from other groups. Ben Aïssa's refusal to partake of Dominique's tobacco underscores this point, as do the frequent references to Islamic law as obliging Muslims to pursue holy war against the French occupiers. Bou Taleb, an Algerian rebel who loves Ben Aïssa's sister Kadidjah in vain, laments: "How crazy I was . . . to seek joy and satisfaction elsewhere than in the triumph of Islam! Allah is punishing me. . . . It is a chastisement that I have earned!" (18). Gautier depicts Islamic law as harsh and retributive, translating a divine imperative not only to punish evil but to seek vengeance for all real or perceived threats to Muslim honor.

Gautier likewise depicts Jewish law, and particularly Jewish family law, as a barrier to interaction with non-Jews. Nathan makes the contrast between the liberal laws of France and the harsh traditional law of Judaism explicit when telling Maurice why he can never marry Léa: "In your country, I know, the Israelites, who have forgotten Talmudic law, make covenants with the idol worshipers; but here, the God of Moses has more faithful servants and there is no friendship between Christian and Jew" (4). The French Jews, according to Nathan, may have thrown off Talmudic restrictions, but in so doing they have ceased to be Jews. As Léa later laments to Maurice, her father's fanatical devotion to Talmudic law supersedes his naturally loving heart. "But Nathan is good," Maurice maintains. "I believe that to be the case," Léa responds, "but his deep study of the Bible and the Talmud, his religious fanaticism, his aversion for Muslims and Christians, occupy his soul entirely" (8). Religious devotion thus compels the Jews, like the Muslims, to hate members of other groups. And it is in relation to family matters—in this case, marriage—that the force of the law comes into clearest focus.

To emphasize the authority of traditional Jewish religious law for the Jews in Algeria, Gautier specifies in the stage directions to the second act, which takes place at the home of Nathan, that a mezuzah hangs on the doorpost to the house: "Suspended in a wooden case, according to Jewish custom, is a roll of parchment containing extracts of the Talmud" (7). Jewish law thus quite literally dominates the scene. Coincidentally (and needless to say, not realistically), the mezuzah happens to contain the exact section of the law dealing with the proper punishment for daughters who marry outside the faith.[39] When Léa informs her father of her love for Maurice, he takes the mezuzah down and reads from it: "Get down on your knees," he commands. "For the book of the law to keep its place at the entrance, this house must be purified! . . . (Coming back toward Léa, reading in trembling voice.) 'The daughter who has given her body and soul to a Nazarene or to an Infidel will be driven away by her family, renounced by her tribe, and considered to be dead'" (11). We know that Gautier's motivation for writing the play came from hearing, during his trip to Algeria, tales of empty tombs in the Jewish cemetery belonging to girls who were treated as dead by families who observed this stricture with a ritualistic exactitude: they mourned their daughters while banishing them from the community.[40] The dramatic force of the play, however, comes from Nathan's struggle to reconcile his fidelity to Jewish law with the demands of his daughter's heart. And it is the heart that wins out: he first agrees to fake Léa's death before finally forgiving her for converting and marrying outside the faith.

Gautier's decision to allow the character of the Jewish father to deviate from Jewish law had profound significance in the context of debates about whether or not French universalism should extend to the indigenous populations in Algeria. As we have seen, despite their initial decision to accord the Muslims and the Jews the same status following the invasion, the French quickly began to see the Jews as more likely than their Muslim neighbors to assimilate to French culture, thanks largely to the efforts of French Jews like Altaras and Cohen. French colonial authorities viewed Algerian Jews as backward and corrupt but as potentially willing and able to reform—which is to say, to accept French law and customs.[41] And, as Schreier has emphasized, the Jews' strategic importance as an oppressed minority who would side with the French against their Muslim oppressors, and thus help facilitate French colonial rule, surely contributed to this perception of their adaptability.

So too did the example of the Jews in the metropole, who had given up their communal autonomy, and renounced the authority of their religious courts, in order to gain citizenship in 1790–91. It stood to reason that the Algerian Jews could transform themselves in a similar manner in order to become French. This process began in the early 1840s, in the period immediately preceding Gautier's first visit to Algeria, which provided him with the source material for the play. In 1841, Algerian rabbis renounced most of their juridical power. The creation of the Algerian consistory in 1847 further contributed to the process of reconciling Talmudic law with French law. In 1851, property cases involving Jews were subjected to the French Civil Code, leaving only family law (divorce and polygamy) as the outstanding areas of disagreement. Property transactions between Muslims, meanwhile, were still regulated by Islamic (shari'a) law.[42]

By the time of Gautier's play, then, the Algerian Jewish community was already being pushed toward reform—especially in legal matters—with the aim of obtaining French citizenship, while the Muslim community remained attached to its religious and legal traditions.[43] When in 1865, a senatus-consult decree for the first time allowed individual indigenous subjects to petition for French citizenship, it made the renunciation of Koranic and Talmudic law a precondition for naturalization. As we have seen, Algerian Jewish reformers and their French advocates were annoyed that this decree treated the Jews the same as Muslims. The reformers thus redoubled their efforts to argue that Jews deserved citizenship because they had successfully assimilated French legal and cultural norms. That very few Algerian Jews (and proportionally even fewer Muslims) after 1865 chose to avail themselves of the offer of citizenship in exchange for renouncing their religious law—which they saw as equivalent to apostasy—indicates that reality differed from the desires of the reformers.[44] Nevertheless, when the Crémieux Decree of 1870 naturalized the Algerian Jews en masse, and with a stroke of the pen forced Jews to obey French law, few Jews complained. Henceforth, the Jews of Algeria would enjoy all the rights accorded to the French or other European settlers, while Muslims retained their separate "personal status" and remained subjected to special ordinances as well as various discriminatory measures.[45]

Gautier's play emphasizes the legal differences separating the three communities—Muslims, Jews, and Christians. It calls attention to the role of law in governing intercultural interaction and explicitly blames the failure of harmony in colonial Algeria on the "fanatical" adherence of Muslims and Jews to their religious laws rather than to enlightened French civil law. Moreover, in keeping with the efforts of Jewish reformers such as Altaras and Cohen, the play advances the notion that the Jews were more amenable to assimilation than their Muslim neighbors. Indeed, literary representations like this one might be said to have played a key role in fashioning these assumptions. The play achieves its goal by turning a spotlight on tensions within the Jewish family, showing Jewish fanaticism as capable of giving way to the forces of French modernity.

The fact that Gautier ventures inside a Jewish home—the second act of the play takes place inside Nathan's house—reflects the perception, also advanced by Altaras and Cohen, that the Jewish family was relatively more open to French cultural norms than its Muslim equivalent. Although the Jewish house remains under the sign of the mezuzah hanging from the doorpost, other features indicate that a certain adaptation to bourgeois French manners and styles has already taken place. When we first see Léa, for instance, she has just set aside a piece of embroidery, the sign par excellence of French womanly domestic accomplishment. Her visibility, both to the other characters and to the audience, offers further indication of her position on the border between oriental and Western conceptions of womanhood. Although she complains to Maurice that "the opportunities to see each other are so rare and so difficult" (5), she manages both to meet her lover and to appear in public.

By contrast, Kadidjah, the Muslim woman, remains veiled throughout the play. As Schreier notes, French colonial authorities treated the veil—which they saw as linked to other elements of Islamic law subjugating women, including divorce and polygamy—as a clear sign of Muslim backwardness and an indication that Muslims remained farther from French standards of civilization than their Jewish neighbors.[46] Whereas Léa captivates Maurice with her beauty, Kadidjah remains both literally and figuratively invisible, both to the other characters and to the audience. When Kadidjah approaches Maurice in the first act, he takes her for a beggar: "What do you want?" he asks her. "Money, no doubt! . . . Here, take this, and let me continue on my way" (6). Maurice's inability to see Kadidjah, which recurs throughout the play despite her increasingly desperate displays of devotion, underscores the play's repeated elevation of the Jewish woman over the Muslim. "What does this veil conceal? a friend? an enemy?" asks Nathan when Kadidjah comes to tell him of his daughter's secret love (9). The play asks this question in many different forms before finally opting to sacrifice the Muslim character so that the French man and Jewish woman can live happily ever after. Kadidjah's eventual substitution for Léa in the sack hurled over the cliff at the end of the play represents the ultimate form of veiling. It repeats a pattern in the play whereby the Jewish woman's freedom comes at the expense of the Muslim woman's confinement.

Just as the play views the relative freedom accorded to women within the Jewish family as a sign that Jews were closer to French standards of enlightened civility than were their Muslim neighbors, so too does it view Jews as more flexible in the application of their backward family laws. When Léa announces her conversion, Nathan at first declares that she must die according to the Talmud: "You have pronounced a death sentence, pitiful wretch!" he tells her. His initial impulse is to carry out the sentence himself despite the fact that Jewish custom allows for the substitution of excommunication for actual execution: "Well, then, unhappy daughter!" Nathan tells Léa. "Come! Come! Because I am the rabbi Nathan, executor of the law!" (11). As we soon discover, however, he decides to violate the law by faking her death, which requires him to lie to the Jewish community. This elaborate ruse signals his elevation of love over law and foreshadows his later decision, in the play's final dramatic tableau, to forgive his daughter for her apostasy: "What does your crime matter to me?" he asks at the end of the play. "I no longer remember it, I have forgotten everything, everything" (27).

Jewish law, of course, is not known for forgiving and forgetting. This seems a very Christian ending to the play, and that's the point: just as Léa has literally accepted Christianity, so too does her father's transformation indicate a willingness to leave behind Old Testament values and Talmudic traditions that the play deems outmoded.[47] This represents Gautier's real departure from more conventional Romantic scenarios. In the Halévy and Scribe opera *La juive* (1835), the Jewish father prefers to allow his daughter to be boiled alive rather than to reveal she is not really Jewish. In Eugénie Foa's novel *La juive* (also 1835), the Jewish father's inability to sanction his daughter's love for a Christian nobleman leads to disaster for the family. By contrast, Gautier allows for a happy resolution to the conflict by showing Nathan—a rabbi, no less—willing to modify Jewish law or to reject it altogether. The Muslim characters, on the other hand, remain bound to what the play depicts as their religious fanaticism. By throwing the bound Kadidjah over the cliff, Ben Aïssa both proves his barbarity and seals his doom: "My sister! my sister!" he moans in the play's last lines. "Oh! I am cursed!" (27).

It is significant that the play ends with a Muslim cursing himself, for Gautier has clearly labored to pin on Muslims the responsibility for their own oppression. Religious fanaticism is the real agent of subjugation in Algeria, according to *La juive de Constantine*, not the French occupying forces. On the contrary, French power emerges as a tool of enlightenment and liberation, especially for women. Here we see the basic principle behind France's "civilizing mission," the idea that spreading enlightenment to conquered populations justifies French colonial endeavors. In *La juive de Constantine*, the rationalizations for colonial domination provided by the French characters contain all the elements—indeed, all the vocabulary—of the *mission civilisatrice* ideology as it would take shape at the end of the century.

As Maurice tells a French civilian who laments the lack of allies among the Muslim population: "Patience, my dear Saint-Aubin, it will come! Barbarism is in the process of disappearing from the world. . . . We are pursuing a holy war of civilization!" Saint-Aubin responds that by expropriating Arab lands, "we are not least serving the cause of humanity. . . . Each acre of land that I reclaim drives back toward the desert two wild beasts: a lion . . . and a bedouin!" (5). Maurice lauds his courage in support of a higher cause: "Destroy in order to build, that should be the motto of the new army!" (6). Later, he tells the Algerian rebel Bou Taleb that "France has stepped foot on African soil to chase away barbarism, and watched by the entire world, she will accomplish her noble task!" (17). Though consumed by the vengeful law of jihad, Bou Taleb worries in secret that the Frenchman may speak the truth: "Will his prophecy come true?" he asks himself (17), confirming for the audience that even those who most resist France's drive to spread civilization know in their hearts that it is both inevitable and morally right.

If the Muslims in the play secretly concede the superiority of French values, the Jewish acceptance of these values constitutes the play's climax and the main thrust of its political message. Gautier's *La juive de Constantine* articulates colonial policies that were only just beginning to take shape in the 1840s. It confronts head-on what would become the principle dilemma of the French colonial endeavor: how to reconcile the civilizing mission—which vaunted the universality of French law and values—with the need to subjugate indigenous populations. The play resolves this contradiction by establishing a hierarchy among the locals: the Jews deserve to be included within the French universal because they have shown themselves willing to assimilate to French culture, whereas the Muslims must remain inferior because of their continued religious fanaticism. In its depiction of the conversion of the *belle juive*, and her eventual marriage to the French soldier, the play thus imagines a union between the Algerian Jews and the French, a happy ending to a courtship that in the 1840s was only just beginning. As the Algerian Jews took their first steps toward accepting French laws and customs at the time the play premiered, they could have only dimly imagined the Crémieux Decree rewarding their efforts with citizenship twenty-five years later. Gautier's play clearly expresses the logic of the process and the inevitability of the outcome.[48]

The Jewish Universal

The universalism at work in Algeria was thus not really universal at all. It excluded Muslims while viewing Jews as worthy of inclusion only because they demonstrated a real or perceived willingness to shed many of their cultural practices. This assimilationist version of French universalism was a far cry from the general principle of equality articulated in the *Declaration of the Rights of Man and the Citizen,* or even from the law that granted citizenship to the French Jews in 1791, which required the dissolution of Jewish communal institutions and courts but made no mention of cultural or religious assimilation as a requirement of enfranchisement. It is perhaps not a surprise, then, that the colonial authorities in Algeria did not look back to 1789 or 1791 when trying to find a model for how to deal with the indigenous populations. Rather, as Schreier points out, they looked to 1806–7, when Napoleon convened the Assembly of Notables and the Grand Sanhedrin with the goal of asserting the limits of Jewish religious law and accelerating the incorporation of Jews into the body of the nation. As we saw at the end of chapter 1, Napoleon did indeed try to make universalism contingent on assimilation, even as his Jewish subjects offered their own original interpretation of these concepts.

"In 1806, the Israelites wished to become French citizens," Louis-Hugues Flandrin, a member of Napoleon III's Conseil d'état, declared before the French Senate in 1865, presenting the law that would allow Algerian Muslims and Jews to gain French citizenship provided they agreed to be bound by French family law. "At the time, they were governed by the Talmud, which, like the Qur'an, sanctified polygamy, repudiation, et cetera. Napoleon I wanted to separate faith and law. He convoked an assembly of notable Israelites, he constituted a great court of the Jewish nation, and on March 2, 1807, the Grand Sanhedrin . . . rendered a doctrinal decision in conformity with the Emperor's thinking. The Israelites then became French citizens."[49] Flandrin, of course, got his history partially wrong: the Jews received citizenship in 1790 and 91 not 1807. And as I showed in chapter 1, the 1791 emancipation decree demanded only that the Jews renounce all their prior privileges, swear an oath of allegiance to the state, and promise to fulfill all the duties imposed on them by the constitution.

But Flandrin was not wrong that Napoleon saw Jewish family law as an obstacle to Jewish integration into the nation, and that he implicitly made the Jews' *continued* citizenship contingent on its renunciation. The members of the Grand Sanhedrin deferred to French law in all civil and family matters, but they did not thereby see themselves as sacrificing Jewish difference. The rulings of the Sanhedrin did not lead to assimilation to Christian culture but rather resulted in a redefinition of Jewish identity. And French Jews became more connected to Jews elsewhere, not less, as a result of the Sanhedrin's affirmation that loyalty to France must take precedence over any other kind of national feeling. This was because the French Jews interpreted loyalty to France to mean loyalty to French universalism, which they saw as seamlessly intertwined with Jewish values and religious doctrines. This faith in universalism led French Jews to take the initiative in spreading universalist French values to Jews abroad. Education was key to this program. Beginning in the 1860s, the Alliance israélite universelle opened schools throughout North Africa and the Near East for Jewish children. The "civilizing mission" to the Jews of Algeria in the 1840s represented a kind of precursor to the Alliance.

If the French Jews pushed a form of assimilation on their Algerian coreligionists as the condition for extending universal rights, it is important to recognize that this was assimilation not to Christianity but rather to their own brand of Franco-Judaism. True, it meant copying bourgeois French manners and adopting the French language. But these were characteristics that had been so thoroughly integrated into French Jewish life that they had long ago lost their Christian connotations. The universalized form of Judaism created by French Jews was rational, decorous, and most of all, it was in French. The French Jews thus did *not* advocate assimilation in Algeria if by this one means encouraging the Algerian Jews to cease being Jews. They did not urge the Algerian Jews to shed their Jewish difference, because in their view, the "fanatical" superstitions and unhygienic living conditions of the Algerians had nothing to do with the universal Judaism they saw themselves as exemplifying.

Moreover, the advocacy on behalf of Jews abroad actually constituted the principle means by which the French Jews asserted their identity and difference as Jews, both in metropolitan France and on the international stage. This paradox is key to understanding the transformation of Algerian Jewry in the nineteenth century. As Leff has shown, the 1830s and '40s saw the rise of a new generation of French Jewish community leaders who boldly asserted their Jewishness in the public sphere.[50] Rachel's brazen performance of her Jewish identity on the stage of the Comédie Française, which I discussed in the last chapter, was part of a larger trend that included Crémieux arguing successfully against the *more judaico*, the special oath that Jews were required to take in court, and unsuccessfully for the abrogation of Jewish communal debts from the Old Regime. He and other communal leaders allied with liberals against the Catholic ultras to promote a version of *laïcité* in which the state would treat France's three recognized religions (Catholicism, Protestantism, and Judaism) in the same manner.[51]

Advocacy on behalf of the Algerian Jews was a natural extension of this fight for equality within France. Crémieux and other French Jewish leaders hardly sought to hide their Jewishness or turn Judaism into a matter of private confession only. On the contrary, they wanted to carve out a public, and equal, place for Judaism in a *laïque* French state. That Judaism did receive equal treatment by the July Monarchy—after 1831, rabbis were put on the state payroll—despite the fact that Jews represented only 0.2 percent of the population signifies the extent to which they succeeded in their task.

The fight led by the metropolitan Jews to make the Algerian Jews French—both in a legal sense, by enfranchising them, and in a cultural sense, by urging them to copy the manners of their French coreligionists—grows out of this activist agenda. Thus the picture I presented at the start of this chapter of universalism growing more hostile to minority difference in the colonies is not quite right, since it overlooks the way in which the effort to "assimilate" the Algerian Jews represented a way of foregrounding Jewish difference in metropolitan France. And by pushing the Algerian Jews to shed the trappings of traditional Jewish identity, the French Jews paradoxically saw themselves as making them *more Jewish*, since the Sanhredrin had redefined Jewishness in universalist terms.

Universalism thus emerges from its encounter with the Jews of Algeria even more varied, even more subject to debate and interpretation, than before. Looked at from the perspective of certain indigenous subjects, universalism no doubt appeared as a homogenizing force and as a tool for colonial exploitation. But looked at from the perspective of the metropolitan Jews who fought to gain rights for their Algerian coreligionists and worked to spread French civilization to Jewish populations in the Muslim world through the auspices of the Alliance israélite universelle, universalism became a tool for preserving and asserting minority difference.[52] If to us today, the name of the Alliance israélite universelle seems like an oxymoron—how can an alliance be both *israélite* and *universelle*?—this was not the case in the mid-nineteenth century, when Jewish identity and French universalism worked in tandem, one reinforcing the other. French universalism would tarnish its reputation in the colonies, where it was increasingly used in a cynical way to justify French domination, but we must be attentive to the ways in which this cynicism coincided, at least for some of its practitioners, with idealist aspirations. Recovering the complexity of this history is all the more important today as the French continue to struggle with the ugly legacies that colonialism wrought.

4
Zola and the Dreyfus Affair

The Dreyfus Affair of the late 1890s represented a crisis not just for French Jews but also for French universalism. Alfred Dreyfus, the Jewish army officer wrongly accused of selling secrets to Germany, eventually managed to prove his innocence and was exonerated, but not before the fundamental tenets of French political culture were put to the test.[1] In the early stages of the Affair, many French people leapt to the twin conclusions that a traitor in the army must be a Jew and that a Jew in the army must be a traitor. "That Dreyfus is capable of treason, I conclude from his race," wrote the nationalist intellectual Maurice Barrès, rejecting a basic postulate of French universalism, that an individual's origin should have no bearing on citizenship.[2] Moreover, once it became clear that Dreyfus had been framed by his superiors, many French people remained willing to sacrifice the civil rights of the individual in order to protect the prestige of the army that had falsely accused him, violating that other sacred universalist principle of equality before the law.

The novelist Émile Zola has gone down in history as one of the great heroes of the Affair—the defender both of Dreyfus and of the principles of equality and justice on which French universalism resides. Zola clearly recognized during the Affair that the rising tide of antisemitism, which began in the 1880s, was a grave threat to the republican values he cherished. For although the Third Republic was declared in 1870, it remained under threat until the end of the nineteenth century from various factions (monarchists, Boulangists, etc.), many of which were openly antisemitic. It thus comes as something of a surprise that just a few years before the Affair, he published a novel entitled *L'argent* (Money, 1890) containing opinions about the Jews that many critics have seen as antisemitic. Literary scholars have tended to excuse Zola's early antisemitism by arguing that he transcended it during the Affair, and they have pointed to the elaborate philosemitism of his final novel, *Vérité* (Truth, 1903), in which a Jewish character wrongly accused of a crime triumphs over his enemies, as proof of this virtuous trajectory.[3] All's well that ends well, this line of reasoning holds. And yet, upon closer inspection, Zola's later writings also contain troubling ideas about the nature of Jewish difference and its place within the French nation.

In this chapter I present a more complicated picture of Zola's repeated attempts to answer the so-called Jewish Question, which asked whether Jews belong in France and if so, on what terms.[4] This was not a rhetorical question for the Dreyfusard novelist. Although Zola believed in the universal rights of all citizens, he also held antisemitic prejudices, rooted in a certain socialist tradition, and displayed at times an antiuniversalist sense that true national belonging was defined, à la Barrès, by blood and soil. One gets the impression reading Zola that the Jews might be citizens, but they were not really French. The solution that eventually allowed Zola to overcome this contradiction was assimilation: the Jews could be incorporated into France, but only by shedding their difference. His version of universalism, I will argue, is antipluralist even as it forcefully defends Jewish rights. Of course, this brand of universalism is not new—it recalls that pre-Revolutionary strain of universalist theorizing that sought to "regenerate" the Jews as the price for their inclusion in the nation. As we will see, however, Zola called for an even more extreme form of assimilation—the complete dissolution of the Jews as a people.

My goal in analyzing Zola's writing about Jews and universalism, I want to emphasize, is not to cast aspersions on his defense of Dreyfus, which I see as nothing short of heroic. Rather, I want to understand the deeper meaning of his magnanimity. To be gained here is not only a clearer picture of the evolution of Zola's attitude toward Jews over the course of his career but also a clearer picture of what was at stake in the fight over universalism in fin-de-siècle France. It was the victory of Zola and the Dreyfusards that led to the separation of churches and the state in 1905 and that enshrined the hard-line form of *laïcité*, hostile to the expression of religious or ethnic difference in the public sphere, which characterizes the "republican universalism" that has become dominant today. What the case of Zola ultimately shows is that the version of universalism that triumphed during the Affair remains haunted by certain aspects of the antisemitism it so successfully opposed.

Jews and Money

In order to trace Zola's complex ideas about the place of Jews in France, I want to begin with his novel *L'argent*, first published serially in the literary periodical *Gil Blas* beginning in November of 1890. In this novel, Zola wrestles with the demon of finance capitalism, which he sees as the root cause of modernity's various social ills. He associates this demon with a dangerous group of foreign invaders: the Jews. All of this, to be sure, Zola derives from other sources. The originality of *L'argent* lies not in the antisemitic stereotypes it perpetuates but in the solutions it offers to the problem of Jewish finance capitalism. These solutions have profound implications both for Zola's development as a novelist and thinker and for the evolution of French universalism.

The eighteenth work in Zola's twenty-volume Rougon-Macquart cycle, *L'argent* takes place in and around the Bourse, the Paris Stock Exchange, during the Second Empire (1852–70). It describes the efforts of a character named Aristide Saccard to launch a Catholic bank, La Banque Universelle, with the twin goals of countering the dominance of Jewish financiers and investing in the Near East. Inspired by his neighbor, the engineer Hamelin, who has spent time in the Levant, Saccard envisions exporting French capital to the Holy Land, funding a series of improvements in transportation, mining, and other industries with the eventual goal of providing the pope with a prosperous refuge should nascent Italian nationalism require the transfer of the Holy See.

It is unclear whether the opportunistic Saccard feels the same level of religious devotion as Hamelin, but he exploits the Catholic angle in order to lure capital from pious speculators, declining aristocrats, and other antisemitic investors frustrated by the dominance of La Haute Banque, that mythical entity otherwise referred to in the novel as La Banque Juive.[5] At first, Saccard's energetic marketing succeeds in boosting the bank's share price to dizzying heights, but soon his overweening ambitions and illegal maneuvers drive La Banque Universelle to ruin. The bank's demise is hastened by the efforts of the all-powerful Jewish banker Gundermann, who sees in Saccard a rival, and who sells shares in the Universelle when the bank is vulnerable. Saccard uses the bank's own cash reserves to buy back its falling shares in a quixotic attempt to halt the tumble but thereby seals the bank's doom. The novel ends with the total collapse of La Banque Universelle, its worthless shares bought up by other Jewish speculators at bargain-basement prices leading to the utter ruin of its many Catholic shareholders.

It is clear from Zola's preparatory notes that as he contemplated his novel about money, he envisioned it also as a novel about Jews. "Don't forget that the Jewish question will be at the root of my subject," he wrote, "because I can't touch on money without evoking the role of the Jews in the past and today."[6] Why, I want to ask, for Zola did "touching" the money question—

with the hint of contamination this implies—necessarily entail discussing Jews? Why was the imbrication of the two unsavory subjects so self-evident? Jews, of course, had acted as moneylenders in Europe since the Middle Ages, fulfilling a role that the Church denied Catholics. Shakespeare's *The Merchant of Venice* testifies to the Renaissance image of the ruthless, usurious Jew. But with the rise of industrial capitalism in the mid-nineteenth century, Jews came to embody a more specific set of monetary associations. Zola's reference to the role played by Jews both "in the past and the present" indicates he was aware of this shift.

In Germany, the philosophers who came to be known, in the early decades of the nineteenth century, as the Young Hegelians considered Judaism to be a religion of self-interest perfectly attuned to the demands of modern capitalism. The Jews, according to Ludwig von Feuerbach and his colleagues, devoted themselves to the single-minded pursuit of wealth and reduced life to a narrow, rational, philistine calculation of profit. They could thus be blamed for the increasing atomization of the individual under capitalism and for the egotism of modern society.[7] Karl Marx, though himself a convert from Judaism, was strongly influenced by the Young Hegelians. In his "On the Jewish Question" (1845), the young Marx argued that Judaism was akin to money worship and must be overcome for true human emancipation to take place. Unlike some of his contemporaries, Marx did not single out specific Jews for blame and did not conceive of Judaism in racial terms. According to the convert, modern Christians were equally guilty of perverting the human spirit: they had become Jewish.[8]

Marx wrote "On the Jewish Question" before he had properly become a Marxist, which is to say, before he had come to recognize class conflict as the true motor of history, rather than the struggle between religions or races. In France, however, certain socialist philosophers shared Marx's early vision of the Jew as the negative force behind capitalist modernity, and they would influence Zola. Charles Fourier, the inventor of the utopian phalanxes, repeatedly denounced the Jews as parasites of the new money economy, although toward the end of his life he hoped that proto-Zionists would implement his utopian vision in Palestine.[9] As we saw in chapter 2, Fourier's follower Alphonse Toussenel published what would come to be considered one of the masterworks of nineteenth-century socialist antisemitism, *Les juifs, rois de l'époque* (The Jews, Kings of the Age, 1845), which denounced the Jews as rootless invaders who had transformed France into their lordly domain through their monetary manipulations. Although Toussenel also at times considered Jews as mere metaphors and included certain Christians (especially Protestants) in his blanket denunciations of "Jewish" capitalism, he did not hesitate to single out the Rothschilds and other actual Jews as the leaders of this new financial feudalism.[10] Both Pierre Leroux and Pierre-Joseph Proudhon, the leaders of the early socialist movement in France, likewise blamed the Jews for corrupting the Christian spirit with their materialism and immoral pursuit of lucre.[11]

In *L'argent*, Zola borrows the equation of the Jew with modern finance capitalism from these socialist antisemites along with a good deal of their rhetoric. At his first entrance in the novel, the German-Jewish banker Gundermann—a clear stand-in for James de Rothschild, head of the French branch of the famous banking house—is described as "the banker king, the master of the Bourse and the world" (53), in terms that recall Toussenel's *Les juifs, rois de l'époque*. But he is far from the only Jewish "king" of capitalism in the novel. A young stockbroker named Nathansohn will succeed, we learn, "since he is a Jew." In order to make it at the Bourse, an aspiring Christian trader laments, "you have to be Jewish." Christians lack the capacity. "We don't have a knack for it, it's our misfortune. . . . What a lousy profession!" another comments (64). Zola's novel shows how Jews dominate not only the top but also the bottom of the financial pyramid. The narrator describes the petty day traders swarming around the Bourse, hoping to scrape together a few francs' profit from small fluctuations, as "a whole filthy Jewish quarter [toute une juiverie malpropre] . . . an extraordinary meeting of characteristic noses [une extraordinaire réunion de nez typiques]" (56).

The racializing of the Jew, the reduction of his portrait to a collection of stereotypical traits ("de nez typiques"), reflects the influence of the new racial pseudo-science that had begun to view Jewishness as a biological destiny in the second half of the nineteenth century. Ernest Renan, the respected author of *The Life of Jesus*, had described the distinctions between Aryans and Semites as early as 1848.[12] And Arthur de Gobineau would marshal anthropological and scientific knowledge toward racist ends in his *Essay on the Inequality of Human Races* of 1853. Edouard Drumont's *La France juive* (Jewish France, 1886), one of the most significant books of the nineteenth century in France, would fuse the economic antisemitism of the utopian socialists with the racial antisemitism of Gobineau.[13] For Drumont, capitalist modernity represented the principal means by which the Jews—whom he characterizes as a horde of foreign invaders—pursued their unrelenting quest to dominate Catholic France. Drumont, it should be clear, conceived of the nation in fundamentally antiuniversalist terms: Frenchness was determined by blood, soil, and religion, and Jews were by definition excluded from it.

Although Zola disapproved of *La France juive*, echoes of Drumont's imprecations against the Jewish takeover of the nation punctuate *L'argent*.[14]

"The empire is sold to the Jews, to the dirty Jews," Saccard fulminates. "All our money is condemned to fall into their gnarled claws" (244). It is true that most such antisemitic diatribes in the novel are voiced by the morally dubious Saccard, and thus do not necessarily represent the views of the narrator or author. The above remark, for example, is framed by quotes making clear that it represents the speech of Saccard. However, other passages in the text would seem to confirm that the narrator might share at least some of the protagonist's hostility to the Jews, if not in its most virulent form, then in a more subtle but no less insidious variant. Describing the origin of Gundermann's wealth, the narrator comments: "In less than a century, the billionaire's monstrous fortune was born, sprouted up, overflowed in that family, through saving and through lucky turns of events" (135). Note the grotesque natural imagery: the Jew's fortune sprouts up like a mushroom, proliferates like a cancer. Note also the unnatural imagery, the emphasis on the "monstrosity" of the Jew's wealth.

That the novel itself, and not just its protagonist, endorses these stereotypes about Jews and money receives further confirmation in the recognition that its many Jewish characters all possess an aptitude for finance that is repeatedly referred to as a racially determined trait, a "Jewish flair" (413). Moreover, the plot of the novel reinforces the view that the Jews are destined to make money. At the end of the novel, after Gundermann and his ilk have driven the Catholic bank to ruin, all the Jewish characters come out on top, whereas the Catholic characters, for the most part, lose everything they have. Even the pale consumptive Marxist revolutionary, Sigismond Busch, the brother of the most repellent of the Jewish bankers, reveals an innate gift for economic calculation that he deploys against the capitalist system dominated by his coreligionists. Note also that he too has a Germanic name, underscoring the Jew's fundamental foreignness.

Zola seems to have lifted from Drumont not just an image of the Jews as a horde of foreign invaders out to plunder France but also many elements of his plot. Indeed, the scandal at the heart of *L'argent* bears a striking resemblance to the real-life 1882 crash of the Union Générale Bank that Drumont had turned into one of his prime pieces of evidence against French Jewry. Zola seems to have originally planned to model the collapse of his fictional bank in *L'argent* as closely as possible on the Union Générale scandal and on the antisemitic explanation for its collapse that Drumont derived from a self-justificatory pamphlet penned by its felonious founder, Eugène Bontoux.[15]

As Richard B. Grant explains, Zola's original outline for the novel cast Gundermann, the banker modeled on James de Rothschild, as the villain of the piece—despite the fact that Rothschild died in 1868, a full decade before the founding of the Union Générale.[16] Zola's original notes not only make Gundermann responsible for bringing down the bank but even go so far as to accuse the Jewish banker of betraying France in favor of Germany. The influence of Bontoux and Drumont is clear: the Jews are not just foreign but are out to destroy France with their ruinous and traitorous greed. In this early conception, Zola had Saccard triumph over Gundermann and "la juiverie," thus rewriting history to lend the paranoid and hateful Bontoux figure the righteous aura of the victor.[17]

By the final version of the novel, however, Zola had modified his views. His thinking on the matter apparently began to change following a series of conversations with the Jewish banker Georges Lévy, who convinced him of the absurdity of blaming a Jewish financial conspiracy for bringing down the Union Générale.[18] In the final version of the novel, Gundermann profits from, but does not provoke, the Catholic bank's failure. The Jewish banker is driven not by animus against Catholics but by a pure desire for profit and the need to eliminate a rival. Most significantly, Gundermann acts alone, in his own individual interest, and not in league with his coreligionists. Although many of those who profit from the bank's collapse in the novel also happen to be Jews, there is no racial drive impelling the Jews to defeat the Catholics in the final version of *L'argent*.

Grant sees Zola's decision to depart from the thesis of Bontoux and Drumont as evidence that he had begun his journey away from antisemitism by the time he finished *L'argent*. I think it reveals something else: namely, the start of a more complex analysis of the place of Jews in modern France. If during his preparations for the novel he saw capitalist modernity as a Manichean battle between the races, the actual novel depicts this battle in more dialectical terms, as an opposition between approaches to finance that points toward a useful synthesis. And if Zola's original plan for the novel was anti-universalist in the way it cast the Jews as a horde of foreign invaders intent on turning France into their feudal domain, the final version offers a more inclusive vision for the French nation, one that holds out a place for Jews within it.

Saccard, the French Catholic, represents the pleasures of the capitalist system, its uncontained desires and unbridled lusts. In this, he is the opposite of the foreign Jews in the novel, such as the ascetic Gundermann, who avoids women and subsists on a diet of milk, as well as of Sigismond Busch, the consumptive revolutionary who wastes away in a monkish cell reading Marx. The narrator makes it clear that the sexual excesses of Saccard are inextricably linked to his capitalist drive, that one fuels the other. And it is this principle of desire, associated here with the Catholic character, that offers an alternative to the cold, rational capitalism of the Jews. As Hamelin's sister, Madame

Caroline, the white-haired angel of purity who eventually succumbs to Saccard's violent desire, realizes (or rationalizes), "without speculation, there wouldn't be big, flourishing, fertile enterprises, no more than there would be children without lust. That excess of passion, all that life spent and wasted in the gutter, is necessary for the very continuation of life" (293). This passion also represents the novel's hope for a future of productive ferment. It is this desire that will permit the nonproductive regions of the Levant to flourish.

But Saccard's lust also produces unfortunate consequences. "It was passion that raised Saccard up and it was passion that would prove his undoing" (329), the narrator announces in terms that elevate Saccard to the status of a Greek hero whose tragic flaw leads to both greatness and downfall. We find out early in the novel that he raped a woman as a young man, producing a degenerate son, Victor, whom Sigismond's brother will use to blackmail him. Saccard's sexual incontinence will bring about not only his downfall but that of his bank as well. Ultimately it is a spurned lover of Saccard's, Baroness Sandorff, who reveals the secret of the bank's vulnerability to Gundermann at the crucial moment, permitting him to capitalize on the bank's weakness to sell its shares. The Catholic Saccard may have the kind of passion that allows for great things to be dreamed, but such desires cannot compete in the modern marketplace with the Jew's calculation and cunning.

So what lesson about money does the novel ultimately teach, with its representation of the Bourse as a clash between Catholics and Jews? The dispassionate logic of the Jews, the product of their racial capacities, eventually destroys the beautiful dreams of the passionate Catholics. Perhaps the solution for these Catholics, the novel seems to imply, is to learn from the Jews, to combine lust and passion with rationality and cunning. Imagine what great things capitalist modernity might produce, the novel leaves us wondering, if such opposites allied. And imagine how strong France could become if instead of following Drumont by conceiving of the Jews as the enemy, as the anti-France, it included them within the national fold and harnessed their powers.

L'argent thus reveals an author in the midst of a conversion of sorts. If Zola began the novel convinced of the dastardly intentions of a bunch of treacherous, foreign Jewish capitalists who control the Bourse, he ended it on a far more ambivalent note. The novel still views the Jews as threatening in their financial savvy, but it accords them a certain respect while also exculpating them from the most damning charges of conspiracy. More importantly, it no longer views them as traitors to France but rather as a source of potential productivity. Zola is thus coming around to a more universalist view of the nation that would include the Jews. According to Grant and other critics, his receding antisemitism helped pave the way for Zola's heroic actions during the Dreyfus Affair, when the famous author bravely took up his pen on behalf of the falsely convicted Jew. A close examination of his journalistic writing published during the Affair, however, once again yields a more complicated picture, one in which Zola's defense of the Jews goes hand in hand with a call for their disappearance.

The Affair

Without a doubt, the many articles that Zola penned during the Dreyfus Affair view antisemitism as the prime culprit in the grotesque judicial error that condemned Dreyfus and in the public hysteria that prevented a revision of the verdict from taking place. In his article "Procès-verbal" (Sworn Statement), published in *Le Figaro* on December 5, 1897, Zola lashes out at the forces that were turning the case into an "affair." While Zola blames the press for distorting the truth and enflaming public opinion, he reserves his real fury for the scourge of antisemitism. "It is the guilty party," Zola declares, denouncing the "barbarous" campaign against the Jews for perverting France's system of justice.[19] In his famous open letter to the president of the republic that came to be known by its most famous words, "J'accuse" (I Accuse), published in January of 1898, Zola shows more circumspection in regard to antisemitism, preferring to denounce the monstrous actions of the army officers responsible for the false conviction rather than delving into their ideological motivations. Nevertheless, he includes a paragraph criticizing the press for inflaming reactionary passions and generating intolerance, "hiding behind odious antisemitism, from which the great liberal France of the rights of man will die if it is not cured of it."[20] A more forceful *anti*-antisemitism can hardly be imagined.

A year before this, however, Zola defended the Jews in rather more curious terms. In an article entitled "Pour les juifs" (A Plea for the Jews), published in *Le Figaro* on May 16, 1896, Zola takes aim not at the architects of the judicial error or Dreyfus's accusers per se but rather at the culture of antisemitism brewing in France. "For a few years now, I have been following the campaign that they are trying to wage against the Jews, with a growing surprise and disgust," he begins the article.[21] He continues by calling this antisemitism "something stupid and blind" and describes it as a throwback to the religious persecutions of the Middle Ages. Once again, one has trouble imagining a more forceful defense of the Jews. Complications arise, however, when Zola explores the phenomenon of antisemitism in greater detail. Zola describes the "prosecution" directed at the Jews for being a "nation within the nation" and forming international links with Jews around the world, thus for not upholding their part of the universalist bargain by refusing to elevate their ties to France over their ties to other Jews. He also examines the charge that they "love money." In less than a hundred years, such antisemites claim, they have appropriated the nation's wealth, becoming a new kind of "royalty." Here Zola once again parrots the rhetoric of Toussenel and Drumont, as he had in *L'argent*, only now the reader detects in these clichés a distinctly ironic tone. Surprisingly, though, instead of denouncing these accusations, Zola concedes their validity. "And all of this is true" (58), he concludes.

Zola follows this concession with an attempt to explain the origins of this "truth" about the Jews. Here he employs the conventional liberal argument, used by apologists since the eighteenth century, that the Jews have become what the Christians made them. Prevented from entering most guilds and professions, the Jews took up moneylending because Christians were forbidden from doing so—and as a way to keep their assets liquid in case they suddenly found it necessary to flee. "Nothing surprising," Zola concludes, that the Jews now find themselves the "masters of capital," with "their brains conditioned" for financial transactions, the product of centuries of training (58).

The question then becomes, for Zola, how Christians should deal with these financial wizards in their midst. As we have seen, the author asked a very similar question in *L'argent*, which depicts the modern French economic sphere as a battle for supremacy waged by passionate Catholics against the cold, rational Jewish kings of the Bourse. I would like to suggest that the solutions Zola explicitly proposes in "Pour les juifs" help shed light on Zola's views that remain more inchoate in that novel. In "Pour les juifs," Zola once again depicts modern capitalism as a war between conflicting races, but he now seems to think that this is a war that Christians should have no problem winning: "What is this? You are more than 200 million Catholics and there are barely five million Jews" (59). The Catholics' superior numbers should guarantee victory if only they knew how to fight. And fight they must if they hope to regain control of their nation's finances from this "nation within a nation," this band of outsiders that has made itself a new aristocracy. "It seems to me that the condions for battle are acceptable" (59), Zola states, in terms that leave little doubt about the bellicose nature of his vision of modernity.

Zola concluded *L'argent* with the Jews victorious and the Catholics in disarray, driven to despair by the superior abilities of a race that has honed its craft over centuries. In "Pour les juifs," he's less willing to accept defeat. Here Zola proposes a surefire method to beat the Jews at their own game: become like them. "When it comes to business, why not be as intelligent and as clever as they are?" he asks (59). Citing his experience at the Bourse while doing research for *L'argent*, he describes the sense of defeatism that had plagued the Catholic stockbrokers. This Zola finds "humiliating." "Nobody is standing in our way," he argues. If Jews have had centuries "to love money and learn to make it, we only have to follow them onto the battlefield, acquire their qualities, and then fight them with their own arms" (59). What satisfaction the Jews must take, Zola proclaims, in seeing their enemies so weak and humble.

The reader might pause here to consider the strangeness of a call to arms against the Jews in an essay that purports to be a plea in their favor. With friends like this, one might say, the Jews hardly need enemies. It is important to recognize, however, that Zola's call for fighting the Jews with their own weapons figures in opposition to what he describes as a worse alternative— outright persecution—which has once again become an option in France. This alternative is worse not only because it is old-fashioned and immoral but also because it is bound to backfire: persecution, Zola reasons, only makes the Jews stronger, turns them into more fearful enemies. Better to work within the liberal universalist tradition, to accord the Jews rights, and then emulate them. Had Saccard attempted to learn from Gundermann instead of fulminating against him, we presume, he might have succeeded in establishing the Catholic Bank after all.

But if the Catholics succeed in becoming more like the Jews, what place does this leave for the actual Jews in the universalist future imagined by Zola? The answer is none. Zola makes his vision of a Jew-free France plain. Through tolerance and imitation, the Catholics will succeed in making the Jews obsolete. "Open our arms wide, realize socially the equality that has been recognized by the Code," Zola commands. This exhortation to universalism is the surefire path to overcoming the Jews' domination. For with Zola's universalist vision comes a desire for assimilation, in the true sense of the term—which is to say, the complete dissipation or eradication of Jewish difference. Zola means this in a fundamental, biological sense: "Embrace the Jews, in order to absorb them and mingle them into us. Enrich ourselves with their good qualities, because they have some. End the war of races by mixing the races. Push for [mixed] marriages, leave it to the children to reconcile the parents" (60). Like Napoleon, Zola seeks to solve the "Jewish Question" by making the Jewish "race" disappear through intermarriage. And Zola displays confidence that the Christians' one true superiority—that of numbers—will allow them to dominate the future gene pool. In Zola's solution to the "Jewish Question," the genetic material of the Jews should be mined for its useful qualities and then discarded. "And that alone is the work of unity, humanity, and liberation" (60), Zola concludes, without irony.

The Universalism of *Vérité*

Zola may have wanted the Jews to disappear, but this desire went hand in hand with a vigorous defense of their rights that put his own well-being at risk. His bombshell article "J'accuse," with its attacks on the army high command, represented a calculated act of self-sacrifice: by accusing his adversaries in such a blatant manner, Zola left them no choice but to prosecute him for libel. And unlike the various trials of Dreyfus for treason held in military courts, which could suppress classified documents, a trial for libel against Zola held in civil court would expose the lack of evidence against the Jewish officer. Zola's gambit worked: his libel trial in 1898 proved the innocence of Dreyfus to everyone acting in good faith, leading the president of the republic to offer the Jewish officer a pardon (Dreyfus would be fully exonerated only in 1906). The libel trial nevertheless returned a guilty verdict for Zola, forcing the writer into exile in London to avoid prison. Stripped of the Legion of Honor, and suffering financially, Zola returned to France in 1899 in time to see the tide of public sentiment turn in favor of Dreyfus.

Zola's final novel, *Vérité*, was published posthumously in 1903, shortly after the author's death by asphyxiation—a supposed accident that some have seen as an act of retaliation for his support of Dreyfus, although this has never been proved. The third in the projected *Four Gospels* cycle of novels, *Vérité* consists of an obvious transposition of the events of the Affair. In place of the Jewish army officer falsely accused of treason, the victim of injustice in the novel is a Jewish schoolmaster (Simon) in the small town of Maillebois accused of murdering a child—his nephew (Zéphirin), who had been raised as a Catholic and who lived with Simon following the death of his parents. When the child is found dead—strangled and apparently raped—the Jewish teacher comes under suspicion despite the lack of evidence against him.

Enflamed by a scandalmongering antisemitic press and manipulated by Church officials anxious to conceal the possible guilt of one of the teachers at a Jesuit school, the crowd of angry townspeople calls for the Jew's head. Like Dreyfus, Simon is sent to a penal colony following his conviction, while his devoted brother David works toward his exoneration. Rejected by the rich Jews to whom he turns for help, David finds his biggest supporter in Marc Froment, a freethinking schoolmaster, who plays the Zola role: Marc overcomes his latent antisemitism to pursue the cause of justice even though it causes a rift with his wife, a practicing Catholic. After many years of struggle, Marc eventually convinces a former student of the Jesuits to admit that a copybook assignment that had been found at the scene of the crime came from his school. Marc slowly wins over most of the citizens of Maillebois, including his wife, who finally recognizes Simon's innocence and the guilt of Brother Gorgias, the Jesuit teacher. Like Dreyfus, Simon has a retrial; he is once again convicted, and he then receives a pardon. He only returns to Maillebois many years later after the townspeople take up a collection to buy him a new house as a reparation, once the full extent of the nefarious plot against him has become clear. The novel ends with a spectacular scene of philosemitism, as the exonerated Jew is greeted exultantly by the townspeople.

Though Zola's longest and last novel, *Vérité* has received comparatively little critical attention. This no doubt has to do with the novel's many artistic flaws, an unrelenting didacticism foremost among them. While Zola never refrained from using his fiction to expound his theories about society and politics, ideology takes center stage in *Vérité*. A true ideological novel, or *roman à thèse*, *Vérité* marshals its plot and characters in service of a relatively straightforward argument against the Church and in favor of secularism, republicanism, and universalism. The true villains in the novel are the Church officials who fan the flames of antisemitism and willingly ruin the life of a humble Jew in order to protect themselves from scandal. Along with Simon and his family, who find themselves driven to misery and despair, the victims in the novel are the townspeople, who are kept in blighted ignorance by the Church and its allies. The heroes, of course, are Marc and his colleagues, who work tirelessly and suffer personally for the cause of truth and justice and who are ultimately able to implement their universalist vision at the novel's end.

In *Vérité*, Zola employs far more convincing arguments against antisemitism than in *L'argent* or even his journalistic writing. The narrator demonstrates repeatedly that antisemitism is the enemy of the political values he holds dear—secularism, republicanism, and universalism. Indeed, it is the repetition of this argument that helps make the novel read like a political tract. Zola seems to have come to the conclusion that antisemitism represents not just an immoral throwback to the injustice of the Inquisition, or an understandable but regrettable feeling that must be overcome in the name of social harmony, but a very modern means of propagating reactionary political views. He seems to have recognized that right-wing ideologues such as Drumont were fanning the flames of Jew-hatred to garner popular support for their opposition to the Third Republic. This should have been apparent to all readers of *La France juive* in 1886, but it took the Dreyfus Affair to drive home the extent to which the right-wing had effected a political sleight of hand: stirring up antisemitism—including leftist stereotypes about Jews and capitalism—to trick the lower classes into endorsing a political program that did not serve their economic interests.[22] Inheritors of the Revolutionary tradition, like Zola, who may have flirted with left-wing antisemitism, emerged from the Affair convinced that defending the Jews was necessary in order to save the republic.[23]

Whereas *L'argent* and "Pour les juifs" had represented modernity as an arena of conflict between Jews and Christians, *Vérité* recasts the nature of the struggle. *Vérité* draws the battle lines not between the races but rather between advocates and adversaries of the republic and its values, principal among them universalism.[24] On one side are the Jews and their protector, the humble republican schoolmaster; on the other are the forces of reaction, the Church leaders and wealthy politicians intent on sowing ignorance and hatred. The Jews are no longer the enemy but rather the victims of the latter's efforts to stir up ancient prejudices to win the people over to their side. Here the Jew becomes the very emblem of the revolutionary struggle. The delirious philosemitism of the novel's end, in which huge crowds acclaim the return of Simon, represents a victory celebration for republican universalism. This new political alignment would seem, then, to mark a definitive evolution for Zola, the positive end point of his virtuous trajectory.

However, a closer examination of the novel complicates this picture. On the surface, *Vérité* seems to refute the equation of Jews and money assumed by Zola in both *L'argent* and "Pour les juifs" by foregrounding a family of poor Jews. Simon, the schoolmaster, makes a modest salary and seems satisfied with his lot. But it is his wife Rachel's family, the Lehmanns, who incarnate a new type for Zola: the Jewish proletarian laborer. Poor tailors, they live in a squalid house on the rue du Trou (Hole Street), in the dankest quarter of Maillebois. Hunched over their piecework, they have the tortured bodies and melancholy souls of the dispossessed.

> Marc constantly felt surprised that such an admirable woman as Rachel, one of so rare a beauty, should have sprung in such a horrid den from needy parents, weighed down by a long heredity of anxious penury.... They led a narrow life full of difficulties, earning a scanty subsistence by dint of hard work for slowly-acquired customers, such as the few Israelites of the region who were in easy circumstances, and certain Christians who did not spend much money on their clothes.[25]

Zola not only describes the Lehmanns as poor but emphasizes that the vast majority of Jews in the region are poor as well. "The gold of France, with which the Jews were said to gorge themselves, was certainly not piled up here" (77), Marc, or perhaps the narrator, muses. The recognition that not all Jews are rich reflects the influence on Zola of his friend the Jewish Dreyfusard Bernard Lazare, who had drawn a distinction between the rich Jewish parvenu and the poor Jewish pariah, who suffers by association with his coreligionists. Other Dreyfusards, such as Charles Péguy, came to a similar conclusion about the suffering of ordinary Jews.[26]

As Zola's narrative progresses, however, the Lehmanns gradually emerge from their impoverished condition. Although immediately after Simon's conviction they lose the few customers they had, by the end of the novel they have achieved a modest prosperity. Twenty years after the conviction of Simon, after he has received a pardon but before his exoneration, his daughter Sarah returns to Maillebois to help her grandfather run the tailor shop. Ten years after that, the "establishment" on the rue du Trou has grown too big for Sarah to oversee it (497). Finally, she sells it to a neighbor (521). Simon, meanwhile, joins his brother David in the exploitation of a marble quarry after his pardon and gains a "little fortune" (521).

Thus, even as Marc labors in the trenches of his small schoolroom to bring enlightenment to the masses, never earning more than a pittance, the Jews in the novel turn toward capitalist pursuits. The narrator never judges their newfound wealth, and indeed, the reader feels happy they have raised themselves out of misery. But the implication remains that the Jews have reasserted their hereditary aptitude for financial success, transforming a teacher into a mine owner and a tailor into a clothing manufacturer. This is how it should be, the novel seems to say; it is only natural.

If *Vérité* ultimately undermines its claim that not all Jews are rich by showing the transformation of its proletarian Jewish characters into capitalists, it also reinforces traditional stereotypes in a less subtle manner. Indeed, certain Jewish characters in *Vérité* seem to have stepped straight out of *L'argent*. I'm referring here to Baron Nathan, the arch-capitalist in the novel, who resembles Gundermann from *L'argent* quite closely. However, given their common model (James de Rothschild), it strikes the reader as odd that in the later, supposedly philosemitic novel, the Jewish capitalist comes off as so much worse than in the earlier, antisemitic novel. For not only does Nathan share Gundermann's lust for lucre, he lacks his positive, redeeming qualities— namely, his probity and rectitude. Nathan becomes one of the novel's chief villains when he cravenly refuses David's request for him to help Simon out of concern for his own social advancement.

Zola makes much of the contrast between the two Jews, Baron Nathan, the capitalist, and Lehmann, the poor tailor. When Marc and David pay a visit to the baron to request his aid, they marvel at the luxury of the surroundings in terms that come straight out of Toussenel. "A king might have dwelt there," the narrator comments.

> And at the sight of that paradise acquired by Jew wealth, at the thought of the splendid fortune amassed by Nathan the Jew moneymonger, Marc instinctively recalled the gloomy little shop in the Rue du Trou, the dismal hovel without air or sunshine, where Lehmann, that other Jew, had been plying his needle for thirty years, and earning only enough to provide himself with bread. (83)

Zola clearly struggles to dissociate Jews from money in *Vérité*, but he can't help representing his selfish capitalist as a Jew. Curiously, in order to make his point that not all Jews are rich, he offers the most repulsive depiction of Jewish wealth in his oeuvre. Something here is amiss.

On the one hand, Zola wants to represent certain Jews as blameless victims of capitalism. This is a new discovery for him, and he trumpets it with the zeal of one who has recognized the error of his previous beliefs. As the narrator says of Jews like Lehmann: "And, ah! how many other Jews there were, yet more wretched than he—Jews who starved in filthy dens. They were the immense majority, and their existence demonstrated all the idiotic falsity of antisemitism, that proscription en masse of a race which was charged with the monopolisation of all wealth, when it numbered so many poor working-folk" (83). On the other hand, Zola cannot help seeing the main oppressor of the downtrodden also as a Jew. For immediately after lamenting the plight of the poor Jews, he once again begins to berate the rich ones: "As soon as ever a French Jew became a great capitalist, he bought a title of Baron, married his daughter to a Count of ancient stock, made a pretence of showing himself more royalist than the king, and ended by becoming the worst of renegades, a fierce anti-semite, who not only denied, but helped to slaughter, his kith and kin" (83). The venom of this portrait is startling, especially because it so clearly distorts its model. Although Rothschild did become a baron, and although the Rothschilds, like most other French people, were slow to recognize Dreyfus's innocence, they did not turn their back on the Jewish community and did not convert, like Nathan. Indeed, a Rothschild always remained at the helm of the French Jewish consistory. And another rich Jewish baron—Reinach—became one of Dreyfus's most ardent defenders.

Zola's rhetoric is at odds with his argument here. He clearly wants to exculpate the Jews from charges of capitalist conspiracy. "There was really no Jew question at all, there was only a Capitalist question—a question of money heaped up in the hands of a certain number of gluttons, and thereby poisoning and rotting the world" (83), the narrator declares in terms that show a major evolution from the preparatory notes to *L'argent*, which had posited an inextricable link between money and Jews. Zola seems to have turned 180 degrees. But the more Zola seeks to free the Jews from old stereotypes of moneymongering, the more they return. In the same passage where he denounces the suffering of the poor Jew Lehmann, he blames the rich Jew Nathan for his selfishness and cupidity. Why, one might ask, does Zola still depict the extreme capitalists, the exemplars of the most craven bourgeois values, as Jews?

The answer can be found in Zola's peculiar analysis of the logic of capitalism. In *L'argent*, Gundermann and his Jewish brethren single-mindedly pursue their own financial interests, which lie in bringing down the Catholic bank. Zola's great *anti*-antisemitic realization—that the Jews do not act in concert, as part of a religious or racial plot, but rather for their own self-interest—transforms the Jew from racial conspirator into emblem of bourgeois individualism. This hyperindividualism of the Jews, which had seemed like a Jewish financial conspiracy in *L'argent*, leads the rich Jews of *Vérité* into a form of self-hatred. Realizing that their true self-interest lies in betraying their brethren to ally with Catholic nationalists, the successful Jewish capitalists become antisemites. Gundermann becomes Nathan. Zola needs his capitalists to be Jews in the later novel since it is the Jews who, according to Zola's theory, display the perverse effects of capitalism most clearly.

In *Vérité*, however, the fault lies not with Jews but with capitalism itself. The only solution to preventing antisemitism from taking hold, Zola makes clear, is to overcome capitalism. This solution, of course, had already been proposed in *L'argent* by Sigismond, the consumptive Jewish revolutionary. But in that novel it never has the lung power to succeed. Too theoretical, it remains tied to a hyperlogical economism. In other words, it remains too Jewish. In *Vérité*, capitalism finds a more formidable foe: Marc Froment, whose name means "yeast," promises to begin a process that will allow a new society to rise. This new society achieves the synthesis of Catholicism and Judaism that Zola had called for implicitly in *L'argent* and explicitly in "Pour les juifs." But whereas in "Pour les juifs" Zola had called on the Catholics to adopt the Jews' hyperrationality, in *Vérité* it is the social solidarity and secular humanism of Marc and his allies that comes to temper the Jewish capitalist drive.

In contrast to Nathan, who refuses to help a fellow Jew in need, the antisemite Marc overcomes his innate hatreds to rally in support of an innocent man. "Nobody could claim exemption from his duty," Marc reflects; "the action of one single isolated individual might suffice to modify destiny. . . . All the members of the nation were jointly and severally interested, for each defended his own liberty by protecting that of his fellow" (353). And this sense of social solidarity, which leads Marc to sacrifice his domestic happiness to defend Simon, eventually triumphs at the end of the novel.

Unlike in *L'argent*, where Sigismond's vision of the communist paradise remains theoretical, in *Vérité* Zola's utopian vision takes on real contours. The novel finishes decades in the future, when Marc's struggle has brought about a true transformation of the country. "And now a France which soon would be all one was being constituted; there would soon be no upper class, no lower class" (568). This vision of a postcapitalist paradise is also very specifically a paradise in which the war between Christians and Jews has ceased to rage: "Thus disappeared the divided France of former times, the France in which there had been two classes, two hostile, ever-warring races, reared, it might have been thought, on different planets, as if they were destined never to meet, never to come to an agreement" (569). And with the end of conflict between the races—a conflict born of capitalism and individualism, and destined to die with it—comes the end of antisemitism.

However, the end of antisemitism, Zola makes plain, also means an end to the Jews. In the last section of the novel, as plans are being made for the triumphant return of Simon to Maillebois, one of the older townspeople makes an antisemitic remark. Another responds: "The Jews, indeed! Why did he speak of the Jews! Antisemitism was dead—to such a degree, indeed, that the new generation failed to understand what was meant when people accused the Jews of every crime. . . . There were no Jews left, since only citizens, freed from the tyranny of dogmas, remained" (542). This vision of a Jew-free republic realizes the universalist dream of a nation of quality-less citizens, free of difference in the eyes of the law, but also in the eyes of each other. We might say that this is the ultimate Jacobin fantasy except that, as we saw in chapter 1, even Jacobins like Robespierre didn't actually call for the Jews to disappear. Zola, however, has no such qualms: "There are no more Jews, for there will soon be no more Catholics," one of the younger generation tells his grandmother. The disappearance of the Jews in this sense is ideological: Jews will cease to exist because their religion—all religion—will cease to exist. Once the French replace faith in God with faith in the republic, all sectarian conflict will end.

But Zola's utopian vision also spells an end for Jews as a race or people. Just as Napoleon wanted to hasten Jewish assimilation through intermarriage, so too does the novel see the fusion of the Christian and Jewish gene pools as the ultimate goal. By the end of *Vérité*, Simon's son Joseph has married Marc's daughter Louise. Simon's daughter Sarah has married one of the Christian townspeople, Sébastien Milhomme. They all produce offspring who gather, along with all the residents of Maillebois, to welcome home Simon. "These constituted the three generations which had sprung from the blood of the innocent man mingled with that of his champions" (549). The fantasy of racial reconciliation called for in "Pour les juifs" here achieves its fictional realization: "Embrace the Jews, in order to absorb them and mingle them into us.... Push for [mixed] marriages, leave it to the children to reconcile the parents" (60). In "Pour les juifs," Zola had called for a kind of genetic takeover: the more numerous Christians will fuse with the Jews, "enriching" themselves with their positive qualities—"because they have some" (60)—and diluting their negative qualities in the vast Christian gene pool. In *Vérité*, since Simon's descendants have no distinguishing qualities whatsoever, and barely exist as characters, one can only presume that this assimilationist solution to the Jewish question will achieve rapid and complete success.

But what to do with Simon himself? What to make of the older generation of Jews, those who suffered antisemitism and thus continue to exist as Jews? The novel shows the townspeople welcoming the Jewish victim back in an orgy of contrition and respect bordering on adulation. "They acclaimed Simon with the wildest enthusiasm," the narrator proclaims. "Glory to the innocent man who had well-nigh perished by the people's fault, and on whom the people would never be able to bestow sufficient happiness!" (560). Remembering how a similar crowd had called out "To death, to death with the Jew!" after Simon's false conviction, the children and grandchildren of the Jew's persecutors had now become his defenders, "striving by dint of sincerity and affection to redeem the crime of their forerunners!" (561).

But if this is philosemitism, it is a philosemitism without Jews. Or rather, the Jew is welcomed back into the national community, here figured in the town of Maillebois, but only as a reminder of past divisions that have been overcome. At the same time that the townspeople herald the Jew's return, they eliminate his difference, bulldozing his former home as a sign of progress. "On the site of the filthy Rue du Trou is a recreation-ground, which the children of the neighbourhood fill with their play and their laughter." Alongside the playground, they construct a new house for Simon—"not a palace, but a modest, bright, cheerful dwelling" (533). The narrator explains that this house would have no "great pecuniary value"; it would not resemble the "château" constructed by Baron Nathan, the feudal lord of finance.

Above the doorframe of this house, they carve an inscription in marble to commemorate Simon's suffering. "Presented by the Town of Maillebois to Schoolmaster Simon," it reads, "in the name of Truth and Justice, and in reparation for the torture inflicted on him" (534). Repentence is a noble sentiment, and one should not look a gift-house in the mouth: Zola surely meant this inscribed lodging to signify a universalist welcoming of the Jew into the national body, as well as a permanent reminder of the suffering he had undergone. But no mention is made that he suffered as a Jew and because of antisemitism. It is hard not to see this house as a kind of museum display, or cage at a zoo, in which the Jew's difference is at once exhibited and erased. His offspring, meanwhile, gladly relinquish the distinctions that made their forebear suffer and that have no positive valence whatsoever.

Zola and the "Jewish Question"

Zola's assimilationist answer to the "Jewish Question" was certainly not the only one being tried or tested in the fin-de-siècle period. At the same time that Zola was writing *Vérité*, his contemporary Theodore Herzl began to lay the foundation of political Zionism. Herzl had renounced assimilationist universalism to espouse a future in which Jews pursue their national destiny apart from Christians.[27] Zola's comrade-in-arms during the Dreyfus Affair, Bernard Lazare, had also come to see Zionism as the answer to antisemitism, as did certain non-Jews in this period.[28] And of course, long before the Affair, the British novelist George Eliot, in *Daniel Deronda* (1876), had offered her own version of Jewish nationalism.

After the Affair, Zola himself began to express conditional support for Zionism. "I find the sentiment that inspires you very noble, the desire to create an asylum for your people," he told a journalist for a Jewish publication in Vienna in 1900.[29] He had his reservations, however, about the practicality of the project, which he considered "utopian." He expressed doubts that the Zionists could organize the mass immigration of Jews to the Palestinian desert and wondered what the Jews would do once they got there. How would they overcome the material and political difficulties, and what would unify people from so many different countries who spoke different languages? But Zola liked utopias and sympathized with the motivations of the early Zionists: "I understand quite well . . . that the Jews who are in unfortunate circumstances are taking pains to improve their situation and, to whatever extent possible, I would lend full support to your project." To be sure, Zola did not believe that Zionism would constitute an attractive option for the Jews of France: "In truth, despite certain social and political pressures, the situation of the Jews in countries like France is not unhappy and, what is more, they are French," Zola told the journalist. "For what reason would they leave their country?"

Zola had other plans for the French Jews. As he set out to write *L'argent*, he saw the Jews as a nation apart, working conspiratorially to dominate French Christians with their financial cunning. As I have shown, however, the completed novel rejects the notion of a Jewish financial conspiracy and offers something resembling admiration for Jewish financial savvy. It even suggests that France might achieve great things if it could harness the capacities of the Jews for productive ends. In "Pour les juifs," written as political antisemitism was reaching a crescendo in the lead-up to the Affair, Zola lays out this vision clearly, proposing that France deal with the threat posed by the Jews by "embracing" them, which is to say incorporating them through imitation and intermarriage. That the Jews would emerge from this "embrace" having shed their difference, which is to say no longer a distinct people, appears as a desirable by-product of Zola's liberal plea.

In *Vérité*—his last word not only on the "Jewish Question" but as a novelist—Zola once again wrestles with the troubling nature of Jewish difference. Here, Zola's answer to the "Jewish Question" involves not only denouncing the nefarious manipulation of antisemitism by the antirepublican, Catholic right but also doing away with Jewish difference once and for all. The Jews may be more or less blameless victims in the partisan struggles of different French factions—and some Jews, especially those who sacrifice their coreligionsts for their own gain, are certainly less blameless than others. But Zola does not imagine that the Jews will have any reason to exist as a distinct people once antisemitism no longer threatens their collective safety. At the end of *Vérité*, the universalist vision of "Pour les juifs" has come to pass, as the future offspring of the republican hero absorb and dissipate the Jewishness of the descendants of the victim he saved from destruction.

For Zola, the defense of the Jews was inseparable from the defense of the republic and its values. And vice versa: the fate of the republic rested on finding a just and equitable solution to the "Jewish Question." That this solution involved the disappearance of the Jews through assimilation, I have argued, can be traced to the deep ambivalence that informed Zola's understanding of the role of Jews within the capitalist economy, an understanding that evolved through the decade of the 1890s without ever shedding its underlying ambivalence. It is important to recognize the complexity of the attitudes that lay behind Zola's defense of Dreyfus, which is still held up as the model of principled engagement by an intellectual in a political cause. That this engagement was motivated in part by what we might now consider to be antisemitic views in no way detracts from Zola's heroic actions. But it should lead us to view Zola's brand of republican universalism in a new light.

The victory of Zola and the Dreyfusards in the ongoing war between left and right—what the French call the "guerre franco-française"—would have profound consequences in France. It helped prevent political antisemitism from gaining the traction that it achieved in Germany—at least until the anti-Dreyfusards took their revenge during the Vichy period. Moreover, the victory of the anticlerical left over the right-wing nationalist Catholics during the Affair led directly to the Combes Law of 1905, which separated churches and the state. It was this law that instituted the version of state secularism, or *laïcité*, that characterizes what I am calling "republican universalism," which has become so dominant in France today that few realize that other forms of universalism, other models for negotiating the relation of the state to its religious and ethnic minorities, used to exist.

Many current defenders of *laïcité* in France today, especially those who wield *laïcité* as a weapon in the war against radical Islam and other forms of minority *communautarisme*, distort the meaning of the Combes Law. It did not, as Jean Baubérot has explained, necessitate the complete elimination of religion and minority difference from the public sphere.[30] But it is not hard to see why the law has been interpreted this way. A certain strain of Dreyfusard thought that lay behind the law—the strain identified with the leading Dreyfusard, Zola—did indeed call for the suppression of Jewish difference and predicate its vision for the universalist future on a radical form of Jewish assimilation. Given the popularity and prestige of Zola as a thinker and writer, it is not hard to see why so many today continue to think that the French republic demands such assimilation not just of Jews but of its other minorities as well. As we will see in the following two chapters, however, Zola's brand of republican universalism would be contested in the middle decades of the twentieth century by thinkers who conceived of other options for France's Jews besides merely blending in.

5

The Jew in Renoir's *La grande illusion*

The period between the two world wars saw major demographic changes in France's Jewish population.[1] Thanks to high levels of immigration, the number of Jews in France doubled, from approximately 150,000 at the end of the First World War to 300,000 on the eve of the Second World War. Polish and Russian Jews seeking better economic conditions in the 1920s were joined by floods of Central European Jews fleeing Nazi persecution after 1933.[2] The interwar period also saw a dramatic increase in the visibility of Jews in the government, which in turn fanned the flames of antisemitism. In 1936, Léon Blum, a literary critic who had embraced politics during the Dreyfus Affair, became France's first Jewish (and first Socialist) prime minister. The rise to power of Blum's Popular Front government enraged the numerous followers of France's homegrown protofascist parties. Members of the Camelots du roi, an openly antisemitic party, nearly murdered Blum on February 13, 1936, shortly before he became prime minister.[3]

In this fraught political environment, debates over the meaning of universalism focused the conflict between left and right. Whether vaunting the *volkish* notion that true Frenchness requires deep "roots" or denouncing the hordes of Jewish invaders, the far right rejected the very foundations of universalism, especially the idea that Frenchness is an ideological affiliation, one that in theory is available to all citizens. For Maurice Barrès and his followers, angered by the outcome of the Dreyfus Affair and the Combes Law of 1905 separating churches and state, Frenchness was defined by *la terre et les morts*, blood and soil, and by the heritage of Catholicism.[4] The right was countered by equally passionate defenders of republican universalism, such as Julien Benda, whose *Treason of the Intellectuals* (1927) castigated thinkers like Barrès for elevating the particular over the universal and the mysticism of race and rootedness over reason. Benda famously equated thinking itself with universalism: he saw defending universalism as the obligation of the intellectual.[5]

In this chapter, I argue that Jean Renoir's *La grande illusion* (The Grand Illusion, 1937), considered by many as one of the greatest films of all time, weighs in on this debate over universalism in significant, if complex, ways. The film tells the story of a group of French soldiers who plot escapes from a series of German prisoner-of-war camps during World War I. Renoir was known as a leftist director, and he had just made a propaganda film for the French Communist Party when he began working on *La grande illusion*. In his autobiography, he makes it clear that he intended the film as an antifascist statement: "It seemed to me that every honest man owed it to himself to combat Nazism. I am a filmmaker, my only possibility for taking part in that combat was a film."[6] No doubt the inclusion of a Jewish character named Rosenthal, played by Marcel Dalio, among the French officers in the film was intended to convey this antifascist message, as was the film's espousal of a doctrine of universal brotherhood transcending the barriers of race, class, and nation.

And yet *La grande illusion*'s representation of the Jew proves highly ambiguous. While the film seems to transcend antisemitic ideology by including the Jewish character within the symbolic national community formed by the French prisoners, it also endows the Jew with a range of negative characteristics reminiscent of antisemitic stereotype. Critics through the years have been discomfited by these stereotypes, puzzled by the apparent recourse to antisemitism in a film that otherwise broadcasts such universalist values. They have tended either to decry the film's representation of the Jew or, like Renoir's great champion, André Bazin, to dismiss it as irrelevant to the film's larger message of universal brotherhood. In what follows, I want to suggest, on the contrary, that these antisemitic stereotypes are both central to the film's meaning and a key to understanding its unique contribution to the debate over universalism. Indeed, it is precisely through the invocation of antisemitic stereotypes, I will argue, that the film makes the case for a kind of universalism built on the acceptance, or inclusion, of Jewish particularity. Renoir's brand of universalism thus marks a departure not just from the antiuniversalism of Barrès and the right but also from the assimilationist universalism of Zola and the republican left.

The Critical Controversy

The entry point of our analysis will be the controversy over the film's depiction of Jews that has divided critics over the decades—a sure sign of the complexity of Renoir's approach to the "Jewish Question." One of the few films Renoir directed that critics greeted favorably upon its initial release, *La grande illusion* garnered glowing reviews in 1937. Certain critics on the right, wary of Renoir's leftist leanings, did fault the film for "a few rather naïve phrases" and for a "rather elementary sociology," but they by and large overlooked issues pertaining to Jewishness.[7] Critics for *Le Candide* and *Ce Soir* mention the presence of a Jewish character, but they do not describe the film as antisemitic.[8] Of course, critics may have overlooked the "Jewish Question" because the film's depiction of the Jewish character so confirmed their prejudices: we are, by definition, blind to our own ideology. To the critic for *Les Nouvelles Littéraires*, for example, all the characterizations in the film, including that of "the rich Jew Rosenthal," seemed "exactly true to type."[9]

A controversy over the "Jewish Question" erupted, however, when the film was rereleased shortly after the Second World War, in 1946. Writing first in the left-leaning *Le Franc Tireur* and then in *L'Ecran Français*, the critic Georges Altman describes his sense of "malaise" watching the film a second time, a malaise that "despite Renoir, despite the beauty of the images, or because of it, changed into amazement and distrust." Altman's discomfiture stems in part from the sympathetic treatment of the Germans in the film, a representation that the ovens of Auschwitz and Dachau have caused him to see in a new light. "Nothing to be done about it," Altman writes. "Our optic has been turned upside down, like many other things in the world." This postgenocide optic also causes the critic to reconsider the film's representation of the Jew: "When *La grande illusion* presents, sympathetically to be sure, the French soldier Rosenthal as an Israelite, but finds it necessary to specify, to underline that he's a Jew, it asks ever so gently the racist question that ended in Auschwitz."[10] In rather hyperbolic rhetoric, Altman accuses Renoir's film of participating in a racist logic, beginning down the road that leads to genocide, even while representing the Jew sympathetically.

Altman's reaction to the film's alleged antisemitism is all the more striking in that many of the references to Rosenthal's Jewishness had been edited out of the 1946 version of the film in an effort to avoid offending postwar sensibilities.[11] Perhaps because of these cuts, other critics at the time did not share Altman's perception. Amid a general critical and popular appreciation of the film, the critic for the left-leaning *Libération* takes special pains to defend *La grande illusion* against Altman's attacks, finding the charge of antisemitism to be "hardly founded" and pointing out that the film's producer was "Israelite," as was the censor who approved the edited version of the film for release.[12]

More striking is the opinion of those arch-antisemites and collaborators, Maurice Bardèche and Robert Brasillach, which runs directly counter to Altman's. In their disturbing but often insightful *Histoire du cinéma* (1943), Renoir occupies an ambiguous place as both a despised mouthpiece for the Popular Front and an accomplished cinematic artist. When they come to *La grande illusion*, which they call the best French film of recent years, their enthusiasm for an acknowledged masterpiece is tempered by what they perceive as the director's philosemitism:

> Some points, here and there, are debatable. The characters are magnificently drawn, and the most original surely is the Jew Rosenthal, courageous, obliging, intelligent, ironical, who fights, he tells us, to sanctify the property that his family has acquired through its ingenuity. Céline was right to see there the "tip of the iceberg," and the first Jew that the Popular Front dared to portray sympathetically as a Jew [en tant que Juif]. All of which is highly disturbing.[13]

The collaborating critics praise certain aspects of Renoir's depiction of "the Jew Rosenthal," approving especially of the Jew's admission of greed and acquisitiveness. They are disturbed, however, by the character's sympathetic qualities. Like their fellow antisemite Céline, whose murderous fantasies about Jewish conspiracy earned him a death sentence in absentia after the war, Bardèche and Brasillach see in Renoir an agent of the Popular Front, which is to say, of *the Jew Blum*.

Despite this criticism from the extreme right, Renoir's film could not completely escape the charge of antisemitism from left-leaning critics when it was next released in 1958, once again to great acclaim. Writing in *Le Canard Enchaîné*, Henry Magnan, while admiring the film overall, faults it for being "a little bit jingoistic, a little bit naïve, and a touch antisemitic."[14] In a later article for *Combat*, Magnan criticizes the overaccentuation of types in the film, again singling out the representation of Rosenthal as interpreted by Marcel Dalio: "Where I feel it the most is in the portrait of the Jew Rosenthal."[15] While regretting the depiction of Rosenthal as supremely rich, ostentatious, and given to complaining (especially during the escape sequence, when the proletarian Frenchman played by Jean Gabin remains stoic), Magnan sees the danger not so much in the specificity of these stereotypes but in the way the film substitutes cliché for characterization: "For me, the very fact of giving him a few well-defined faults forces us to generalize and impute them to all of his coreligionists." Magnan argues that because the film presents certain characters as "prototypes of the social class (and even the race) that they are supposed to represent," it too blatantly asks its viewers to see Rosenthal, along with his defects, as emblematic of all Jews. "And the oily appearance of Dalio doesn't help matters," he adds.

The Jewish question was foremost on André Bazin's mind when he wrote an important analysis of *La grande illusion* in *Radio Cinéma Télévision* in 1958. The legendary film critic begins his review of the film by describing how the new version restored the scenes relating to Rosenthal's Jewishness that had been cut in the 1946 version.[16] Bazin invokes Altman's charge of antisemitism right from the start of his article, only to dismiss it as a misguided aftereffect of the War: "Only the sensibility of the aftermath of the Liberation can explain judgments that are so contrary to the spirit of the film.... In 1946 the message of *La Grande Illusion* still couldn't be fully grasped."[17] This message, according to Bazin, is a theme dear to Renoir, one that he frequently described in interviews, namely that "men are less separated by vertical barriers of nationalism than by the horizontal cleavage of cultures, races, classes, professions, etc." As described by Bazin, Renoir's theory that vertical divisions (of nationalism) matter less than horizontal ones (of race, class, culture), often referred to by later critics, implies that race *does* remain a fundamental division between men and thus might seem to contradict the *anti*-antisemitic "spirit" that Bazin attributes to the film. Nevertheless, Bazin sees any critical focus on race as a distraction from the film's message of universal brotherhood.

In general, Bazin's view of the film has triumphed. Subsequent cinema scholars have discussed the film's treatment of the Jewish character in passing, but to my knowledge there has been no sustained analysis of the question of antisemitism in Renoir's oeuvre. And the question of antisemitism is indeed that—a question, one that we have seen depends, to some extent, on the perspective of individual viewers. In the following sections, I will present both sides of this question through a close and contextualized analysis of the film's depiction of the Jew. I will show how *La grande illusion* raises and tries to answer a series of questions about Jewishness and the nation, questions that circulated in various ways and through various discourses in France in the late 1930s. While the mere asking of these questions (Does the Jew belong in France? If so, on what terms?), regardless of the answers the film provides, may seem to our present-day eyes to implicate the film in an antisemitic and antiuniversalist logic, I will ultimately suggest that the film escapes from this logic by subtly undermining the exclusionary categories on which such a logic depends. And in so doing, I'll argue, it makes the case for an open form of universalism in contrast to the orthodoxies of both right and left.

Jews on Film

A first step in evaluating the film's representation of the Jew would involve comparing it to other cinematic depictions of Jews from the time. Rémy Pithon's work on the image of the Jew in French cinema of the 1930s allows us to perceive the truly exceptional nature of Renoir's representation. Pithon describes how the first half of the 1930s saw numerous depictions of Jews on the screen, mainly in a comic register.[18] Explicit references to Jews in French cinema nearly disappeared, however, during the second half of the decade. This disappearance is all the more striking in that the same period saw a vast increase in the vehemence of antisemitic rhetoric in the popular press.

The Stavisky Scandal of 1934, in which a Jewish businessman committed suicide after the revelation of his links with corrupt politicians, as well as the rise to power of the Popular Front government of Léon Blum in 1936, both provoked a torrent of antisemitic writing as well as actual physical violence in France. The Stavisky Scandal caused a right-wing riot outside the Chamber of Deputies in which fourteen people were killed. As mentioned above, Blum was attacked by a mob incited by the right-wing thugs five months before becoming prime minister. To explain the sudden disappearance of the Jew from the French screen in the late 1930s, Pithon suggests that filmmakers may have feared fanning the flames of this violent antisemitism. He further hypothesizes that the heavy concentration of Jews in the Parisian cinema world—a concentration that increased in the late 1930s as Jewish refugee producers and directors, such as Fritz Lang and Max Ophuls, flocked to France—led to greater reticence and caution.[19]

Pithon goes on to show, however, that despite the *explicit* disappearance of the Jew, several films of the period included characters marked by what he calls a "vague Jewishness." In these films, characters had Jewish connotations even if they were not explicitly named as Jews, especially if the actors playing them had played Jews in the past. Pithon's prime example of a connotated actor is Marcel Dalio, who was known for playing shady "foreign" (métèque) characters in such films as Julien Duvivier's *Pépé le Moko* (1936) and Robert Siodmak's *Cargaison blanche* (1937) as well as onstage.[20] Even if these characters were vaguely foreign rather than explicitly Jewish, Pithon argues that they had Jewish associations for the average viewer of the time.

Viewed in this context, *La grande illusion* stands out all the more strongly as one of the only films from the late 1930s to depict Jews explicitly and to confront head-on the question of their place within French society. According to Pithon, Renoir's clear intention was to combat antisemitism with the representation of Rosenthal as a sympathetic Jew.[21] Whether or not he succeeded in his mission, however, Pithon leaves in doubt. By casting Dalio as Rosenthal, for example, Renoir may have compromised his intentions, since audiences at the time would have perceived the actor as sinister because of his prior roles. And by depicting Rosenthal as supremely rich, Renoir plays into popular prejudices against Jews. For Pithon, the lesson of *La grande illusion* is that "even if one tried, in the 1930s, with the best intentions in the world, to portray the Jew sympathetically, it was impossible to avoid resorting to stereotypes."[22] But is antisemitism really so inescapable an ideology? And is the film really so blind to its effects? To absolve the film of antisemitism in this manner is to view it, in a sense, as a failure. In my analysis of the film that follows, I want to emphasize the highly elaborate and even self-conscious nature of the film's portrayal of Jewishness. Rather than view the depiction of the Jew as the film's blind spot, I will show it to be one of the lenses through which its meaning can be seen most clearly.

Profiling the Jew

The debate over the film's depiction of Jews turns on the issue of stereotypes, the most obvious of which is Rosenthal's extreme wealth. The recipient of packages from home loaded with expensive foodstuffs while a prisoner of war, Rosenthal is introduced as a figure of ostentatious privilege. Presiding over a table set up in the prison dormitory, he doles out delicacies from fancy Parisian restaurants to his fellow French officers, including the new arrivals, the aristocratic de Boieldieu (Pierre Fresney) and the proletarian Maréchal (Jean Gabin). The men accept "Rosenthal's kindness," with an appreciation not untinged by resentment.[23] "I've never eaten so well in my life," states one officer, but Maréchal declares that he prefers bistro fare to the gastronomic luxuries of Maxim's and Fouquet's. As numerous critics have pointed out, Rosenthal's display of alimentary largesse quickly becomes a pretext for the portrayal of class difference among the French officers, another of the film's themes that has aroused much critical debate.[24] Maréchal, a mechanic who has risen through the ranks, emerges as the spokesman for traditional French values of simplicity and thrift, values clearly opposed to Rosenthal's expensive tastes.

In the scene following the prison lunch sequence at which Rosenthal shares his packages (colis) from home, Maréchal and the engineer (Gaston Modot) discuss their fellow prisoners. While the engineer wonders about de Boieldieu's trustworthiness (they refer to him as "the monocle," mocking his affected eyepiece), Maréchal inquires about Rosenthal's wealth. "He must be well off," Maréchal states, inviting elaboration. The engineer proceeds to explain that Rosenthal's family are "the great Rosenthal bankers," while Rosenthal himself runs a "big fashion business." Rosenthal is thus linked to not one but two professions that were stereotyped as Jewish in 1930s France. Rosenthal's role as garmento, it should be noted, serves a specific function as the plot unfolds, for it is his Parisian *maison de couture* that provides the officers with the case of women's dresses they will wear in their theatrical performance later in the film. (The association with female fashion might also serve to feminize his character, which I will comment on below.) But if Rosenthal's profession as couturier is narratively necessary, his banking background is stereotypically necessary, since the association of Jews and finance had such deep roots in French culture.[25]

Oddly, however, Rosenthal is not explicitly named as a Jew in the early scenes of the film. The words *juif* (Jew) and *Israélite* (Israelite) are not mentioned even as Rosenthal's character comes to embody an increasing number of antisemitic clichés. Instead, his heavily coded name serves as substitute for any overt reference to his racial or religious identity. The film lays particular stress on the name "Rosenthal" right from the start, in the first scene set in the POW camp when the Germans distribute packages to the French officers. The accentuating of the Jewish name, with its Germanic tonalities, implicitly links the Jew with the enemy and stands in contrast to the film's treatment of the names of the other French officers. With the exception of Maréchal and de Boieldieu, these "French" names are passed over quickly or not mentioned at all.

The name "Rosenthal," constantly repeated by the various characters who discuss his wealth, ostentation, and banking connections, comes to serve as a substitute for the word "Jew," which the film withholds. The word "Jew," then, remains an absent but overdetermined signifier in the first half of the film, standing for an accumulation of (mostly negative) attributes, while the name "Rosenthal" functions as what psychoanalysis would call a fetish, a site where knowledge about these attributes is at once displayed and repressed. Like all overdetermined figures, the word "Jew" becomes so laden with meaning that its eventual manifestation late in the film, when hurled as an insult by Maréchal, contains all the impact of the return of the repressed. By continually circling around the Jewish question without naming it specifically, moreover, the film seeks to create a kind of complicity with the viewer over the tacit recognition of Rosenthal's difference.

This complicity implicates the viewer in an antisemitic logic, a logic of exclusion, that is key to understanding the film's intervention in the debate over universalism. If the French officers form a symbolic nation in the sense that they represent different classes and occupations, a cross-section of French society, one kind of difference—Jewish difference—is shown to be more different than the rest. The viewer is encouraged to perceive this difference as a series of signals and signs that set Rosenthal apart from the other officers and that add up to more than class distinction. In this manner, then, the film seems to embrace a Barrèsian antiuniversalism, a vision of the nation based on deterministic notions of religion and ancestry to which the Jew can gain only provisional entry. It will become the goal of the second half of the film to break down or transcend this model by explicitly thematizing the inclusion of the Jew within the symbolic nation formed by Maréchal and by undermining the category of race itself.

Throughout the first half of the film, however, both the other officers and Rosenthal himself engage in a game of circumlocution that insists on pointing to an identity that nevertheless remains unspecified. The absence of the word "Jew" is felt in the oddness of the dialogue, characterized by apparent non sequitur. An example of this pattern occurs in the scene in which the officers take a break from digging a tunnel to discuss their reasons for wanting to escape from the German camp. Maréchal states in characteristically unselfish terms that he wants to escape so as to rejoin the war effort and prevent others from dying. For de Boieldieu, a camp is to be escaped from just as a tennis court is to be played on. The aristocrat then asks: "What do you say, Rosenthal? As a sportsman?" (Et vous, Rosenthal? Vous qui êtes un sportif?).[26] This unmotivated reference to Rosenthal's athletic prowess (nothing thus far indicates that Rosenthal is athletic, although we later learn that he hunts) gives way to antisemitic innuendo, when the actor (Julien Carette) chimes in: "Him! He was born in Jerusalem." Through the metonymical association of Jews with Jerusalem, the actor moves a step closer to literalization, to naming Rosenthal's Jewishness as such. He also thereby calls into doubt Rosenthal's patriotism and courage by implying that since he was "born in Jerusalem," Rosenthal is not really French and thus cannot really want to return to a country that is not his own.

Rosenthal's deadpan answer to both the actor and the aristocrat about where he was born at once acknowledges the hidden subtext of the dialogue and perpetuates the game of circumlocution. "No, in Vienna," he responds; "my mother was Danish, my father Polish, naturalized French." The humor of Rosenthal's response derives from the fact that even while denying that he is from Jerusalem, he all the more emphasizes that he is Jewish by referring to his cosmopolitan, partly Eastern European, and hence highly coded, parentage.[27] "Old Breton nobility," adds Maréchal, showing that he too can joke about Rosenthal's Jewishness, this time by naming a seeming opposite. But Rosenthal has the last laugh: "It's possible," he declares, and then abruptly shifts registers, putting an end to the series of displacements. Speaking as the parvenu immigrant he is, although still stopping short of owning his Jewishness specifically, he accuses the other officers, "of old French stock," of not possessing a hundred square meters of their country while the Rosenthals in thirty-five years of residence in France have acquired three castles along with their hunting grounds and picture galleries of "authentic" ancestors. All of that, he concludes, is certainly worth fighting for. De Boieldieu comments, bemused, that the question of patriotism viewed in that manner is certainly very unique.

Rosenthal's speech provides the cornerstone of the case that would see the film as antisemitic and antiuniversalist. Not only is Rosenthal ostentatiously wealthy and involved in the stereotypically Jewish professions of banking and clothing but, foreigners in France, his family has used its wealth to lay hold of the French patrimony. This reference to the Rosenthals' rapaciousness calls to mind the viciously antisemitic diatribes of Édouard Drumont, who in his best-selling *La France juive* (Jewish France, 1886) had denounced what he saw as a Jewish takeover of the nation. Not content with the three castles and their hunting grounds, Rosenthal hints at an even more threatening possession, the future entry of his family into the very aristocracy they have displaced through the appropriation of their portraits. Although the word "Jew" has still not been spoken, the character of Rosenthal has come to typify the image of the Jew as dangerous, foreign interloper. His very brazenness and unapologetic boast, in spite of his bonhomie, seem calculated to arouse the worst fears of French audiences in the late 1930s, who were all the more alert to the threat of Jews taking over France following the rise to power of Léon Blum.

Renoir buffs will recognize in the reference to Rosenthal's châteaux and aristocratic ancestors an intertextual anticipation of Renoir's later film *La règle du jeu* (The Rules of the Game, 1939), in which the same actor who plays Rosenthal, Marcel Dalio, plays an eccentric marquis, Robert de La Chesnaye, who invites guests for a hunting party on his estate. In *La règle du jeu* we discover, through some servant gossip, that the marquis's family tree contains a Rosenthal, as if to signal that the threat of polluting the aristocracy alluded to in *La grande illusion* has come to pass. In his autobiography, the Jewish Dalio describes the daring of Renoir's casting him against type in *La règle du jeu*, as well as his own nervousness at the challenge of playing an aristocrat, in terms that recall Rosenthal's speech in *La grande illusion*: "So here I am, Marcel Blauschild, called Dalio, about to depart for the Sologne where I will become the marquis Robert de La Chesnaye and take possession of 'La Colinière,' my ancestral castle." While in retrospect Dalio's performance as La Chesnaye seems of the utmost brilliance, the actor's outsider status lending the character a remarkable poignancy, Renoir's doubts at the time led to the reference to the marquis's Jewish ancestry, which, we learn from Dalio, was a late addition to the script: "With me, he [Renoir] needed to be reassured, to be certain that he hadn't made a mistake, to be able to justify the marquis de La Chesnaye beneath my Levantine features. Still in doubt, he added a scene in which we learn through some servant gossip that I'm half Jewish."[28]

Unlike *La grande illusion, La règle du jeu* was not well received by audiences or critics at the time of its initial release. And the peculiarly Jewish marquis posed a particular problem. According to a critic in *Les Annales*: "The choice of actors renders the whole enterprise even stranger. M. Dalio plays the role of the marquis; to portray a country gentleman, they went and got the little Israelite officer from *La Grande Illusion*!"[29] Even if the reference to an ancestor named Rosenthal did not immediately call to mind the Jewish character in *La grande illusion* for viewers of the later film, Dalio's presence in both films seems to have made the Jewish connection between them inescapable. Indeed, the presence of this highly connotated actor did not go unremarked by Bardèche and Brasillach, who, writing in *L'Action Française*, saw in the later film "an astonishing Dalio, more Jewish than ever, at once attractive and sordid."[30] The antisemitic critics carry a mimetic or realist reading of cinema to an extreme, refusing to see the actor as playing a character or the film as a fiction. For Bardèche and Brasillach, the presence of Dalio makes *La règle du jeu* a film not about the aristocracy at all but about the Jew's inescapable foreignness: "Another odor rises in him from the depth of the ages, another race that does not hunt, that possesses no castle, for whom the Sologne means nothing. Never perhaps has the foreignness [l'étrangeté] of the Jew been as forcefully or as brutally depicted."[31] For these critics, it is the threat of the Jew taking over the patrimony of France, a threat alluded to in *La grande illusion* and carried out in *La règle du jeu*, that provokes such hostility. Even if Renoir raised this threat in order to defuse it, as I will suggest below, he nevertheless played into passions and prejudices of the antiuniversalist camp, the camp that would deny the Jew's right to belong in France on account of his difference.

If Rosenthal's boasts about his acquisitiveness provide rather obvious fodder for critics intent on seeing *La grande illusion* as antiuniversalist and antisemitic, closer inspection reveals more subtle, and perhaps for that reason more troubling, ethnic stereotyping. In *The Jew's Body*, Sander Gilman describes how a tradition of antisemitic discourse stretching back to the nineteenth century in France and Germany purported to read racial difference as a series of physical signs. "In the world of nineteenth-century medicine, this difference becomes labeled as the 'pathological' or 'pathogenic' qualities of the Jewish body."[32] In *La grande illusion*, Rosenthal bears many of these signs of Jewish degeneration. Gilman devotes a chapter to what he calls "the Jewish disease," syphilis, a sickness that had begun to be perceived as a crisis in

Germany by the 1920s and '30s but that had already been viewed as a national catastrophe by the French a half century before, where it originally had aristocratic and intellectual associations. According to Gilman, the deadly qualities of syphilis eventually became associated in the mindset of the period with the Jew,[33] a link underscored in *La grande illusion*, during a conversation among the French prisoners about the nature of infectious disease, when Rosenthal announces that he contracted "the pox" from a society friend of his mother. ("Everything gets democratized," de Boieldieu comments snidely.)

Gilman devotes an entire chapter to the Jew's supposedly deformed feet, which represented another sign of inferiority for both German and French antisemites. The idea that the Jew's feet bear a resemblance to the cloven foot of the devil can be traced back to the Middle Ages,[34] but in France this association received renewed emphasis during the Dreyfus Affair in the 1890s, when antisemitic caricaturists capitalized on the alleged traitor's name, depicting him as a three-toed demon. According to Gilman, the pathognomonic foot of the Jew, now diagnosed as flat rather than cloven, took on a new significance in the nineteenth century when it seemed to exclude the Jew from military service, and hence from citizenship in the nation-state. Moreover, the condition of intermittent claudication (limping produced by insufficient blood flow to the outer extremities), identified first by Jean-Martin Charcot, the French founder of modern psychiatry, also came to be considered a Jewish nervous disorder in the late nineteenth century.[35]

The limp that Rosenthal develops while fleeing with Maréchal through the German countryside taps into these stereotypes. The product of an injury rather than a congenital weakness or nervous symptom—the film shows the moment when Rosenthal hurts himself in close-up, as if to guard against these other explanations—the Jew's lame foot nevertheless acts an impediment (so to speak) to his escape, and hence to the accomplishment of his military duties. It risks jeopardizing his life and that of his comrade, who must stop to help him along. The Jew's clumsiness—Maréchal will later call him "maladroit"—partakes in stereotypical notions about the Jewish body, highlighting to what extent de Boieldieu's attribution of athleticism to Rosenthal was ironic. At home neither in his own body nor in nature, Rosenthal once again contrasts unfavorably with Maréchal, the physically and morally healthy Frenchman.

This contrast is instructive, for while Maréchal grew up in the inner city —he refers proudly to his origins in the proletarian 20th arrondissement of Paris—he is nevertheless able to establish an immediate bond with the cow that belongs to Elsa (Dita Parlo), the German woman who shelters the two escaping Frenchmen while they wait for Rosenthal's foot to heal. "You smell like my grandfather's cows," Maréchal tells the animal, revealing a connection with the soil, a bond all the more "natural" because it is shown to be hereditary. While hiding out on the farm, Maréchal is continually shown stretching in the out-of-doors, looking out at the rolling hills, whereas Rosenthal remains confined by domestic space on account of his injury. Maréchal is filmed against deep-focus landscapes suggesting an affinity with nature; Rosenthal is continually framed or bounded by windows and doors, a sign of his association with culture. While Maréchal engages in rustic farm occupations, Rosenthal occupies himself by teaching the German woman's daughter to count, in German. Stereotypical ethnic divisions of labor thus find their echo in these scenes as both men revert to their ancestral occupations: Maréchal returns to his peasant roots, just as Rosenthal exercises his innate talent for the calculation associated with banking.

Rosenthal displays other deficiencies as well. Reduced to the role of interpreter between Maréchal and Elsa, he watches passively as their mutual attraction turns into a love affair. The feminization of Rosenthal's character, already hinted at through his association with female fashion, is even more accentuated during the scenes on the German farm, when his virility suffers further compromise. As Gilman points out, antisemitic discourse represented male Jews as at once overly libidinous and as castrated (circumcision was often associated with castration in the popular mindset).[36] Rosenthal's injured foot might thus symbolize a kind of symbolic castration, an exclusion of the Jew from the erotic triangle, allowing the two blond, blue-eyed Christians of different nationalities to consummate what the film presents as a natural bond between them.[37] The emasculation of the Jew is all the more striking in that an early treatment for the film, in which Maréchal escapes with a fellow Christian, has them share the affections of the German woman.[38]

Of all the elements of the Jewish body marked by antisemitic discourse, however, the nose stands out as the most visible and identifiable. As Linda Nochlin has shown, the curved nose became such a common symbol for designating Jews, and by extension a range of unsavory occupations associated with Jews, such as moneylending, that even Jewish artists such as Camille Pissarro used it as a shorthand to designate capitalist exploitation.[39] *La grande illusion* makes much of Rosenthal's nose, or rather, of Marcel Dalio's. Renoir (and his director of photography, Christian Matras) film Gabin and Dalio differently, the former often facing the camera and the latter in profile, his aquiline appendage given full prominence.[40] Dalio's silhouette becomes all the more marked in the scenes when Rosenthal's "race" is at issue, such as when he describes the Jewish tendency toward pride from behind and slightly to the right of Gabin, who faces the camera head-on. The accentuation of this feature typifies the film's almost obsessive focus on Jewish stereotypes with negative connotations. Indeed, the film seems to harp on Rosenthal's differences—both physical and cultural—as if to manifest every possible reason for excluding him from the symbolic national unit formed by the other men.[41]

Symbolic Inclusion

However, Rosenthal is *not* excluded from this symbolic unit. Like the Revolutionaries I examined in chapter 1, who pointed to the Jews' myriad "vices" but nevertheless offered them citizenship, Renoir adopts what might be called an "even so" strategy toward universalism: yes, the Jews are different, but they still deserve to be included within the embrace of the French universal. And, as for the Revolutionaries, the Jew's difference actually becomes valuable for Renoir as a way of demonstrating the reach of the universal, just how inclusive it can be. In *La grande illusion*, we see a return to a more pluralistic understanding of French universalism, one that accepts Jewish difference without trying to assimilate it away. But to understand how the film makes this statement, it is necessary to unpack further its complex representation of the Jew.

First, we must recognize that while the film might harp on Jewish difference in stereotyped ways, it portrays all cultural differences in clichéd terms. This is true of the various nationalities in the German camp: the English are described as plum-pudding eaters, the Russians as vodka drinkers, etc. Each of the individual French officers, moreover, embodies a series of stereotypes characteristic of his class or profession. While most of these are less pejorative or threatening than the characteristics associated with the Jew, some might in fact be seen as worse. De Boieldieu's monocle, English cigarettes, and inability to use the familiar form *tu* even to his wife and mother, for example, represent the typical trappings of the effete and painfully remote aristocrat.

Eventually de Boieldieu redeems himself by transcending his stereotype, confirming through his heroic gesture of self-sacrifice that the values associated with his class are doomed to extinction. Acting as a decoy and allowing himself to be shot so that Maréchal and Rosenthal can escape, de Boieldieu forges a link with his fellow French officers that makes any criticism of his haughty manners seem trivial. So too, however, does the film depict Rosenthal rising above the stereotype of Jewish acquisitiveness through generosity. Although he brags of his family's vast fortune, he shares his wealth by feeding his fellow officers. Indeed, the film compensates for Rosenthal's Jewish deficiencies by endowing him with a series of positive personal qualities that earn him the esteem of his comrades as well as the sympathies of the viewer. When

Maréchal returns from solitary confinement, the camera cuts to a close-up of Rosenthal's face, showing him wipe a tear away at the sight of his friend's haggard appearance.[42] As we have seen, moreover, Rosenthal is deeply patriotic and eagerly takes on the project of escape, displaying great personal courage. When von Rauffenstein (Erich von Stroheim), the aristocratic German commander of the second and supposedly escape-proof prisoner camp, makes a disparaging comment about Maréchal and Rosenthal, de Boieldieu defends his countrymen: "They are very good soldiers," he declares.

This affirmation of the Jew as soldier, in the mouth of an aristocratic career officer, had a particularly strong resonance for the French in 1937. Jews had served in the French army since the time of the Napoleonic Wars, but the Dreyfus Affair opened a rift between the Jews and the military that did not close easily.[43] Although the Jewish captain falsely accused of treason was eventually pardoned and rehabilitated into the army (Dreyfus served in the First World War and died in 1935, shortly before the filming of *La grande illusion*), many Jews felt that their military aptitude had been called into question. De Boieldieu's recognition of Rosenthal as a good soldier, and, perhaps even more importantly, the lack of distinction made between him and Maréchal in regard to their soldiering skills, signals the film's acceptance of Jewish military virtue and its normalization of the Jewish soldier.

Returning to the comparison between Rosenthal and de Boieldieu, we recognize that although the Jewish character embodies a series of negatively connoted stereotypes, these deficiencies are perceived as less negative than those of the aristocrat. Whereas Rosenthal is genial and generous, de Boieldieu is distant, at times rude and snobbish, and earns the mistrust—even the dislike—of his fellow soldiers. Once again, Maréchal, the embodiment of the average Frenchman, provides the terms for gauging the relative merits of the two men. In a crucial scene, Maréchal tells Rosenthal that he would prefer escaping with him rather than de Boieldieu. With de Boieldieu, Maréchal says, "I can't let myself go. I'm not free." Maréchal contends that their different "education" erects a barrier between them: "There is a wall between us." Maréchal's highly charged metaphorical language assimilates the French class structure to the German prison, suggesting that class differences, what Renoir and later Bazin would call horizontal divisions, count at least as much as, if not more than, national or racial frontiers.

Interestingly, Maréchal does not experience Rosenthal's wealth as a similar wall. While we know little about Rosenthal's education, I would point out that he and Maréchal speak in a similar manner. Their linguistic similarity is displayed most clearly at the moment of greatest tension in their relationship: when Maréchal threatens to abandon Rosenthal because of his twisted ankle, he mimics the Jew's exact words. As Rosenthal intones, "I slipped. . . . Not my fault" [J'ai glissé. . . . C'est pas ma faute], Maréchal echoes, "You slipped. . . . I know you slipped" [T'as glissé. . . . Je sais que t'as glissé]. The mirroring words underscore the fundamental bond between the two men in spite of the temporary rupture. Their familiar mode of address and colloquial constructions, moreover, contrast with the highly proper and formal French of de Boieldieu (who would never address his fellow officers with *tu*, much less *t'*[44]), as well as with the English that de Boieldieu speaks with fellow aristocrat von Rauffenstein. Although later he will reveal that he also speaks German, Rosenthal might thus in some way be seen as closer to an "authentic" kind of Frenchness than the scion of an ancient French bloodline, who reveals a greater linguistic affinity with the German nobleman and with a transnational aristocracy of English-speaking, horse-racing privilege. The traditional antisemitic charge of cosmopolitanism, of not being sufficiently rooted, as Barrès would have it, is thus ironically shifted in *La grande illusion* from the Vienna-born Jew to the representative of the old French nobility. This move echoes the way the Revolutionaries enfranchised Jews while driving aristocrats from France.

Maréchal returns to the issue of Rosenthal's generosity in his explanation of why he feels closer to him than to de Boieldieu. Rosenthal, however, dismisses his generosity as a function of pride. "I'm very proud of my rich family," he explains. Rosenthal then engages in a remarkable reflection on the nature of antisemitic stereotyping (although still without mentioning the word "Jew"): "People think that our great fault is avarice. A serious error. We are often very generous. But alas, along with that quality, Jehovah has heavily endowed us with the sin of pride." For the viewer attempting to decode the film's stance on Jews, this scene is highly ambiguous. On one level, Rosenthal's statement may be understood as an internalization of the antisemitic gesture of viewing the Jews as a group tinged by collective defect that marked the discourse not only of the Jews' critics but of many of their defenders as well. On the other, the Jew explicitly contradicts the stereotype of Jewish avarice, or rather replaces it with pride, an arguably less offensive sin. The possibility of Rosenthal's irony complicates the question, opening the potential for his subversion of the very act of speaking of Jews as a group at all. The ambiguity of the scene resolves itself, however, when Maréchal brushes aside Rosenthal's entire disquisition: "Those are all just stories. I don't give a damn about Jehovah." Maréchal thus dismisses Rosenthal's rhetoric about the Jews as precisely that, as mere rhetoric, "just stories," substituting a clear expression of friendship for what perhaps might be seen as a (Jewish?) splitting of hairs.

Viewers inclined to see Maréchal's gesture of friendship toward Rosenthal (and over de Boieldieu) as a sign of the film's acceptance of the Jew receive confirmation during the climactic scenes following the escape. First, however, Maréchal and Rosenthal put their friendship (and Maréchal's dismissal of Jewish difference) to the test. De Boieldieu has just nobly sacrificed himself so that his compatriots can get away. Setting out through the German countryside in the middle of winter with only a few lumps of sugar, Maréchal and Rosenthal experience extreme privation. When Rosenthal hurts his foot and cannot keep up, Maréchal threatens to abandon him after first venting his rage. Calling Rosenthal a *colis*, thus symbolically returning the packages the Jew has shared, Maréchal states baldly that he cannot stand Jews: "Jews! I never could stand them!" [Les juifs, j'ai jamais pu les blairer!]. The first time the word "Jew" is mentioned in the film, it hits Rosenthal, and the viewer, like a slap in the face, redounding with all the pent-up fury of a broken taboo. "A little late to realize it," comments Rosenthal sardonically as Maréchal leaves him behind to die in the snow. The viewer is momentarily left with the impression that all the expressions of goodwill have been a pretense and that the fundamental antipathy of the true Frenchman toward the Jew has finally been revealed. Then follows a justly celebrated scene in which Rosenthal sings loudly to cover his misery. We see him alone in close-up. The body of Maréchal then appears in the frame like a guardian angel. He gently helps his friend to walk slowly. "You really can't go on?" Maréchal asks tenderly. "Oh, it's all right," Rosenthal replies, and the bond between the two men, temporarily broken, is reforged of much stronger stuff.

Maréchal's generosity, his unwillingness to abandon his injured Jewish friend even at the risk of his own life, stands as the film's moral centerpiece. The fact that it comes immediately after the one overt expression of antisemitism in the film would seem to signal Renoir's elevation of human sympathy over hate and prejudice. His antisemitism brought into the open and thereby dissipated, Maréchal illustrates the film's message of universalism, a message made all the stronger, like their bond of friendship, by the venting of repressed animosity. This typical Frenchman's gesture of inclusion also would seem to represent an ideal France open to minority and marginality, a symbolic inclusion of racial difference within the nation.

Maréchal's gesture has all the more significance in that the original treatment for the film showed Maréchal escaping with a non-Jewish officer named Dolette (indeed, it did not include a Jewish character at all). As Dalio recounts in his autobiography, the tensions between his character and Maréchal were a last-minute addition to the script, made during the shooting.[45] The addition of the Jewish theme in the highly charged political atmosphere of the late 1930s no doubt signals the filmmakers' courageous willingness to take a stand against antisemitism. The transformation of Dolette into Rosenthal and the inclusion of Maréchal's antisemitic diatribe endow his later affirmation of the human bond with a universalist message of acceptance winning out over antisemitic prejudice.

One could certainly argue, however, that the Jew's inclusion in the nation is shown to depend on the precarious magnanimity of the non-Jew. Moreover, the act of asking whether the Jew belongs in the French nation might seem by its very nature antisemitic. After all, this was the question asked by Barrès, whose *volkish* vision of Frenchness in *Scènes et doctrines du nationalisme* (1902) excluded recent immigrants such as Rosenthal.[46] In his novel *Les déracinés* (The Uprooted, 1897), Barrès showed the debilitating effects, both for individual subjectivities and for the health of the nation, of rootless cosmopolitanism. Indeed, in its focus on a group of young Frenchmen cut off from their homeland, analyzing the links that tie them to the nation while trying to return to it, *La grande illusion* might be seen as a kind of reworking of *Les déracinés*, but one that subverts the novel's main thesis by offering a different model of Frenchness—one based not on a deterministic model of ancestry but on a universalist affirmation of shared values and patriotic acts, one that explicitly includes the Jew.

Crucially, moreover, the film's universalism is not of the type that seeks to ignore the Jew's difference or make it disappear. It is here that the antisemitic clichés of the first half of the film prove so important, for by endowing Rosenthal with every conceivable Jewish stereotypical trait, but including him anyway within the symbolic nation, the film calls for a kind of French universalism that includes difference within it. Renoir's universalism is thus not that of Grégoire: Rosenthal is not asked to change or regenerate in order to become French. Nor is it that of Zola: Rosenthal's difference is not seen as something that must be made to disappear. Renoir's universalism is much closer to that of the Revolutionaries who saw Jewish difference as key to defining just how universal French universalism could be.

We glimpse something like an affirmation of this model of universalism at the very end of the film, in the final exchange between Maréchal and Rosenthal, once they have left the protected paradise of the German farm and as they prepare to cross over the border into freedom in Switzerland. As they say good-bye, perhaps for the last time should German guards shoot them while they make haste for the frontier, Maréchal calls Rosenthal a "dirty Jew" (sale juif), and Rosenthal counters by hurling the less loaded epithet of "old goat" (vieille noix). Given the significance that the word "Jew" has taken on over the course of the film, first as a site of repressed anxiety and later, during the escape scene, as the insult that marks their temporary rupture, its return at the film's close as an endearment shows how far the men, and the viewer, have come. Rendered harmless through the film's thematization and exploration of antisemitic stereotype, the taboo term now has the power not to divide but to unite. As the last word Maréchal speaks to Rosenthal in the film, "Jew" serves as a sign of their friendship, as a mark of the Jew's integration into French culture, not just in the universalizing manner that would deny Jewish particularity but, as Céline would lament, *as a Jew*.

The notion that the film does not merely tolerate Jewish difference but actually values it receives confirmation from the recognition that Rosenthal, more than any other character in the film, serves as a stand-in for the filmmaker, for Renoir himself. I am referring here not only to the fact that Renoir, like Rosenthal during the escape, walked with a limp following an injury received during the First World War. The film itself points to the resemblance between character and director in the Christmas scene on the farm where Rosenthal and Maréchal are hiding out while waiting for the Jew's foot to heal. The scene begins with a close-up on a miniature manger with a male voice describing the various members of the Holy Family. The camera then pulls back to reveal the Jew arranging the crèche like a director setting props. He then insists on shutting off the lights while cranking up the Victrola and telling Maréchal and Elsa where to stand. With lights, sets, music, and actors in place, the scene is ready for its audience, Elsa's daughter Lotte. Making Rosenthal into a director points to the extent to which his outsider status (both as Jew and as interpreter for the lovers) is viewed in the film as a source of creativity and productivity.

The playful nature of the Christmas scene also helps us see how the film views race itself as a kind of role-playing. While Rosenthal's pride in the crèche may seem either ironic or blasphemous, the genuine care and interest he takes in its creation is that of an artist able to see universal beauties beneath surface differences. "Isn't my little angel sweet?" Rosenthal asks Maréchal as he arranges the figures in the manger. "And the little Jesus? My blood brother [mon frère de race]." Like Rosenthal's previous forays into racial theorizing, this line has its ambiguities. On one level, the reference to race smacks of pseudo-scientific categorizing. On another, it reminds audiences that Jesus himself was Jewish. But beyond either of these two literal readings, the line undercuts any antisemitism it may seem to espouse. Dalio's delivery, accompanied by a smile (once again viewed in profile) directed at Maréchal, contains an unmistakably ironic tinge. In the intimacy of the domestic setting, where he not only controls the two languages spoken but also directs the others' actions, Rosenthal's invocation of his Jewish "race" reveals its playfulness, its theatricality. Just as during the earlier theatrical performance, in which men dressed as women succeed in arousing the silent respect (and titillation) of the assembled prisoners, certain forms of identity—gender or, in this case, race—are seen as a kind of illusion, inessential in the face of a deeper humanity. The film thus undermines the very categorization that underpins the exclusionary logic of Barrès and his avatars.

The argument that the film invokes racial categorization only to undermine it would seem to be upheld by the way the act of racial stereotyping is represented in the film. Or rather, by whom. For, as we have seen, it is frequently Rosenthal himself who gives voice to the discourse on Jews. It is Rosenthal, for example, who describes his family's acquisitions, and not without a tinge of irony. It is Rosenthal, moreover, who describes Jews as more prideful than avaricious, while Maréchal dismisses such a debate as "just stories." And Dalio's heavily ironic delivery of the line referring to Jesus as his "blood brother [frère de race]" indicates that the audience should view such racial categorization with the same kind of distance.

A similar if more subtle distancing from the pseudo-scientific discourse on race occurs earlier in the film, when the German commandant, von Rauffenstein, conducts a surprise inspection of the French officers' barracks. After being tricked by the Frenchmen, who manage to hide a rope for escape, von Rauffenstein, before exiting, turns to one of the French officers, a scholar who has obsessively been working on a translation of Pindar. The German measures the man's skull and then declares, "Poor old Pindar." Phrenology, of course, served as a tool of Nazi racial "science" and would provide the justification for the German conquest of certain "inferior" peoples, including the French, and extermination of others, including the Jews, during the Second World War. The film seems to mock this racial discourse by showing von Rauffenstein, the dupe, to be its exponent. A further level of irony might be perceived by those who notice a black officer among the prisoners, his race never commented upon, and by those who know that Erich von Stroheim, the celebrated film director who plays the racist Prussian aristocrat, was the son of a Jewish hat merchant from Vienna.

Conclusions

Unlike Pithon, then, who suggests that Renoir resorts to antisemitic cliché unconsciously, I would argue that *La grande illusion* invokes the discourse of antisemitism strategically. My reading thus has more in common with that of Daniel Serceau, who maintains that the film invokes antisemitic stereotypes in order to neutralize them. "You can't combat prejudices if you refuse to recognize them,"[47] Serceau concludes. But I have argued that *La grande illu-*

sion does more than just neutralize negative stereotypes. If the film represents the Jew both positively and negatively, it does so in order to intervene in debates about the nature of French universalism. In response to antiuniversalist antisemites—like Drumont, Barrès, Bardèche, Brasillach, or Céline—who advocate a *volkish* model of the nation predicated on rootedness, the film welcomes the Jew into a symbolic community. And in response to assimilationist universalists, like Grégoire or Zola, who welcome the Jews on the explicit or implicit condition that they transform themselves, the film stipulates that they should be accepted *as Jews*, which is to say without shedding their difference. The Jew may be ostentatiously rich, he may bear the marks of physical degeneration, but as long as he demonstrates his willingness to contribute to the national project, he deserves to be included. Indeed, Renoir goes so far as to suggest that the Jew's difference—including antisemitic stereotype—can become a source of creativity and inspiration.

Renoir, in other words, resurrects the more open form of universalism first postulated during the French Revolution and exemplified by the discourse surrounding the actress Rachel during the July Monarchy. At a time when the battle lines between right and left in France had become hardened as never before, Renoir rejects both right-wing nationalism and the rigid form of republicanism, hostile to all forms of difference, that many saw as the only way to resist fascism. His vision of friendship between the physically and morally healthy proletarian officer and the egregiously wealthy and physically "degenerate" Jew stakes out a new model for the nation, one composed not of abstract, featureless individuals beholden only to the state but of embodied subjects, complete with their particularities, and accepting of each other in spite of—or even perhaps because of—these defects.

But what if viewers miss this level of complexity? What if they retain only the image of the Jew as a hooked-nose plutocrat? Recent film theory has insisted that it is viewers in historically and materially specific situations who ultimately determine a film's meaning.[48] And, as we have seen, certain viewers through the years have indeed failed to recognize the subtlety of Renoir's handling of the "Jewish Question," viewing it instead as antisemitic. For Pithon, *La grande illusion* proves that filmmakers may end up resorting to antisemitic stereotypes despite their best intentions. I think the film teaches a different lesson—namely, that filmmakers cannot, despite their best intentions, ultimately control or fix the meaning of their representations. They lack the power to determine how their representations will be received or to what use their images will be put. Perhaps Renoir deserves to be blamed for creating a representation that is too subtle, too complex, too liable to be read in the wrong way. Perhaps also his famous realist style is the true culprit: the realist codes employed by Renoir naturalize a certain image of the Jew, encouraging viewers to accept rather than question the representation.

Cinematic depictions, particularly realist ones, have a way of escaping the limits prescribed to them, just as audiences have a way of retaining not the subtle message of a film but its more overt images, particularly if these confirm rather than unsettle long-standing prejudices. The picture of Rosenthal as a large-nosed capitalist may have made a greater impression on viewers than his ironic disquisitions on race or the gesture of harmony between him and Maréchal at the film's end. To illustrate this concluding point, I'd like to turn once more to an anecdote from the autobiography of Marcel Dalio, the actor who played Rosenthal (and La Chesnaye).

In the spring of 1940, Dalio was waiting in Portugal, like so many other French Jews, for a visa to the United States—or England, or Mexico, or any other country that would take him. Like so many other French Jews, he had abandoned a promising career after the fall of France and was now desperate to leave Europe. One night, in a bar called the Avenida, frequented by French Jews (and thus not unlike Rick's Bar in *Casablanca*, a film in which he would later play a supporting role), Dalio ran into an old friend who told him that he had done well to flee Paris ahead of the Germans. For, according to this friend, Dalio's face was now plastered on posters all around the place de l'Opera that purported to show the French how to identify Jewish physical characteristics. Overnight he had gone from being a typical French Jew to being a *prototypical* French Jew—public enemy number one.

The Nazis chose Dalio as the image of the criminalized, deviant Jew not —or not merely—because of his profile but because his cinematic roles, including and especially in Renoir's two films *La grande illusion* and *La règle du jeu*, had helped fix an image of the Jew in the minds of the French public. Should Renoir therefore be considered an antisemitic filmmaker? A historically informed reading would answer no. But did his films lend themselves to antisemitic uses under particular circumstances? Unfortunately, history seems to answer yes. Despite what may have been Renoir's wish to include the Jew within the symbolic nation, his image returned in grotesque form, appropriated by the fascist menace it was meant to counter. Perhaps, ultimately, it is not so much Renoir as film itself, the medium, which is to blame for Dalio's plight, because of the ease with which its images can be isolated, divorced from the subtleties of narrative, captured as a still and splashed on a poster.[49] Dalio did, however, at least manage to find some humor in his predicament: the actor notes feeling a certain pride that, for once, he got top billing.[50]

6

Sartre's "Jewish Question"

There is something poignant—touching but also sad—about the reactions of the first Jewish readers to Jean-Paul Sartre's *Réflexions sur la question juive* (*Anti-Semite and Jew*).[1] Written in the immediate aftermath of the liberation of Paris in the fall of 1944, and published in 1945 and '46, Sartre's philosophical essay seems to have moved survivors simply by talking about Jews with a modicum of sympathy and respect.[2] For Claude Lanzmann, the future director of the documentary *Shoah*, Sartre's philosophical essay provided a psychic liberation more powerful than the actual physical liberation from the Nazi occupation. "I remember I walked the streets differently," Lanzmann said later; "I could breathe again, because the simple fact that the war was over had not changed the way one felt inside."[3] The philosopher Robert Misrahi writes of *Réflexions* that "after the Nazi night . . . the emotion and admiration of readers were evidently considerable. You could even say we felt astonishment or profound surprise, so used were we (by 'we' I mean Jews) to hatred and scorn."[4]

The almost messianic gratitude certain French Jewish readers felt toward Sartre's text clearly stems from its contrast with the way Jews had been attacked for decades by the nationalist right in France. In this chapter, I want to suggest that at least part of the gratitude that French Jews felt toward *Réflexions* also stems from its contrast with the way Jews were being defended by the republican left. As much as *Réflexions* offers up a devastating critique of antisemitism as a philosophical position, so too does it deliver a devastating critique of Zola's brand of republican universalism that we examined in chapter 4. What really moved Sartre's early Jewish readers, and what still makes the text powerful today, I want to suggest, lies in its departure from a mode of discourse that defends the Jews as individuals but not as Jews, a mode of discourse that assumes that Jewish specificity, Jewish difference, must be suppressed as a precondition for full participation in the French nation.

Scholars who have analyzed *Réflexions*, and there have been many, have tended to focus on the first section—the portrait of the antisemite—which they have seen as a signal achievement, one of the most important and original contributions to the theoretical understanding of antisemitism produced in the postwar era.[5] No less a commentator than Emmanuel Levinas, writing in 1947, called Sartre's approach to the problem of antisemitism "wholly new."[6] Recently, scholars such as Susan Suleiman have also devoted attention to the more problematic third section of Sartre's text—the portrait of the Jew—accusing it of perpetuating some of the same antisemitic stereotypes it attempts to dismiss.[7] I will consider these sections in turn but will also examine closely the short and relatively underappreciated second section of the text, the portrait of the Jew's principal defender, whom Sartre labels the "democrat." This section of the text contains a particularly biting attack on the type of republican universalism, epitomized by Zola, that became dominant after the Dreyfus Affair.[8]

Sartre's attack on republican universalism renews the more pluralist tradition of dealing with Jewish difference that has existed in France since the time of the Revolution. But while the other examples of this more pluralist tradition that I have pointed to in previous chapters—like the discourse surrounding the actress Rachel, the efforts of the Alliance israélite universelle, or the depiction of the Jew in the film *La grande illusion*—can be found on the spectrum of universalist approaches to minority difference that I identified in the introduction, Sartre broke new ground by rejecting universalism outright and by theorizing the implications of this stance. Of course, Sartre was not the first intellectual to reject universalism, but he was the first major thinker to do so *from the left*, which is to say that Sartre rejects republican universalism not in the name of *volkish* rootedness, as Maurice Barrès or Charles Maurras had done, but out of a concern for the ability of minorities to feel included within the nation without having to repress what makes them different.[9] Sartre calls his model a "concrete liberalism" and opposes it to the form of universalism, which began during the Enlightenment but took its definitive form with Zola, that represses minorities under the guise of welcoming them. Sartre's model constitutes a very real innovation and represents a genuine turning point in the history both of French universalism and of France's relation to its Jews.

But just as certain recent scholars have revealed the extent to which Sartre fails to escape completely from the antisemitism he criticizes, so too will I point to a rather surprising return to a hard-line, assimilationist universalism in the fourth and final section of *Réflexions*. The portrait of Sartre that emerges from this chapter will thus not be without its contradictions. Nevertheless, I will emphasize that what really matters in our understanding of Sartre's text is less its logical or ideological consistency than the effect that it had on generations of readers. For while Sartre may have undermined his rejection of assimilation in the final pages of *Réflexions*, readers seem by and large to have ignored this backpedaling and responded instead to his call for a "concrete liberalism" in the book's earlier sections. This is especially true of Sartre's Jewish readers who saw in *Réflexions* an intellectual justification for their assertion of the right to difference that marked the last decades of the twentieth century.

The War on the Jews

During World War II, a hundred and fifty years of Jewish emancipation in France came to an abrupt end. Almost immediately following the German invasion in June of 1940, the new French puppet government established in Vichy passed its first piece of anti-Jewish legislation, abrogating a law that banned racial attacks. Over the next several years, the Jews in both the Nazi-occupied northern zone and in the Vichy-controlled zone in the south (which was also occupied by the Nazis after 1942) experienced increasingly harsh persecution. Jews were dismissed from government employment and excluded from certain professions in both zones by a law of October 3, 1940. Jewish property was confiscated, or "aryanized," beginning with a decree of October 18, 1940. The first mass roundups, or *rafles*, affecting primarily foreign-born Jews, began in May 1941. Eventually native-born French Jews were targeted as well. In June of 1942, Jews were required to wear the yellow Star of David insignia—a visible departure from the French universalist practice of not distinguishing among citizens based on race or religion. Arrested, often by French police or militia, and detained in concentration camps in France, Jews eventually faced deportation to death camps in the east. The first convoy containing French Jews left for Auschwitz on March 27, 1942. In total, 75,721 Jews were deported from metropolitan France during the war, including 11,600 children.[10] Only a few thousand survivors returned.

Beginning immediately after the liberation of Paris in August 1944, the newly installed provisional authorities, led by Charles de Gaulle, began to "purge" those who had collaborated with the Nazis, subjecting them to trial, prison, and in some cases execution.[11] At the same time, however, the rhetoric of de Gaulle and his followers minimized French participation in the crimes of the Occupation while emphasizing—or exaggerating—the heroic role of French resistance fighters in an attempt to reunify a splintered nation. It took the sleuthing of an American historian, Robert O. Paxton, to uncover the full extent of Vichy's participation in the Nazi's "final solution" to the "Jewish Question."[12] Paxton's pioneering work in the 1970s helped unleash a kind of national obsession with Vichy and the Holocaust that the historian Henry Rousso has dubbed the "Vichy Syndrome."[13] Hundreds of books and films about the war have appeared every year since the 1970s—a phenomenon that has yet to show signs of abating.

Scholars have also brought to light the role of intellectuals during the war, and particularly their responsibility for the crimes against the Jews. Some of the most notorious French antisemitic writers, such as Robert Brasillach and Louis-Ferdinand Céline, were tried for collaboration and condemned after the war. As has become clear, these writers did not merely import a German genocidal mentality but rather drew their inspiration from more local sources. Alice Kaplan and David Carroll have shown how writers like Brasillach and Céline, along with other antisemitic writers in the 1930s, such as Pierre Drieu la Rochelle, Lucien Rebatet, and Thierry Maulnier, transformed the theses of such fin-de-siècle heroes of the anti-Dreyfusard right as Maurice Barrès, Charles Maurras, and Édouard Drumont into a form of homegrown French fascism.[14] As we will see, these protofascist writers are among Sartre's prime targets in *Réflexions*: Sartre identifies their "syncretic" vision of the national character, defined by a mystical relation to French soil and an opposition to all forms of economic, political, and cultural modernity, as the principal elements of an organicist, determinist, antiuniversalist vision of the nation designed to exclude the Jews.[15]

If Sartre took a clear stand against antisemitism and collaboration after the liberation, his actions during the war itself have lately elicited a certain degree of controversy. Although he would later depict the occupation as a time of existential struggle when all French people, including writers, were called upon to take sides, during the war Sartre did not always act in the most honorable of ways.[16] Like the vast majority of French people, Sartre did not participate actively in the resistance. Perhaps more damningly, he accepted a position teaching philosophy at the Lycée Condorcet that had been vacated by a Jew forced to resign as a result of the racial laws (whether or not Sartre knew he was replacing a Jew remains in doubt).[17] Writers like Sartre, however, must be judged not only by their actions but also by their words. Here too, scholars have disagreed in their judgments. For some, the fact that he continued to publish and have his plays performed under the Nazi regime of censorship makes him guilty of at least a passive form of collaboration. For others, however, the plays he wrote during the war contain a veiled critique of the Occupation that makes him more a hero than a villain.[18]

Réflexions sur la question juive appeared just as the Gaullist myth of France as a nation of resistance fighters was taking shape. In the name of national unity, many politicians and writers glossed over the specific hardships faced by Jews during the war, preferring instead to speak of the collective suffering of the nation and especially of the martyrdom of those who had fought in the resistance. Many Jews who had survived the war in France, and many of those who returned from deportation, accepted this pact of silence, glad for their Jewishness to pass—for once—unnoticed and to meld into the national collective. Other French Jews found themselves too traumatized to speak of their experience, while still others just wanted to get on with their lives. To those Jews who felt oppressed by this silence, however, Sartre's recognition of their suffering provided a welcome relief.[19]

In *Réflexions*, Sartre describes what he perceives as a silence surrounding the genocide as one of his primary motivations for taking up the "Jewish Question." "Now all France rejoices and fraternizes in the streets," Sartre says of the period following the liberation; "the newspapers devote whole columns to stories of prisoners of war and deportees. Do we say anything about the Jews? Do we give a thought to those who died in the gas chambers at Lublin? Not a word." According to Sartre, the reason for this silence is clear: it is "because we must not irritate the anti-Semites."[20] He goes on to relate an anecdote concerning the reaction he received to an article published in the *Lettres Françaises* immediately after the war in which he had mentioned the Jews in a list of those who had suffered at the hands of the Nazis.[21] "Several Jews thanked me in a most touching manner," Sartre declares, noting that he found their gratitude disturbing, the sign of a profound sense of Jewish unease. "How completely must they have felt themselves abandoned, to think of thanking an author for merely having written the world 'Jew' in an article!" (72). For Sartre, then, the goal of *Réflexions* was to break the silence surrounding Jewish suffering and to provide French Jews with a new sense of security, a new self-confidence.

Turning now to Sartre's text, I want to explore the highly original and effective ways that Sartre goes about achieving this aim. Sartre divides *Réflexions* into four parts, each of which identifies a different actor in the ongoing drama surrounding the "Jewish Question." In the first part, Sartre provides a harsh psychological portrait of the antisemite. The second part of the text shifts focus to attack the Jew's traditional ally, whom Sartre labels "the democrat," but whom we recognize as the republican universalist in the mold of Zola. His real target here, as we shall see, is the tradition of republican universalism that defends the Jew as an individual but ultimately seeks to erase his difference through assimilation. In the third section, Sartre provides a portrait of the Jew, whom he defines in negative terms as someone seen as Jewish by others and to whom he attributes a number of negative characteristics. This turns out to be a portrait of the "inauthentic Jew," who becomes in Sartre's schema the mirror image of the antisemite by attempting to flee the reality of his "situation" through assimilation. It is this attempt to flee or deny the Jew's situation that Sartre says produces the negative qualities associated with Jewishness. The "authentic Jew," on the other hand, would assume his situation, embrace his difference, and thereby cease to embody negative stereotypes. Sartre provides a portrait of the "authentic Jew" in the fourth and final section, where he also reveals that a long-term and collective solution to the "Jewish Question" can only come through socialist revolution.

Réflexions is famous for turning the tables on the antisemites, subjecting them to the same kind of scrutiny to which they long subjected the Jews. I will argue that a great part of the originality of Sartre's text lies in the way it turns the tables on the Jews' defenders as well, subjecting traditional French forms of anti-antisemitism to a harsh critique. Sartre makes the critique of French republican universalism the focus of the second section, but as I will now show, this critique is evident from the very start and in fact can be found throughout the text.

Portrait of the Antisemite

Sartre begins the first section of *Réflexions* with an attack on the way well-meaning liberals have gone about defending the Jews since the Enlightenment. The problem, he argues, lies in their "analytic spirit" (8). Sartre's target here, in a general sense, is rationalism itself, the confidence that all problems can be solved through the application of reason. According to Sartre, however, the analytic mindset operates according to a certain procedure, by breaking down entities into their composite parts. The analytic response to antisemitism posits that hatred of the Jew represents only one element in the larger composite of the intellectual and psychological makeup of the antisemite. Antisemitism would thus constitute a mere subjective opinion or taste according to this model, equivalent to a fondness for fishing or ideas about the condition of the natives in Africa. This Sartre considers a mistake: antisemitism represents, according to him, a choice of one's very being. To combat antisemitism, then, it is necessary to combat the antisemite's very being, to indict not just his opinions but his entire psychological profile.

The analytic opponent of antisemitism, according to Sartre, assumes the antisemite to be governed by the same objective, rational spirit that governs him. He believes that he can refute the antisemite's ideas with logic and statistics. "In such wise, anti-Semitism appears to be at once a subjective taste that enters into combination with other tastes to form a personality, and an impersonal and social phenomenon which can be expressed by figures and averages" (9). Antisemites, for example, might denounce the supposed underrepresentation of Jews in the French army during World War I, or the overrepresentation of Jews among French bankers, and the analytic anti-antisemite would counter with other statistics proving these notions false or exaggerated. Believing that antisemitism constitutes a rational opinion based on objective facts, the analytic anti-antisemite musters economic, historical, or political arguments in the hope of bringing the antisemite around to his way of seeing the world.

According to Sartre, this constitutes a grave error, for antisemitism is not rational and therefore not susceptible to objective arguments and counter-demonstrations of facts. On the contrary, antisemitism represents an illogical or prelogical mindset that judges regardless of facts. It is a "passion" masquerading as an opinion: "Anti-Semitism in its most temperate and most evolved forms remains a syncretic whole which may be expressed by statements of reasonable tenor" (10). Antisemitism cannot be countered with logic that is foreign to it. It must be fought with its own weapons.

Sartre introduces here a key term, "syncretic," which represents the opposite of "analytic."[22] According to Sartre, whereas analytic reasoning breaks down a problem, or a person, into parts, syncretic thinking (which I won't call reasoning) sees entities in holistic terms. According to the antisemite, who is always a syncretic thinker, the Jew is not evil because he's a banker or fails to fight in the war, but rather he fails to fight in the war or charges usurious interest because he's a Jew and therefore evil. The antisemite thus cannot be dissuaded from his passion by statistics showing the number of Jews in the army, or by the demonstration that Christians lend money at interest as well, because for him there will always be a special kind of Jewish cowardice or rapaciousness. He has "adopted in advance a certain idea of the Jew" (13). His hatred is a priori; it precedes experience, and therefore the traditional weapons used against it, rooted in Enlightenment rationalism, must by necessity fail to reach their target.

Sartre clearly has in mind certain very specific examples of syncretic antisemitism, including Barrès and Maurras at the fin de siècle and Brasillach and Céline in the 1930s, who posited a deterministic model of Frenchness rooted in tradition and the soil. Their brand of antisemitism is classically syncretic:

just as they view the Jew as an organic whole, whose every action is conditioned by his Jewishness, so too do they see Frenchness as organically linked to an ensemble of determinants.[23] For syncretic thinkers, a person's way of being or actions cannot be separated from the conditions that determine his existence, whether biological, historical, or social. We remember the maxim of Barrès cited in chapter 4: "That Dreyfus is capable of treason, I conclude from his race."[24] According to this model, one cannot change one's nationality because one cannot change one's essence. It is impossible, therefore, to *become* French, just as it is impossible to cease to be Jewish. This model of Frenchness, of course, is in complete opposition to the universalist, republican model, inherited from the Revolution, that sees Frenchness as an ideological affiliation and that accords citizenship, in theory, to anyone.

One of Sartre's most radical maneuvers in *Réflexions* consists in turning the syncretic approach back on the antisemite. Whereas analytic antiantisemitism fails because it seeks to convince the antisemite of the logic of its position, the syncretic critique of antisemitism focuses not on this or that fact or statistic concerning the Jews but on "the personality of the antiSemite" (8). Sartre treats antisemitism not as a discrete opinion that can be separated from other tastes or preferences but rather as an essential personality trait. He depicts the antisemite as a criminal who fears his own freedom and who chooses hatred of the Jew as a means of providing his life with an imaginary kind of coherence. Sartre refuses to reason with the antisemite as to the merits of the Jew but rather aims to put the antisemite himself on the defensive by revealing the fundamental cowardice of his worldview. Sartre thus talks to the antisemite in his own language, attacking him as a *type*. Just as the antisemite characterizes the Jew as an aggregate of negative characteristics, so too will Sartre show the antisemite to be a composite of weaknesses, phobias, and petty resentments.

Antisemitism, Sartre states, is not a response to the real situation of the world but rather an attempt to deny reality by attributing to the Jew magical powers of evil. This Manichean worldview proves comforting to the antisemite because it relieves him of all responsibility for thinking on his own. According to Sartre, from an existentialist perspective, the antisemite fears discovering the world as it is: "If all he has to do is to remove Evil, that means that the Good is already given. He has no need to seek it in anguish, to invent it, to scrutinize it patiently when he has found it . . . or, finally, to shoulder the responsibilities of the moral choice he has made" (44). Sartre's antisemite is thus not just dishonest and deluded; he is fundamentally a coward—afraid not so much of Jews as of thought itself.

This attack on the person of the antisemite represents a significant departure from the prior modes of defending the Jews we have examined in previous chapters. Levinas was right to call it "wholly new" in its focus and its methods. One might, however, question its efficacy. Without a doubt, Sartre's approach succeeds in discrediting antisemitism as an *intellectual* program, as a philosophy. After *Réflexions*, it is hard to imagine intellectuals like Brasillach, or anti-intellectuals like Céline (who nevertheless remain tied to an intellectualized worldview they critique), continuing to attract adherents to their antisemitic creed among elite university students, the *jeunesse d'écoles*, as they had in the 1930s. But the cowardice that Sartre attributes to the antisemite is very much an *intellectual* cowardice. One might therefore doubt whether the attack would really hit home against those who scorn rational argument altogether—and Sartre admits that these are the majority of antisemites.

But if Sartre's attack on antisemitism may be less effective than he thinks, his attack on a certain French philosophical tradition stemming from the Enlightenment does indeed hit the target. Sartre undermines not just a rationalist approach to the "Jewish Question" but a rationalist approach to *any* question. This is why *Réflexions* constitutes not a deviation from Sartre's larger philosophical program but rather a central part of it: as other scholars have shown, Sartre's analysis of the "Jewish Question" in many ways offers a concrete example of the more abstract ideas he presents in his monumental treatise *L'être et le néant* (Being and Nothingness, 1943).[25] Indeed, the deeper one enters into *Réflexions*, the more one wonders whether the "Jewish Question" is not a mere pretext for Sartre to dismantle fundamental ways of approaching problems and fundamental philosophical and political structures, including and especially French universalism.

Portrait of the Jew

Let us now skip to the controversial third section of the text, in which Sartre attempts to define the Jew. This section begins with another critique of the analytic spirit of Enlightenment rationalism, which now is shown not just to break down ideas to their component parts but also to reduce identity to the minimal features that constitute "human nature." Enlightenment rationalism recognizes only a single, identical, abstract individual, which, according to Sartre, necessarily excludes what defines the Jew as different. It overlooks the specific features that Jews have in common, whether biological (racial), psychological, historical, social, or cultural. The analytical mode of defending the Jews that grows out of this Enlightenment tradition, a mode typified by Zola's universalist utopia at the end of *Vérité*, does not recognize what we today would label "ethnicity" as a defining category of identity. And according to Sartre, any attempt to propose an answer to the "Jewish Question" that refuses to acknowledge Jewish ethnic difference is doomed to failure. Not only does such an approach attempt to wish away the features that make antisemites hate Jews, but it also fails to acknowledge what causes Jews to continue to band together as a group or community.

Just as in the first section of the text, Sartre attempts here to appropriate the antisemite's syncretic approach to human identity in order to define the Jew. "We are in agreement with the anti-Semite on one point: we do not believe in 'human nature'; we cannot conceive of society as a sum of isolated molecules; we believe that it is necessary to consider biological, psychical, and social phenomena in a spirit of synthesis" (59). Sartre thus radically departs from the assimilationist model of French universalism that seeks to grant Jews rights as individuals by abstracting them from their communal or group affiliations. For Sartre, there is no such thing as an isolated, abstract individual. On the contrary, he readily admits that Jews constitute a group with defining features.

Jewish difference matters for Sartre, but he is at pains to define it. Right from the start, he dismisses the most obvious thing Jews have in common: the Jewish religion. Sartre sees the practice of Judaism as having almost entirely disappeared in France: "Religion is here only a symbolic means. At least in Western Europe the Jewish religion has been unable to resist the attacks launched by rationalism and by the Christian spirit" (66). Even Jewish atheists, Sartre contends, find themselves in an antagonistic relationship with Christianity, not Judaism, since Judaism has so little importance as a religious philosophy. Judaism as a religion is only a vestigial aspect of Jewish difference.

Likewise, Sartre denies that the Jewish people share a common history: "Its twenty centuries of dispersion and political importance forbid its having a *historic past*" (66, his emphasis). Sartre means history here in the Hegelian sense of consciousness of a national history: "If it is true, as Hegel says, that a community is historical to the degree that it remembers its history, then the Jewish community is the least historical of all" (66–67). All that the Jews possess, according to Sartre, is a memory of their martyrdom. This qualifies them, at most, as being "an abstract historical community" (66), but such a weak bond does not really qualify as a defining characteristic of the group.[26] It should be noted that Sartre would later admit to having known very little about Judaism or the history of the Jewish people when he wrote *Réflexions*.[27] In an interview with Benny Lévy at the end of his life, moreover, he spoke approvingly of the Jewish messianic tradition.[28] Nevertheless, it remains the case that in *Réflexions*, Sartre defines Jewishness almost purely as a set of psychological, and also biological, characteristics.

As many of Sartre's recent critics have noted, however, in so doing Sartre comes perilously close to adopting antisemitic stereotypes of the Jew. "I shall not deny that there is a Jewish race," Sartre writes before immediately qualifying his statement: "But we must understand each other at once" (60–61). Sartre's qualifications amount to distinguishing between "certain inherited physical conformations that one encounters more frequently among Jews than among non-Jews," which Sartre considers evident, and "intellectual and moral traits," which Sartre also considers evident but does not accept as the product of biology. He further qualifies this statement by acknowledging that not all Jews have the same physical characteristics and that it might be more accurate to speak of "Jewish races" in the plural (61).

As Susan Suleiman has pointed out, the text's enumeration of the supposed physical characteristics of the Jew verges on antisemitic stereotype.[29] Speaking of an acquaintance of his who possesses the "'marked Semitic type,'" a phrase which Sartre prudently puts in scare quotes, he notes his "hooked nose," "protruding ears," and "thick lips" (61), caricatural features that Sartre does not find it necessary to set off in quotes. Indeed, as Suleiman remarks, Sartre slips easily in the text from a discourse of skepticism regarding race ("but we must understand each other at once") to one that accepts racial typologies of the Jew that legitimate science had debunked by the time Sartre wrote *Réflexions*.[30] Through a series of qualifications that he then disqualifies—as in the sentence "However that may be, even admitting that all Jews have certain physical traits in common" (62)—Sartre winds up conceding the existence of common physical characteristics among Jews only one page after having said that all Jews do not possess common physical characteristics.

Sartre denies, however, that Jews possess *inherited* intellectual or moral qualities as their attackers allege: "I believe in it no more than I do in ouija boards" (61), he writes mockingly. And yet Sartre accepts that Jews do share a list of negative intellectual and moral qualities with which the most hardened antisemite could find little fault. These include a predilection for rational argument and for money, a tortured relation to their bodies, a lack of tact, and a general disquietude. The difference between Sartre's portrait of the Jewish character and the antisemite's portrait lies in the origin of these characteristics: while the antisemite sees them as inherited racial features, Sartre sees them as the product of the Jew's "situation." This concept of situation is key to Sartre's approach to the "Jewish Question." It refers to the ensemble of factors that govern the position of Jews in society. These may include certain biological (racial) features, but they also include all the social, historical, cultural, and economic features that determine how Jews experience the world.

Thus while the antisemite might view "the Jew's special relationship to money" (126) as a racially inherited trait, Sartre sees it as a response to the Jews' diasporic condition. As we have seen, a whole tradition of Enlightenment liberalism stretching from Dohm and the Abbé Grégoire down to Zola argued similarly that the Jews were forced into moneylending by Christians who barred them access to more noble professions. But Sartre digs deeper. Behind the Jews' supposed love of money, he detects an attraction to the universal system of exchange that money represents. The Jewish attraction to money developed, according to Sartre, as a defense against the appropriation by Christians of more particular forms of value, such as land. For Sartre, there is an affinity between the Jews and the universal that stems from their "situation" and is not directly traceable to any biological defect.

This is not to say that the Sartrean notion of situation excludes race, for certainly the Jew's supposed curved nose, protruding ears, and thick lips constitute relevant factors impacting how the Jew functions in the world. But whereas the antisemite sees all the Jew's characteristics, including moral and intellectual ones, as the product of race, Sartre sees only physical characteristics as racial or biological. "We must therefore envisage the hereditary and somatic characteristics of the Jew as one factor among others in his situation, not as a condition determining his nature" (64). For Sartre, physical characteristics are merely one among many aspects—and not the most important one—that constitute Jewish difference. Moreover, for Sartre, there is no correlation between physical and moral/intellectual characteristics. Whereas the antisemite sees the two as inextricably linked in a syncretic whole in the Jew, Sartre points out that the antisemite would not see the presence of a curved nose in a Christian as indicating a corresponding love of money or hairsplitting casuistry. "But in that case the whole theory crumbles" (62), because this proves that the physical is not in fact inextricably associated with the moral/intellectual.

Sartre also points to another significant difference separating his approach to the problem of Jewish identity from that of the antisemite: his view of the Jew is not Manichean. He does not attribute to the Jew magical powers of evil. He does, nevertheless, view the features that constitute Jewish identity as essentially negative. As Suleiman remarks, he substitutes a "determinism of situation" for one of race.[31] The Jew feels perpetual guilt, Sartre tells us. The Jew relies too much on reason. The Jew splits hairs. The Jew denies his body. The Jew lacks grace and tact. The Jew has a "special relationship" with money (126). To be sure, Sartre nuances his descriptions of the intellectual/moral traits of the Jew so as to distinguish them from crass antisemitic caricature: we learn that the Jew loves money not for its own sake, like the miser, but out of a taste for abstraction.

Despite the imposition of an existentialist philosophical vocabulary, Sartre's main point is basically identical to Grégoire's and Zola's: Christian mistreatment has caused the Jew's degeneration. Even Sartre's famous negative definition of the Jew—"The Jew is one whom other men consider a Jew" (69)—is really just another way of reformulating the idea that the antisemite's treatment shapes the Jew's character. Indeed, once could argue that Grégoire constructed a theory of the Jew's "situation" *avant la lettre* by describing the multiple factors (cultural, social, economic, biological) that oppress the Jew and cause him to behave in degenerate ways. Sartre may characterize antisemitic discourse as a hostile "gaze," and the Jew's response as an "avenue of flight" (93), but the practical examples he gives of the result of this existentialist struggle mirror almost exactly the examples found in the universalist defenses of the Jews in the Enlightenment tradition.

Sartre does differ from Grégoire and his ilk, however, in drawing a distinction between "authentic" and "inauthentic" Jews. According to Sartre's theory, only inauthentic Jews embody the negative stereotypes he enumerates. These stereotypes result from the Jew's attempt to flee his situation. As we have seen, this still makes the negative aspects of the Jew's character the fault of the antisemite, as Grégoire had postulated. But this also seems to allow the Jew at least the possibility of avoiding deformation and remaining Jewish by choosing to become an authentic Jew. Choosing authenticity means, for Sartre, refusing to flee the Jewish situation: "Authenticity for him is to live to the full his condition as a Jew" (91). This constitutes a major departure from Grégoire, Zola, and the assimilationist mode of French universalism. For Sartre, the "authentic Jew" will not seek to shed his Jewishness, through regeneration, intermarriage or any other form of assimilation. On the contrary, the "authentic Jew" will affirm or celebrate his difference.

Since Sartre has defined the Jew's situation in entirely negative terms, however, this choice doesn't allow the Jew much room to maneuver. Because the Jew, according to Sartre, has no religion or history of his own, his choice of authenticity implies not choosing to live according to Jewish religious laws or to share in Jewish culture but rather accepting the negative situation imposed on him by the antisemite: "He accepts to live in a condition defined precisely as being unlivable because he derives pride from humiliation" (91, translation modified). Choosing to become an authentic Jew, for Sartre, means little more than embracing abjection.

Sartre thus appears to reject the assimilationist bargain whereby Jews agree to copy the manners and beliefs of the dominant society in exchange for equality. For Sartre, this strategy is precisely the problem: it is the attempt to deny Jewishness that produces the negative characteristics in the first place. Negative Jewish stereotypes result from the Jew attempting to flee his situation. It is paradoxically by accepting these stereotypes, by refusing to "flee," that the Jew will in fact cease to embody them. Sartre thus deals a fierce blow to the assimilationist mode of French universalism, but as I will show in the next section, he does not follow his own logic through to the end. Indeed, just as we think that Sartre has banished assimilationist universalism, it returns through the back door.

Authenticity and Assimilation

As in the portraits of the antisemite and the Jew in the first and third parts, Sartre's portrait of the Jew's main defender (the "democrat") in the second section of the text takes aim at the republican model of French universalism, which has its roots in the Revolutionary period but found its definitive instantiation in Zola. This section contains a critique of those who defend the Jews out of allegiance to the principles of liberty, equality, and fraternity, and to the ideal of a nation composed of abstract, homogenous individuals. Sartre finds this line of defense weak at best: "The Jews have one friend, however, the democrat. But he is a feeble protector. No doubt he proclaims that all men have equal rights; no doubt he has founded the League for the Rights of Man; but his own declarations show the weakness of his position" (55). Written at the very moment that the League for the Rights of Man, originally formed during the Dreyfus Affair, was being reconstituted following its dissolution by Vichy, Sartre's provocative statement flies in the face not just of the postwar mobilization in the name of human rights but of the French revolutionary tradition itself.[32]

According to Sartre, the problem with the "democrat" is, once again, his analytic approach to defining the Jew: "In the eighteenth century, once and for all, he made his choice: the analytic spirit" (55). This is to say that the democrat sees all men as abstract individuals, bearing the same rights and unencumbered by any of the particular attachments and affiliations that reactionaries like Barrès and Maurras understood to determine subjectivity: "He has no eyes for the concrete syntheses with which history confronts him," Sartre says of his democrat. "He recognizes neither Jew, nor Arab, nor Negro, nor bourgeois, nor worker, but only man—man always the same in all times and all places" (55). Whereas Barrès and Maurras attribute identity to an ensemble of quasi-mystical qualities emanating from a spiritual connection to the soil, Sartre locates identity in a historical set of determinants. But Sartre nevertheless agrees with his reactionary adversaries that the democrat is wrong to ignore these contingencies in his determination to recognize only a single, abstract, homogenous individual.

Difference matters for Sartre. According to him, the democrat errs by refusing to take into account the particularities that define human beings and that encourage them to band together as a group. "He [the democrat] resolves all collectivities into individual elements. To him a physical body is a collection of molecules; a social body, a collection of individuals" (55). When antisemites attack the Jews as a collectivity, or attack a Jew for being part of this collectivity, which is to say, for being a Jew, the democrat's response is to defend him as an individual. The problem with this response to the "Jewish Question," for Sartre, is that it denies the specificity of the Jew's situation, the ensemble of cultural, historical, religious, and political factors that shape his subjectivity and make him part of a group whether he likes it or not: "The democrat, like the scientist, fails to see the particular case; to him the individual is only an ensemble of universal traits. It follows that his defense of the Jew saves the latter as man and annihilates him as Jew" (56). Here Sartre comes a step closer to identifying the real problem with the democrat's universalizing defense of the Jew: it is tied to what he calls "a politics of assimilation."

Assimilation—whether in its radical form, which strives toward the total disappearance of Jewish difference, or in its milder form, which seeks the relegation of Jewish specificity to the private sphere—remains the goal of Sartre's democrat. What the democrat ultimately wants is a nation of abstract, homogenous individuals loyal only to the state. According to Sartre, the antisemite's hostility and the universalist's defense amount to much the same thing for the Jew: "There may not be so much difference between the anti-Semite and the democrat. The former wishes to destroy him as a man and leave nothing in him but the Jew, the pariah, the untouchable; the latter wishes to destroy him as a Jew and leave nothing in him but the man, the abstract and universal subject of the rights of man and the rights of the citizen." Sartre even goes so far as to detect a latent antisemitism in the democrat: "He is hostile to the Jew to the extent that the latter thinks of himself as a Jew" (57). He points to the way the democrat criticizes all forms of Jewish collective political and social organization as inimical to the republican social contract. Sartre reports hearing some democrats, who had deplored the Nazi persecution of the Jews, fear that the Jews would emerge from the Nazi genocide with a renewed sense of Jewish solidarity that would clash with the loyalty to the state demanded by the universalist republic. The choice for the Jews, then, is dire: either be killed at the hands of the Nazis or assimilate at the behest of the democrats. Either way they disappear as a group. "Between his enemy and his defender, the Jew is in a difficult situation: apparently he can do no more than choose the sauce with which he will be devoured" (58).

Sartre's critique of the democrat is, I have been arguing, a critique of the way a certain brand of French universalism has defended the Jews from the Enlightenment through the Dreyfus Affair. In previous chapters, I critiqued this brand of universalism in terms very similar to Sartre. Although Sartre no doubt believed that Revolutionaries like Clermont-Tonnerre and Robespierre epitomized this type of assimilationist universalism, I have shown that they were more open to difference, more pluralist, than has previously been assumed. But I have shown that Zola did indeed defend the Jews with an aim to making them disappear. His final novel, *Vérité*, imagines a future in which the descendants of a Jewish schoolteacher wrongly accused of murder (a stand-in for Dreyfus) would intermarry with the children of his Christian defender, leading to the disappearance not only of antisemitism but also of the Jews as a distinct people. "The Jews, indeed! Why did he speak of the Jews!" one of Zola's characters says in the utopian future of the novel's conclusion. "Anti-Semitism was dead—to such a degree, indeed, that the new generation failed to understand what was meant when people accused the Jews of every crime.... There were no Jews left, since only citizens, freed from the tyranny of dogmas, remained."[33] Sartre himself could not have written a better description of the kind of republican universalism he opposes. While there have been notable exceptions to this model throughout French history—and one of my goals in this book is to point to a countertradition of French universalism that welcomes Jewish difference—Sartre is correct that a certain articulation of French universalism, which became dominant after the Dreyfus Affair, does in fact demand assimilation of the Jews.

Sartre's *Réflexions* thus represents a swing of the pendulum back toward the embrace of difference that prevailed in the pre-Dreyfus era—in the response of certain critics to the Jewish actress Rachel, for example—or that continued to exist as a countertradition in the interwar period, such as in *La grande illusion*. Sartre strikes a blow against the assimilationist form of universalism by advocating for what he calls a "concrete liberalism" (146) that would accept and even value Jewish difference: "It is with his character, his customs, his tastes, his religion if he has one, his name, and his physical traits that we *must* accept him" (147, his emphasis), he says of the Jew. Sartre likewise lands a blow against the assumption that Jews should assimilate in grateful appreciation for being included in the nation. He calls for the Jews to remain Jews even while affirming their fundamental right to be French. Sartre's existentialist philosophy, based on the fundamental singularity of individuals, has no use for a type of universalism that emphasizes sameness and homogeneity.

And yet, in a surprising last-minute reversal, Sartre seems to advocate the very procedure he denounces: he ends the text by calling for assimilation after all, noting that it will follow inevitably and naturally from socialist revolution. In the fourth and final section of *Réflexions*, Sartre shifts registers from a psychological and phenomenological explanation of antisemitism—placing emphasis on how the antisemite views the world—to a materialist one that sees the "Jewish Question" as a corollary to, or rather a distraction from, the economic question: "Anti-Semitism is a mythical, bourgeois representation of the class struggle" (149), Sartre proclaims. Echoing the old Marxist description of antisemitism as the "socialism of fools,"[34] Sartre describes how the bourgeois ruling class encourages hatred of the Jews in order to trick the working class into ignoring the real cause of their oppression. Like orthodox Marxists, Sartre believes that hatred of the Jews would disappear with the disappearance of capitalism: "In a society whose members feel mutual bonds of solidarity, because they are all engaged in the same enterprise, there would be no place for it" (149–50). Given that Sartre's ideological adhesions later caused him to be slow to recognize and denounce certain Communist crimes, including the persecution of Jews in the Soviet Union, it comes as no surprise that he failed to notice that antisemitism did not disappear with the Russian Revolution.[35]

But given that Sartre has just provided a sustained attack on the assimilationist brand of universalism, it may come as a surprise that at the end of *Réflexions*, he seems to see Jewish assimilation as the inevitable—and desirable—outcome of a future socialist revolution in France: "Thus the authentic Jew who thinks of himself as a Jew because the anti-Semite has put him in the situation of a Jew is not opposed to assimilation any more than the class-conscious worker is opposed to the liquidation of classes" (150). For Sartre, the Jew would—and more importantly *should*—cease to view assimilation as problematic once antisemitism has ceased to exist. The Jew who is constituted as a Jew by the antisemite would no longer have any reason to so define himself once the antisemite no longer considers him as such. Like the worker who renounces his affiliation with other workers once the revolution has put an end to the class struggle, so too would the Jew cease to desire an affiliation with other Jews once antisemitism has disappeared. Once non-Jews have truly accepted the Jew's difference, the Jew would no longer require that acceptance: "And if that acceptance is total and sincere, the result will be, first, to make easier the Jew's choice of authenticity, and then, bit by bit, to make possible, without violence and by the very course of history, that assimilation to which some would like to drive him by force" (147). Sartre's call for a "concrete liberalism" that welcomes the Jew as a Jew is thus a temporary measure; the real goal is a society in which such differences no longer signify: "It is for the Jews *also* that we shall make the revolution" (182, his emphasis).[36]

Sartre's "wholly new" defense of the Jews thus comes to resemble the very model it appears to reject. In particular, his assertion that antisemitism would disappear following the socialist revolution bears a striking resemblance to the theories of Zola, who likewise saw antisemitism as an outgrowth of class struggle: "There was really no Jew question at all, there was only a Capitalist question—a question of money heaped up in the hands of a certain number of gluttons, and thereby poisoning and rotting the world," Zola declares in *Vérité*. Significantly, the necessary precondition for the assimilation of the Jews that Zola forecasts in the utopian conclusion of that novel is an end to class struggle, just as it is for Sartre: "And now a France which soon would be all one was being constituted; there would soon be no upper class, no lower class" Zola predicts.[37] Even while purportedly critiquing the figure of the republican universalist who defends the Jew but calls for his assimilation, Sartre winds up adopting the exact same thesis, and using almost precisely the same language, as that paragon of republican universalism, Zola.

Naomi Schor points to a similar paradox in Sartre's thought: although Sartre ostensibly argues against universalism in *Réflexions*, his Marxism forces him to return to it.[38] "If existentialism is by definition an anti-universalism," Schor writes, "Marxism is not." Sartre's allegiance to Marxism thus motivates him to accept a political category he has just renounced (universalism), although certainly, for Sartre, the Marxist universal is not the same thing as the republican universal if only because the latter accepts the world as it is while the former depends on a new form of social organization. "From a Marxist perspective universalization is an ongoing process, the universal, a utopian goal," Schor explains.[39] Nevertheless, for the Jews, the result of the Marxist universal as imagined by Sartre would be the same as the one advocated by the democrat: assimilation, disappearance as a distinct group. Sartre might object that the Marxist form of assimilation is fundamentally different from the democratic one because it is not coerced, but it is hard to understand how their results would not be identical. Once again, the Jew has only to choose with what sauce he will be devoured.[40]

Beyond Universalism

To reveal Sartre's betrayal of his own argument, however, should not invalidate the power of that argument. For despite Sartre's equivocations and reversals, it is undeniable that his text had a profound effect on the "situation" of Jews in postwar France by encouraging them to affirm their difference. "We are many, from François Jacob to Simone Veil, from Edgar Morin to Claude Lanzmann and Robert Misrahi, to have recognized ourselves in the Sartrean text," wrote the Algerian-born Jewish journalist Jean Daniel of the effect of Sartre's text on his generation of intellectuals, who all came to affirm their Jewishness in public ways.[41] In the remainder of this chapter, I want to step back from my analysis of the text itself in order to examine, briefly, its legacy: how did *Réflexions* help change the French intellectual landscape, and particularly the French Jewish intellectual landscape? How did it alter the way that Jews were viewed in France and the way that Jews viewed themselves? *Réflexions* constitutes one of the most significant defenses of the Jews in the French tradition, I want to suggest, not just because of its actual arguments but also because its readers took it so seriously and attempted to follow its mandate in ways that Sartre himself could not have envisioned when he wrote it.[42]

First, I want to emphasize once again that although Sartre may have conceived it as a temporary measure, his concept of "concrete liberalism" did in fact represent a significant departure from a certain republican universalist model that expected Jews to assimilate in exchange for equal treatment. Although he seems ultimately to have wished for Jews to assimilate in the utopian future, Sartre called on Jews in the present to affirm their Jewishness in an open manner and obligated France to welcome the Jews as citizens on those terms. Sartre's respect for Jewish difference in the present moment thus recalls the pluralist models of defending the Jews I have pointed to in previous chapters, even though those models were by and large formulated within the republican universalist tradition, whereas Sartre ostensibly positions his text against that tradition.

It is true that for Sartre, Jewishness did not have positive connotations at the time that he wrote *Réflexions*, so that "choosing oneself as a Jew" signifies little more, in this text, than affirming the negativity of the Jewish situation, or in Sartre's terms, deriving "pride from humiliation" (91). This is not exactly a call for multiculturalism, and it's not clear that Sartre would have welcomed an actual renewal of Jewish religious and cultural identification at the time he wrote his text. As Jonathan Judaken and others have documented, Sartre knew relatively little about Judaism when he wrote *Réflexions* and based his portrait of the Jew on the limited number of highly assimilated Jews in his circle. His essentially negative view of Jewishness thus sprang from observing the degree to which these Jews had no positive relation to their religion or culture.[43] In conversations with Benny Lévy at the end of his life, however, Sartre declared his affinity for certain elements of the Jewish messianic tradition in what constitutes an admission of a positive basis for Jewish identity, a recognition that the Jewish religion, and Jewish history and culture, have something worth affirming other than abjection.[44] But many of Sartre's contemporary readers, it seems, simply ignored Sartre's ill-informed and overly negative view of Jewishness in *Réflexions* and sought to affirm Jewish authenticity on their own, more positive terms.

They were helped, paradoxically, by the Holocaust itself, which generated a climate that was far more welcoming, or at least less overtly hostile, to Jews and Judaism than what had prevailed before the war. In 1944, the novelist and essayist George Bernanos quipped, "Antisemite: this word increasingly fills me with horror. Hitler dishonored it once and for all," indicating the extent to which the Nazi genocide discredited antisemitism as an ideology for a certain kind of intellectual.[45] Indeed, if antisemitism on the right did not disappear in the second half of the twentieth century, it was displayed publicly mainly by fanatics and provocateurs, such as Jean-Marie Le Pen, whose seeming delight in shocking the left with his antisemitic quips served as a useful bogeyman against which the Socialists could mobilize.[46] Statistics confirm that actual physical violence against Jews diminished significantly in the postwar period.[47] The decline of open antisemitism that prevailed for five decades after 1945 created a safer space for the experiments with Jewish affirmation that would mark the last quarter of the twentieth century.[48] It offered French Jews a unique opportunity to take Sartre up on his suggestion and to proclaim their right to difference, their *droit à la différence*, which became the rallying cry for the Gallic form of multi-culturalism.[49]

To be sure, the renewal of Jewish identity in postwar France was not a purely intellectual affair. It also resulted from demographic factors. Although deeply traumatized by wartime persecution, the French Jewish community reconstituted itself relatively quickly as Jews surfaced from hiding or returned from exile. France became the only European country to have a bigger Jewish population after the war than before it. The relatively large number of survivors was bolstered by the arrival, following decolonization in the 1950s and '60s, of roughly 235,000 Jews from North Africa (mainly Algeria, Tunisia, and Morocco).[50] Many of these Jews felt less constrained by the traditional circumspection concerning public displays of Jewish identity that had long characterized the metropolitan brand of Franco-Judaism. The arrival of these North African Jews reinvigorated dwindling Jewish communities throughout France and repopulated synagogues and Jewish schools.[51] As Esther Benbassa remarks, unlike the Ashkenazim, who had resided in France for generations, the new arrivals were on the whole more religious and less willing to confine their Judaism to the private sphere.⁵² They greatly hastened the drive toward Jewish "authenticity" in the Sartrean sense even if they had not read a word of Sartre.

But for many postwar French Jews, the drive to authenticity took on an intellectual cast. Judith Friedlander has described how the Colloquium of French-Speaking Jewish Intellectuals, founded in 1957, and the Cercle Gaston-Crémieux, founded in 1967, both sought to renew the bonds of Jewish learning in what had become the biggest Jewish community in Europe.⁵³ To those who sought authenticity in Jewish religious sources, the teachings of the Lithuanian-born Emmanuel Lévinas offered guidance. Jacques Derrida would devote significant attention to Levinas's work and in his own philosophic project, elaborated from the 1960s to the 2000s, would attempt to redefine the nature of Jewish identity for a postmodern, postreligious age.⁵⁴

To others, however, the imperative to affirm Jewish authenticity expressed itself in solidarity with Israel as it fought numerous wars against its Arab neighbors. The Six-Day War (June 1967) represented a turning point for many French Jews who viewed the conflict in Sartrean terms, including Raymond Aron, Sartre's classmate at the École normale supérieure, who supposedly served as his model for the assimilated French Jew in *Réflexions*.⁵⁵ For these Jews, including Aron, the war ignited an intense concern for Israel's survival and fear of another massacre of the Jewish people on the order of the Holocaust. These feelings were intensified by a press conference given on November 27, 1967, by Charles de Gaulle, in which the president of the republic referred to the Jews as an "elite people, sure of itself and domineering," terms that de Gaulle would later claim to be a form of praise but that at the time struck observers as redolent of antisemitic stereotype. Moreover, de Gaulle seemed to include French Jews within this "people," thus contradicting the republican universalist principle of not distinguishing among French citizens based on race or religion. It seemed to create a distinction between the Jews and other French people, to separate the Jews from the body of the nation, an impression that a later French prime minister, Raymond Barre, haplessly confirmed in 1980 when he described the bombing of the synagogue on the rue Copernic as "a heinous act against Jews in a synagogue that struck four innocent Frenchmen crossing the street." It is not hard to see why some Jews began to see republican universalism as hollow in this period and to regard Judaism as a more concrete form of identity.⁵⁶

As Lawrence Kritzman has shown, essayists and fiction writers in the 1960s, '70s, and '80s would find new ways of heeding Sartre's call for Jewish affirmation.⁵⁷ Indeed, for a range of writers, Jewish identity would be conceived in Sartrean terms. Albert Memmi, the Tunisian-born Jewish writer and philosopher, chose to work in an explicitly Sartrean paradigm in his exploration of the psychological effects of colonization and antisemitism, including his *Portrait d'un juif* (Portrait of a Jew, 1962).[58] Memmi's semiautobiographical novel, *La statue de sel* (The Pillar of Salt, 1953) reads as a dramatization of the existential dynamic described in *Réflexions*: at first the young protagonist attempts to flee his Jewish condition by cathecting onto French culture, but in the end his confrontation with various forms of discrimination, including internment in a Nazi prison camp, forces him to confront his Jewish identity head-on and produces what we assume is the detailed exploration of Jewish identity in the novel we have just read.

Patrick Modiano's novel *La place de l'étoile* (1968) represents another sustained engagement with Sartre's text, only this time in an absurdist, darkly comic vein. Modiano attempts to take Sartre literally: the protagonist of the novel, Raphaël Schlemilovitch, embraces all the various abject identities foisted on the Jew in a *reductio ad absurdum* of the Sartrean notion that the Jew exists only in the eyes of the antisemite. He becomes, in turn, a cosmopolitan, a traitor, a collaborator, and a pimp before winding up on the couch of Sigmund Freud, who tells him: "Here, I want you to read the penetrating essay of your compatriot Jean-Paul Schweitzer de la Sarthe:[59] *Réflexions sur la question juive*. It is absolutely necessary that you understand one thing: THE JEW DOES NOT EXIST."[60] Since Jewishness is only a projection of antisemitic fantasies, Schlemilovitch's entire identity must be nothing more than a fiction. "You are not a Jew, I'm telling you," Freud says. "You are merely suffering from a hallucinatory delirium, phantasms, nothing more, a very minor paranoia." Confronted with this denial of his very being, Schlemilovitch declares himself nostalgic for the antisemitism of Céline, who at least allowed Jews their existence. Modiano's novel reflects the way a generation of French Jews who came of age after the war used Sartre's text as a springboard for their idiosyncratic attempts to redefine Jewishness in spite of the philosopher's limited notions of what such attempts should entail. Paradoxically, in its very negativity, Modiano's novel announces a new voice for French Jews, a comedic one that strives to break free from the mirthless existential choice of evasion or abjection Sartre saw as the Jew's dilemma in the modern world.[61]

Like Modiano, Alain Finkielkraut belongs to the generation born immediately after the war that came of age around 1968. His *Le juif imaginaire* (The Imaginary Jew, 1983) dramatizes yet another Sartrean struggle with Jewish affirmation. The essay describes the author's various failed or wrongheaded attempts to affirm his Jewish identity—mainly by claiming the legacy of his Polish family's suffering during the Holocaust, which he describes as an "imaginary" form of identity because he himself did not experience it—before finally turning to the study of *Yiddishkeit*, the lost world of his murdered Eastern European Jewish relatives, as a way to forge a more authentic way of being Jewish in the modern world. Like Memmi and Modiano, Finkielkraut takes up Sartre's call to become an authentic Jew but seeks to move beyond the philosopher's purely negative notion of what this would or should entail.

These works joined a host of others focused on Jews and Judaism in finding a receptive audience in France. In what might be interpreted as a Sartrean virtuous circle, in which a weakening of antisemitism promotes greater Jewish authenticity, which leads in turn to greater acceptance of the Jews, the 1980s and '90s saw Jewish-themed works enter the cultural mainstream. The response to Lanzmann's film *Shoah* in 1985 surely represents the highwater mark of this new cultural philosemitism. Sartre's companion, Simone de Beauvoir, set the tone in her review of the film, calling it "a pure masterpiece."[62] Following the success of the film, the word "Shoah" immediately entered the French lexicon as a substitute for "Holocaust," which came to be seen as too theological, too Christian. *Shoah* was thus a key moment in the elevation of Jewish suffering to the status of a paradigm in France.

As I have argued, Sartre's *Réflexions sur la question juive* contributed to the decline of republican universalism's prestige in the second half of the twentieth century. The events of the postwar years—especially decolonization—may have accelerated the shift, but Sartre provided its intellectual justification. By pointing to the complicity of republican universalism in the very forms of prejudice it sought to overcome, Sartre helped create a climate in which difference could be affirmed and valued. He made such affirmation the responsibility of the minority group, and he made the acceptance of difference the responsibility of the majority culture. What Sartre could not have imagined is the perverse side effect of this rejection of republican universalism: the perceived competition among minority groups that would follow from their simultaneous affirmations of difference, one result of which has been a dramatic rise in antisemitism in the early years of the new millennium.[63] Nor, certainly, could Sartre have imagined that the response to this rise in antisemitism, among intellectuals from across the political spectrum, would be yet another pendulum swing back to the same model of universalism—the subject of the next chapter—that Sartre had sought to discredit once and for all.

7

Finkielkraut, Badiou, and the "New Antisemitism"

Universalism fell out of favor among French politicians and academics at the end of the last millennium. After Sartre's critique of the way the republican universalist defends the Jew as a man only to destroy him as a Jew, it became more difficult to speak in terms that denied minority particularism, even when such language was intended to help minorities gain rights. The discrimination faced by people of North African descent, particularly after France began to allow entire families rather than just workers to settle in the 1970s, contributed to a feeling that universalism's message of equality masked deeply entrenched animosities directed at specific ethnic and religious groups.[1] These factors helped produce the outpouring of criticism of republican universalism during the commemoration of the bicentennial of the French Revolution in 1989, as revisionists highlighted the supposedly "totalitarian" legacies of Jacobinism. By the 1990s, the "right to difference," *le droit à la différence*, had become a watchword as minorities, including Jews, began to demand recognition of their voice, and their claims to group affiliation, in the public sphere.

The new millennium, however, has seen a return to hard-line, assimilationist versions of universalism, hostile to difference. Much of this neo-universalist discourse has come in response to what scholars have labeled the "new antisemitism," or the "new judeophobia," the well-documented rise in antisemitic incidents perpetrated mostly by young Muslim men since 2000.[2] Defenses of universalism in the face of rising antisemitism can be found across the political spectrum, even if the meaning of the concept changes depending on the political persuasion of its defenders. Those in the center and on the center right often see republican universalism, and its corollary *laïcité*, as the antidote to France's difficulties integrating its large and growing

Muslim minority. Their response to minority "incivility," including Muslim attacks against Jews, involves denouncing what they see as the Muslim tendency to assert religious solidarity over allegiance to France. Certain thinkers on the far left of the political spectrum, meanwhile, look to a Marxist form of universalism as a rampart against a supposedly excessive Jewish persecution complex, whether manifested in Holocaust commemoration or in what they take to be exaggerated fears of the "new antisemitism."

Despite their differences, all these contemporary universalists demonize minority *communautarisme* as the adversary. *Communautarisme* in French implies the voluntary identification by members of minority groups with other members of their group, and the privileging of ethnic or religious affiliation over national affiliation. It is usually translated into English as "communalism" or "identitarianism" and is meant to conjure the image of an Anglo-American-style multiculturalism in which ethnic and religious minorities supposedly fight each other for recognition, to the exclusion of other forms of collective solidarity.[3] The new French universalists oppose such communal splintering along ethnic and religious lines in the name of a higher form of identification, whether with the republic (for those more in the center or on the left), the nation (for those more on the right), or some abstract cosmopolitan ideal (for those on the far left).

In this chapter, I examine how two highly publicized philosophers, Alain Finkielkraut and Alain Badiou, have responded to the problem of the "new antisemitism" with a call for a return to universalism. In most ways, these thinkers could not be more different. The son of Holocaust survivors and a recently elected member of the Académie française, Finkielkraut was attracted to the anarchical spirit of May 1968 as a young man but has increasingly moved to the center right, defining himself as a hard-line defender of *laïcité* and critic of Muslim *communautarisme*. A former Maoist who has remained true to his far-left ideals, Badiou has defended Muslim rights in France, including the right to wear the veil, but has denounced many forms of Jewish communal identification, including Zionism, Holocaust commemoration, and concern about the "new antisemitism."[4] Both Finkielkraut and Badiou vaunt universalism as the answer to France's current ethnic tensions. And although their versions of universalism differ in ways that I will unravel in the pages that follow, both philosophers overlook the more flexible, pluralistic models for reconciling the universal and the particular that I have pointed to in the preceding chapters.

The "New Antisemitism"

The attack on the kosher supermarket in Paris in January 2015, which followed close upon the murder of the cartoonists at *Charlie Hebdo*, may have shocked the world, but to those familiar with the problem of antisemitism in France, it did not really come as a surprise. Observers had registered a dramatic increase in violence directed against Jews in France beginning in 2000. If French antisemitism seemed to have all but disappeared during the 1990s, the first decade of the new millennium saw France become the capital of the "new antisemitism."[5] The torture and murder of Ilan Halimi in 2006, the slaying of three children and their teacher at a Jewish school in Toulouse in 2012, and the attack on the Jewish Museum of Brussels by a French Muslim in 2014 were not isolated incidents but rather part of a highly disturbing trend. Figures from the Kantor Center for the Study of Contemporary European Jewry at Tel Aviv University show that in 2012, France had by far the largest number of antisemitic acts in the world, more than double that of any other country.[6]

Almost all of these acts of violence have been committed by a very specific segment of the population: what the French refer to as youth "issued from immigration" (issu de l'immigration), which is to say young Muslim men whose families (usually their parents or grandparents) immigrated to France from North Africa. Many observers have linked the sudden increase in violence in 2000 to a general sense of Muslim disaffection in France, as well as to the start of the Second Intifada in the territories of the West Bank occupied by Israel. According to these observers, young French Muslim men, inflamed by media coverage of events in the Middle East, seek vengeance for their feelings of dispossession by committing violent acts against Jews, despised both as stand-ins for the Israeli military and as examples of a well-integrated, economically superior minority group in France.[7] But while the periods immediately following flare-ups in the Middle East—such as after Israeli attacks on Gaza in 2008–9, 2012, and 2014—have indeed seen an increase in antisemitic incidents in France, the sociologist Michel Wieviorka has noted that antisemitic violence in France has taken on an "autonomous" character and cannot be tied to specific events.[8]

The French government has denounced this new wave of violence against Jews in forthright terms, and major events such as the Toulouse shootings and the kosher supermarket massacre have aroused widespread sympathy for Jewish victims. But intellectuals in France have not agreed about the significance of these attacks. Their responses fall mainly into two camps. On the one side are those who, like Finkielkraut, denounce the current situation as a "crisis" and place blame squarely on radical Islamists, on the young men they influence, and on their apologists on the far left. On the other side are the far leftists themselves, foremost among them Badiou, who have sought to minimize the rise in antisemitism and to expose the ideological investments of those who call attention to it.

This debate is not about the facts. Those who seek to minimize the "new antisemitism" do not dispute the number or nature of the attacks against the Jews in France since 2000. Nor do they dispute the origin of this violence, which they agree can almost always be attributed to youth of Muslim background in France's disadvantaged suburbs. Rather, they dispute the degree to which this situation constitutes a crisis. For Finkielkraut, the Muslim perpetrators of violence against the Jews, and their apologists on the far left, threaten not just the Jews but France itself—and in particular, as we shall see, France's identity as a republic. To Badiou, the rhetoric surrounding the "new antisemitism"—indeed, the very term itself—is invested in a Jewish *communautariste* or identitarian position that constitutes no less a threat than the violence it denounces.

In what follows, I will argue that this debate represents the latest battle in the ongoing war over universalism in France. I will suggest that it is not a coincidence that the Jews once again serve as the pretext for this attempt to define the nature of the universal, since the Jews have continually played this role since the time of the Revolution of 1789. In many ways, the debate over the "new antisemitism" reveals itself to be highly overdetermined by the history I have attempted to uncover in the preceding chapters. It is my hope that this history will shed light on the current debate and that this debate will in turn help bring many of the issues I have discussed into clearer focus.

Finkielkraut and Neorepublicanism

Alain Finkielkraut was one of the first French intellectuals to call attention to the "new antisemitism," and his writing on the subject has had a major impact on subsequent debates. He is the author of over thirty books and is a frequent media presence in France, as well as a member of the Académie française. A specialist in the history of ideas, he has long been an outspoken critic of postmodernism and multiculturalism.[9] His career has not been without controversy, notably after an interview he gave to the Israeli newspaper *Haaretz* in 2005, following a series of riots in the suburbs of Paris, in which he called the French national soccer team "black, black, black" (a satiric reference to the epithet *black, blanc, beur*, or "black, white, Arab," used to celebrate the team's multiethnic origins) and later apologized for the insensitivity of his remarks.¹⁰ He has also been accused of trying to have his cake and eat it too, of criticizing *communautarisme* in French Arabs while hosting a talk show on a Jewish radio station.¹¹ An outspoken supporter of Israel, he advocates the two-state solution, and his views on Jewish identity have always been complex. As we saw in the last chapter, his *Le juif imaginaire* (The Imaginary Jew, 1981), offers an indictment of Jews of his generation, born after the war, who base their identity on Holocaust suffering they did not themselves experience. In some ways, it could be said to have presaged the "Holocaust fatigue" said to be one of the causes of the "new antisemitism."¹²

The title of Finkielkraut's *Au nom de l'Autre: Réflexions sur l'antisémitisme qui vient* (In the Name of the Other: Reflections on the Coming Antisemitism) alludes to a danger looming on the horizon, although he makes clear that this danger had already begun to arrive in France by 2002, when he published the book. The agents of the new wave of antisemitism Finkielkraut forecasts are young Muslims, the residents of "sensitive urban zones" (cités sensibles) who are very often themselves the victims of racism and discrimination. Finkielkraut, however, is interested not in what motivates their hatred of Jews but in the ideology that attempts to justify their violence to the French public. His main target is not radical Islamism so much as the apologists for Islamism on the far left.

The "Réflexions" in Finkielkraut's title recalls Sartre's *Réflexions sur la question juive*, but Finkielkraut sees the "new antisemitism" as quite different from the old version analyzed by Sartre. Whereas the force of Sartre's critique of antisemitism was directed at the traditional antisemitism of the far right, at those who loathe the Jew for not belonging—for being "other," eternal nomads and wanderers, alien to the soil of France—Finkielkraut shows how the situation has now almost completely reversed. In the decades following the Nazi genocide, there was a concerted effort in Europe to reject all forms of fascism. According to Finkielkraut, however, this worthy project led to a glorification of the "other" and to an exaltation of the very features formerly despised in the Jews as a diasporic people: cosmopolitanism, nomadism, wandering.¹³

According to Finkielkraut, the obsession with the Jew's otherness creates a divide between different modes of "being Jewish"—between the "nomadic" and the "grounded," the "ethical" and the "ethnic," the diasporic and the Zionist. This opposition has informed a range of far-left, anti-Zionist thinkers, from Jean-François Lyotard to, more recently, Judith Butler and Enzo Traverso, who all celebrate the supposed nomadism of theoretical Jews while deploring the attachment of real Jews to the land of Israel.¹⁴ As Finkielkraut notes, the anti-Zionist far left reappropriates the negative stereotype of Jewish cosmopolitanism borrowed from the old antisemitism, the better to criticize Jews for failing to live up to it: "Their cosmopolitan vocation is no longer denounced, but on the contrary exalted, and, with a pained vehemence, they are reproached for betraying it. It is lamented that Jewishness is no longer what it used to be, with the admirable exception of a handful of righteous people."[15] The celebration of alterity and territorial dispossession, according to Finkielkraut, has had the perverse effect of transforming the Palestinians into the new Jews. And the obvious implication of transforming the Palestinians into Jews is that the Israelis must play the role of Nazis, which is to say the archenemy of a Europe on guard against a recurrence of fascism.[16]

According to Finkielkraut, the far left blames the Jews for coming to nationalism too late, after fascism had discredited all claims to territorial or ethnic belonging: "These inveterate nomads are not accused of conspiring to uproot Europe. On the contrary, as latecomers to autochthony, they are deplored for having regressed to the stage that Europeans were at before remorse set in and they were forced to place universal principles above territorial sovereignties."[17] Finkielkraut sees a curious process at work here, whereby the supposedly Jewish trait of nomadism gets universalized and de-Judaized in order to stigmatize actual Jews for remaining bound to the particular—to chosenness, election, the land, and a particular country (Israel). This repeats the gesture of Saint Paul and the early Christians who opposed the universalism of the church to the particularism of Jewish law, tradition, and ethnically defined identity.[18] As we will see, it is not a coincidence that Badiou makes Paul his patron saint. Just as Paul rejected the *juif charnel*, the carnal Jew, in favor of a spiritualized Judaism, which is to say Christianity, so too does the far left fault Zionism for being obstinately attached to a specific land and to a tribal identity, forms of particularism that have been superseded in the new postnational world order: "Once again it is the heredity, the tribalism, of the carnal Jew that gets called into question," writes Finkielkraut.[19] The "antisemitism to come" is in this sense a throwback to the earliest form of Christian universalist anti-Judaism.

Finkielkraut's analysis of the problem of antisemitism in contemporary France is penetrating and prescient. But there is also something ironic about his critique. For while denouncing the antisemitic universalism of the anti-Zionists, Finkielkraut himself remains obstinately attached to a different kind of universalism, the French republican kind. Finkielkraut's ire at the anti-Zionists stems, I would argue, from their claim to have superseded (in Pauline fashion) his cherished republican universal by revealing it to be too French, which is to say tied to a specific national context and to a specific form of nationalism that was born during the Revolutionary period and that reached its zenith at the end of the nineteenth century. The philosophers of the far left denounced by Finkielkraut are anti- or postnationalist, meaning that they reject the old French republican form of universalism as a false universalism, still bent on drawing boundaries, on instituting separate rights for citizens and foreigners, on creating distinctions between us and them. For Finkielkraut, by contrast, true liberty can only be conceived in a national context.

Let us turn for confirmation of this hypothesis to Finkielkraut's *L'identité malheureuse* (Unfortunate Identity, 2013). Here Finkielkraut argues that Muslim hatred of Jews in France always seems to accompany a hatred of France itself, and that neither animosity can be excused by the discrimination directed at Muslims in France or by Israel's treatment of the Palestinians: "It is necessary, *a fortiori*, to guard against interpreting the anti-French sentiment that is spreading in France as a reaction of legitimate self-defense against exclusion, and antisemitism, which more and more frequently accompanies it like an unfortunate retort . . . as a response to the very real scandal of Israel's oppression of the Palestinian people."[20] Finkielkraut's real, and perhaps quixotic, goal in this book is to assert pride in French identity in the face of both antifascist suspicions of national belonging and anticolonial critiques of French arrogance. How, Finkielkraut asks, can the French be attentive to the dangers of ethnocentrism, and sensitive to the demands of the other, without falling victim to self-hatred and thereby sacrificing what is truly valuable in French civilization?

This is ultimately a book about the possibility of French republican universalism in the new millennium. Finkielkraut's goal is not to argue that there is value in French civilization in the way that there is value in any civilization—this would be the cultural relativist position, which he disdains—but rather that there is something *universally* valuable in French civilization. He defends the currently controversial position that some (French) ideas are in fact universally true and deserve to be defended against ideas from other cultures, particularly when representatives of these cultures attempt to assert their ideas on French soil. The main French value that Finkielkraut thinks needs defending is *laïcité*, which he takes to mean the radical eradication of religion and ethnicity from the public sphere, and which he sees as threatened by Muslims wearing the veil in public school. He writes movingly of his own experience in French public school, which allowed the son of Polish Jewish immigrants to succeed precisely because the school did not permit ethnicity and religion to matter, and contrasts this with the current educational climate, in which a respect for "alterity" accompanies a general decline in expectations and standards. The veil should be banned, he argues, out of respect for French *laïque* traditions, which see the school as a place where freedom *from* religion, and not just freedom *of* religion, is possible, and where women should not be confined by the misogynistic standards of Islam. He also defends the veil ban in the name of the rather more dubious French tradition of gallantry, which allows men to express their esteem for women by flirting with them, an act of generosity that a headscarf apparently renders impossible.

In *L'identité malheureuse*, Finkielkraut traces a history of the French universal, and of challenges to it, from the French Revolution through the Dreyfus Affair, and through to decolonization. His project thus mirrors my own, although he denigrates the pluralism I seek to locate within the French tradition of universalism. Finkielkraut shows how first Joseph de Maistre and Edmund Burke, and later Maurice Barrès, attacked the Revolution's notion of universalism in the name of pluralism and the specificity of individual cultures: "For the nationalist writer, as for romantic thinkers, humanity is written in the plural. . . . There is therefore no law that is applicable to all men. The universal is a trap, a rational abstraction, a dangerous abstraction of the mind" (90–91). Cultural relativism, hostile to what Finkielkraut sees as the republican brand of universalism underpinning Jewish emancipation, ultimately led to the persecution of the Jew, first on an individual level in the Dreyfus Affair and then on a collective scale during Vichy. Following the horror of the Holocaust, European conscience recognized the danger of this relativist or extreme pluralist position and swung back toward the republican universal, with its assumption of assimilation as a precondition for welcoming minorities. But the painful experience of decolonization then exposed the danger of republican universalism and revealed how a belief in one truth could also lead to a sense of cultural superiority and dehumanization of the other. The pendulum thus swung so far back again that it has rejected universalism altogether: "Postcolonial Europe is a sober Europe that has sworn never to take another drink. It has arranged that not a drop of the alcohol of universalism remains in its current cosmopolitanism" (101). The current far-left fetishization of "alterity" is the product of this latest pendulum swing away from republican universalism.

According to Finkielkraut, the pendulum has swung too far. France has taken the acceptance of the other to mean a hatred of the self. He borrows the term "oikophobia," literally the hatred of one's own home, from the conservative English philosopher Roger Scruton in order to designate the opposite of xenophobia.[21] Although he admits that some degree of respect for the other is necessary, Finkielkraut thinks that the French are wrong to refuse to defend any core beliefs or any idea of Frenchness whatsoever: "The cosmopolitan individuals that we suddenly became have lost the habit of saying *we.*" France must combat the temptation of ethnocentricity "without at the same time succumbing to the penitential temptation of detaching ourselves from ourselves in order to atone for our sins" (134). Finkielkraut thus calls for a return to a kind of French nationalism. However, the national identity he defends so vigorously is not the Barrèsian one of soil and blood but rather the tradition of eighteenth-century universalism and twentieth-century *laïcité.*

For Finkielkraut, then, the antisemitism and general "incivility" of certain French Muslims might come as a response to discrimination, or from exposure to radical jihadist ideology, but the real problem lies elsewhere. Ultimately, he blames the non-Muslim French for failing to require allegiance to French national identity and for ceasing to believe in it themselves. In particular, he targets those on the far left, along with well-meaning centrists, for trying to accommodate "otherness" by ceasing to emphasize the positive values—the universal values—that have defined France for the last two hundred years. These values, principally *laïcité,* are what enabled different kinds of French people to coexist more or less peacefully despite great cultural differences. And they are what he believes might offer a counterweight to the dangerous *communautarisme* that encourages members of minority groups to express solidarity only with members of their group and hostility to all others.

Finkielkraut has faced a great deal of criticism for his views. As I pointed out above, he was essentially called a racist after his "black, black, black" comment, and his continued perceived hostility to immigrants has earned him the enmity of more than just those on the far left.[22] His call to ban the veil in public schools, which he makes essential to the defense of French values in *L'identité malheureuse,* has come under fire from those who consider it an infringement of religious freedom.[23] As Joan Wallach Scott has pointed out, not in reference to Finkielkraut in particular, although I think her comments apply particularly well to him, those who seek to ban the veil on the grounds that it oppresses women have not shown themselves particularly concerned about other feminist issues. She also points out that there seems to be a slippage in much French republican discourse between the headscarf worn by Muslim girls in school and the kind of veil that totally covers the face.[24] The argument made by Finkielkraut that the veil inhibits human interaction, including interaction between the sexes, might apply to the veil but not to the headscarf. Scott's real problem with the neorepublican fixation on the veil, however, lies in the way that it targets the cultural and religious beliefs of one minority population (Muslims). Scott is radically opposed to Finkielkraut's brand of universalism in the sense that she argues that we (and by we, she means the French) need to acknowledge difference in ways that call into question the certainty and superiority of our own views.[25]

In *L'identité malheureuse*, Finkielkraut mentions Scott by name in discussing her intervention during the Strauss-Kahn affair, but the whole book might be seen as an implicit response to the kinds of arguments she makes against banning the veil and to her antiuniversalism.[26] For Finkielkraut, it all comes down to two competing versions of universalism and its corollary, *laïcité*. The model that Finkielkraut labels "liberal secularism," which prevails in the rest of the Western world and which Scott defends, allows the veil to be worn in school on the grounds that "everyone must be able to practice his or her religion, to inhabit his or her difference, and to manifest his or her convictions without interference from the state" (52). But France is not the rest of the world: it follows the model of "republican secularism," which according to Finkielkraut insists on the elimination of religion in the public sphere. Whereas the rest of the West insists on the freedom *of* religion, France alone allows for freedom *from* religion—and, by extension, from *communautarisme*. Finkielkraut, as we have seen, does not refrain from asserting the superiority of the French republican model.

In a book devoted to the problem of Muslim antisemitism, and to the French state's reaction to it, the French journalist Nicolas Weill discusses the dangers of Finkielkraut's brand of republican universalism. "The problem is that a decade of defensive exaltation of the 'republican model' . . . has ill prepared intellectuals and politicians for self-criticism in this arena. But the ritual denunciation of '*commautarisme*' no longer suffices."[27] For Weill, the French cannot simply say that ethnic and religious communities do not matter. Instead of ceaselessly advocating a militant *laïcité*, the French state must fundamentally reconsider its relation to minority groups. In order to manage the current crisis, the state and its leaders must "openly practice a politics that seeks to balance the demands of different groups."[28] It must emphasize that republicanism is not synonymous with hostility to minorities but rather incarnates positive values such as "civility," personal liberty, and equality.

I share Weill's view of the problem of taking universalism and *laïcité* to mean hostility to minority difference. I also think that in addition to having the effect of alienating minority groups, such a view reduces the complexity that has attached historically to these concepts. Finkielkraut falls into this trap in *L'identité malheureuse* when he characterizes the history of universalism as the history of the opposition to particularism, whether by Burke and de Maistre or by Barrès. As I have tried to show throughout this book, there is more to the history of universalism in France than this. There have been many moments in French history when universalism and minority particularlism have been thought to mutually reinforce each other. Even *laïcité*, which Finkielkraut sees as the most important of French values, has not always meant the exclusion of religion from the public sphere. As Jean Baubérot has shown, and as I have repeatedly stressed in this book, there have been multiple *laïcités* in France; the concept has evolved over time. To take a certain twentieth-century version of universalism and *laïcité* as the only model available is to accept a voluntary impoverishment and a shutting down of options. This does not mean acceding to the Anglo-American, liberal model of secularism at the expense of the French republican one but rather means seeing that different possibilities exist even within the *exception française*. I will discuss some of these other models below, at the end of this chapter.

Badiou's Universalism

Finkielkraut offers a sharp critique of the young men of North African origin who transport the Second Intifada to the Parisian suburbs. But he saves his true wrath for the anti-Zionists of the French far left who provide them with ideological cover. If Muslim youth in the "sensitive urban zones" have failed to understand what Republican citizenship demands of them, and if French Islam has likewise failed to laicize itself into a consistorial "confession" subservient to a secular state, the postmodern thinkers of the far left have committed the much worse sin of undermining republican universalism, and with it the very foundations of the French nation. The *communautarisme* of Muslims might be explained—although not explained *away* in relativizing fashion certainly—as a vestige of a less evolved political and cultural sensibility, but the conscious attempt by the far left to subvert the values of republican France, for Finkielkraut, amounts almost to a form of treason.

Given the force of this critique, it thus comes as no surprise that thinkers on the far left have returned fire, denouncing their accusers in no less angry terms. What might come as a surprise, however, is the extent to which they accuse their accusers of the same crime of which they are accused: betraying universalism.[29] But whereas the target of neorepublicans like Finkielkraut is Muslim *communautarisme*, the far left attacks Jewish forms of communal adhesion. In this section, I explore how one thinker in particular, Alain Badiou, has placed himself at the center of these debates. Known mainly as a philosopher of "the event," of subjectivity, and of aesthetics, Badiou's radical political positions have made him a hero to many on the far left both in

France and in the United States.[30] In recent years, he has written extensively on Jews, denouncing not just Zionism but all forms of Jewish *communautarisme* in ways that have earned him the enmity of a range of adversaries, including Finkielkraut, Eric Marty, and Jean-Claude Milner. As I will detail below, critics have accused him of crossing the line from anti-Zionism to antisemitism. Badiou has responded vigorously to these attacks, accusing his "inquisitors" of deploying the charge of antisemitism against him in order to discredit his criticism of Israel and thereby to further the ends of Jewish *communautarisme*, which for him means Israeli and American imperialism.

To get to the heart of Badiou's theories on Jews and universalism, I will work backward, beginning with his more recent interventions. In 2011, Badiou teamed up with the journalist Éric Hazan to denounce the discourse surrounding the "new antisemitism" in *L'antisémitisme partout: Aujourd'hui en France* ("*Anti-Semitism Everywhere*" in France Today).[31] Badiou and Hazan intend their ironic title to designate not the actual increase in antisemitism in contemporary France but rather the supposed atmosphere of hysteria surrounding it, in which "inquisitors" seek to condemn Muslim perpetrators and their defenders on the far left to further their *communautariste* political agenda.

In this short and polemical book, Badiou and Hazan don't actually deny that Jews have been victimized and synagogues burned: "The notion of a 'wave of anti-Semitism' was not entirely without foundation," they allow. "It is undeniable that the years from 2002 to 2004 saw insults against Jews, hostile graffiti, wooden crates burned outside synagogues, and fights among youths."[32] However, they admit the existence of these attacks only barely, by using ungainly negative grammatical constructions, by confining the antisemitism to a two year period, and by minimizing the actual physical violence directed against Jews. Even in admitting the existence of some minor "insults," Badiou and Hazan reduce their significance to "fights among youths," as if Jews were equally to blame for the attacks directed against them. They are masters at giving with one hand and taking away with the other: "We do not take any acts of this kind lightly," they maintain, but then add, "Yet nothing happened that a reasonable person would see as particularly serious, nothing irreparable" (5), as if a certain amount of violence against Jews should be considered normal or acceptable, and as if only another "irreparable" event like the Holocaust would really justify the label "antisemitism."

Not only do Badiou and Hazan dismiss the gravity of the attacks against the Jews; they also purport to explain the attacks by reading the minds of the young Muslims who perpetrate them. Badiou and Hazan concede that "a large section of black and Arab French youth" in France hate Jews but explain that they do so because they consider Palestinians their brothers "for obvious historical reasons" (13), as if hating Jews in France follows logically from Israel's actions in the West Bank. They are justified in this hatred, Badiou and Hazan state, because Israel calls itself a "Jewish state," thus implicating Jews the world over in its policies. Moreover, many Jews in France *do* identify with Israel, which makes the hatred of the "black and Arab French youth" all the more understandable, since "an attentive and politicized eye is needed to understand that a large number of Jews do not consider that state their own" (14, translation modified). Aside from the implication that attacking Jews in France who identify with Israel is justified, Badiou and Hazan are quite condescending toward the young Arabs and blacks they defend, whom they consider unable to make basic moral and political distinctions: "For a young French person, Arab or black, son or daughter of a Maghrebian or African peasant who came to France in the last few decades as a worker and living on a blighted housing estate, it is not so easy to disassociate the persecutory practice of Israel as a state from the Jewish label that is granted it by almost universal agreement" (14). In other words, they imply that young Muslims are too ignorant to direct their hatred toward the proper target. Badiou and Hazan dismiss this hatred as "political but not well politicized" (une politique mal politisée) and denounce any attempt to label it as "antisemitism" as "an operation of stigmatization" (14), which they imply is itself racist and prejudiced.

However, Badiou and Hazan did not write *Antisémitisme partout* to excuse the misdirected political animosities of a bunch of poor minorities in the suburbs. Their real motivation is to defend themselves, which is to say the French far left, against charges of aiding and abetting criminals with their anti-Zionist rhetoric. They devote the rest of the book to debunking the accusations of their adversaries by exposing their hidden motivations. Badiou and Hazan name names—Finkielkraut, Lanzmann, Glucksmann, Lévy, Milner, Taguieff, Jean Birnbaum, Adler, and Éric Marty—most of whom, they point out, originally come from the left themselves, their political credentials enabling them to denounce those on the (farther) left with more credibility. On the one hand, Badiou and Hazan allege, discussion of antisemitism in France serves to distract from Israel's repressive policies in the West Bank.[33] On the other, Israel itself serves as a distraction from the even more sinister designs of the United States.[34]

Now, to accuse these intellectuals of acting out of a concern for the interests of Israel or the United States is tantamount to accusing them of shirking their responsibility as intellectuals to defend a higher truth. It is tantamount to accusing them of *communautarisme*, of privileging particular ties—whether to the Jews or to the West—over obligations to the universal. Badiou had already elaborated explicitly on this point in an earlier book, *Circonstances 3*, subtitled *Portées du mot "juif"* (Uses of the Word "Jew," 2005), really a collection of essays written from the 1980s to the present, to which an essay by Cécile Winter has been appended. The introduction to this work, presumably written by Badiou shortly before publication, at first sounds more genuinely concerned about, and less willing to excuse, the recent rise of antisemitism in France's Muslim population: "For now, suffice it to say that the existence of this type of anti-Semitism is not in doubt, and that the zeal with which some deny its existence—generally in the name of supporting the Palestinians or the working-class minorities in France—is extremely harmful."[35] But this disclaimer is clearly intended to protect the author from charges of doing if not exactly that, then something analogous: namely denying that antisemitism should be studied, or indeed named, at all.

Badiou maintains that antisemitism should not be examined separately from other racisms, for to do so places "the word 'Jew,' and the community claiming to stand for it, . . . in a paradigmatic position with respect to the field of values, cultural hierarchies, and in evaluating the politics of states" (159). He means by this that any attempt to say that the persecution of Jews is unique or not the same as racism against blacks or Arabs—and he's mainly referring to the discourse surrounding the "Shoah," although he interestingly collapses this discourse into the discourse surrounding the "new antisemitism"—commits the sin of according to a single community, the Jewish community, a paradigmatic or "transcendental" significance, which is a violation of universalism.[36] The theorists of the "new antisemitism" and the guardians of Holocaust memory have done precisely this—aided by the complicity of the media: "Today it is evident that a strong intellectual current, featuring bestselling publications and considerable media impact, indeed maintains that the fate of the word 'Jew' lies in its communitarian transcendence, in such a way that this destiny cannot be rendered commensurable with those of other names that, within the registers of ideology, or of politics, or even of philosophy, have been subject to conflicting assessments" (159). The advantage of according such privileged status to the word "Jew" is that it allows those who act in its name (read: Israel) to commit crimes with impunity: "The grace of having been an incomparable victim can be passed down not only to descendants and to the descendants of descendants but to all who come under the predicate in question, be they heads of state or armies engaging in the severe oppression of those whose lands they have confiscated"

(160). In other words, like the excessive focus on Holocaust memory, the attempt to call attention to Muslim antisemitism enables Israeli aggression by casting the Jews as victims.

For Badiou, then, Jews must not denounce violence directed at them as Jews, or speak about such violence in the past, because to do so makes claims on world sympathy and thereby provides Israel with cover to commit crimes against humanity. But Badiou goes further: his explicit goal is to abolish the "name" of the Jews, which is to say, Jewish identity as such. Now, to be fair, Badiou in theory opposes any "identitary predicate" (prédicat identitaire), any identity label attached to people or to states, not just Jewish identity. But he especially opposes the Jewish identity label because, in his view, the Nazi experience has made it particularly toxic. According to Badiou, the Jews who identify overtly as Jews become Nazis because they are using a word that Hitler used.[37] In the text signed Cécile Winter, included in Badiou's book, the word "Jew" is referred to as "the Master-Signifier of the New Aryans."[38] Winter, who proclaims her own Jewishness by disavowing it with what Badiou admiringly calls a "rare violence,"[39] thus becomes another in the line of Jewish coauthors (along with Hazan and Ivan Segré[40]) whose Jewish identity helps legitimate Badiou's attack on Jewish identity. Badiou seems to believe that if some Jews agree with his attempt to expunge the very "name" of the Jews, then it must not be antisemitic to do so. Note Badiou's hypocrisy in proudly naming his coauthor as a Jew when it serves his purposes despite his supposed hostility to such identity labels.[41]

Unlike others who display such a virulent opposition to Israel, Badiou seems driven less by a concern for Palestinian suffering than by an almost abstract quest for philosophical purity.[42] In Badiou's philosophical utopia, all identity distinctions, all community formations, and all national allegiances will be overcome. He calls for an extreme version of universalism in which the abstract individual exists free from all determinations. But, in what amounts to antisemitic exceptionalism, the classic operation whereby Jews are held to a different standard from others, in *Portées du mot "juif"* Israel is the only state Badiou blames for its nationalism, just as the Jews are the only people he blames for their *communautarisme*. Badiou is quite open about this singling out of the Jews, because, like Saint Paul, he makes the Jews into a metaphor both of what the universal should be—"In the meantime, we can try . . . to agree upon a meaning for the word 'Jew' that would have universal import" (165)—and of all that the universal is not.

Badiou accomplishes this by splitting the "real" Jews, the ethical or spiritual or universalist Jews, from the false or ethnic or particularist Jews who are tied to the forms of Jewish identity Badiou derisively groups under the acronym SIT (for Shoah, Israel, Tradition).⁴³ As we have seen, this is the same procedure practiced by a range of postmodern theorists who fetishize Jewish nomadism. Only those Jews Badiou thinks have broken with Jewish tradition or identity are therefore "universal" Jews, and in this camp he places Spinoza, Marx, and Freud. In the other camp he puts (nearly) the entire state of Israel, which becomes, in the title of the first chapter in the book, "the country in the world where there are the fewest Jews," by which he means the fewest "real" or "universal" Jews.

Badiou did not develop these ideas about the Jews and universalism in response to the rise of the "new antisemitism" in the 2000s. On the contrary, some of the essays in *Portées du mot "juif"* date back to the early 1980s. Similarly, his 1997 book *Saint Paul: La fondation de l'universalisme* (Saint Paul: The Foundation of Universalism), written before the outbreak of the "new antisemitism," contains the crux of the arguments he would later put forth during the antisemitism debates.⁴⁴ Unlike *Portées du mot "juif"* or *Antisémitisme partout*, the *Saint Paul* book does not seem like hasty journalistic or polemical writing. On the contrary, it gives the impression of being a fully developed argument and thus helps us to see the extent to which Badiou's thinking about the Jews and universalism proves central to his larger philosophical enterprise. Moreover, Badiou makes it clear from the start of the Saint Paul book that his motivation in writing it lies here, in the contemporary political resonance of what Paul had to say about the Jews and universalism, and not in the properly Christian religious dimension of Saint Paul's teaching, which Badiou dismisses as a mere fable. This is not a book about salvation through Christ, much less a book about the religious politics of the Roman world in the first millennium. It is a deliberately anachronistic book, a book focused on the intellectual, political, and social horizon of contemporary France, as he makes clear in the first chapter, "Paul: Our Contemporary."

Badiou locates the essence of Paul's teaching in his famous statement of religious universalism, "There is neither Jew nor Greek, there is neither slave nor free, there is neither male nor female; for you are all one in Christ Jesus" (Gal. 3:28). Indeed, Badiou's entire book can be understood as a gloss on this statement, which he interprets as announcing the existence of a new kind of subject, a subject "devoid of all identity" except that made possible through a single "event" that cannot be proven (the resurrection of Christ). According to Badiou, just as Paul replaces the concreteness of Jewish law, engraved in stone and manifest in physical signs (circumcision), with the abstractness of Christian law based on faith alone, so too does he create a subject who transcends the tribal, ethnic, national identity of the Jews, or any kind of terrestrial determination whatsoever, including class and gender. This is the basis of universalism both in Paul's time and in our own: "What is essential for us is that this paradoxical connection between a subject without identity and a law without support provides the foundation for the possibility of a universal teaching within history itself."[45] Whereas the Jews had tied truth to the law, which Badiou claims was only ever particular or applicable to the Jews alone, Paul makes truth available to all believers: "Paul's unprecedented gesture consists in subtracting truth from the communitarian grasp, be it that of a people, a city, an empire, a territory, or a social class" (5). Paul, in other words, frees truth from the *communautarisme* of the Jews.

Badiou hammers home the connection with the contemporary intellectual scene in France. Our present, he declares, is all about "the progressive reduction of the question of truth (and hence, of thought) to a linguistic form, judgment." Badiou links the drive toward relativism, the argument that each culture or group has its own truth, with the rise of the ideology of victimization, which also leads to the defeat of the universal: "All access to the universal . . . collapses when confronted with this intersection between culturalist ideology and the 'victimist' [victimaire] conception of man" (6). Now, as Carolyn J. Dean and others have shown, the "'victimist' conception of man" derives from the competition among minority groups in France for recognition of their past suffering, a competition that began with the success of the Jews in elevating the "Shoah" to the status of what Badiou labels a transcendental signifier of suffering.[46] Badiou, as we have already seen, decries in *Portées du mot "juif"* the way that "unprecedented extermination is held to be paradigmatic," endowing the word "Jew" with a "nominal sacralization" (159–60). The real problem with the *communautarisme* that results from the competition among victims, we now learn, is that it relativizes truth. It erects one law for the (Jewish) community and another law for outsiders. And for the true philosopher, as for the saint, truth must be one or it must not be.

Badiou's hostility to relativism would seem to place him in the camp of the critics of postmodernism, making him an odd bedfellow of Finkielkraut, who made largely the same point in *La défaite de la pensée* (The Defeat of the Mind, 1987). Only Badiou takes care to distinguish his version of universalism from the French republican universalism defended by Finkielkraut and his ilk. Their universalism, according to Badiou, is a false universalism. It purports to be universal, but like the law of the Jews, it is applicable only to those who belong to the nation—in this case French. It treats foreigners differently from French people: "The law thereby falls under the control of a 'national' model devoid of any real principle, unless it be that of the persecutions it initiates" (*Saint Paul*, 9). For Badiou, there is no real difference between the laws of the French republic and the laws of the Vichy state (or by implication, the Nazi state): both rely on "identitarian verification," "police monitoring," and other procedures to determine who deserves to benefit from supposedly universal laws. "The unique *political* real proper to the word 'French,' when the latter is upheld as a founding category in the state, is the increasingly insistent installation of relentlessly discriminatory measures targeting people who are here, or who are trying to live here" (8). Whereas Finkielkraut and other theorists of the "new antisemitism," such as Shmuel Trigano, argue that there is no liberty possible outside of the national framework, for Badiou, there is no liberty possible within it.

However, the problem with French republican universalism runs deeper: it not only upholds a form of identity (the national community) that is a contradiction of true universalism, but it also helps uphold *capitalism*, another false universal purporting to reduce everything to an abstract equivalence but in reality relying on inequalities to benefit a single class. That the ideology of republican universalism, and along with it modern nationalism, took shape during the Revolution of 1789, which employed the language of the universal (democracy, human rights, etc.) but in fact benefited the bourgeoisie by sweeping away the political obstacles to the reign of modern industrial capitalism, is hardly a coincidence for Badiou. He insists on opposing both liberal democracy and capitalism along with nationalism: "No, we will not allow the rights of true-thought to have as their only instance monetarist free exchange and its mediocre political appendage, capitalist-parliamentarianism, whose squalor is ever more poorly dissimulated behind the fine word 'democracy'" (7). Badiou is in many ways the intellectual heir of the nineteenth-century socialists Alphonse Toussenel and Karl Marx, whose opposition to capitalist modernity also took the form of anti-Judaism.

For Badiou, the "identitarian fanaticism" in contemporary France is the product of the Jewish obsession with the "Shoah," although its roots run much deeper—indeed, it represents a fundamental aspect of Judaism, its founding principle, according to Badiou. Judaism is the original particularism; it is the ultimate *communautarisme*. It establishes different laws for Jews and non-Jews. It is all about making distinctions based on tribal criteria. This was what Paul overcame. Badiou wants to make a similar gesture by reinstating a genuine *philosophical* universalism (as opposed to French republican universalism, which is a universalism in name only). This requires rejecting competing minority identities. However, unlike neorepublicans such as Finkielkraut, Badiou does not see the solution in banning religious practices, such as wearing the veil, in order to defend French republican institutions. He dismisses the "sorry affair of the foulard" (8) as a product of the "persecutory real proper to identitarian logic." Those who fulminate against veiled girls, he argues, want a "uniform dictatorship of what they take to be 'modernity'" (11).[47] As Éric Marty comments, the *laïcité* of the French republicans, for Badiou, is no better than religion; in fact, it is worse, because it is used in a persecutory way against immigrants.[48]

Badiou wants to break both with the *communautarisme* of the Jews and the petty persecutions of the French republicans by asking: "What are the conditions for a *universal singularity*?" (13). This was Paul's question, Badiou tells us, as he tried to free the truth from the strict enclosure of the Jewish community of his time. Paul proclaims "a universal singularity" against "prevailing abstractions" (14), which for him were the laws of the Jews and for us now are nationalism and capitalism and identity politics (all still associated, for Badiou, with the Jews). Thus Badiou's seeming tolerance for the signs of religious identity (the veil) do not indicate a softened stance on particularism, an overcoming of the opposition between the universal and the particular that I have argued structures most French thought on the question of minorities. On the contrary, like Sartre, he is willing to accept religious and cultural manifestations (especially when they come from oppressed groups, like Muslims) as a necessary stage on the path to a higher universal, the overcoming of capitalism—which, as for Sartre, will presumably result in minorities gladly surrendering the vestiges of their identity.[49]

It is not the least perverse aspect of Badiou's philosophy that despite his fundamental hostility to all forms of Jewish identity except that which defines itself as an explicit negation of Jewish identity, he presents himself as a philosemite, a defender of the Jews. As he articulates his goal in *Portées du mot "juif,"* he wants to protect the "Jews" from themselves. "A 'goy' [non-Jew] says it passionately: to him, saving the name of the Jews is essential, since it has to do with his own conceptual and active determination" (170). This involves detaching the "Jews" from their Jewish identity because all identity, but especially Jewish identity, is inherently fascist. In Badiou's view, Hitler has won if the "Jews" conceive of themselves in racial or ethnic or even, it seems, religious terms. For Badiou, "Jewishness" has no meaning prior to fascism and no meaning beyond it.[50] First and foremost, however, Badiou proposes to save the Jews by making them realize that the state of Israel is not a "Jewish" state; rather, "the principal threat to the name of Jews comes from a state calling itself Jewish" (169). Israel, once again, is guilty of the crime of "hostility to wandering, to minorities, to the universal, to revolutions" (170). But as Badiou points out, these are the crimes of which all states are guilty. In this sense, all states are antisemitic, according to Badiou, because the "Jew" represents both that which persecutes the universal and that which is persecuted in it. Badiou's goal here, as throughout his work, is to oppose the bad, particularist incarnation of the "Jew" to the good, universalist one, which involves rejecting actual Jews, or at least those who have not disavowed their affiliation—the "predicate" or identitarian label—which amounts to the same thing.

Responses to Badiou

Badiou's disquisitions on Jewish identity have not gone unanswered. Finkielkraut has been one of his primary critics, noting how Badiou's neo-Pauline universalism repeats the gesture at the heart of Christian antisemitism—the rejection or transcendence of the "carnal Jew" in favor of a supposedly higher, spiritual force. Badiou replaces this Christian supersessionism with a Marxist one: he calls for "a new universal church," this one "radically secular [laïque], progressive, democratic, but placed under the explicit patronage of Saint Paul." But at the heart of this new supersessionism still lies a hostility to "carnal" Jews who refuse to renounce land, history, tradition, etc. Finkielkraut describes how Badiou's "celebration of the wandering, diasporic, minority, Luftmensch, winged vagabond, ungraspable Jew leads him, and many others with him, to a repulsion, a disgust before the stubbornness of the carnal Jew." In addition to uncovering the Christian antecedents of Badiou's hostility to Jewish identity, Finkielkraut helps us to see that Badiou's opposition to Israel is not on the order of the political. It is metaphysical, and therefore the Israeli-Palestinian conflict cannot be resolved through political means for Badiou, but only through a radical transcendence of Jewish identity—along with all those who lay claim to it.[51]

The literary scholar Éric Marty has offered one of the most detailed responses to Badiou, in *Une querelle avec Alain Badiou, philosophe* (A Quarrel with the Philosopher Alain Badiou, 2007), where he engages specifically and at length with Badiou's theses in *Portées*, as well as in *Bref séjour à Jérusalem* (Brief Stay in Jerusalem, 2003), which is written in part as a response to the anti-Zionism of Jean Genet, but which I think also responds implicitly to the arguments made by Badiou and others on the far left against Israel, the "new antisemitism," and Jewish *communautarisme* more generally. I refer the reader to these two works, which I will discuss briefly as a way of bringing this chapter to a conclusion. I'd like to suggest that Marty's critique is so compelling because it focuses on Badiou's conception of universalism, but also that Marty himself remains tied to a conception of the universal that perhaps limits his approach to the problem.

In *Bref séjour à Jérusalem*, Marty asks why French intellectuals have taken the lead in denouncing Israel as a racist, imperialist state. Why, he asks, have

French thinkers taken it upon themselves not only to denounce Israel's policies but also to denounce Israel's very existence, its right to be a state and certainly its right to be a *Jewish* state? The answer, according to Marty, lies in the clash between two types of universalism, or rather, in the inability of French universalists to understand other forms of universalism, including—especially—the Jewish form. "In the 'metaphysics of nations,' France is no doubt the country least able to understand the proper name that is Israel. That visceral incomprehension stems quite simply from the fact that France is the bearer, holder, and perhaps also the founder of a type of universality that is antagonistic to that which founds the name of Israel."[52] In other words, French intellectuals are so used to thinking of themselves as the sole repositories of the universal, they are so used to the French universal being *the* universal, that they cannot see any other forms of it, or rather, they see any other forms of it as especially egregious violations of what they take to be the universal.

How, Badiou and his ilk ask, can there be a universal belonging to a single people? Does not the notion of election preclude the universal by binding salvation to a particular group? As we have seen, Badiou seems to think so, and this represents the primary reason he looks to Paul as a model, for it was Paul who sought to overcome the election of the Jews by making salvation available to all through Christ. Badiou thus seeks to perform the *laïque* equivalent of Paul's gesture of supersession. But this, according to Marty, constitutes a misreading of Paul, for Paul always saw himself as a Jew and always thought that salvation came through the Jews. For Paul, the sacrifice of Christ was a repetition of the sacrifice of Isaac by Abraham, an "event" that Badiou passes over in his attempt to make the word "Jew" devoid of any other meaning besides the racist one Hitler attached to it. Paul said there is "neither Jew nor Greek," but he also said immediately after: "And if you are Christ's, then you are Abraham's offspring, heirs according to promise" (Gal. 3:29). As Marty explains, the universality declared by Paul is "in no manner the bourgeois declaration of the rights of man," but nor is it a declaration that the abstract individual, devoid of all particularity, would be "the measure or standard of the universal" (74). Paul, moreover, did not renounce his belonging to a particular people. "I myself am an Israelite, a descendant of Abraham, a member of the tribe of Benjamin," he wrote in the Epistle to the Romans (2:1).

As Marty explains, the Jews have their own version of the universal that passes through the singularity, the particularity, of a people. Paul derives his notion of the universal from within the Jewish tradition, where the notion of election does not always have the tribalist connotation that Badiou assigns to it and where the word "Jew" means more than a petty particularity. "If Badiou were to take on the word 'Jew' in its true genealogy, which is extremely complex and foundational, he would come up against the experience of the word 'Jew' as a signifier beyond any predicate" (73). And moving from the ancient to the modern, Marty points out that the current Jewish population of Israel is likewise far from the homogenous purity Badiou taxes the Jews, those new "Aryans," with trying to achieve; rather, it contains an enormous ethnic, cultural, religious, and linguistic diversity. Israel is inherently cosmopolitan, even while defining itself as a Jewish state.

According to Marty, French intellectuals cannot believe that there can be a universalism different from their own. For Badiou, who purports to reject the French republican model, universalism still means homogeneity: "All people are the same and all people are like us" (61). Universalism, for Badiou, is not a process, something one strives for, but a state of being, a fact. It was this very arrogance of the French approach to the universal that led so many to see it as a mere alibi masking a quest for imperial domination. After decolonization, Marty postulates, French intellectuals began to perceive the bad faith of their claims to universality, but instead of abandoning it, they transferred it onto the third world. The republican universal of Zola became the cosmopolitan universal of Badiou without really changing its stripes. The victims of colonial violence became the new symbols of the universal through their suffering. And in this schema, Israel could only play the role of the imperial aggressor, when it was not a mere pawn of the capitalist superpower.

As Marty points out, such was not always the case. The original idea for Zionism did not spring, as propaganda would have it, from some misguided effort after the Holocaust to make the Arabs suffer for the crimes of Europe but rather was intended to allow the Jews to have a national homeland like other peoples. Indeed, Zionism was born during the Dreyfus Affair and was inextricably linked to the quest for universal justice incarnated in that struggle.[53] Moreover, at its origins, Israel was conceived as a kind of socialist utopia, as well as a bastion of democracy in a region of repressive autocratic states. For these reasons, until the 1960s, Israel was beloved by the universalist left, especially in France. All this is certainly true, even if Marty glosses over the degree to which Israel's own policies—including the occupation of the West Bank but also the shift away from a socialist ideal—were in part responsible for the change in its reputation in much of the world.

To a certain extent, I think that Marty exaggerates the differences between the French and the Jewish—or rather, the Israeli, and the difference is a big one—brands of universalism. For modern Israel, like modern France, was conceived as a way for the universal to take shape within a national context. Its mission was to allow the Jews to attain to the universal via nationalism, the idea being that they would no longer be condemned to the particular, the tribal, the ethnic once they were allowed to have a homeland like everyone else. This was the model for universalism that France pioneered during the Revolution of 1789. The problem, therefore, is not that French intellectuals like Badiou cannot recognize a different form of the universal in modern Israel but that they see their own reflection all too clearly. Israel, for Badiou, represents everything that the modern world has shown to be wrong with nationalism.

Badiou rejects both Israeli universalism and the French republican variety, which I think he would see as part and parcel of the same wrongheaded attempt to draw boundaries around what cannot or should not be bounded and which he clumsily associates with fascism, or Nazism, or Pétainism. Marty is on firmer ground when he implies that despite his critique of French republican universalism, Badiou remains very much its prisoner. That is to say, Badiou cannot see universalism as anything other than a state of being, the flat idea that "all people are the same and all people are like us" (61). This is why he reduces universalism to antiparticularlism. Universalism, for Badiou, is the rejection of the tribal and the ethnic. It is a negativity always opposed to *communautarisme* and unable to signify without it. Hence the important role the Jews play in his philosophy, since their stubborn particularism is necessary to provide universalism with its other.

But as Marty rightly shows, the Jewish tradition at its origin offers the possibility for an alternate form of universalism, one that does not see itself as the opposite of the particular. The Jewish tradition, according to Marty, teaches that not all people are the same and that in this difference lies the key to the elaboration of a higher, universal truth. This is something that Badiou overlooks. For, as Marty points out, difference does not preclude equality. On the contrary, there can be no equality without difference, for you need two things that are different in order to declare them equal. As I have shown throughout this book, a certain strain of French universalism has always realized the truth of this insight and has always fought—against both the right and the left—to allow for difference within it. Universalism is thus not a state of being but a struggle. To lose sight of this struggle, to allow universalism to become a rigid caricature, is to condemn it to irrelevance.

As Jean-Claude Milner—another sparring partner of Badiou as well as his occasional coauthor[54]—has explained, we need to distinguish between the "easy universal" of Badiou, a universal modeled on Saint Paul, on supersessionism, on the repression of all forms of minority particularity, and a more "difficult universal," one that is derived from particularity and that takes difference into account. Whereas various forms of the "easy universal," including Marxism and Maoism, European progressivism, and American democracy, have failed to prevent violence and persecution, the "difficult universal" has the potential to act as an "obstacle to the worst."[55] According to Milner, such a "difficult universal" would seek in difference, and particularly Jewish difference, the ground for a more inclusive form of universality, one that does not demand conversion or conformity in return.[56] "Not only is the time ripe for the thinking through of the difficult universal," Milner tells us, "but the return of the name of the Jew obliges us to such a thinking through."[57]

Conclusion

"Je suis juif"

The twin attacks on *Charlie Hebdo* and the Hypercacher supermarket in Paris on January 7 and 9, 2015, by French terrorists with Islamist ties produced an outpouring of grief, sympathy, and outrage. An estimated two million people attended a "rally of national unity" at the place de la République on January 11, joined by millions more at similar marches throughout France and the world. Commentators stressed that not since the liberation of France from the Nazis, or perhaps not since the French Revolution itself, had so many French people come together in such a public way.[1] The phrase "Je suis Charlie" (I am Charlie) could be seen on signs at demonstrations and on social media throughout the world—a visible indication not just of solidarity with the murdered cartoonists at the satirical newspaper but also of support for free speech and resistance to religious dogmatism. Amid this remarkable affirmation of universalist values, however, could also be signs declaring support for two other sets of victims whose universal significance was perhaps less clear: "Je suis policier" (I am a police officer), in homage to the police agents gunned down by the killers, and "Je suis juif" (I am Jewish), in recognition of the antisemitic nature of the second attack.

As I thought about ways to conclude a book that argues for the possibility of reconciling French republican universalism with minority difference, these "Je suis juif" signs kept coming to mind. They struck me as an emblem of the continuing importance of Jews to the ever-evolving nature of French universalist discourse, but their exact meaning in the contemporary context demanded further explanation. Were the signs merely a last-minute recognition that cartoonists were not the only ones who died in the attacks? Were they an "afterthought," as one American Jewish critic put it, in the sense that the real values that the millions of marchers rallied to were free speech and *laïcité*, not the right of Jews to shop in a kosher grocery store without fearing for their lives?[2] Did the signs mask an unwillingness to confront the growing problem of Islamist antisemitism even as they expressed sympathy for its victims, as this critic alleged? Or did they in fact signal an awakening to the specific dangers that Jews in France faced? If this were the case, in what way did they signal this? Did they follow the classic model of the Dreyfusards in defending the Jewish victim in universalist terms and hence in seeking to erase Jewish difference beneath the guise of defending it (as Sartre accused the "democrat" of doing)? Or did those "Je suis juif" signs point to something more? Did they signal a recognition that it was possible in France to be both universal and particular, to be both "Charlie" and "juif," at the same time?

In this book, I have argued that questions about the nature of Jewish difference have haunted the imagination of French universalism since the eighteenth century, and that the solutions proposed to these questions can be plotted on a continuum between assimilation and pluralism. During the French Revolution, debates over extending citizenship to the Jews crystallized conflicts over just how universal the Revolution would be. Along with those who argued that the Jews must assimilate to merit civil rights, others sought to include them within the nation despite—or perhaps on account of—their difference. For these theorists of the universal, the strange customs of the Jews did not contradict the values of universalism but rather revealed universalism's flexibility and reach. In the nineteenth century, this more pluralist notion of universalism—and its corollary, *laïcité*—continued to exert force, even as universalism faced contradictions in the colonies. The victory of the Dreyfusards at the start of the twentieth century signaled a setback for the forces of nationalist and religious reaction who would exclude the Jews from the nation outright and led to the separation of churches and the state in 1905. But this triumph of the left enshrined a hard-line, assimilationist form of universalism, which has been synonymous with the values of the French republic ever since. French republicanism came to mean the evacuation of difference from the public sphere. Jews and other minorities would be included in the French nation, but only as individuals, shorn of their distinctive attributes and communal affiliations. Despite attacks on this hard-line universalism through the years, by Sartre and those minorities who proclaimed their "right to difference" in his wake, most political actors and thinkers in France today assume a fundamental opposition between the universal and the particular.

So how then to interpret the "Je suis juif" signs at the "national unity" rallies in January 2015? Did they contradict this assumption? Did they seek to overturn the opposition by restoring difference to the universal? To begin to answer this question, it must be recognized that "I am"–type statements of solidarity with victims have a long history. To American ears, they echo John F. Kennedy's famous "Ich bin ein Berliner" (I am a Berliner) speech of June 26, 1963, in support of West Germany after the construction of the Berlin Wall. To the French, however, they more readily recall the slogan heard during the revolutionary events of May 1968: "Nous sommes tous des juifs allemands" (We are all German Jews). A specific reference to the German-Jewish background of the French student leader Daniel Cohn-Bendit, the slogan also recalled in a more general way the suffering of German Jews during World War II.³ To the *soixante-huitard* radicals, the German Jews symbolized martyrdom at the hands of fascism and offered a convenient if hyperbolic shorthand for expressing their sense of frustration at the repressive policies of the center-right government of Charles de Gaulle.

As Sarah Hammerschlag has shown, the "Nous sommes tous des juifs allemands" slogan both called attention to the specific plight of Jews and universalized it in a way that some observers found troubling.⁴ To thinkers like Maurice Blanchot and Jacques Rancière, the identification of young French radicals in 1968 with the suffering of the German Jews signaled a voluntary dispossession of the privileges of rootedness, an embrace of the cosmopolitanism of the Jews that the far right had always stigmatized.⁵ However, to Alain Finkielkraut, who participated in the demonstrations in '68 but who later rejected many of the movement's core principles, the slogan "We are all German Jews" turned the Holocaust into a fashionable symbol that could be appropriated by any group claiming victim status. And once anyone could claim the victim status of the Jew, Finkielkraut argued, it was just a short step to seeing actual Jews as Nazis, since according to many on the far left, the Palestinians were the newly sacralized victims, the real Jews.⁶

The "Je suis juif" slogan of 2015 inherits many of these ambiguities. On the one hand, like its predecessor from 1968, the "Je suis juif" slogan might be said to universalize the status of the Jewish victims. One might allege that it allows their victimhood as Jews to be appropriated, to be turned into a universal moral lesson, and hence to be divorced from the experience of real Jews trying to survive in France in the face of growing antisemitic violence. If everyone is a Jew, then what happens to actual Jews? What if real Jews don't want to play the role of victim? What if they support Israel? Would the crowds in the place de la République still identify with them? Or does the crowd's identification with Jews only extend to dead Jews or to the "ethical" Jews who share their supposedly universal values?

On the other hand, we might ask, what would it have meant if there had *not* been "Je suis juif" signs at the self-described "unity rally"? If those signs had not gone up, the antisemitic nature of the attack on the Hypercacher market would have been passed over in silence. The Jews would have been excluded from the demonstration of unity. It is important, I think, to see those "Je suis juif" signs as a response to the "Je suis Charlie" signs. By this I mean that in the French context, where there is a tradition of identification with the victims of certain crimes that are seen to threaten universalist values, it was necessary to identify also with the Jewish victims of the second attack and to call attention to the fact that they were targeted as Jews. While there is a danger that the mass identification with the Jewish victims erases their particularity, there is perhaps a greater danger in *not* identifying with them. If the response of the French public was to universalize the tragedy, then at least they were including the Jews in the universal.

It might also be noted that there is a difference between the "we" of 1968 and the "I" of today. It is certainly possible, I think, to read the "Je suis Charlie" and "Je suis juif" signs as a refusal of the drive to universalize victimhood by making suffering collective, as well as a refusal of the nationalism driving the "national unity" rally itself. Many in France were disgusted by what they saw as the government's co-opting of the rally for partisan political ends. Certainly some of those holding these signs were speaking in their own name, as individual subjects horrified by the killings, and not in the name of French universalism or any other official political ideology.

To conclude this book, I want to look closely at the official government response, or at least at one instance of it: the speech delivered by the French prime minister, Manuel Valls, to the French National Assembly on January 15, 2015, a few days after the attacks and the "national unity" rally, in a special session held in honor of the victims.[7] Valls is a Socialist, but from a more conservative side of the party than President François Hollande, whose economic policies he has criticized. Valls's repeated calls to address the growing problem of antisemitism in certain segments of France's large Muslim population have gained the admiration of Jewish leaders around the world.[8] His speech, I want to suggest, offers a new twist in the ongoing story of the relation of French universalism to Jewish difference.

Delivered with passionate emphasis to a full house, Valls's speech on one level follows a familiar script: it views the attacks not only as an assault on cartoonists or Jews but as a strike against the values of French republican universalism. "It is really the spirit of France, its light, its universal message that they wanted to destroy," Valls declares. This "universal" French spirit or message, Valls makes clear, includes the holy trinity of republican values—liberty, equality, and fraternity. Indeed, he refers to these Revolutionary values throughout the speech and even makes explicit reference to the French

Revolution itself as a model for the kind of resistance to darkness and oppression that the attacks demand. The singing of the "Marseillaise" in the National Assembly, he insists, delivers the message that France remains "worthy of its history." Valls goes on to enumerate a number of other familiar republican values that he sees as under attack. In slaying journalists, police agents, and Jews, he says, the Islamists were really targeting "freedom of expression," "the vitality of our democracy," "republican order," "tolerance," and, last but definitely not least, "*laïcité*."

This last term—*laïcité*—turns out to be the key value that the Islamists sought to target, according to Valls, and he returns to it at multiple points throughout the speech. It is *laïcité* above all that the rise of Islamism most threatens. And it is *laïcité* that constitutes the only possible response to the January attacks and the only defense against future ones. "And finally," Valls says toward the end of the speech, "the response to the emergency our society faces must be strong and without hesitation: the Republic and its values. And these are my final words. These values are first and foremost *laïcité*, which is the gauge of unity and tolerance." One of the few concrete things that he proposes the French state should do in response to the crimes committed, aside from increasing police surveillance, is to devote more attention to the teaching of *laïcité* in French public schools: "One message should resonate at every level of the national education system ... *laïcité* ! *laïcité* ! *Laïcité*, because it is the heart of the Republic and therefore of the school." And he does not hesitate to say that those who need the lessons most are Muslims: "It is really a debate at the heart of Islam, which Islam must have in its heart," he declares.

As we have seen throughout this book, French *laïcité*, like universalism, has a history and has meant different things over time. In the nineteenth century, it simply meant that the state must treat France's three main religions equally. Over the course of the twentieth century, however, it came to mean the absence of all religion from the public sphere. Valls pays lip service to the idea that *laïcité* means the freedom *of* religion as well as the freedom *from* religion: "*Laïcité*, yes, *laïcité*, the freedom to believe or not to believe." But it is really the freedom *from* religion that he sees as the heart of the matter, because in the following sentence in the speech, he avers that the real motive for the attacks—and the real reason the French republic has become a prime enemy of radical Islam—is the French commitment to a neutral public sphere, a public sphere free of religion. "And let us proudly declare our allegiance to that principle since we are being attacked because of *laïcité*, because of the laws that we passed forbidding religious symbols in school, prohibiting the total face covering. Let us take responsibility for these laws because they are what will help us to become stronger." So, for Valls, France is being attacked because of its commitment to *laïcité*, which he equates to the law forbidding the wearing of "ostentatious" religious symbols in public schools and the law forbidding the *niqab* in public places.[9]

Valls thus seems to embrace and defend the kind of hard-line hostility to religious or ethnic difference that became synonymous with French universalism in the twentieth century. Again, this is the kind of rhetoric that one has come to expect from a leader of the French republic. It is the kind of response that draws a line in the sand between "us" and "them," between the republic and the minority *communautarisme* that threatens it. And yet, upon closer inspection, Valls also seems to transcend this horizon of expectation. At certain key moments in the speech, he departs from the expected script by seeming to indicate a more open attitude toward minority difference. He does this first at the very opening of the speech when he enumerates the targets of the attack, whom he describes as journalists, police officers, Jewish French people (Français juifs), and salaried employees "in their diversity of origin, opinion, and belief." The "diversity" of the victims, he says—and by this, he surely means not just that many Jews were killed but also that one of the slain police officers was Muslim, although he does not say this explicitly—testifies to the inclusiveness of the French state and to its tradition of welcoming minorities within a universalist framework. It is through their diversity, he suggests, that the victims become "so many symbols" of French republican values, including and especially *laïcité*.

It is hard not to hear in Valls's ode to unity in diversity an implicit rejection of an earlier prime minister's ill-chosen words condemning the bombing of the synagogue on the rue Copernic by anti-Zionist terrorists in 1980. As we have seen, Prime Minister Raymond Barre said in a press conference after the attack that terrorists had meant to strike Jews and had instead killed "innocent French people" crossing the street. Whereas Barre's rhetoric had seemed to draw a distinction between Jews and French people, and had implied that only the latter are innocent, Valls takes pains to describe the victims of the kosher supermarket attack as *Français juifs* (Jewish French people), thus emphasizing their Frenchness, and to stress that in attacking Jews, the terrorists had in fact attacked "the entire national community." In a sense, both prime ministers violated the rules of republican universalist discourse by singling the Jews out at all: the state is not supposed to make distinctions among its citizens based on religion or ethnicity. But whereas Barre transgressed by implying that Jews do not form part of the national community, Valls did so by stressing that the nation is composed of diverse members and by underlining this diversity.

A more surprising transgression of the usual rules of republican discourse, however, came during the long portion of Valls's speech devoted to the fight against antisemitism. Jewish leaders around the world have praised this section of the speech because of the ways that Valls calls attention to a problem that many feel has not received enough attention.[10] Valls echoes these critiques by acknowledging that there was not enough outrage after the kidnapping and murder of Ilan Halimi or after the shootings at the Jewish school in Toulouse in 2012. And unlike President François Hollande, who caused consternation in certain quarters by saying that the January 2015 attacks had "nothing to do with the Muslim religion,"[11] Valls feels no compunction about placing the onus on Muslim religious leaders to help resolve the crisis: "It is really a debate at the heart of Islam, that Islam must have in its heart." Valls goes on to underline the importance of combating antisemitism in order to keep the Jews from leaving France: "Without the Jews of France, France would no longer be France. And we all must proclaim this message loud and clear." The Jews are thus central to France, not just as abstract citizens, interchangeable with all other subjects of the state, but as Jews.

The surprising transgression of republican discourse I am referring to, the moment that made me rewind to listen to the speech again, came when he described the multiple ways that French Jews have been made to feel insecure in recent years. How to accept, he asks, that in the land that first emancipated the Jews, and that became one of the lands of their martyrdom during World War II, that Jews can no longer feel safe as Jews? "How can we accept," he goes on, "that our compatriots or that a Tunisian citizen, whose father sent him to France so that he would be safe while buying bread for Shabbat, should die because they are Jews?" It was the Hebrew word for Sabbath that surprised me here as much as the reference to the specificity of Jewish religious ritual. If the French republic has always promised to protect the religious practices of members of all faiths, it has not always enumerated these practices so specifically or done so using the language of its religious minorities. Indeed, it is quite rare to hear the prime minister of France address the National Assembly using a Hebrew word.

And he does so twice. The second time comes a paragraph later when he is describing how certain schoolchildren resist the Holocaust education mandated by the French state: "And how can we accept that, in certain elementary schools or high schools, you can't teach what the Shoah is?" While one could argue that the more surprising thing is that the French state has mandated Holocaust education to begin with, it is still surprising to hear the Jewish genocide referred to by its Hebrew name in the National Assembly. It is far more common in French republican discourse to refer to the Holocaust euphemistically as the "deportation," as if the true horror the victims of Auschwitz faced was being expelled from France, not being gassed and incinerated. It was Claude Lanzmann, director of the epic documentary *Shoah*, who helped this Hebrew word enter the French lexicon, in part because he objected to the redemptive overtones of the conventional term "Holocaust" (which means "burnt offering") and in part to call attention to the Jewish specificity of the event by naming it in a Jewish language.

One might say that these are a few insignificant words in a long speech, but language matters in France as perhaps in no other country. Language is the medium of French universalism. It was the global reach of the French language that made the ideals of the French Enlightenment and of the French Revolution universal in the first place. And just as France fights today to protect the values it associates with this tradition—first among them, according to Valls, *laïcité*—so too does it fight to maintain the prestige and integrity of the French language, in part by banning or discouraging the use of foreign words.[12] To include the language of a minority religious group in a speech at the National Assembly is thus a very surprising thing.

But are these words—along with the sentiment they express, their emphasis on the importance of Jews to France as a nation—indicative of an opening to minority difference within a universalist framework? Do they signal a swing of the pendulum back toward the more pluralist model of universalism preached by certain Revolutionaries, exemplified by Rachel, and foregrounded by Renoir? Do they recall the "concrete liberalism" of Sartre? The answer is not a simple one. At first glance, the invocation of these Hebrew terms does seem to suggest that for Valls, *laïcité* may in fact mean freedom *of* religion and not just freedom *from* religion. These words may in fact signal that French universalism could work to welcome minority difference rather than suppress it. One hears in these words an echo of the Revolutionaries who sought to include a group as different as the Jews as a way to show just how universal their model of universalism could be.

Of course, over and over again in this book I have shown how theorists of universalism who appear to welcome minority difference one minute wind up arguing for its dissolution the next. Sartre is the most blatant example of this bait-and-switch tactic, with his call for a "concrete liberalism" giving way to a hope for the voluntary assimilation of the Jews following a Marxist revolution. If there's one thing that the history of French universalism teaches, it is to be wary of such Trojan horses. There have been models of universalism that allow for difference throughout French history, but they are more the exception than the rule. Even well-meaning defenders of the Jews often have difficulty finding room for their difference.

And on closer inspection, it indeed appears that Valls is less open to minority difference than his remarks about the Jews would indicate. He is not, it must be pointed out, open to minority difference *as such*: his speech does not value Muslim difference in the same way that it values Jewish difference. On the contrary, Valls devotes a significant portion of the speech to enjoining Muslim religious authorities and intellectuals to urge their disaffected young coreligionists to conform to republican values: "But, indeed, when real urban ghettos are forming, where people live only with other people like them, where the only virtue that is extolled is that of withdrawing from society, where the state is no longer present, how to encourage people to look toward the Republic, to grasp the fraternal hand that it extends?" Given his equation of *laïcité* with the "veil law," we can guess what this "fraternal hand" would offer. The one positive reference to Muslim particularism in the speech comes when he says that like many in the audience, he too has "French friends of Muslim culture and religion." But the anecdote he then tells is of this unnamed friend saying, after the attacks, that he is ashamed to be Muslim. Likewise, although Valls does make a possible allusion to the Muslim background of one of the police officers killed, mentioning "the diversity of backgrounds and of origins" of the police victims, he concludes, in typical republican universalist fashion, by subsuming this difference within the French whole: "Before the coffins, next to their families, there were only three colors, those of the national flag." Clearly, there are limits to the kind of minority difference Valls can imagine including within the French universal, at least at this difficult moment.

Rather than recalling Rachel or Renoir, Valls's speech more readily calls to mind France's policies in colonial Algeria. As we saw in chapter 3, French colonial authorities and metropolitan authors made a show of including Algeria's indigenous Jews within the French universal while denying this possibility to the much larger community of indigenous Muslims on the grounds that they were less willing or able to adopt French republican values. In some ways, Valls's otherwise very admirable speech repeats a classic move of French republican universalism, which is to play the (good) Jewish minority against the (bad) Muslim minority. This is perhaps forgivable in a speech following an antisemitic attack perpetrated by radical Islamist extremists. We must, however, be aware of the extent to which Valls's differential treatment of Jews and Muslims forms part of a larger and pernicious tendency on the part of the French state, one with a long history.

But I don't think we should therefore overlook the openness he displays to Jewish difference. Nor, of course, do I think we should dismiss it as the result of "Jewish influence," as one political figure quipped.[13] The point of Valls's speech is to make the case that antisemitism threatens the values of the

French republic. And it does so not for the traditional reasons raised by the Dreyfusards and by generations of French republicans—that it is wrong to single out certain French citizens for their religious or ethnic difference—but rather, and much more radically, because their religious and ethnic difference actually matters to the republic. Jews belong in France, Valls maintains, and they belong not only as abstract individuals, shorn of any distinguishing characteristics, but rather as flesh-and-blood beings who buy kosher food on "Shabbat" and whose relatives died in the "Shoah." If Valls at moments in the speech implies that *laïcité* connotes the evacuation of religious difference from the public sphere, he also makes a point of bringing this difference back, at least in its Jewish incarnation, and giving it pride of place in his speech.

My point here, as throughout this book, is not to argue that these words translate easily into actions. I am not implying that they are enough to keep French Jews from emigrating to Israel or even from feeling fear when shopping in a kosher supermarket. Similarly, I have not tried to argue that in the past the rhetorical inclusion of Jewish difference translated into philosemitic policies, or to deny that French universalism in its dominant form has been hostile to differences of all sorts. Rather, I have tried to show that the discourse of universalism has not always meant the same thing to everyone, that moments of disagreement with the dominant form of the ideology have existed from the beginning. These moments may have existed only as discursive possibilities, reflected in moments of political speeches, novels, or films. But their existence offers an important alternative to the dominant discourse and a model that might be summoned at moments of crisis, like our own, when instead of resorting to familiar slogans that exclude or erase the other, another option is needed.

Notes

Introduction

1. I have refrained from naming the perpetrators of these attacks in order to deny them posthumous celebrity.

2. Most estimates place the Muslim population at 5–6 million (or roughly 10 percent of the French population) and the Jewish population at around 500,000. For a history of immigration to France, see Gérard Noiriel, *Le creuset français: Histoire de l'immigration, XIXe–XXe siècles* (Paris: Seuil, 1988). For a wide-ranging overview of the problems minorities face in contemporary France and of French attitudes toward immigrants, see Alec G. Hargreaves, *Multi-Ethnic France: Immigration, Politics, Culture, and Society* (New York: Routledge, 2007).

3. Mayanthi L. Fernando describes discursive as well as more tangible forms of discrimination (in housing, policing, the criminal justice system, employment, and education) directed against Muslims in France today in *The Republic Unsettled: Muslim French and the Contradictions of Secularism* (Durham: Duke University Press, 2014).

4. David A. Bell underscores that "violence by young, alienated Muslims, directed at Westerners . . . and against Jews, is by no means a singularly French phenomenon" in "The French Dilemma," *Dissent* (Spring 2015): 119.

5. I am using "ideology" in the general sense of "the integrated assertions, theories and aims that constitute a sociopolitical program." *Merriam-Webster's Collegiate Dictionary*, 10th ed. (Springfield, MA: Merriam-Webster, 1993), 575.

6. For a lucid discussion of how the Revolution made use of Enlightenment theories of universal rights, see Michael Rapport, "Robespierre and the Universal Rights of Man, 1789–1794," *French History* 10, no. 3 (1996): 305–6.

7. Naomi Schor discusses the abstract nature of the universalist subject in "Universalism," in *The Columbia History of Twentieth-Century French Thought*, ed. Lawrence Kritzman (New York: Columbia University Press, 2006), 345.

8. Patrick Weil provides a vigorous defense of French republican universalism, and of the French republic's policy of strict religious neutrality, in *Le sens de la république* (Paris: Bernard Grasset, 2015).

9. In *La laïcité falsifiée* (Paris: La Découverte, 2014), Jean Baubérot describes the use of *laïcité* as a "mask" by Marine Le Pen to camouflage the far right's hostility to immigrants (13).

10. A law passed on March 15, 2004, bans the wearing of "ostentatious" religious symbols in French public schools, including the veil, the *kippa*, and large crucifixes. Fernando offers a perceptive analysis of such deployments of power by French republican secularism. For a critique of secularism as a form of political rule in the West, also see Talal Asad, *Formations of the Secular: Christianity, Islam, Modernity* (Stanford: Stanford University Press, 2003).

11. In *Rhinestones, Religion, and the Republic: Fashioning Jewishness in France* (Stanford: Stanford University Press, 2014), Kimberly A. Arkin describes recent threats to the republican universalist consensus on minority difference, including efforts by young Sephardic French Jews to classify their Jewish identity in racial terms.

12. Patrick Weil declares, "There is no Jewish or Muslim community. Jews and Muslims can spend time together, even live together. But there is no community. There are only individuals with differing degrees of identification" (*Le sens de la république*, 112).

13. The Jacobins were a club that came to dominate Revolutionary politics and established a dictatorship under Maximilien Robespierre during the Reign of Terror (1793–94). Among their goals was the creation of a centralized and secular state, which has led many today to use "Jacobin" in a loose sense to refer to the centralizing and secularizing aspects of the current French republic. On the historical Jacobins, see Patrice Higonnet, *Goodness beyond Virtue: Jacobins during the French Revolution* (Cambridge: Harvard University Press, 1998).

14. Joan Wallach Scott makes a similar point in *Parité! Sexual Equality and the Crisis of French Universalism* (Chicago: University of Chicago Press, 2005), when she notes how partisans in debates over the nature of republicanism in the 1980s and 1990s tended to reify the Jacobin model (12).

15. Pierre Birnbaum writes that the fate of the Jews became a test case for "the universalist and homogenizing values of the French Revolution," and that the place of the Jews "at the heart of the national imaginary remains central in the history of modern France: from one century to the next, a number of key social conflicts are structured around their representation." Birnbaum, *Les deux maisons: Essai sur la citoyenneté des juifs (en France et aux Étas-Unis)* (Paris: Gallimard, 2012), 22.

16. In *The Figural Jew: Politics and Identity in Postwar French Thought* (Chicago: University of Chicago Press, 2010), Sarah Hammerschlag discusses "the significance of the Jew as a French cultural and political symbol" (6), particularly of the opposition between the universal and the particular.

17. Shmuel Trigano, *La république et les juifs après Copernic* (Paris: Les Presses d'aujourd'hui, 1982), 74.

18. David Feldman remarks on the convergence between Jewish nationalist critiques of emancipation and Zygmunt Bauman's postmodern critique of modernity's hostility to difference in "Was Modernity Good for the Jews?" in *Modernity, Culture, and "the Jew,"* ed. Bryan Cheyette and Laura Marcus (Cambridge: Polity Press, 1998), 171–87. Bauman's critique can be found in *Modernity and the Holocaust* (Cambridge: Polity Press, 1989) and *Modernity and Ambivalence* (Cambridge: Polity Press, 1991).

19. Wendy Brown, *Regulating Aversion: Tolerance in the Age of Identity and Empire* (Princeton: Princeton University Press, 2006), 66.

20. Ibid., 66, 52.

21. One of the first to argue that French Jews did not actually assimilate in the nineteenth century was Phyllis Cohen Albert in "Ethnicity and Jewish Solidarity in Nineteenth-Century France," in *Mystics, Philosophers, and Politicians: Essays in Jewish Intellectual History in Honor*

of Alexander Altmann, ed. Jehuda Reinharz and Daniel Swetschinski (Durham: Duke University Press, 1982), 24–74. Also see Pierre Birnbaum, "Between Social and Political Assimilation: Remarks on the History of the Jews in France," in *Paths of Emancipation: Jews, States, and Citizenship*, ed. Pierre Birnbaum and Ira Katznelson (Princeton: Princeton University Press, 1995), 121. In *Rites and Passages: The Beginnings of Modern Jewish Culture in France, 1650–1860* (Philadelphia: University of Pennsylvania Press, 2004), Jay R. Berkovitz shows that many French Jews remained bound by religious tradition after their emancipation. Comparing France, Germany, and Britain, Feldman argues that "it is clear that the ambition of modern states to purge themselves of ethnic, religious, linguistic and cultural diversity has been grossly overestimated" ("Was Modernity Good for the Jews?" 176).

22. In *The Jews of the Republic: A Political History of State Jews in France from Gambetta to Vichy*, trans. Jane Marie Todd (Stanford: Stanford University Press, 1996), Pierre Birnbaum shows how elite French Jews in the Third Republic balanced high-profile government service with active participation in Jewish communal life.

23. See the chapter "Jewish Identities in the Age of Romanticism" in Lisa Moses Leff, *Sacred Bonds of Solidarity: The Rise of Jewish Internationalism in Nineteenth-Century France* (Stanford: Stanford University Press, 2006), 81–116.

24. Brown writes: "As bourgeois French Jews devoted themselves to becoming French and to identifying with Frenchness . . . their connection to and identification with Jews in other lands [was] necessarily attenuated. . . . Thus, the process of trying to become French while racially marked as Other involved not just disavowing Jewish belief, practice, or the nation, but disidentifying with one's most victimized brethren" (*Regulating Aversion*, 57).

25. Aron Rodrigue describes the goals of the alliance in *French Jews, Turkish Jews: The Alliance Israélite Universelle and the Politics of Jewish Schooling in Turkey, 1860–1925* (Bloomington: Indiana University Press, 1990). On the creation of the Alliance, also see Leff, *Sacred Bonds of Solidarity*.

26. In *French and Jewish: Culture and the Politics of Identity in Early Twentieth-Century France* (Oxford: Littman Library of Jewish Civilization, 2008), Nadia Malinovich describes how French Jews between the Dreyfus Affair and World War II attempted "to express their particularism fully while simultaneously holding on to the values of republican universalism" (8–9) by creating a variety of Franco-Jewish associations as well as Jewish-inflected literature in French.

27. Emmanuelle Saada discusses some of the shifts in the meaning of assimilation, especially as it pertained to colonial subjects, over the course of the nineteenth century in *Empire's Children: Race, Filiation, and Citizenship in the French Colonies*, trans. Arthur Goldhammer (Chicago: University of Chicago Press, 2012), 109–10.

28. In *The Politics of the Veil* (Princeton: Princeton University Press, 2007), Joan Wallach Scott describes French universalism as "positing the sameness of all individuals, a sameness that is achieved not simply by swearing allegiance to the nation but by assimilating to the norms of its culture." In contrast to the French model of universalism, Scott wants "to insist instead that we need to acknowledge difference in ways that call into question the certainty and superiority of our own views" (12–13, 19).

29. Étienne Balibar, "Y a-t-il un 'néo-racisme'?" in Étienne Balibar and Immanuel Wallerstein, *Race, nation, classe: Les identités ambiguës* (Paris: La Découverte, 1997), 36–37.

30. Gary Wilder avoids the tendency to simplify and reify universalism by arguing that French republican ideology was always riven by an "antimony," or internal contradiction, be-

tween the universal and the particular, between the desire to abstract away minority difference and the concurrent tendency to "differentiate and primitivize subject populations." Gary Wilder, *The French Imperial Nation-State: Negritude and Colonial Humanism between the Two World Wars* (Chicago: University of Chicago Press, 2005), 10.

31. "To be sure, republican *laïcité* distances itself from the idea of tolerance," Finkielkraut writes of the fact that France is the only Western country to ban the veil in public schools. Alain Finkielkraut, *L'identité malheureuse* (Paris: Stock, 2013), 53.

32. Among Finkielkraut's targets in *L'identité malheureuse* is Joan Wallach Scott (66).

33. Ibid., 111–12.

34. "Looked at through the lens of romanticism for the other, the new social norm of diversity conjures a France where origins are only permitted if they are exotic and where a single identity is considered unreal: national identity" (ibid., 113).

35. In *La république et les antisémites* (Paris: Bernard Grasset, 2004), Nicolas Weill argues that the "militant *laïcité*" that has come to define French republicanism is not a sufficient response to the challenges posed by the recent wave of Muslim antisemitism. As I do here, he suggests that "a retrospective analysis of the relation of the State to its communities becomes necessary" (12).

36. Jean-François Chanet, *L'école républicaine et les petites patries* (Paris: Aubier, 1996).

37. Stéphane Gerson has likewise shown how during the Third Republic, regional affiliations, or pride in the "*petite patrie*," was seen not as an obstacle to national unity but rather as a "gateway to the *grande patrie*." Gerson, *The Pride of Place: Local Memories and Political Culture in Nineteenth-Century France* (Ithaca: Cornell University Press, 2003), 10.

38. Mona Ozouf, *Composition française: Retour sur une enfance bretonne* (Paris: Gallimard, 2009).

39. In her inquiry into the dominant mode of secular rule and how it works to exert power and control over minorities in France, Fernando disputes that the "new *laïcité*" is so different from the historical form (20–21).

40. Baubérot, *La laïcité falsifiée*, 49. Also see Jean Baubérot, *Histoire de la laïcité en France* (Paris: Presses Universitaires de France, 2000), 28.

41. My statistical information comes from Paula Hyman, *The Jews of Modern France* (Berkeley: University of California Press, 1998), 56, 116, 137, 194.

42. David Nirenberg, *Anti-Judaism: The Western Tradition* (New York: Norton, 2013), 2.

43. Ibid., 3.

44. Nirenberg writes that Marx's theory of Jewish capitalism "depends on and reproduces deep continuities with Christian figures of Judaism" (ibid., 431).

45. Ibid., 3.

46. Ronald Schechter, *Obstinate Hebrews: Representations of Jews in France, 1715–1815* (Berkeley: University of California Press, 2003), 47. Schechter borrows the term "good to think" from Claude Lévi-Strauss, *Totemism*, trans. Rodney Needham (Boston: Beacon Press, 1963), 89.

47. Unlike Jewish emancipation, enacted in two decrees, black emancipation in France was long and drawn-out. The Revolutionary Constituent Assembly declined at first to end slavery in the colonies. On May 15, 1791, it voted to grant civil rights to free blacks and mulattoes who were born of free parents. Following a slave revolt in Saint-Domingue (later Haiti), the revolutionaries rescinded these rights in September 1791. The Legislative Assembly reinstated these rights but did not end slavery. Eventually the Jacobin-led National Convention voted to end slavery on February 4, 1794. Slavery would then be reinstated by Napoleon, before being finally outlawed during the Revolution of 1848. From this point on, blacks had full rights.

48. Despite the efforts of pioneering feminsts like Olympe de Gouges, who wrote a *Declaration of the Rights of Woman and the Female Citizen* (1791), women did not gain the right to vote in France until 1944.

49. In *The Abbé Grégoire and the French Revolution: The Making of Modern Universalism* (Berkeley: University of California Press, 2005), Alyssa Goldstein Sepinwall discusses how since "gender difference was viewed as fixed, women were not seen as capable of regeneration to the same degree as even long-hated groups like Jews or people of color" (7). In *Parité!*, Scott likewise notes that "sexual difference, in the person of the woman, was not included in the list of traits that could be abstracted for purposes of citizenship" (16). In *The Anatomy of Blackness: Science and Slavery in an Age of Enlightenment* (Baltimore: Johns Hopkins University Press, 2011), Andrew S. Curran describes how Enlightenment philosophes marshaled scientific theories of black difference to help negotiate the contradiction between liberalism and slavery.

50. Saada describes the way that efforts to categorize mixed-race (*métis*) children in France's colonial empire reveal "deep tensions in the practices by which nationality was defined—tensions that were largely invisible in the metropolitan context" (*Empire's Children*, 6). I would argue that debates about Jews made some of these tensions visible in the metropole as well.

51. For a study of French Jewish positions in the debate over secularism in the nineteenth century, see Zvi Jonathan Kaplan, *Between the Devil and the Deep Blue Sea? French Jewry and the Problem of Church and State* (Providence, RI: Brown Judaic Studies, 2009).

Chapter 1

1. I am using "assimilation" here in an anachronistic sense. In *Empire's Children: Race, Filiation, and Citizenship in the French Colonies*, trans. Arthur Goldhammer (Chicago: University of Chicago Press, 2012), Emmanuelle Saada argues that it was only in the course of the nineteenth century that "assimilation" in French came to mean the "transformation of all the social institutions of a civilization and a race" (109). As I show, in the eighteenth century, the term used for this type of transformation was "regeneration."

2. Ahad Ha'Am (pseud. Asher Zvi Hirsch Ginsberg), founder of Cultural Zionism, referred to the condition of the emancipated French Jews as "spiritual slavery under the veil of outward freedom." *Selected Essays of Ahad Ha'Am*, trans. Leon Simon (1912; New York: Simon & Schuster, 1970), 177. Cited in Gary Kates, "Jews into Frenchmen: Nationality and Representation in Revolutionary France," in *The French Revolution and the Birth of Modernity*, ed. Ferenc Fehér (Berkeley: University of California Press, 1990), 106. Arthur Hertzberg offers a more modern version of this tendency in *The French Enlightenment and the Jews* (New York: Columbia University Press, 1968), where he declares: "The era of Western history that began with the French Revolution ended in Auschwitz" (5). Hertzberg reiterates this critique in "The Totalitarian Legacy of the French Revolution," *Patterns of Prejudice* 2, no. 3 (1968): 20–34. Jonathan Frankel provides a helpful overview of the historiography of Jewish emancipation in "Assimilation and the Jews in Nineteenth-Century Europe: Towards a New Historiography?" in *Assimilation and Community: The Jews in Nineteenth-Century Europe*, ed. Jonathan Frankel and Steven J. Zipperstein (Cambridge: Cambridge University Press, 1992), 1–37.

3. François Furet, *Interpreting the French Revolution*, trans. Elborg Forster (Cambridge: Cambridge University Press, 1981).

4. A prime example is Shmuel Trigano, "The French Revolution and the Jews," trans. Scott Lerner, *Modern Judaism* 10 (1990): 171–90. Trigano had already developed his critique in *La république et les juifs après Copernic* (Paris: Les Presses d'aujourd'hui, 1982), where he reads

Revolutionary debates over emancipation to conclude that "the Jew as such is essentially *persona non grata* [interdit de séjour] in France" (74).

5. Robert Badinter is typical of this tendency: "The revolutionary project of emancipation was indeed to make the Jews disappear in Man, just as the provinces were supposed to dissolve in the Nation, and, in a more vast way, the Nation in humanity." Badinter, *Libres et égaux . . . : L'émancipation des juifs sous la Révolution française (1789–1791)* (Paris: Fayard, 1989), 14. On this historiographic controversy, see Lawrence Scott Lerner, "Beyond Grégoire: A Third Discourse on Jews and the French," *Modern Judaism* 21 (2001): 199–215; Ronald Schechter, *Obstinate Hebrews: Representations of Jews in France, 1715–1815* (Berkeley: University of California Press, 2003), 2–5; and Alyssa Goldstein Sepinwall, *The Abbé Grégoire and the French Revolution: The Making of Modern Universalism* (Berkeley: University of California Press, 2005), 229–30. On the Jewish nationalist critique of emancipation and its link to the postmodern critique of modernity, see David Feldman, "Was Modernity Good for the Jews?" in *Modernity, Culture, and "the Jew,"* ed. Bryan Cheyette and Laura Marcus (Cambridge: Polity Press, 1998), 171–87.

6. Hertzberg, *French Enlightenment*, 287.

7. Pierre-Louis de Lacretelle, *Plaidoyer pour Moyse May, Godechaux & Abraham Lévy, juifs de Metz. Contre l'Hôtel-de-ville de Thionville & le Corps des Marchands de cette ville* (Brussels, 1775; rpt. Paris: Lipschutz, 1928), 4. Subsequent references appear in the text.

8. Pinto, a Sephardic Jew who lived in Holland, published the *Apologie de la nation juive* in 1762, and the *Traité de la circulation et du crédit* in 1771, which defended Jewish mercantile practices against the physiocrats. The *Apologie* was a response to an article on the Jews published by Voltaire in 1756 (which would later form part of his *Essai sur les moeurs*) and led to a polemic with Voltaire. Valabrègue, a Jew from Avignon, published his *Lettre ou réflexions d'un milord* defending the Jews anonymously in 1767. Both writers blame Jewish mercantile practices on Christian persecution through the centuries. See Hertzberg, *French Enlightenment*, 61–62, 179–82.

9. "But let us keep from believing that they can thereby receive a decree of grace, a decree of regeneration" (35). Whereas Rita Hermon-Belot gives Lacretelle credit for being the first to urge the secular regeneration of the Jews, Sepinwall argues, I think correctly, that he is using the term "regeneration" in a strict theological sense. He is in fact arguing that including the Jews in civil affairs will *not* lead to their religious regeneration. Hermon-Belot, "Préface," in Grégoire, *Essai sur la régénération physique, morale et politique des juifs*, ed. Rita Hermon-Belot (Paris: Flammarion, 1988), 25. Sepinwall, *The Abbé Grégoire and the French Revolution*, 262n19.

10. Sepinwall, *The Abbé Grégoire and the French Revolution*, 64.

11. On Dohm's economic theories, see Jonathan Karp, *The Politics of Jewish Commerce: Economic Thought and Emancipation in Europe, 1638–1848* (Cambridge: Cambridge University Press, 2008), 122–31.

12. Cited in Jonathan Hess, *Germans, Jews, and the Claims of Modernity* (New Haven: Yale University Press, 2002), 5.

13. Hess describes Dohm's influence on the French Revolutionaries in ibid., 5.

14. Honoré-Gabriel de Riquetti, comte de Mirabeau, *Sur Moses Mendelssohn, sur la réforme politique des juifs: Et en paritculier sur la révolution tentée en leur faveur en 1753 dans la grande Bretagne* (London, 1787). Reprinted in *La Révolution française et l'émancipation des juifs* (Paris: Éditions d'histoire sociale, 1968), vol. 1. Subsequent references appear in the text.

15. In *Jewish Destinies: Citizenship, State, and Community in Modern France*, trans. Arthur Goldhammer (New York: Hill & Wang, 2000), Pierre Birnbaum argues that Mirabeau was the only French thinker to accept Jewish particularism (24). Likewise, Lerner sees Mirabeau as ex-

emplifying a "third discourse" between those who sought to banish the Jews and those who sought to assimilate them ("Beyond Grégoire," 200).

16. Birnbaum describes how one of the entrants, d'Haillecourt, a procureur in the Parlement of Metz, suggested deporting the Jews to Guyana, and another, a monk named Chaix, argued that the Jews should not be killed but "tamed by having their beaks and claws snipped" (ibid., 14).

17. Sepinwall, *The Abbé Grégoire and the French Revolution*, 62.

18. Henri Grégoire, *An Essay on the Physical, Moral, and Political Reformation of the Jews; A Work crowned by the Royal Society of Arts and Sciences at Metz* [translator unknown] (London: C. Forster, 1791), 36. Subsequent references appear in the text.

19. Sepinwall argues "that revolutionary universalism was made possible only through the mechanism of regeneration" (*The Abbé Grégoire and the French Revolution*, 7).

20. On Grégoire's campaign against linguistic diversity and his effort to extinguish regional languages and dialects of French, see David A. Bell, *The Cult of the Nation in France: Inventing Nationalism, 1680–1800* (Cambridge, MA: Harvard University Press, 2001), 175–82. Sepinwall notes that Grégoire's language politics "suggested that universalism involved not only political inclusion but also cultural melting" (*The Abbé Grégoire and the French Revolution*, 97).

21. Claude-Antoine Thiéry, *Dissertation sur cette question: Est-il des moyens de rendre les juifs plus heureux et plus utiles en France?* (Paris: Knapen Fils, 1788), 85–86. Reprinted in *La révolution française et l'émancipation des juifs* (Paris: Éditions d'histoire sociale, 1968), vol. 2. Subsequent references appear in the text.

22. "Should we not above all conserve for Christianity the preeminence and the empire that belong to it?" (84).

23. Lerner, for instance, refers to Hourwitz as also contributing to the "third discourse" that sought to give Jews rights while maintaining the integrity of Jewish identity, as opposed to those who wanted to assimilate the Jews and those who wanted to exclude them ("Beyond Grégoire," 203). Frances Malino argues that Hourwitz "refused to accept that Jews cease to be Jews as the price of their citizenship" in "The Right to Be Equal: Zalkind Hourwitz and the Revolution of 1789," in *From East and West: Jews in a Changing Europe, 1750–1870*, ed. Frances Malino and David Sorkin (New York: Basil Blackwell, 1990), 93.

24. Zalkind Hourwitz, *Apologie des juifs en réponse à la question: Est-il des moyens de rendre les juifs plus heureux et plus utiles en France?* (Paris: Gattey, 1789), 86. Reprinted in *La révolution française et l'émancipation des juifs* (Paris: Éditions d'histoire sociale, 1968), vol. 4. Subsequent references appear in the text.

25. On Napoleon's "infamous decree," see Paula Hyman, *The Jews of Modern France* (Berkeley: University of California Press, 1998), 46–47.

26. Malino, "The Right to Be Equal," 90. Malino also provides a fascinating biographical portrait of Hourwitz in *A Jew in the French Revolution: The Life of Zalkind Hourwitz* (Cambridge, MA: Blackwell, 1996).

27. Schechter, *Obstinate Hebrews*, 7.

28. Ibid., 67.

29. Schechter points out that the Constituent Assembly debated Jewish emancipation on more than thirty-two occasions in the first two years of the Revolution (ibid., 154). Kates also argues that the Jews became "symbols of something else" to the Revolutionaries, namely a proxy for debates over extending democracy ("Jews into Frenchmen," 109). In *Anti-Judaism: The Western Tradition* (New York: Norton, 2013), David Nirenberg includes a chapter on the Revolu-

tion and discusses "how figures of Judaism did new work and gained new meaning in moments of radical transformation that had little to do with Jews" (362).

30. In *Sacred Bonds of Solidarity: The Rise of Jewish Internationalism in Nineteenth-Century France* (Stanford: Stanford University Press, 2006), Lisa Moses Leff also points out that the "regeneration" argument did not ultimately succeed in motivating the Revolutionaries to emancipate the Jews (22).

31. Badinter, *Libres et égaux*, 87.

32. The Parlement of Metz refused to register the edict unless it excluded the Jews. In 1788, the king assigned Guillaume-Chrétien de Lamoignon de Malesherbes to issue a report on the Jews of the east, and he corresponded with Grégoire on the subject. Malesherbes sought ways to incorporate the Jews into the nation by eliminating all but their religious difference, but his report was superseded by the events of the Revolution. See ibid., 88–97.

33. On the conflict over the *cahiers* and participation by the Sephardic Jews in the elections for the Estates General, see Richard Ayoun, *Les juifs de France: De l'émancipation à l'intégration (1787–1812)* (Paris: L'Harmattan, 1997), 25–26.

34. Marcel Gauchet, *La Révolution des droits de l'homme* (Paris: Gallimard, 1989); Sepinwall, *The Abbé Grégoire and the French Revolution*, 90.

35. Cited in Ayoun, *Les juifs de France*, 29.

36. "It is the way the nations have treated the Jews that forces them to become perverse. If something should surprise us it is that they are not even more so." Henri Grégoire, *Motion en faveur des juifs* (Paris: Belin, 1789), 12. Reprinted in *La révolution française et l'émancipation des juifs* (Paris: Éditions d'histoire sociale, 1968), vol. 7. Subsequent references appear in the text.

37. For a discussion of the role of "dietary difference" in Revolutionary debates over citizenship, see Pierre Birnbaum, *La république et le cochon* (Paris: Seuil, 2013).

38. The name "Jacobin" derived from the Revolutionary club that leased space from Jacobin monks beginning in October 1789. Some historians date the term to the growth of the club's network after 1790, although Patrice Higonnet sees Jacobinism as an "esprit révolutionnaire" that was already present at the start of the Revolution. *Goodness beyond Virtue: Jacobins during the French Revolution* (Cambridge, MA: Harvard University Press, 1998), 7.

39. In his "Letter to the Hebrew Congregation of Newport," Washington stated that "all possess alike liberty of conscience and immunities of citizenship."

40. *Opinion de M. Le Comte Stanislas de Clermont-Tonnerre, député de Paris: Le 23 décembre, 1789*, in Ayoun, *Les juifs de France*, 66. Subsequent references appear in the text.

41. A similar impulse motivated the Constituent Assembly to enact the Civil Constitution of the Clergy on July 12, 1790, effectively subordinating the Catholic Church to the state. See Leff, *Sacred Bonds of Solidarity*, 26.

42. Ibid., 25.

43. David Sorkin, "The Count Stanislas de Clermont-Tonnerre's 'To the Jews as a Nation . . .': The Career of a Quotation" (Jerusalem: Leo Baeck Institute, 2012), 19–20.

44. In "Israelite and Jew: How Did Nineteenth-Century French Jews Understand Assimilation?" in *Assimilation and Community: The Jews in Nineteenth-Century Europe*, ed. Jonathan Frankel and Steven J. Zipperstein (Cambridge: Cambridge University Press, 1992), Phyllis Cohen Albert argues that Clermont-Tonnerre asked Jews to give up their corporate structure, not their Jewish identity (91).

45. Frederic Cople Jaher, *The Jews and the Nation: Revolution, Emancipation, State Formation, and the Liberal Paradigm in America and France* (Princteon: Princeton University Press, 2002), 67.

46. On speech acts, see J. L. Austin, *How to Do Things with Words* (Cambridge, MA: Harvard University Press, 1975).

47. Cited in Ayoun, *Les juifs de France*, 109.

48. Bell, *The Cult of the Nation in France*, 15.

49. Ibid., 204. The sociologist Dominique Schnapper provides a definition of the nation that might be said to derive from this French Revolutionary model: "The nation is defined by its ambition of transcending particular belongings by means of citizenship and of defining the citizen as an abtract individual, without particular identification and qualification, over and above all concrete determinations." Schnapper, *Community of Citizens: On the Modern Idea of Nationality*, trans. Séverine Rosée (New Brunswick, NJ: Transaction Publishers, 1998), 35.

50. Jaher similarly argues that in the Revolutionary debates, the Jews became "a metaphor for French society" (*The Jews and the Nation*, 80).

51. Léonard Gallois, ed., *Réimpression de l'ancien Moniteur depuis la réunion des États-Généraux jusqu'au Consulat*, vol. 2 (Paris: Bureau central, 1840), 471.

52. Badinter, *Libres et égaux*, 149.

53. In "Ethnicity and Jewish Solidarity in Nineteenth-Century France," in *Mystics, Philosophers, and Politicians: Essays in Jewish Intellectual History in Hhonor of Alexander Altmann*, ed. Jehuda Reinharz and Daniel Swetschinski (Durham: Duke University Press, 1982), 249–74, Phyllis Cohen Albert describes how French Jews retained their Jewish identity into the nineteenth century.

54. Maurice Samuels, *Inventing the Israelite: Jewish Fiction in Nineteenth-Century France* (Stanford: Stanford University Press, 2010).

55. Higonnet notes that Jacobin thinking about Jews and Jewishness developed along two lines: while the religion itself was condemned (along with other religions), individual Jews were welcomed as citizens—and hundreds of Jews became Jacobins. If individual Jews were persecuted by the Revolutionaries, it was mostly because of their political opinions (*Goodness beyond Virtue*, 236–37). Michael Rapport analyzes the relation between Robespierre's commitment to universal rights during the early phase of the Revolution and his later exclusionary nationalism in "Robespierre and the Universal Rights of Man, 1789–1794," *French History* 10, no. 3 (1996): 303–33.

56. M. J. Mavidal, ed., *Archives parlementaires de 1787 à 1860*, Première série (1787 à 1799), 10:757. References in the next two paragraphs are to this page.

57. Jean-Sifrein Maury (1746–1817) was a Catholic priest and member of the Académie française elected to the Estates General by the clergy.

58. *Archives parlementaries* 10:779. The next quotation is also from this page.

59. Cited in Ayoun, *Les juifs de France*, 113.

60. Cited in ibid., 123.

61. Cited in ibid., 124.

62. Adrien Duport was elected to the Estates General by the nobility and became an influential voice in the Constituent Assembly. Opposed to the execution of the king, he split with the Jacobins to form the Feuillant party in July 1791.

63. *Archives parlementaires* 31:372. All subsequent references to this debate are to this page.

64. Jean-François Rewbell (1747–1807) was a deputy representing the Third Estate from Colmar.

65. Michel-Louis-Étienne Regnaud de Saint-Jean d'Angély (1761–1819) was elected to the Estates General by the Third Estate. Like Duport, he opposed the king's execution and fled during the Terror.

66. On the September 1791 debate, see Leff, *Sacred Bonds of Solidarity*, 28, and Malino, *A Jew in the French Revolution*, 112–13.

67. Schechter, *Obstinate Hebrews*, 156.

68. Kates, "Jews into Frenchmen," 108–9.

69. The final emancipation decree, as amended by Broglie, is cited in Ayoun, *Les juifs de France*, 135.

70. Kates, "Jews into Frenchmen," 103–4.

71. According to Leff, "Berr saw a seamless relation between Judaism and French constitutionalism" (*Sacred Bonds of Solidarity*, 29).

72. On Bonald, see Hyman, *The Jews of Modern France*, 39, and Leff, *Sacred Bonds of Solidarity*, 32.

73. Simon Schwarzfuchs, *Napoleon, the Jews, and the Sanhedrin* (London: Routledge and Kegan Paul, 1979), 49.

74. The first Assembly of Jewish Notables was composed of eighty-two delegates representing the Jews of France and the parts of Germany and Italy that were under French control. The Grand Sanhedrin had seventy-one members, including many of the same notables, along with leading French and Italian rabbis who Napoleon hoped would lend the rulings an air of religious authority. Hyman, *The Jews of Modern France*, 43.

75. In chapter 3, I show that family law became a site of conflict between the Jews of Algeria and the French occupying authority since divorce, which was permitted under Jewish law, was banned in France from 1816 to 1884. During the Empire, however, divorce was still legal in France, so there was less of a conflict for the Sanhedrin in this regard.

76. The following year, however, he issued the so-called Infamous Decree of 1808, which nullified most loans made by Jews to non-Jews in Alsace and Lorraine and prevented Jews in these provinces from hiring replacements for army service. Hyman, *The Jews of Modern France*, 46–47; Schwarzfuchs, *Napoleon, the Jews, and the Sanhedrin*, 120–21.

77. Hyman, *The Jews of Modern France*, 43.

78. According to Schwarzfuchs, it is clear that Napoleon's questions to the Sanhedrin "had only one common aim: to compel the Jews to choose between their religious law and the duties of patriotism" (*Napoleon, the Jews, and the Sanhedrin*, 57).

79. For example, rabbis were encouraged to preach only in French and to wear black cassocks, similar to those worn by priests. These efforts by elite reformers to eliminate Jewish difference were strenuously resisted by the orthodox majority. See Phyllis Cohen Albert, *The Modernization of French Jewry: Consistory and Community in the Nineteenth Century* (Hanover: Brandeis University Press, 1977).

80. See Phoebe Maltz Bovy, "'Embrasser les juifs': Jews and Intermarriage in Nineteenth-Century France (1792–1906)" (Ph.D. diss., New York University, 2013).

81. Leff, *Sacred Bonds of Solidarity*, 34.

82. Cited in Jean Baubérot, *Histoire de la laïcité en France* (Paris: Presses Universitaires de France, 2000), 29.

Chapter 2

1. "And on the antique stage, formerly despised / Where Racine emits his fluty sighs / Where Corneille in Roman verse commands / Their Rachel lights up at the din of our hands."

2. Jules Janin, *Rachel et la tragédie* (Paris: Amyot, 1858), 71. The Comédie-Française was also known as the Théâtre-Français.

3. Phyllis Cohen Albert, *The Modernization of French Jewry: Consistory and Community in the Nineteenth Century* (Hanover: Brandeis University Press, 1977), 23.

4. Janin, *Rachel et la tragédie*, 142.

5. In this chapter, I have been inspired by Rachel Brownstein's book on Rachel's career, *Tragic Muse: Rachel of the Comédie-Française* (New York: Knopf, 1993). She discusses the Purim performance of *Esther* on 134–35. L. Scott Lerner also discusses this production in "Jewish Identity and French Opera, Stage and Politics, 1831–60," *Historical Reflections/Réflexions Historiques* 30, no. 2 (2004): 276.

6. Rachel first played the title role in Racine's tragedy *Bérénice*, about a first-century Jewish queen and her ill-fated love for the Roman emperor Titus, in 1844.

7. Jules Janin, "Théâtre-Français. Esther—Mlle Rachel," *Journal des Débats*, March 4, 1839, 1. Brownstein also discusses this review (*Tragic Muse*, 135). Françoise d'Aubigné, marquise de Maintenon, was the morganatic second wife of Louis XIV and very influential at court. She commissioned *Esther* from Racine to be performed by the girls of the Saint-Cyr school in 1689.

8. I am hardly the first scholar to call attention to Rachel's Jewishness. Aside from Brownstein and Lerner, an exhibit (and accompanying catalog) entitled "Rachel, une vie pour le théâtre (1821–1858)" at the Musée d'art et d'histoire du Judaïsme (March 1–May 31, 2004) focused on this aspect of Rachel's story. In her essay for the catalog volume, "'L'enfant du miracle': Ambivalences du discours sur les origines de Rachel et de son géni," (Paris: Adam Biro, 2004; 71–87), Anne Hélène Hoog describes how Rachel's early biographers saw in her Jewishness proof that the Revolution's mission of equality had worked—that anyone could achieve greatness. In a later article, Hoog shows how Rachel's itinerary from poor immigrant to grand tragedienne epitomized the way a generation of French Jews assimilated via a cathexis with French language and culture. "Le marge, l'exemple et l'exception: Le parcours d'Élisa Félix dite Mademoiselle Rachel," *Romantisme* 125 (2004): 91–101.

9. Christine Piette, *Les juifs de Paris (1808–1840): La marche vers l'assimilation* (Québec: Laval, 1983), 50.

10. Sephardic Jews in the southwest and the Jews in Provence were more acculturated and did speak French. Several of the most prominent Jews in the 1830s and '40s came from these communities: the Péreire brothers were from Bordeaux, and Adolphe Crémieux was born in Nîmes.

11. Julie Kalman describes this as "a golden age" compared to other periods in Jewish history in *Rethinking Antisemitism in Nineteenth-Century France* (Cambridge: Cambridge University Press, 2010), 6.

12. These were Achille Fould, Adolphe Crémieux, and Lieutenant Colonel Max Cerfberr.

13. General accounts of the integration of French Jews during the nineteenth century can be found in Esther Benbassa, *The Jews of France: A History from Antiquity to the Present*, trans. M. B. DeBevoise (Princeton: Princeton University Press, 1999), 96–133; and Paula Hyman, *The Jews of Modern France* (Berkeley: University of California Press, 1998), 53–90.

14. Jean Baubérot, *Histoire de la laïcité en France* (Paris: Presses universitaires de France, 2000), 28.

15. Halévy would later score another triumph with *Le juif errant* (1852), based on the novel by Eugène Sue.

16. Most sources, from the nineteenth century and today, refer to Pasta as Jewish. See, for example, Philip V. Bohlman, ed., *Jewish Musical Modernism, Old and New* (Chicago: University of Chicago Press, 2008), ix. However, Kenneth Stern's self-published biography, *Giuditta Pasta: A Life on the Lyric Stage* (Palm Springs: Operaphile, 2011), maintains that no actual evidence

of her Jewishness exists beyond her Old Testament name. Likewise, I have found no proof that Falcon was actually Jewish.

17. N. N., "Madame Iffla," *Les Archives Israélites* (1842): 235.

18. Mlle Judith was born Julie Bernat (1827–1912). *Mémoires de Madame Judith de la Comédie-Française et souvenirs sur ses contemporains. La vie d'une grande comédienne. Rédigés par Paul Gsell* (Paris: Jules Tallandier, 1911).

19. "Théâtre Français. *Esther*, tragédie de Racine. Mlle Rachel," *Le Corsaire*, March 2, 1839, 2. A satirical *petit journal, Le Corsaire* was the main organ of literary bohemia. It refers to Jews quite often in this period, mostly to mock what it sees as their unsavory financial activities.

20. According to Brownstein, "Rachel flaunted her Jewishness as something that looked good on her, therefore was quite good enough for anyone" (*Tragic Muse*, 190).

21. Ibid., 51.

22. Brownstein describes how it is thought that Rachel's parents gave most of their children names that combined the saints' calendar and the Old Testament: Sophie-Sarah, Élisa-Rachel, Adélaïde-Lia, and Mélanie-Dinah. All four women dropped the Christian part of their names when they went onstage. Rachel's younger siblings Raphaël and Rébecca only had Old Testament names (ibid., 49). Mlle Judith, born Julie, was given her stage name by Rachel's father. For short biographical sketches of many nineteenth-century French actors, see Henry Lyonnet, *Dictionnaire des comédiens français* (1904; Geneva: Slatkine, 1969).

23. On Jewish conversions in this period, see Thomas Kselman, "Turbulent Souls in Modern France: Jewish Conversion and the Terquem Affair," *Historical Reflections/Réflexions historiques* 32, no. 1 (Spring 2006): 83–104; and Ari Joskowicz, *The Modernity of Others: Jewish Anti-Catholicism in Germany and France* (Stanford: Stanford University Press, 2013), 156. Todd M. Endelman states that between 1814 and 1848, there were no more than 160 conversions from Judaism in Paris (by comparison, Berlin had about 65 a year). He attributes the relative unpopularity of conversion in France to the lack of benefit to be gained from it. Endelman, *Leaving the Jewish Fold: Conversion and Radical Assimilation in Modern Jewish History* (Princeton: Princeton University Press, 2015), 73.

24. An article in June 1841, for example, noted that after a performance in England, Rachel asked the Duke of Wellington to speak in favor of the Jews. In September of that year, the *Archives* noted that her presence at High Holiday services at the consistorial synagogue "made a strong impression" (585).

25. Janin, *Rachel*, 521.

26. Léon Poliakov, *Histoire de l'antisémitisme*, vol. 2 (Paris: Calmann-Lévy, 1981), 206–11.

27. One notice concerning the caprices of the Jewish star singers of the Opéra notes, "Mlle Falcon will return if she can, Mme Stoltz will go where she wants, Mlle Nathan will perform when it pleases the Synagogue." *Courrier des Théâtres*, February 7, 1839, 3. Another notice refers to the "blind cupidity" and "incendiary kikishness" (juiverie incendiaire) of Cerfberr, the Jewish director of the Opéra Comique. *Courrier des Théâtres*, February 1, 1840, 4.

28. Balzac's novel (published between 1838 and 1847) included very similar phonetic transcriptions of the Jewish banker Nucingen's accent.

29. *Courrier des Théâtres*, March 30, 1840, 4.

30. In his "Fifth Letter of a Humorist," subtitled "The Complicities of an Adjective," the Jewish writer Ben-Lévi (pseud. Godchaux Baruch Weil) urges the use of *Israélite* instead of *juif* because the dictionary of the Académie française defines *le juif* as "a man who practices usury." *Les Archives Israélites* (1842): 147.

NOTES TO CHAPTER 2

31. *Courrier des Théâtres*, February 15, 1840, 3.

32. *Courrier des Théâtres*, March 1, 1839, 3. The March 1 quotations that follow come from the same source.

33. *Courrier des Théâtres*, March 2, 1839, 3.

34. *Courrier des Théâtres*, March 3, 1839, 4.

35. In 1846, the *Journal des Débats* was the fifth-largest French newspaper, with an average circulation of 9305. Claude Bellanger, *Histoire générale de la presse française*, vol. 2, *1815–1871* (Paris: Presses Universitaires de France, 1969–76), 146.

36. Jules Janin, "Théâtre-Français. Esther—Mlle Rachel." *Journal des Débats* (March 4, 1839), 1. The quotations from Janin that follow come from the same source. Brownstein also discusses this review (*Tragic Muse*, 135).

37. Jonathan Freedman, *The Temple of Culture* (New York: Oxford University Press, 2000), 30.

38. Richard Wagner, *Prose Works*, trans. William Ashton Ellis (1850; London: Kegan Paul, 1907), 3:84. One of Wagner's prime targets was Meyerbeer.

39. Victor Hugo, preface to *Hernani* (Paris: Gallimard, 1995), 32.

40. Borel was also the author of an earlier and much more philosemitic text, in which he praised the beauty and purity of Jewish women. Pétrus Borel, "Dina, la belle juive," in *Champavert: Contes immoraux* (Paris: Eugène Renduel, 1833), 205–92.

41. Jonathan Frankel describes the Damascus Affair, in which Jews were accused of having killed an Italian monk and his servant, as a "cause célèbre" in *The Damascus Affair: "Ritual Murder," Politics, and the Jews in 1840* (Cambridge: Cambridge University Press, 1997), 1.

42. Pétrus Borel, "Marinette et Gros-Réné. M. Samson et Mlle Rachel. Phèdre en proie à la synagogue. Nouvelles larmes de Racine," *Le Journal du Commerce*, July 15, 1844, 2. The following quotations from his review come from this source.

43. Drumont gives an appreciative summary of Borel's review of Rachel and writes, "Poor unhappy man! The Jews, as is their custom, pursued him all his life, hunted him down like a wild beast." *La France juive: Essai d'histoire contemporaine, tome premier* (1886; Beirut, Lebanon: Éditions Charlemagne, 1994), 253.

44. Martine Lavaud, *Théophile Gautier: Militant du romantisme* (Paris: Honoré Champion, 2001), 489.

45. Théophile Gautier, "Mlle Rachel," *Le Moniteur Universel*, January 11, 1858.

46. Brownstein, *Tragic Muse*, 76.

47. Ibid., 77. In *How to Be French: Nationality in the Making since 1789*, trans. Catherine Porter (Durham: Duke University Press, 2008), Patrick Weil describes how children born of French parents abroad had French nationality if they established residency in France (25).

48. Janin, *Rachel et la tragédie*, 24.

49. In "L'enfant du miracle," Hoog describes how according to Janin, "Rachel's Jewish origins put her among the oriental princesses of the tragedies" (79).

50. As Freedman points out, Rachel played a similar role for Matthew Arnold and Henry James in the Anglo-American context (*Temple of Culture*, 49). Arnold devoted a series of sonnets to Rachel, viewing her as a synthesis of ancient and modern, Jewish and classical elements: "Sprung from the blood of Israel's scattered race . . . Tricked out with a Parisian speech and face . . . Imparting life renewed, old classic grace . . . While by her bedside Hebrew rites have place." *The Poetical Works of Matthew Arnold* (New York: Thomas Y. Crowell, 1897), 171. In *Culture and Anarchy* (1869), Arnold had described culture as a conflict between Hellenic and Hebraic elements.

51. Antoine de Latour, "Mlle Rachel," *Revue de Paris* 60 (December 1838): 271. The following quotations come from this source.

52. Lisa Moses Leff, *Sacred Bonds of Solidarity: The Rise of Jewish Internationalism in Nineteenth-Century France* (Stanford: Stanford University Press, 2006), 82. Leff describes the philosemitism of the 1830s and '40s in her chapter "Jewish Identities in the Age of Romanticism," 81–116.

53. Wendy Brown, *Regulating Aversion: Tolerance in the Age of Identity and Empire* (Princeton: Princeton University Press, 2006), 56.

54. M. A., "Théâtre-Français. Rentrée de Mlle Mars. Continuation des débuts de Mlle Rachel," *Le Courrier Français*, October 29, 1838, 1. The following quotations come from this source.

55. For example, a caricature by Marcellin published in *Le Journal pour Rire* on November 20, 1852, shows Rachel with a gigantic forehead riding atop a *caisse* containing her equally outsized receipts. Reproduced in Brownstein, *Tragic Muse*, 198.

56. The phrase comes from a lecture delivered on March 10, 1899, to the Ligue de la patrie française by Maurice Barrès, "La terre et les morts. Sur quelles réalités fonder la conscience française" (Paris: Bureau de la patrie française, 1899).

57. David A. Bell describes the creation of this new conception of the nation during the French Revolution in *The Cult of the Nation in France: Inventing Nationalism, 1680–1800* (Cambridge, MA: Harvard University Press, 2001).

58. Brownstein writes that Rachel's detractors claimed she was "nothing but a banner for reactionaries to mass behind" and describes how certain legitimist critics praised her rejuvenation of tragedy. Those on the left disapproved of the way she pronounced the word *peuple* in Corneille's *Cinna* but liked that she addressed King Louis-Philippe, who saw the play, as *monsieur* (*Tragic Muse*, 127–28).

59. Of course, Napoleon also adopted neoclassicism as the visual style of his un-democratic empire.

60. Janin, *Rachel et la tragédie*, 470.

61. Lerner writes that when declaiming the "Marseillaise," "the actress whom Sainte-Beuve had described ten years earlier as 'Mademoiselle Rachel, juive' had become 'notre Rachel,' dramatizing the Republican, patriotic spirit as no one else could. . . . Rachel was both a Jewish incarnation of the quintessentially French and a modern French Jewess." Citing Brownstein (*Tragic Muse*, 183–97), he also notes that coins and medallions representing the feminine symbol of the Republic, Marianne, were drawn in her image (279).

62. Rachel's correspondence, which I consulted at the Comédie-Française archive, contains several letters to Adolphe Crémieux.

63. Crémieux had gained his reputation by defending Jewish causes, such as outlawing the *more judaico*, the special oath required of Jews in court, and intervening in the Damascus Affair. See Leff, *Sacred Bonds of Solidarity*, 54–56.

64. Janin, *Rachel et la tragédie*, 471.

65. Brownstein describes her "series of Napoleonic amorous connections," including Napoleon's illegitimate son (by the Polish Countess Walewska) and Charles-Louis-Napoleon Bonaparte, the future Napoleon III (*Tragic Muse*, 15).

Chapter 3

1. Alice L. Conklin, *A Mission to Civilize: The Republican Idea of Empire in France and West Africa, 1895–1930* (Stanford: Stanford University Press, 1997), 10. Examples of this re-

NOTES TO CHAPTER 3

cent works that have informed my understanding of the relation of colonialism to republican ideology include Emmanuelle Saada, *Empire's Children: Race, Filiation, and Citizenship in the French Colonies*, trans. Arthur Goldhammer (Chicago: University of Chicago Press, 2012); Todd Shepard, *The Invention of Decolonization: The Algerian War and the Remaking of France* (Ithaca: Cornell University Press, 2006); and Gary Wilder, *The French Imperial Nation-State: Negritude and Colonial Humanism between the Two World Wars* (Chicago: University of Chicago Press, 2005).

2. Michael Shurkin examines France's treatment of Algerian Jews from the perspective of liberalism in "French Nation Building, Liberalism, and the Jews of Alsace and Algeria, 1815–1870" (PhD diss., Yale University, 2000). He argues that "Jews, more than any other minority, tested nineteenth-century France's response to difference" and that France's illiberal policies in Algeria were actually consistent with the way liberalism was articulated as an ideology in the metropole (5–6).

3. Joshua Schreier, *Arabs of the Jewish Faith: The Civilizing Mission in Colonial Algeria* (New Brunswick: Rutgers University Press, 2010), 1–2.

4. In *Sacred Bonds of Solidarity: The Rise of Jewish Internationalism in Nineteenth-Century France* (Stanford: Stanford University Press, 2006), Lisa Moses Leff argues that French Jewish support for the "civilizing mission" in the colonies "formed an integral part of the project of securing French Jewish rights in France" (155).

5. Schreier, *Arabs of the Jewish Faith*, 11.

6. Algeria had roughly 15,000 to 17,000 Jews at the time of the French invasion in 1830. France had 70,000 Jews in 1831 and 85,910 in 1845. On French population statistics, see Phyllis Cohen Albert, *The Modernization of French Jewry: Consistory and Community in the Nineteenth Century* (Hanover: Brandeis University Press, 1977), 4. On Algerian population statistics, see Schreier, *Arabs of the Jewish Faith*, 25.

7. Christine Piette estimates that there were roughly 9,000 Jews in Paris in 1840 out of a total population of 900,000 to 1 million. Piette, *Les juifs de Paris (1808–1840): La marche vers l'assimilation* (Québec: Les Presses de l'Université Laval, 1983), 50. Albert estimates the percentage of Jews in Paris in the period 1836–41 as 0.88 percent (*The Modernization of French Jewry*, 25).

8. Saada, *Empire's Children*, 100. Christopher L. Miller surveys the opinions and attitudes of French writers toward slavery in *The French Atlantic Triangle: Literature and Culture of the Slave Trade* (Durham: Duke University Press, 2008).

9. Schreier, *Arabs of the Jewish Faith*, 2.

10. Saada, *Empire's Children*, 100.

11. Ibid., 100–101.

12. Schreier, *Arabs of the Jewish Faith*, 1–2.

13. Patrick Weil, *How to Be French: Nationality in the Making since 1789*, trans. Catherine Porter (Durham: Duke University Press, 2008), 209–10. Also see Judith Surkis, "Propriété, polygamie et statut personnel en Algérie coloniale, 1830–1873," *Revue d'Histoire du XIXe Siècle* 41 (2010): 27–48; and Schreier, *Arabs of the Jewish Faith*, 2–3, 143–47.

14. Aron Rodrigue, *French Jews, Turkish Jews: The Alliance Israélite Universelle and the Politics of Jewish Schooling in Turkey, 1860–1925* (Bloomington: Indiana University Press, 1990), 8.

15. Aron Rodrigue describes how French Jews considered their Algerian coreligionists not as "distinctively different or 'other,' but essentially as extension of 'self.'" Rodrigue, "Comment" to Eli Bar-Chen, "Two Communities with a Sense of Mission: The Alliance Israélite Universelle and the Hilfsverein der deutschen Juden," in *Jewish Emancipation Reconsidered: The French and*

German Models, ed. Michael Brenner, Vicki Caron, and Uri R. Kaufmann, (London: Leo Baeck Institute, 2003), 123.

16. Anonymous letter, dated May 31, 1840, in *Les Archives Israélites* (1840): 269.

17. Anonymous, "Lettre sur l'état des juifs d'Algerie et sur les moyens de les tirer de l'abjection dans laquelle ils sont tombés," in ibid., 476.

18. Anonymous, "Lettre sur l'état," 537. Schreier discusses this letter (*Arabs of the Jewish Faith*, 124).

19. These terms were used in an 1851 report on the Algerian Jews by the French rabbi Michel-Aaron Weill. Cited in Pierre Birnbaum, "French Jews and the 'Regeneration' of Algerian Jewry," in *Jews and the State: Dangerous Alliances and the Perils of Privilege*, ed. Ezra Mendelsohn (New York: Oxford University Press, 2003), 90. Schreier also discusses this letter (*Arabs of the Jewish Faith*, 140–41).

20. Schreier, *Arabs of the Jewish Faith*, 45.

21. Birnbaum calls the Altaras and Cohen report a "key text" in the history of Jewish emancipation (88). Schreier (*Arabs of the Jewish Faith*) also devotes significant attention to it.

22. Jacques-Isaac Altaras and Joseph Cohen, "Rapport sur l'état moral et politique des Israélites de l'Algérie et des moyens de l'améliorer," in *Les juifs d'Algérie et la France (1830–1855)*, ed. Simon Schwarzfuchs (Jerusalem: Institut Ben-Zvi, 1981), 68. Subsequent references appear in the text.

23. Rodrigue writes that "French Jewry saw in Algerian Jewry not only a poor, traditional, 'backward' Jewish community, but it saw itself as it had existed a generation or two before" ("*Comment*," 124).

24. Schreier, *Arabs of the Jewish Faith*, 3.

25. Ibid., 54.

26. Sarah Abrevaya Stein, *Saharan Jews and the Fate of French Algeria* (Chicago: University of Chicago Press, 2014), xiv.

27. According to Gautier's account, the more experienced dramatist Parfait constructed the outline of the play, while Gautier himself wrote the dialogue. Charles Lovenjoul, *Histoire des oeuvres de Théophile Gautier* (Paris: Charpentier, 1887), 1:351.

28. Claudine Lacoste-Veysseyre, ed., *Théophile Gautier: Correspondance générale, 1846–48* (Geneva: Droz, 1988), 121. Lovenjoul reproduces Gautier's feuilleton describing the origins of the play from *La Presse*, November 16, 1846 (*Histoire* 1:351).

29. Jules Janin, "La semaine dramatique," *Journal des Débats*, November 16, 1846. Not all critics were hostile. The review in *L'Artiste* defended Gautier (November 22, 1846, 46–47).

30. R., "Théâtres, *La Juive de Constantine*, drame en cinq actes et six tableaux de M. Théophile Gautier," *Le Constitutionnel*, November 16, 1846.

31. French forces captured Constantine in 1837.

32. As many critics at the time noted, despite Gautier's effort to endow the play with the local color he absorbed during his trip to Algeria the previous year, this and other plot elements seem oddly reminiscent of Shakespeare's *Romeo and Juliet*.

33. Théophile Gautier and Noël Parfait, "La Juive de Constantine, drame anecdotique en cinq actes et six tableaux," *Magasin théâtral* (Paris: Marchant, 1846), 10. Subsequent references appear in the text.

34. These include the enormously popular Scribe and Halévy opera *La juive* of 1835, as well as Balzac's novel *La Cousine Bette*, which was being serialized in *Le Constitutionnel* during the run of Gautier's play.

35. The Jewish writer Eugénie Foa's short story "La Kalissa" (1833) ends with a woman being placed in a sack and tossed into the sea. On Foa, see Maurice Samuels, *Inventing the Israelite: Jewish Fiction in Nineteenth-Century France* (Stanford: Stanford University Press, 2010), 37–73.

36. According to Altaras and Cohen, French officers seek out Algerian Jewish women for "their remarkable beauty" ("Rapport," 100).

37. See the discussion of Gautier's antisemitic writings in chapter 2.

38. "*La Juive de Constantine*, drame en six actes, par Théophile Gautier," *Les Archives Israélites* (1846): 769–76. The review is signed David-Wolf-Bénédic-Lazares-Sohn, an obvious pseudonym. It seems to be the work of Ben-Lévi (pseud. Godchaux Weil), whose frequent contributions to the journal in the 1840s employ a similar playful style and treat similar subjects. On Ben-Lévi, see Samuels, *Inventing the Israelite*, 74–111.

39. In reality, a mezuzah contains not extracts from the Talmud but rather short passages from the Bible's Book of Deuteronomy, including the *Shema Yisrael* prayer.

40. Gautier describes how the inspiration came from a story he heard, during his trip to Constantine, about Jewish girls being mourned by their families after marrying Christians, which struck him as a perfect subject for a melodrama. Cited in Lovenjoul, *Histoire des oeuvres de Gautier*, 349.

41. Schreier, *Arabs of the Jewish Faith*, 2.

42. Ibid., 51–55.

43. This assimilation involved a strong cultural component as well: new schools for Jewish children were founded that made French the primary language of instruction. On the Alliance Israélite schools, see Rodrigue, *French Jews, Turkish Jews*.

44. Only 142 out of the 33,000 Jews in Algeria were naturalized between 1865 and 1870. By 1878, only 435 Muslims out of more than 3 million had accepted citizenship. Schreier, *Arabs of the Jewish Faith*, 173.

45. Not all Algerian Jews welcomed this transformation of their status: one Algerian Jew was brought to trial for insisting on his rights to take a second wife, claiming he had done so before the law of 1870 officially denied him the right to do so. Ibid., 143.

46. Ibid., 149.

47. The parallel between Léa's emergence from her tomb and the resurrection of Christ reinforces the play's Christian overtones.

48. In her brief discussion of the play, Nicole Savy likewise argues that it places "Modern Jews . . . on the side of the West, which the Crémieux Decreet will later make official." *Les juifs des romantiques* (Paris: Belin, 2010), 100.

49. Cited in Schreier, *Arabs of the Jewish Faith*, 171.

50. Leff, *Sacred Bonds of Solidarity*, 81–83.

51. Leff writes that the concept of secularism in mid-nineteenth-century France championed by Crémieux and other Restoration liberals "was one that considered Judaism, Protestantism, and Catholicism equally dignified, equally universalist moral codes appropriate for civic education and for public expressions of religious sentiment, and thus equally worthy of state support" (ibid., 40).

52. In "Jewish Solidarity in Nineteenth-Century France: The Evolution of a Concept," *Journal of Modern History* 74 (March 2002), Lisa Moses Leff argues that for nineteenth-century French Jews, "adopting a universalist ideology did not erase their minority identity; instead, it provided a new language for its expression" (61).

Chapter 4

1. Accounts in English of the Dreyfus Affair include Jean-Denis Bredin, *The Affair: The Case of Alfred Dreyfus*, trans. Jeffrey Mehlman (New York: George Braziller, 1986); and Ruth Harris, *Dreyfus: Politics, Emotion, and the Scandal of the Century* (New York: Henry Holt, 2010).

2. Maurice Barrès, *Scènes et doctrines du nationalisme* (Paris: F. Juven), 1:152. Cited in Zeev Sternhell, *Maurice Barrès et le nationalisme français* (Paris: Éditions Complexe, 1972), 264.

3. Richard B. Grant, "The Jewish Question in Zola's *L'Argent*," *PMLA* 70, no. 5 (December 1955): 955–67.

4. Numerous other critics besides Grant have examined the "Jewish Question" in Zola's oeuvre. See, for example, Alain Pagès, "Émile Zola contre l'antisémitisme: Réflexions sur la question juive," in, *Les intellectuels face à l'affaire Dreyfus alors et aujourd'hui*, ed. Roselyne Koren and Dan Michman (Paris: L'Harmattan, 1998), 63–74. More recently, Dorian Bell analyzes the imperial subtext in Zola's writing about Jews, including *L'argent* and *Vérité*, in "Beyond the Bourse: Zola, Empire, and the Jews," *Romanic Review* 102, nos. 3–4 (January 2013), 485–501.

5. Emily Apter notes that in the mid-nineteenth century, the term "La Haute Banque" "designated roughly twenty affiliated banking firms directed by Jewish (and some Protestant) financiers." She also discusses the "economic xenophobia" of Zola's *L'argent* (396–401). Apter, "Speculation and Economic Xenophobia as Literary World Systems: The Nineteenth-Century Business Novel," in *French Global: A New Approach to Literary History*, ed. Christie McDonald and Susan Rubin Suleiman (New York: Columbia University Press, 2010), 394.

6. See notes by Henri Mitterand in his edition of Émile Zola, *L'argent* (Paris: Gallimard Folio, 1980), 519. All references to *L'argent* come from this edition and are cited in the text.

7. Robert Wistrich, *Socialism and the Jews: The Dilemmas of Assimilation in Germany and Austria-Hungary* (New York: Oxford University Press, 1985), 23.

8. Karl Marx, "On the Jewish Question," in *Karl Marx: Early Writings*, trans. and ed. T. B. Bottomore (New York: McGraw-Hill, 1964), 12–63.

9. On the antisemitism of Fourier and his disciples, see Léon Poliakov, *Histoire de l'antisémitisme* (Paris: Calmann-Lévy, 1981), 2:203–5.

10. Alphonse Toussenel, *Les juifs rois de l'époque: Histoire de la féodalité financière* (Paris: L'École sociétaire, 1845).

11. Jacob Katz, *From Prejudice to Destruction: Anti-Semitism, 1700–1933* (Cambridge: Harvard University Press, 1980), 127.

12. On racist ideology in the work of Renan and others, see Poliakov, *Histoire de l'antisémitisme*, 163–71.

13. Published by Flammarion, Drumont's two-volume denunciation of the Jewish presence in French political and cultural life sold 65,000 copies in the first year and roughly 100,000 copies by 1914. Elisabeth Parinet, *La librairie Flammarion, 1875–1914* (Paris: Imec, 1992), 256.

14. Grant cites a letter by Alphonse Daudet, who had helped get *La France juive* published at the prestigious house of Flammarion, describing Zola's criticism of Drumont's antisemitic best seller ("The Jewish Question," 955). Apter details how Zola "drew on the whole paranoid association of Jews and money that would become the stock-in-trade of anti-Dreyfus propagandists," including Drumont ("Speculation and Economic Xenophobia," 396).

15. Eugène Bontoux, a former employee of the Rothschilds, founded the bank in 1878. André Wurmser describes the Union Générale scandal as the model for *L'argent* in his introduction to Mitterand's edition of the novel (10).

16. Note that Zola had to set the novel in this earlier period because his Rougon-Macquart series was supposed to take place entirely during the Second Empire (1852–70).

17. Grant, "The Jewish Question," 955.

18. Ibid., 961.

19. Émile Zola, "Procès-verbal," in *L'Affaire Dreyfus: La vérité en marche* (Paris: Flammarion, 1994), 85.

20. Émile Zola, "Lettre au Président de la République," in ibid., 122.

21. Émile Zola, "Pour les juifs," in ibid., 57. Subsequent references appear in the text.

22. On the political uses of antisemitism in this period, see Philip Nord, *Paris Shopkeepers and the Politics of Resentment* (Princeton: Princeton University Press, 1986).

23. Katz, *From Prejudice to Destruction*, 300.

24. Bell shows how Zola also casts antisemitism as an obstacle to republican universalism's colonial endeavors ("Beyond the Bourse," 496).

25. Émile Zola, *Truth*, trans. Ernest A. Vizetelly (Amherst, NY: Prometheus Books, 2002), 77. Subsequent references appear in the text.

26. On the figure of the Jewish pariah in Lazare and Péguy, see Sarah Hammerschlag, *The Figural Jew: Politics and Identity in Postwar French Thought* (Chicago: University of Chicago Press, 2010). Alain Finkielkraut describes Péguy's significance in *Le mécontemporain* (Paris: Gallimard, 1991).

27. Although it has long been said that Hezl's Zionist awakening was inspired by the Dreyfus Affair, which he covered as a reporter for an Austrian newspaper, scholars have recently argued that his notes and journals do not indicate he was particularly preoccupied by the Affair. See Shlomo Avineri, *Herzl's Vision: Theodor Herzl and the Foundation of the Jewish State*, trans. Haim Watzman (New York: Blue Bridge, 2013).

28. On Lazare and Zionism, see Nelly Wilson, *Bernard Lazare* (Paris: Albin Michel, 1985).

29. This interview with Zola by Nahum Sloschtsch, who translated several of Zola's novels into Hebrew, appeared under the title "Emile Zola. On Zionism," in German in the *Oesterreichische Wochenschrift*, February 16, 1900. I cite from Nelly Wilson's French translation in "Propos de Zola sur le sionisme," *Cahiers Naturalistes* 40 (1970): 152–53.

30. Jean Baubérot, *La laïcité falsifiée* (Paris: La Découverte, 2014), 16.

Chapter 5

1. This chapter reworks arguments originally made in my article "Renoir's *La Grande Illusion* and the 'Jewish Question,'" *Historical Reflections/Réflexions Historiques* 32, no. 1 (Spring 2006): 165–92.

2. Paula Hyman, *The Jews of Modern France* (Berkeley: University of California Press, 1998), 137.

3. Pierre Birnbaum describes how right-wing parties in the interwar period identified Léon Blum, and Jews more generally, with the universalist values of the Third Republic, including and especially *laïcité*. *Un mythe politique: La 'république juive' de Léon Blum à Pierre Mendès-France* (Paris: Fayard, 1988), especially 350–56.

4. Maurice Barrès, *La terre et les morts: Sur quelles réalités fonder la conscience française* (Paris: Bureau de la patrie française, 1899). Originally given as a lecture to the Ligue de la patrie française, March 10, 1899.

5. "The cult for the particular and the scorn for the universal is a reversal of values quite generally characteristic of the teaching of the modern 'clerks,' who proclaim them in a far higher

sphere of thought than politics." Benda's target here is the philosophy of Henri Bergson, who happened to be Jewish. Julien Benda, *The Treason of the Intellectuals*, trans. Richard Aldington (New Brunswick, NJ: Transaction Publishers, 2014), 60.

6. Jean Renoir, *Ma vie et mes films* (Paris: Flammarion, 1974), 113.

7. See Jean Barreyre's review in *Le Jour*, June 10, 1937.

8. See Jean Fayard's review in *Le Candide*, June 17, 1937, and Pierre Bonnel's review in *Ce Soir*, June 12, 1937.

9. *Les Nouvelles Littéraires*, June 1, 1937.

10. *L'Écran Français*, September 4, 1946.

11. According to Bazin, the love scenes between Maréchal and the German woman, Elsa, were cut along with the references to Rosenthal's "race" for the 1946 version. André Bazin, *Jean Renoir*, ed. François Truffaut, trans. W. W. Halsey II and William H. Simon (New York: Simon & Schuster, 1971), 60.

12. *Libération*, September 7, 1946. The producers of *La grande illusion* were Frank Rollmer and Albert Pinkevitch. In *Jean Renoir: The French Films, 1924–1939* (Harvard University Press, 1980), Alexander Sesonske quotes Renoir as saying that Pinkevitch made suggestions about "how a Jew would act and what he would say in that situation" during filming (285).

13. Maurice Bardèche and Robert Brasillach, *Histoire du cinéma* (Paris: Denoël, 1943), 346. Alice Kaplan discusses their assessment of *La grande illusion* in *Reproductions of Banality: Fascism, Literature, and French Intellectual Life* (Minneapolis: University of Minnesota Press, 1986), 145.

14. *Le Canard Enchaîné*, August 10, 1958.

15. *Combat*, October 18, 1958.

16. Renoir and his coscriptwriter, Charles Spaak, were able to reconstruct the film for its re-release in 1958 based on a negative that had been seized by the Germans during the occupation and recovered in Munich by the Americans after the war.

17. *Radio Cinéma Télévision*, November 2, 1958. This article was collected, along with many of Bazin's other writings on Renoir, for the volume edited by Truffaut (*Jean Renoir*) cited above.

18. The best-known examples include the four films by the director André Hugon, about a family of Jewish merchants named Lévy, made between 1930 and 1936. See Rémy Pithon, "Le juif à l'écran en France vers la fin des années trente," *Vingtième Siècle* 18 (1988): 89–99.

19. Pithon quotes Renoir's reponse to a questionnaire in *Pour Vous*, November 1, 1939, calling attention to all the "producers with names ending in -ich and in -zy" [producteurs en -ich ou en -zy] who dominated the Parisian cinema world (92–93).

20. After he fled to Hollywood, Dalio would ironically be cast as a stereotypical Frenchman in such films as *Casablanca*, Darryl Zanuck's *Wilson* (in which he played Georges Clemenceau), *On the Riviera*, and *Sabrina*.

21. Rémy Pithon, "L'image du juif dans le cinéma francais des années trente," in *Cinéma et judéité*, ed. Annie Goldmann and Guy Hennebelle (Paris: Cerf, 1986), 140.

22. Pithon, "L'image du juif," 141.

23. The translations of the film's dialogue are my own.

24. Scenes of eating often serve an important function in Renoir's films. See Raphaëlle Moine, "Nourritures de Jean Renoir," in *Nouvelles approches de l'oeuvre de Jean Renoir*, ed. Frank Curot (Montpellier: Université Paul Valéry, 1996), 134. I would note that it is during the servant's dinner scene in *La règle du jeu* that the marquis's Jewish origins are revealed.

25. Hyman describes how the role of Jewish bankers, and especially that of the Rothschilds,

was "greatly inflated by antisemitic opinion, which saw the development of finance and industrial capitalism as a Jewish plot" (*The Jews of Modern France*, 93).

26. Certain (paranoid?) ears might hear in the seemingly unmotivated *sportif* (sportsman) a rhymed displacement for the repressed word *juif* (Jew).

27. If the Polish origins of the father identify Rosenthal with Jewish stereotype, the reference to the Danish mother is more difficult to parse. Given the small number of Danish Jews, it may suggest that the character is only half-Jewish.

28. Marcel Dalio, *Mes années folles*, récit recueilli par Jean-Pierre Lucovich (Paris: Jean-Claude Lattès, 1976), 127–29.

29. Cited in ibid., 131–32.

30. Cited in ibid., 132.

31. Cited in ibid.

32. Sander Gilman, *The Jew's Body* (New York: Routledge, 1991), 39.

33. Ibid., 219.

34. Ibid., 39.

35. Ibid., 54–57. Also see Jan Goldstein, "The Wandering Jew and the Problem of Psychiatric Antisemitism in Fin-de-Siècle France," *Journal of Contemporary History* 20 (1985): 541. Goldstein describes how one of Charcot's disciples, Meige, would draw on case studies of a number of Jewish patients who had fled to France from Eastern Europe, often on foot, to diagnose what he referred to as a "Jewish Wandering Disease."

36. Gilman writes, "Central to the definition of the Jew—here to be understood always as the 'male' Jew—is the image of the male Jew's circumcised penis as impaired, damaged, or incomplete and therefore threatening" (*The Jew's Body*, 96).

37. Rosenthal teaches Maréchal to say that Lotte (Elsa's daughter) has blue eyes in German. Along with "strikt verboten," this mispronounced phrase forms the extent of the Frenchman's German vocabulary. The phrase "Lotte hat blaue Augen," repeated as a term of endearment between the lovers, might also be seen to underline the "racial" difference between them and the brown-eyed Rosenthal.

38. See "An Early Treatment of Grand Illusion" in the appendix to Bazin's *Jean Renoir*, 181.

39. Linda Nochlin, "Degas and the Dreyfus Affair: A Portrait of the Artist as Anti-Semite," in *The Dreyfus Affair: Art, Truth, Justice*, ed. Norman L. Kleeblatt (Berkeley: University of California Press, 1987), 96–116. On the Jewish nose, also see Gilman, *The Jew's Body*, chapter 7.

40. Pithon makes a similar point: "Dalio is often filmed differently from the other characters." He also suggests that Dalio was typecast "based on his silhouette" (*Le juif à l'écran*, 97).

41. For François Garçon, this use of cliché is antisemitic and may betray a hidden or repressed antisemitism in Renoir himself. See Garçon, *De Blum à Pétain: Cinéma et société française (1936–1944)* (Paris: Cerf, 1984).

42. According to Daniel Serceau, this moment counters the effect of the Jew's negative associations with wealth. "A-t-on le droit de montrer un banquier juif au cinema?" in *Cinéma et judéité*, ed. Annie Goldmann and Guy Hennebelle (Paris: Cerf, 1986), 143.

43. There were high-ranking Jewish officers in the French army as early as the July Monarchy. During the Third Republic, there were twenty-five Jewish generals. Pierre Birnbaum, *The Jews of the Republic: A Political History of State Jews in France from Gambetta to Vichy*, trans. Jane Marie Todd (Stanford: Stanford University Press, 1996), 45–53. Also see Hyman, *The Jews of Modern France*, 94.

44. While *tu* is the familiar form of address, *t'* is a contraction used only in popular speech.

45. Dalio, *Mes années folles*, 91.

46. Barrès would modify his views somewhat as a result of Jewish patriotism in the First World War. In *Les diverses familles spirituelles de la France* (1917), he declared that "many Israelites, settled among us for generations, and centuries, are natural members of the national body." Cited in Paula Hyman, *From Dreyfus to Vichy: The Remaking of French Jewry, 1906–1939* (New York: Columbia University Press, 1979), 50. One can still wonder whether a recent immigrant such as Rosenthal, in spite of his patriotism, would be included in Barrès's "national body."

47. Serceau, "A-t-on le droit de montrer un banquier juif au cinéma?" 143.

48. Among many examples of this critical position, see the chapter entitled "Viewers Make Meaning" in Marita Sturken and Lisa Cartwright, *Practices of Looking: An Introduction to Visual Culture* (Oxford: Oxford University Press, 2001).

49. Tom Gunning has shown how the technologies of photography and cinema functioned as a means of fixing identity by tying it to a particular body and were used by the police as a means of tracking criminals. See Tom Gunning, "Tracing the Individual Body: Photography, Detectives, and Early Cinema," in *Cinema and the Invention of Modern Life*, ed. Leo Charney and Vanessa Schwartz (Berkeley: University of California Press, 1995), 15–45.

50. In French, he says he was "seul à l'affiche." Dalio, *Mes années folles*, 146–48.

Chapter 6

1. A more literal translation of the title would be "*Reflections on the Jewish Question*," but the English edition bears the title *Anti-Semite and Jew*.

2. Sartre published the first part of the text, "Portrait of the Antisemite," in *Les Temps Modernes* in December 1945, shortly after the start of that journal. The entire text was published by Paul Morihien in November 1946. New editions were published by Gallimard in 1954, 1961, and 1986. See Michel Rybalka, "Publication and Reception of *Anti-Semite and Jew*," *October* 87 (Winter 1999): 167.

3. Lanzmann interview in *Les Temps Modernes* (April 1982): 1710. Quoted (and translated) in Susan Rubin Suleiman, "The Jew in Jean-Paul Sartre's *Réflexions sur la question juive*: An Exercise in Historical Reading," in *The Jew in the Text*, ed. Linda Nochlin and Tamar Garb (New York: Thames & Hudson, 1995), 201. Pierre Vidal-Naquet also recalls feeling profound admiration for Sartre's text in "Sartre et la question juive: Réflexions d'un lecteur de 1946," in *Sartre et les juifs*, ed. Ingrid Galster (Paris: La Découverte, 2005), 49.

4. Robert Misrahi, "Sartre et les juifs: Un bienheureux malentendu," in Galster, *Sartre et les juifs*, 64.

5. Seth L. Wolitz describes Sartre's "groundbreaking accomplishment" (122) in "Imagining the Jew in France: From 1945 to the Present," *Yale French Studies* 85 (1994): 119–34. Max Silverman also discusses the significance of Sartre's analysis of the antisemite and of its reception in "'Killing Me Softly': Racial Ambivalence in Jean-Paul Sartre's *Réflexions sur la question juive*," in *Antisemitism and Philosemitism in the Twentieth and Twenty-First Centuries: Representing Jews, Jewishness, and Modern Culture*, ed. Phyllis Lassner and Lara Trubowitz (Newark: University of Delaware Press, 2008), 49. In *Affective Genealogies: Psychoanalysis, Postmodernism, and the "Jewish Question" after Auschwitz* (Lincoln: University of Nebraska Press, 1997), Elizabeth J. Bellamy sees Sartre's text doing for France what Adorno and Horkheimer's *Dialectic of Enlightenment* from the same period did for Germany—namely showing the roots of antisemitism within the nation's philosophical heritage.

6. "The most striking feature of Sartre's fight resides less in his victory than in the new weapons he deploys. They are wholly new. Anti-Semitism is attacked with existentialist arguments. . . . Sartre's general philosophy is nothing but an attempt to think mankind in its spiritual being, its historical, economical, and social situation, without treating it as a mere object for thought. This philosophy recognizes that the mind is tied by commitments that are not structured as knowledge. Commitments that are not thoughts—that's existentialism!" Emmanuel Levinas, "Existentialism and Anti-Semitism," trans. Denis Hollier and Rosalind Krauss, *October* 87 (Winter 1999): 28. This text by Levinas constitutes his introduction to Sartre's lecture published in the June 1947 issue of *Les Cahiers de L'Alliance*, the journal of the Alliance israélite universelle.

7. Along with Suleiman's essay cited above, Pierre Birnbaum offers perhaps the most harsh condemnation of the third section of *Réflexions* in "Sorry Afterthoughts on *Anti-Semite and Jew*," *October* 87 (Winter 1999):, 89–106.

8. In *The Figural Jew: Politics and Identity in Postwar French Thought*, Sarah Hammerschlag makes a similar point: "The argument that Sartre critiques here is essentially the argument of the Dreyfusards, as exemplified by Zola's *J'accuse*" (83).

9. Hammerschlag describes Sartre's decisive contribution to the "revalorization of the figure of the rootless Jew in post-1945 France" (ibid., 73). She points to Bernard Lazare and Charles Péguy, both of whom came to affirm the distinctive nature of Jewish difference during the Affair, as precursors (54–67).

10. Paula Hyman, *The Jews of Modern France* (Berkeley: University of California Press), 161.

11. On the "purge" of intellectuals, see Alice Kaplan, *The Collaborator: The Trial and Execution of Robert Brasillach* (Chicago: University of Chicago Press, 2000). Also see Philip Watts, *Allegories of the Purge: How Literature Responded to the Postwar Trials of Writers and Intellectuals in France* (Stanford: Stanford University Press, 1998).

12. See Robert O. Paxton, *Vichy France: Old Guard and New Order, 1940–1944* (New York: Knopf, 1972) and Paxton and Michael Marrus, *Vichy France and the Jews* (New York: Basic Books, 1981).

13. Henry Rousso, *Le syndrome de Vichy, 1944–198–* (Paris: Seuil, 1987).

14. Alice Kaplan, *Reproductions of Banality: Fascism, Literature, and French Intellectual Life* (Minneapolis: University of Minnesota Press, 1986); David Carroll, *French Literary Fascism: Nationalism, Anti-Semitism, and the Ideology of Culture* (Princeton: Princeton University Press, 1994).

15. Barrès gave a famous lecture to the antisemitic Ligue de la patrie française entitled "La terre et les morts" on March 10, 1899 (see note 4 to chapter 5 above). Zeev Sternhell discusses the ideology of French fascism in *Neither Right nor Left: Fascist Ideology in France* (Berkeley: University of California Press, 1986).

16. "Never were we more free than under the German occupation," Sartre wrote in *La république du silence*. "Each of our acts had the weight of commitment [engagement]." Cited in Jonathan Judaken, *Jean-Paul Sartre and the Jewish Question: Anti-Antisemitism and the Politics of the French Intellectual* (Lincoln: University of Nebraska Press, 2006), 113. Judaken provides a comprehensive discussion of Sartre's position on Jewish subjects throughout his career.

17. Ingrid Galster, "Sartre et la 'question juive': Réflexions au-delà d'un controverse," *Commentaire* 89 (Spring 2000), 141–47. Also see Galster, *Sartre, Vichy et les intellectuels* (Paris: L'Harmattan, 2001), 79–94. On the Condorcet affair, see Judaken, *Jean-Paul Sartre and the Jewish Question*, 49–51; and Maurice Samuels, "J'accuse Sartre," *Lingua Franca* 10, no. 7 (October 2000): 8–9.

18. Judaken discusses the "gray zone" (*Jean-Paul Sartre and the Jewish Question*, 51) of Sartre's politics and publishing during the occupation (49–105).

19. In *Le mythe du grand silence* (Paris: Fayard, 2012), François Azouvi shows that in fact the Jewish genocide received a great deal of attention in postwar France.

20. Jean-Paul Sartre, *Anti-Semite and Jew*, trans. George J. Becker (New York: Schocken Books, 1965), 71. Subsequent references appear in the text. Azouvi quotes this line from Sartre and argues that "it is as if the very character of the event had produced by anticipation the sentiment of forgetting into which, it was believed, it would inevitably fall" (*Le mythe du grand silence*, 10).

21. The essay is "La république du silence," which appeared on the front page of the inaugural issue of *Les Lettres Françaises*, September 9, 1944, 1. Suleiman discusses this reference in "Rereading Rereading: Further Reflections on Sartre's Réflexions," *October* 87 (Winter 1999): 135.

22. A version of the opposition between analytic and syncretic propositions stretches back to Kant's *Critique of Pure Reason* (1781).

23. On Barrès and the philosophy of rootedness, see Hammerschlag, *The Figural Jew*, 31–41.

24. Maurice Barrès, *Scènes et doctrines du nationalisme* (Paris: F. Juven), 1:152. Cited in Zeev Sternhell, *Maurice Barrès et le nationalisme français* (Paris: Éditions Complexe, 1972), 264.

25. Judaken notes that the analysis of antisemitism "reconstitutes the basic categories of Sartre's *Being and Nothingness*: antisemitism is an inauthentic response to man's situation in the world and being-with-others" (*Jean-Paul Sartre and the Jewish Question*, 132). Hammerschlag also reads *Réflexions* in the light of Sartre's philosophical treatise (*The Figural Jew*, 80–92).

26. Denis Hollier points out that Sartre is not entirely wrong in saying that the Jewish sense of the recent past (the diasporic period) is weak. Citing Yosef Yerushalmi's *Zakhor*, Hollier notes that the Talmudic tradition tends to see the postdiasporic era as empty time, unworthy of historiography. Hollier, "Mosaic: Terminable and Interminable" *October* 87 (Winter 1999): 157. On the rise of modern Jewish historiography, see Yerushalmi, *Zakhor: Jewish History and Jewish Memory* (Seattle: University of Washington Press, 1982), 86; and Maurice Samuels, *Inventing the Israelite: Jewish Fiction in Nineteenth-Century France* (Stanford: Stanford University Press, 2010), 217–21.

27. Judaken, *Jean-Paul Sartre and the Jewish Question*, 243.

28. Judaken writes that what was "most shocking" in the interviews Sartre gave with Benny Lévy, published as *Hope Now* (1980), "was how the infamous atheist stressed the importance to non-Jews like himself of the Jewish concept of the coming of the Messiah" (ibid., 227).

29. "Yet, his very use of the term 'Jewish race' in a pseudo-scientific sense, and his association of it with physical characteristics that 'can be recognized by any Frenchman,' . . . strike me as troubling." Suleiman, "The Jew," 211.

30. Ibid., 210–11.

31. Suleiman, "Rereading Rereading," 132.

32. Founded in 1898 by Ludovic Trarieux to defend Dreyfus and oppose antisemitism, the league was dissolved by Vichy and reconstituted clandestinely by a group that included René Cassin. For two recent historical accounts of the discourse of human rights in the aftermath of World War II, see Jay Winter, *René Cassin and Human Rights: From the Great War to the Universal Declaration* (Cambridge: Cambridge University Press, 2013); and Samuel Moyn, *The Last Utopia: Human Rights in History* (Cambridge: Harvard University Press, 2012).

33. Émile Zola, *Truth*, trans. Ernest A. Vizetelly (Amherst, NY: Prometheus Books, 2002), 542.

34. Often attributed to Ferdinand August Bebel (1840–1913), the saying was in fact common

in German Social Democratic circles in the 1890s. Richard J. Evans, *The Coming of the Third Reich* (New York: Penguin, 2005), 496.

35. Sartre's friend from the École normale supérieure, Raymond Aron, offers a condemnation of the romance of French intellectuals with Communism in *L'Opium des intellectuels* (Paris: Calmann-Lévy, 1955). Tony Judt discusses Sartre's failure to protest Communist antisemitism, and the failure of intellectuals on the French left to recognize the definiciencies of the Communist system more generally, in *Past Imperfect: French Intellectuals, 1944–1956* (Berkeley: University of California Press, 1992), 184–86.

36. Silverman analyzes this dynamic in Sartre's text: "Emancipation in the form of 'authenticity' (choosing one's individual identity freely rather than reacting, in bad faith, to imposed images) involves, ultimately, transcendence of difference as a prerequisite for a (nondifferentiated) classless society" ("'Killing Me Softly,'" 56).

37. Zola, *Truth*, 83, 568.

38. As Silverman likewise puts it: "Despite his espousal of the cause of oppressed groups in their struggle against Western universalism, Sartre demonstrates, in *Réflexions*, that he is, fundamentally, a universalist himself" ("'Killing Me Softly,'" 55).

39. Naomi Schor, "Anti-Semitism, Jews, and the Universal," *October* 87 (Winter 1999): 113.

40. Denis Hollier defends Sartre on the charge of backsliding on the question of assimilation by arguing that when Sartre calls for the Jews' assimilation, he does not mean the end of Jewish identity, but rather the end of the Jews' lack of history (in the Hegelian sense). In Sartre's schema, according to Hollier, Jews would not assimilate into French society but rather, via Israel, into the normality of being a people with a state of their own. This positing of a Zionist subtext to Sartre's essay, which was written four years before Israel became a state, seems to me far-fetched. Hollier, "Mosaic," 155.

41. Jean Daniel, "Le retour de Sartre," *Le Nouvel Observateur*, January 13–19, 2000, 6. Cited in Judaken, *Jean-Paul Sartre and the Jewish Question*, 240.

42. Bellamy similarly argues that the positive revaluation of the Jew in postmodern French thought derives in part from Sartre's *Réflexions*. "It could be argued that the process of 'imagining the Jew" in postwar France begins with Sartre" (*Affective Genealogies*, 16). Wolitz writes that "Sartre's opuscule of 1946 [i.e., *Réflexions*] must be recognized as the basis of most intellectual debate in France concerning the Jew and his representation for the next forty years" ("Imagining the Jew in France," 123).

43. Judaken, *Jean-Paul Sartre and the Jewish Question*, 243. According to Judaken, even in a lecture Sartre gave as early as 1947 at the Alliance israélite universelle, he "softened his emphatic tone and language, acknowledged the existence of a unique Jewish culture" (242).

44. Judaken describes how the interviews with Benny Lévy caused a scandal because Sartre reassesses some of his key concepts (ibid., 226–39).

45. Georges Bernanos, "Encore la question juive" (1944), in *La grande peur des bien-pensants* (Paris: Le Livre de Poche, 1998), 397–99. Bernanos was an admirer of Drumont, Barrès, and Maurras into the 1930s before becoming an ardent antifascist.

46. Along with other forms of Holocaust denial, Le Pen famously called the gas chambers a "detail" in the history of the war. He has been been convicted by French courts of inciting racial hatred on multiple occasions.

47. Michel Wieviorka cites statistics from the Commission nationale consultative des droits de l'homme showing that there were fewer than one hundred antisemitic attacks in the second half of the 1990s. *La tentation antisémite: Haine des juifs dans la France d'aujourd'hui* (Paris:

Éditions Robert Laffont, 2005), 31. The resurgence of antisemitism after 2000 will be discussed in the next chapter.

48. Wieviorka summarizes surveys of antisemitic attitudes to show that while there may not have been fewer antisemites in the late twentieth century, they were less open about it (ibid., 31–40).

49. Phyllis Cohen Albert remarks that "in general, the value of difference has been acclaimed in periods when antisemitism was perceived as minimal," in "The Right to Be Different: Interpretations of the French Revolution's Promises to the Jews," *Modern Judaism* 12, no. 3 (October 1992): 250.

50. Esther Benbassa, *The Jews of France: A History from Antiquity to the Present*, trans. M. B. DeBevoise (Princeton: Princeton University Press, 1999), 186.

51. Although between 25 and 30 percent of the North African Jews settled in Paris, others chose Marseilles, Lyons, and diverse smaller cities (ibid., 188).

52. Ibid., 187.

53. Judith Friedlander, *Vilna on the Seine: Jewish Intellectuals in France since 1968* (New Haven: Yale University Press, 1990). Also see Sarah Hammerschlag's forthcoming book, *Sowers and Sages: The Renaissance of Judaism in Postwar Paris*.

54. Derrida discusses Levinas in texts ranging from the essay "Violence et metaphysique" (1964) to *Adieu à Emmanuel Lévinas* (1997). Derrida explores questions of his own Jewish identity in numerous texts, such as *Glas* (1984) and *Circonfession* (2004). Another Algerian-born Jewish philosopher, Hélène Cixous, would meditate on Derrida's Jewishness in *Portait de Jacques Derrida en jeune saint juif* (2001).

55. Raymond Aron collected his articles written during this period in *De Gaulle, Israël et les juifs* (Paris: Plon, 1968).

56. In *La république et les juifs après Copernic* (Paris: Les Presses d'aujourd'hui, 1982), Shmuel Trigano describes how the rue Copernic bombing crystallized for him a growing dissastisfaction with the French republican universalist model: "On the one hand, the lawful State and the courts were not able to protect the Jews, and on the other, they forbid them to defend themselves" (20). Also see Benbassa, *The Jews of France*, 189.

57. Kritzman describes the ways in which Memmi, Finkielkraut, and Derrida work within and against the Sartrean paradigm in "Critical Reflections: Self-Portraiture and the Representation of Jewish Identity in French," in *Auschwitz and After: Race, Culture, and "the Jewish Question" in France*, ed. Lawrence D. Kritzman (New York: Routledge, 1995), 98–118.

58. Wolitz, "Imagining the Jew in France," 123–25.

59. This fanciful name plays on Sartre's familial connection to Albert Schweitzer (Schweitzer was Sartre's mother's cousin).

60. Patrick Modiano, *La place de l'étoile* (Paris: Folio, 1968), 209. The title of the novel, literally "The Place of the Star," contains a double meaning: it refers to both a locality in Paris and the location on the body where the Nazi yellow star was affixed during the war.

61. In "Patrick Modiano: A French Jew?" *Yale French Studies* 85 (1994), Ora Avni calls Modiano's *La place de l'étoile* an "exemplary" novel about the conflicted identities of French Jews in the late twentieth century (230).

62. Simone de Beauvoir, "La mémoire de l'horreur," *Le Monde*, April 28–29, 1985, 12.

63. Carolyn J. Dean describes the "competition among victims" in *Aversion and Erasure: The Fate of the Victim after the Holocaust* (Ithaca: Cornell University Press, 2010).

Chapter 7

1. Patrick Weil describes the change in French immigration policies in the 1970s in *Le Sens de la République* (Paris: Bernard Grasset, 2015), 28–29.

2. Pierre-André Taguieff uses the term "Judeophobia" to designate hatred of Jews that is ideological in focus and takes the form of anti-Zionism. Taguieff, *La nouvelle judéophobie* (Paris: Mille et une nuits, 2002), 25.

3. Denis Lacorne describes the often distorted French view of American multiculturalism in *La crise de l'identité américaine: Du melting-pot au multiculturalisme* (Paris: Fayard, 1997).

4. Lawrence Kritzman offers a penetrating critique of both Badiou and Finkielkraut in "The Jews Who Are Not One: Politics and Intellectual Life in France," *Contemporary French and Francophone Studies* 17, no. 2 (March 2013): 141–53.

5. According to the Commission nationale consultative des droits de l'homme, the number of antisemitic acts in France rose from fewer than 100 between 1995 and 1999 to 743 in 2000 alone. After dropping in 2001, this number then rose to 932 in 2002 and has stayed high during the decade since. Michel Wieviorka, *La tentation antisémite: Haine des juifs dans la France d'aujourd'hui* (Paris: Éditions Robert Laffont, 2005), 31.

6. Kantor Center, *Antisemitism Worldwide 2012: General Analysis*, http://kantorcenter.tau.ac.il/sites/default/files/doch-all-final-2012.pdf.

7. Maud S. Mandel provides an essential study of the "evolution and political meaning" (2) of the conflict between Muslims and Jews in postwar France in *Muslims and Jews in France: History of a Conflict* (Princeton: Princeton University Press, 2014). She notes the decline of universalist rhetoric, noting that "Muslims and Jews have both moved away from republican models of cultural integration" and that the shift "in French identity politics has led to more vocal and politicized minority expression, challenging republican norms in place since the Revolution" (153).

8. Wieviorka, *La tentation antisémite*, 32.

9. Finkielkraut's *Défaite de la pensée* (Paris: Gallimard, 1987) laments the decline of universalism, which he equates with "civilization," in the face of the "barbarism" of postmodernism and multiculturalism.

10. The interview appeared in English in *Haaretz* on November 18, 2005. Excerpts appeared in French in *Le Monde* on November 23. Daniel Ben-Simon, "French Philosopher Alain Finkielkraut Apologizes after Death Threats," *Haaretz*, November 27, 2005.

11. Ivan Segré, *La réaction philosémite ou la trahison des clercs* (Paris: Nouvelles Éditions Lignes, 2009), 17.

12. Carolyn J. Dean, *Aversion and Erasure: The Fate of the Victim after the Holocaust* (Ithaca: Cornell University Press, 2010), 61. Dean writes that "the singling out of Jewish memory as a threat to other kinds of memory may also be related to recent defenses of the universal republic and its commitment to abstract citizenship against particular ethnic and group identifications of all sorts (that is, against liberal pluralism, in which the interplay of individuals and collectives with diverse interests define the meaning of the state)" (62).

13. The model for the postmodern glorification of the Jew as nomadic other is Maurice Blanchot. In *The Infinite Conversation*, trans. Susan Hanson (Minneapolis: University of Minnesota Press, 1993), Blachot writes, "The Jew has throughout time been the oppressed and the accused. He is, he has been, the oppressed of every society" (123). Sarah Hammerschlag describes this revalorization in *The Figural Jew: Politics and Identity in Postwar French Thought* (Chicago: University of Chicago Press, 2010), 4–11.

14. See Jean-François Lyotard, *Heidegger et "les juifs"* (Paris: Galilee, 1988); Enzo Traverso, *La fin de la modernité juive: Histoire d'un tournant conservateur* (Paris: La Découverte, 2011); Judith Butler, *Parting Ways: Jewishness and the Critique of Zionism* (New York: Columbia University Press, 2013). Bruno Chaouat offers a trenchant critique of leftist philosophical anti-Zionism in "Antisemitism Redux: On Literary and Theoretical Perversions," in *Resurgent Antisemitism in Global Perspectives*, ed. Alvin Rosenfeld (Bloomington: Indiana University Press, 2013), 118–39.

15. Alain Finkielkraut, *Au nom de l'autre: Réflexions sur l'antisémitisme qui vient* (Paris: Gallimard, 2003), 21.

16. Finkielkraut, "Les vicissitudes du juif charnel," *Cahier d'Études Levinassiennes* 6 (2000): 233.

17. Finkielkraut, *Au nom*, 22.

18. For another take on Paul's teaching, which doesn't see him as anti-Jewish, see Daniel Boyarin, *A Radical Jew: Paul and the Politics of Identity* (Berkeley: University of California Press, 1994).

19. Finkielkraut, "Vicissitudes," 242.

20. Alain Finkielkraut, *L'identité malheureuse* (Paris: Stock, 2013), 189. Subsequent references appear in the text.

21. Roger Scruton, *England and the Need for Nations* (London: Civitas, 2004), 33–38.

22. See, for instance, Robert Stam and Ella Shohat, *Race in Translation: Culture Wars around the Postcolonial Atlantic* (New York: NYU Press, 2012), 166.

23. Shmuel Trigano has criticized the "symbolic fixation" on the veil and other Muslim breaches of *laïcité*, which he sees as an "easy outlet" designed to make the problem of Muslim incivility seem religious when in fact it is cultural and political. According to Trigano, Judaism and Christianity suffer when Islam's failure to abide by the rules of French secularism gets blamed on religion in general. Shmuel Trigano, *La démission de la république: Juifs et Musulmans en France* (Paris: Presses Universitaires de France, 2003), 29–31.

24. Joan Wallach Scott, *The Politics of the Veil* (Princeton: Princeton University Press, 2007), 4.

25. Ibid., 19.

26. Finielkraut, *L'identité malheureuse*, 66.

27. Nicolas Weill, *La république et les antisémites* (Paris: Bernard Grasset, 2004), 11.

28. Ibid., 12.

29. We see this strategy deployed most cynically by Tariq Ramadan, the Swiss Muslim theologian, whose essay from 2003, "Critique des (nouveaux) intellectuels communautaires" (Critique of the [New] Identitarian Intellectuals) accuses "some French Jewish intellectuals" (des intellectuels juifs français) who denounce antisemitism, principally Finkielkraut, of acting out of narrow Jewish interests rather than properly universal ones. The essay was refused by France's major newspapers and published instead on the website oumma.com on October 3, 2003.

30. Christian Delacampagne, "Alain Badiou (1937–)," in *The Columbia History of Twentieth-Century French Thought*, ed. Lawrence Kritzman (New York: Columbia University Press, 2006), 402. For a sympathetic treatment of Badiou's thought, and of his relation to other thinkers coming out of the '68 nexus, see Bruno Bosteels, *Alain Badiou, une trajectoire polémique* (Paris: La Fabrique, 2009).

31. Chaouat discusses this text by Badiou and Hazan in, "Antisemitism Redux," 125–27.

32. Alain Badiou and Eric Hazan, *"Anti-Semitism Everywhere" in France Today*, in Alain Badiou, Eric Hazan, and Ivan Segré, *Reflections on Anti-Semitism*, trans. David Fernbach (London:

Verso, 2013), 4. Subsequent references appear in the text. Originally published as *L'antisémitisme partout: Aujourd'hui en France* (Paris: La Fabrique, 2011).

33. "Denouncing the 'wave of anti-Semitism' was a good way to distract attention from the bloody Operation Defensive Shield [Rempart]" (4).

34. Badiou and Hazan ask if those who denounce antisemitism "are fully aware of being, for their part, a specialist detachment of intellectuals in the service of the present forms of reactionary domination, under the protection of the US army and with the state of Israel as the advance post in the face of barbarism" (23).

35. Alain Badiou, "Uses of the Word 'Jew,'" in *Polemics*, trans. Steve Corcoran (London: Verso, 2011), 158. Subsequent references appear in the text. Originally published as *Circonstances 3: Portées du mot "juif" suivi de Cécile Winter, signifiant-maître des nouveaux aryens* (Paris: Éditions Léo Scheer, 2005).

36. Philippe Zard points out that not one of the major authors who has located in Judaism a kind of antidote to Nazism—such as Thomas Mann, Elie Wiesel, or Emmanuel Levinas, among many others—has ever sought to "sacralize" Jewish suffering or to use it to gain impunity for Israel. Philippe Zard, "Un étrange apôtre: Réflexions sur la question Badiou," *Plurielles* 13 (2007): 89–96.

37. As Zard notes, "The thesis is simple but the reasoning is false: from the premise that the Nazis turned the predicate 'Jew' into the watchword of a genocidal project, Badiou deduces that they are the *inventors* of said predicate" (ibid., 89).

38. "The Master-Signifier of the New Aryans" comes from the title of Winter's essay.

39. Badiou writes in his introduction, "Cécile Winter engages in an intimate wrangle of a rare violence with the word 'Jew'" ("Uses of the Word 'Jew,'" 165–66).

40. Segré, an Israeli philosopher and student of Badiou, is the author of two books in French denouncing discourse on the "new antisemitism" and discourse on the Shoah as part of a plot to further the aim of American imperialism coded as a "defense of the West." A translation of selections from these books has been published in English in the same volume with Badiou's *"Anti-Semitism Everywhere."*

41. Badiou describes Winter: "In the eyes of certain glorifiers of this name [i.e., Jew], none doubt that she would constitute what they call a 'negative Jew'" ("Uses of the Word 'Jew,'" 166).

42. See Philippe Raynaud, *L'extrême gauche plurielle: Entre démocratie radicale et révolution* (Paris: Autrement, 2006), 152–53.

43. Hammerschlag offers a compelling critique of Badiou's diatribe against Jewish identity and of his neo-Pauline universalism (*The Figural Jew*, 261–67). Also see Maxime Decout, *Écrire la judéité: Enquête sur un malaise dans la littérature française* (Paris: Champ Vallon, 2015), 272–73.

44. Raynaud argues that Badiou's embrace of Paul must be seen in the context of debates among the ex-Maoist *normaliens*, and especially in relation to Benny Lévy's critique of Paul in *Le meurtre du pasteur: Critique de la vision politique du monde* (Paris: Grasset, 2002). Raynaud, *L'extrême gauche plurielle*, 156.

45. Alain Badiou, *Saint Paul: The Foundation of Universalism*, trans. Ray Brassier (Stanford: Stanford University Press, 2003), 5. Subsequent references appear in the text. Originally published as *Saint Paul: La fondation de l'universalisme* (Paris: Presses Universitaires de France 1997).

46. Dean, *Aversion and Erasure*.

47. See Badiou's article "Derriere la Loi fouladière, la peur," *Le Monde*, February 21, 2004.

48. Eric Marty, *Une querelle avec Alain Badiou, philosophe* (Paris: Gallimard, 2007), 38.

49. Marty also discusses the relation of Sartre's notion of the Jew to Badiou's (ibid., 90).

50. As Marty puts it, Badiou cannot distinguish between the Jew and the "youpin" or Yid: "To take pride in being Jewish participates in the same predicatory process as antisemitic discrimination. Declaring oneself a Jew follows the same logic as obeying an antisemitic injunction" (ibid., 57).

51. Finkielkraut, "Vicissitudes," 243. David Nirenberg also describes how Pauline supersessionism provides a template for Western anti-Judaism in *Anti-Judaism: The Western Tradition* (New York: Norton, 2013), 60.

52. Eric Marty, *Bref séjour à Jérusalem* (Paris: Gallimard, 2003), 60–61. Subsequent references appear in the text.

53. In *Proust among the Nations: From Dreyfus to the Middle East* (Chicago: University of Chicago Press, 2011), Jacqueline Rose argues that Zionists drew precisely the wrong lesson from the Dreyfus Affair, which had shown the danger of nationalist ideologies. Rose thus follows Butler and Traverso in splitting "ethnic" (bad) and "ethical" (good) Jews.

54. They recently published together a set of interviews with Philippe Petit in which they debate issues such as universalism. Alain Badiou and Jean-Claude Milner, *Controverse: Dialogue sur la poitique et la philosophie de notre temps* (Paris: Seuil, 2012).

55. Jean-Claude Milner, *Le juif de savoir* (Paris: Éditions Grasset & Fasquelle, 2006), 222.

56. One of the main goals of the philosophical project of Emmanuel Levinas might also be seen as an attempt to think through a "difficult universal" from within the Jewish tradition. On Levinas's struggle with the universal versus particular binary, see among others, Hammerschlag, *The Figural Jew*, 117–65.

57. Milner, *Le juif de savoir*, 212.

Conclusion

1. Natalie Nougayrède, "Paris Unity Rally," *Guardian*, January 11, 2015, http://www.theguardian.com/commentisfree/2015/jan/11/paris-unity-rally-for-fraternity-and-freedom.

2. The historian Deborah Lipstadt wrote: "It just seemed that throughout all the collective mourning, the Jews who were targeted and killed *because they were Jews* were an afterthought—and would always remain so." Lipstadt, "Hypocrisy after the Paris Terror Attacks," *Tablet*, January 16, 2015.

3. Jonathan Judaken describes how the protesters took the "Nous sommes tous des juifs allemands!" slogan from a poster made by the action committee at the École des Beaux-Arts. Some of these posters showed Cohn-Bendit's face. *Jean-Paul Sartre and the Jewish Question: Anti-Antisemitism and the Politics of the French Intellectual* (Lincoln: University of Nebraska Press, 2006), 220.

4. Sarah Hammerschlag, *The Figural Jew: Politics and Identity in Postwar French Thought* (Chicago: University of Chicago Press, 2010), 1–7.

5. Blanchot called it an "inaugural speech-event, opening and overturning borders," in "Les actions exemplaires," *Comité*, October 1, 1968. Cited in Hammerschlag, *The Figural Jew*, 5. Hammerschlag discusses how for Rancière, "the students refused to identify with their own interest, their own social status, or their own nation-state" (5). See Jacques Rancière, *La mésentente* (Paris: Galilée, 1995), 173.

6. Finkielkraut describes how Jews are accused of betraying their "cosmopolitan vocation" and their claim to victim status in *Au nom de l'autre: Réflexions sur l'antisémitisme qui vient* (Paris: Gallimard, 2003), 21. Hammerschlag describes how for Finielkraut, the 1968 slogan used

"Judaism as an emblem for victim and outsider, an emblem whose content is easily transferable" (*The Figural Jew*, 5).

7. "Allocution de Manuel Valls, premier ministre. Séance spéciale d'hommage aux victimes des attentats," Assemblé nationale, January 13, 2015, Service Communication, Hôtel Matignon. All references to the speech are from this document.

8. The Anti-Defamation League, for example, has circulated an open letter thanking Valls for his efforts to combat antisemitism. See http://www.adl.org/sp/condemn-european-anti-semitism/#.VQxPf440pkg, accessed March 20, 2015.

9. The so-called "veil law," passed on March 15, 2004, forbids the wearing of "ostentatious religious symbols," including the Muslim headscarf, the Jewish *kippa*, and large crucifixes, in public schools. On the controversy over this law, see Joan Scott, *The Politics of the Veil* (Princeton: Princeton University Press, 2007). Another law, passed by the French Senate on September 14, 2010, forbids the wearing of a complete face covering (*niqab*) in public places.

10. In "Hypocrisy after the Paris Terror Attacks," Lipstadt writes, "World leaders, including our own, have been decidedly reluctant to identify this problem. What needs to be said is that there is a problem in a segment of the Muslim world."

11. Jean Birnbaum discusses Hollande's assertion in "Attentats djihadists: 'Rien à voir' avec les musulmans?" *Le Monde*, February 11, 2015.

12. Naomi Schor describes how "French government institutions continue to adhere to a discredited linguistic universalism and wage an increasingly ineffective campaign to ward off the encroachment of the new Latin, the new universal linguistic idiom, English." Schor, "Universalism," in *The Columbia History of Twentieth-Century French Thought*, ed. Lawrence Kritzman (New York: Columbia University Press, 2006), 345. Schor is referring to the "Loi Toubon" of August 4, 1994, mandating the use of the French language in official government publications, advertising, commercial contracts, and other contexts.

13. Roland Dumas, the foreign minister under François Mitterand, made headlines after Valls's speech by telling an interviewer that Valls was "under Jewish influence" (sous l'influence juive), a reference to the Jewish origins of his wife. "Roland Dumas et 'l'influence juive' de Manuel Valls," *Libération*, February 16, 2015.

Index

Abd El-Kader, 83
Academy of Metz, 24–25, 27–29, 203n16
Adler, Alexandre, 174
Adorno, Theodor, 218n5
affirmative action, 4
Albert, Phyllis Cohen, 40, 198–99n21, 204n44, 205n53, 211n7, 222n49
Algeria: 1830 French invasion of, 73, 75, 76; assimilation of Jews versus Muslims in, 81; citizenship for Jews but not Muslims and, 88; civilizing mission and, 79, 81, 82, 90–91, 93; European immigration to, 75; Jewish family law and, 206n75; Muslim law versus French law in, 86; revolts in, 82. *See also* Algerian Jews
Algerian Jews: versus Algerian Muslims, 76–78, 80–82, 87–90, 91, 194; assimilation and, 74, 79, 80–81; citizenship for, 81–82, 213n44; civilizing mission and, 93; civil law versus religious law and, 81, 88–89; communal autonomy and, 79; conditions among, 77, 78–79, 212n23; Crémieux Decree and, 74, 83; as dhimmis, 74; divorce and polygamy and, 76, 78–80, 88, 213n45; French Jews and, 74, 76–78, 86, 88, 211–12n15, 212n23; French language and, 213n43; as indigenous population, 74–77; Jewish consistories and, 78, 88; Jewish universalism and, 93; Jewish women's freedom and, 89–90; in *La juive de Constantine* (Gautier and Parfait), 82–91; liberalism and, 211n2; as middlemen, 78; origins of, 74; under Ottoman rule, 74–75; population of, 75, 211n6, 213n44; regeneration of, 77–82; strategic importance of for France, 87–88. *See also* Jews and Judaism
Alliance israélite universelle, 8, 93, 94, 140, 221n43
al-Qaeda in Yemen, 1

Altaras, Jacques-Isaac, 78–82, 84, 87, 89, 212n21, 213n36
Altman, Georges, 119–20, 121
Anti-Defamation League, 227n8
antisemitism: in 1930s popular press, 122; in Abbé Grégoire's description of Jews, 25–26; anti-antisemitism and, 103, 111, 121, 144–47, 152–56; Communism and, 155, 221n35; criticism of Israel as, 173; Dreyfus Affair and, 103, 115, 128; Émile Zola and, 7, 95–96, 101–3, 107, 109, 111–12, 115, 214n14; in France versus Germany, 115; of French right versus left, 139; *La grande illusion* (film) and, 118–21, 124–28, 132–35, 136–37; Islamic, 187, 200n35; Judeophobia and, 223n2; in late twentieth century, 221–22nn47–48; minimization of, 2, 173, 175–76; misreading of the Talmud and, 28; models of Frenchness and, 67; new antisemitism and, 162–66, 170, 173–75, 181, 188, 223n5, 224n29, 225n40; versus other racisms, 175–76; Pauline supersessionism and, 226n51; pseudo-scientific racial categorization and, 135–36; psychological portrait of, 143; in *Réflexions sur la question juive* (Sartre), 140–41, 144–47, 149–50, 158, 220n29; roots of in philosophy, 218–19nn5–6; socialism and, 99, 155–56, 220–21n34; terrorism and, 189–90, 192; in theater and theater criticism, 51, 55–61, 63, 69, 85, 98, 209n43; as threat to republican ideals, 95, 194; Union Générale Bank scandal and, 100–101; union of economic and cultural forms of, 61; value of Jewish difference and, 222n49; Zionism versus, 114
Apter, Emily, 214n5, 214n14
Arkin, Kimberly A., 198n11
Arnold, Matthew, 209n50
Aron, Raymond, 159, 221n35

Asad, Talal, 198n10
Assembly of Jewish Notables, 47, 48, 92, 206n74
assimilation: 1775 lawsuit of the Jews of Metz and, 19–22; versus acculturation, 74; after World War II, 143; in Algeria, 74, 79, 80–81, 88–89, 91; assimilationist universalism and, 151–55, 162; blacks and women and, 14, 33, 201n49; civic improvement and, 22–23, 29; coaxed versus coerced, 28; dissolution of Jews as a people and, 105, 115, 116, 193; emancipation of Jews and, 17–18, 23, 29; in exchange for rights and inclusion, 7–8, 17, 20; French language and, 213n43; human rights and, 9; intermarriage and, 48, 112; Jewish consistories and, 47–48; Jewish difference and, 74, 93, 96; meaning of, 199n27, 201n1; Napoleonic precedent for colonial assimilation and, 92; as necessary for citizenship, 81, 88, 140; as neither required of nor pursued by Jews, 40–41, 46; political, 22–23, 24, 36–37, 45; regeneration and, 20–21, 22, 26, 33, 80, 201n1, 202n8; religious conversion and, 27; socialist revolution and, 155–56; universalism and, 4–11, 13–14, 74, 83, 92, 118, 139–41, 148, 187; Zionism versus, 114. *See also* assimilationist-pluralist continuum
assimilationist-pluralist continuum: 1775 lawsuit of the Jews of Metz and, 21; Academy of Metz and, 24–25, 27–29; Émile Zola and, 96, 140; the "Jewish Question" and, 18, 24; models of French universalism and, 9; nature of Jewish difference and, 187; poles of, 9; Sartre and, 140, 157; theater criticism and, 63; Zalkind Hourwitz's "third discourse" and, 203n23
Aubigné, Françoise d', 207n7
Austin, J. L., 205n46
Avineri, Shlomo, 215n27
Avni, Ora, 222n61
Ayoun, Richard, 204n33, 204n35, 204n40, 205n47, 205nn59–61
Azouvi, François, 220nn19–20

Badinter, Robert, 30, 40, 202n5
Badiou, Alain: abolition of Jewish and other identity and, 176, 180; antisemitism as distraction from Israel's violence and, 174, 225nn33–34; *L'antisémitisme partout* ("Anti-Semitism Everywhere") by, 173–75; anti-Zionist far left and, 172–73, 174–75; on capitalism and nationalism, 179; on ethical versus ethnic Jews, 176–77; Israel and nationalism and, 184; Jean-Claude Milner and, 173, 184, 226n54; minimization of antisemitism and, 175–76; on new antisemitism, 173–74, 175; as philosemite, 180; *Portées du mot "juif"* (Uses of the Word "Jew") by, 175–77, 180; responses to, 181–85; Saint Paul and, 167, 176–83, 225n44; *Saint Paul* by, 177–80; on terrorist attacks, 165; universalism and, 163, 172–81, 182–83, 184–85; uses of the word *Jew* and, 225n37, 225n41; veil controversy and, 179–80
Balibar, Étienne, 9
Balzac, Honoré de, 56, 208n28
Bardèche, Maurice, 119–20, 127, 137
Barre, Raymond, 159, 191
Barrès, Maurice: antisemitic models of Frenchness and, 67, 145–46; *Les déracinés* by, 134; Dreyfus Affair and, 95, 146; homegrown French fascism and, 142; Jewish "race" and, 136; moderation of antisemitic views of, 218n46; national belonging defined by blood and soil and, 96, 117–18, 124–25, 170; rootless cosmopolitanism and, 132, 134; source of identity and, 152–53; universalism and, 124–25, 137, 140, 169, 171
Barreyre, Jean, 216n7
Barthélemy, Auguste-Marseille, 50, 206n1
Baubérot, Jean, 11–12, 116, 172, 197n9
Bauman, Zygmunt, 11, 198n18
Bazin, André, 118, 120–21, 131, 216n11
Beauvoir, Simone de, 161
Bebel, Ferdinand August, 220–21n34
Bell, David A., 37–38, 197n2
Bell, Dorian, 112, 215n25
Bellamy, Elizabeth J., 218n5, 221n42
Bellanger, Claude, 209n35
Benbassa, Esther, 158
Benda, Julien, 117–18, 215–16n5
ben Israel, Menasseh, 23
Ben-Lévi (pseud. Godchaux Baruch Weil), 208n30, 213n38
Bergson, Henri, 215–16n5
Berkovitz, Jay R., 198–99n21
Bernanos, George, 158, 221n45
Berr, Berr Isaac, 31, 45–46
Berr, Cerf, 21
Birnbaum, Jean, 174
Birnbaum, Pierre, 198–99n21, 212n19, 217n43, 227n11; on French Jews' visit to Algeria, 212n21; on Jews and the French national imaginary, 198n15; on Jews and universalism, 215n3; Jews' dietary difference and, 204n37; Mirabeau's acceptance of Jewish particularism and, 202–3n15; preservation of Jewish identity and, 199n22; on *Réflexions sur la question juive* (Sartre), 219n7
blacks: antisemitism versus other racisms and, 175; emancipation of in France, 200n47; Enlightenment theories of difference and, 201n49; in French colonies, 75; in *La grand illusion* (film), 136; rights and citizenship for, 38, 75–76; as unassimilable, 14, 33
Blanchot, Maurice, 188, 223n13, 226n5

Blum, Léon, 117, 122, 126, 215n3
Bohlman, Philip, 207–8n16
Bonnel, Pierre, 216n8
Bontoux, Eugène, 100–101, 214n15
Borel, Pétrus, 60–63, 68–69, 72, 209n40, 209n43
Bosteels, Bruno, 224n30
Bovy, Phoebe Maltz, 48
Boyarin, Daniel, 224n18
Brasillach, Robert, 119–20, 127, 137, 142, 145–46
Brenner, Michael, 211–12n15
Broglie, Victor-François, duc de, 41–42, 43–44
Brown, Wendy, 8, 9, 66, 199n24
Brownstein, Rachel, 54, 64, 207n3, 208n20, 208n22, 210n58, 210n65
Burke, Edmund, 169, 171
Butler, Judith, 166, 226n53

Camelots du roi, 117
capitalism: in *L'argent* (Zola), 98–99, 101, 110–12; associated with Jews, 13, 98–99, 129, 138, 216–17n25; as false universalism, 179; in *Vérité* (Zola), 110–12
Cargaison blanche (film), 122
Charney, Leo, 218n49
Caron, Vicki, 211–12n15
Carroll, David, 142
Cartwright, Lisa, 218n48
Casablanca (film), 138, 216n20
Cassin, René, 220n32
Catholics and Catholicism: in *L'argent* (Zola), 97–98, 99–102, 104–5, 111; assimilation to, 4; ban on money lending and, 13; Concordat and, 47; conversions from Judaism to, 54; disappearance of religion and, 112; Dreyfus Affair and, 115; France as fundamentally Catholic and, 59; freeing France from grip of, 10; groups excluded from the Church and, 34–35; as original universalism, 2–3, 13; prohibitions against religious displays and, 4, 198n10; state nonrecognition of Church and, 36; subordination of church to state and, 204n41; as superseding Jewish particularity, 13; *Vérité* (Zola) and, 106–7. *See also* Christians and Christianity
Céline, Louis-Ferdinand, 120, 137, 142, 145–46
Cercle Gaston-Crémieux, 159
Cerfberr, Max, 52, 207n12, 208n27
Chaix (monk), 203n16
Chanet, Jean-François, 11
Chaouat, Bruno, 224n14, 224n31
Charcot, Jean Martin, 128, 217n35
Charles X, 73
Charlie Hebdo attack, 1–2, 164, 186, 188–95, 197n1
Chateaubriand, François-René de, 60
Cheyette, Bryan, 198n18, 202n5

Christians and Christianity: banning of crucifixes in public schools and, 227n9; Christian instruction for Jews and, 27; Christians' historical oppression of Jews and, 20, 22–24, 26, 28, 32, 41, 151, 202n8; Christian universalism versus Jewish particularity and, 167, 179, 181; dhimmis and, 74; election and salvation and, 182–83; Jews' conversion to, 21, 27, 87, 208n23; Judaism's role in Christian theology and, 13; leaving Jews no occupational choice but moneylending and, 20, 26, 35–36, 150–51; Protestants and, 3, 34, 47; Saint Paul and universalism and, 177–78; supersessionism and, 181, 182, 184, 226n51; violations of French secularism and, 224n23. *See also* Catholics and Catholicism
citizenship: for Algerian Jews but not Muslims, 81–82, 83, 88; assimilation as necessary for, 81, 88; for blacks, 75–76; civil versus religious law and, 92–93; communal autonomy and, 36–37, 45, 204n44; Crémieux Decree and, 74; establishment of French nationality and, 209n47; family law and, 92–93; financial versus religious requirements for, 38, 41, 45; freedom versus, 76; groups eligible for and excluded from, 38, 44, 45; for indigenous people of Algeria, 76, 81, 82; Jews born as citizens and, 52; *lettres patentes* from Old Regime and, 43; nation defined by ideology not blood and, 37–39; naturalization of Algerian Jews and Muslims and, 213n44; oath of allegiance and, 45; regeneration as unnecessary for, 39–40, 45, 130; for Sephardim versus Ashkenazim, 43–44; for women, 76
civil rights. *See* human rights
Cixous, Hélène, 222n54
Clemenceau, Georges, 216n20
Clermont-Tonnerre, Stanislas Marie Adélaïde, comte de: acceptance of Jewish difference and, 18, 39–40, 42, 67; antisemitic language about Jews and, 42; assimilationist universalism and, 154; on civil rights for Jews, 17; equality before the law and, 34–35; exculpating Jews by blaming Christians and, 35–36; humanitarian ideals of, 41; imperative versus conditional manner of speaking and, 37, 39; on Jews and citizenship, 36–37, 38, 204n44; misinterpretation of speech by, 40; religious liberty and, 35
Cohen, Joseph, 78–82, 84, 87, 89, 212n21, 213n36
Cohn-Bendit, Daniel, 188, 226n3
Colloquium of French-Speaking Jewish Intellectuals, 159
colonialism and imperialism: Algeria versus other colonies and, 75; antisemitism as obstacle to, 215n24; civilizing mission and, 76, 77, 79, 82, 90–91, 211n4; fate of indigenous populations and, 75, 76, 91, 92; French republicanism and,

colonialism and imperialism (*continued*) 73; invented nature of French colonial categories and, 82; literature and, 82; mixed-race children and, 201n50; Napoleonic precedent for assimilation in, 92; native subjects versus citizens and, 76; physical violence and, 82; "rights of man" and, 73; slavery and, 75, 200n47; universalism and, 94, 183; veiled women in, 89–90. *See also* Algeria
Combes Law, 115–16, 117
Comédie-Française, 50–51, 54–56, 61, 63, 68, 93
communautarisme: competition among victims and, 178; versus freedom from religion, 171; of Israel's defenders, 174–75; Israel's opponents and, 181; of Jews versus others, 176; versus *laïcité*, 116, 163, 170, 171; of Muslims, 172; new antisemitism and, 165, 173; as threat to the republic, 4, 191; universalism and, 163, 178, 184
Communism, 155, 221n35
Conklin, Alice, 73, 79
Constituent Assembly, 30–34, 38, 41–45, 203–4n29, 204n41
Corneille, Pierre, 50–51, 64, 66–69, 71
Corsaire, Le, 54, 208n19
Crémieux, Adolphe: Algerian Jews and, 78, 81–82, 88, 91, 93–94; conversions of family members and, 54; equal treatment of France's religions and, 213n51; golden age of Franco-Judaism and, 52; as minister 71; *more judaico* and, 93; National Assembly and, 52, 207n12; origins of, 207n10; Rachel Félix and, 71, 210n62; reputation of, 210n63. *See also* Crémieux Decree
Crémieux Decree, 74, 82, 83, 213n48
Curot, Frank, 216n24
Curran, Andrew S., 201n49

Dalio, Marcel: appearance of, 129, 135, 217n40; in *Casablanca* (film), 138; cast as stereotypical Frenchman, 216n20; in *La grand illusion* (film), 118, 120, 122, 133, 135–36; in *La règle du jeu* (film), 126–27
Damascus Affair, 209n41, 210n63
Daniel, Jean, 157
Daudet, Alphonse, 214n14
David, Jacques-Louis, 68
Dean, Carolyn J., 178, 222n63, 223n12
Declaration of the Rights of Man and the Citizen, 3, 31, 33, 34
decolonization, 161, 169, 183
de Gaulle, Charles, 141–42, 143, 159, 188
Delacampagne, Christian, 224n30
Delacroix, Eugène, 66
de Latour, Antoine, 65, 66, 210n51
de Maistre, Joseph de, 169, 171
Derrida, Jacques, 159, 221n54, 222n57
d'Haillecourt, 203n16

difference. *See* Jewish identity; right to difference; universal versus particular
Dohm, Christian Wilhelm, 21–24, 26, 35, 202n13
Douglas, Kirk, 54
Dreyfus, Alfred. *See* Dreyfus Affair
Dreyfus Affair: anti-Dreyfusards of Vichy period and, 115, 142; antisemitism and, 72, 103, 115, 128, 146, 195; assimilationist universalism and, 140, 154, 187; caricaturists and, 128; Catholic right versus anticlerical left and, 115; cultural relativism and, 169; Dreyfusards and, 108–9; Émile Zola and, 95, 96, 103, 106–7, 115, 154, 219n8; erasure of Jewish difference and, 187; Franco-French war and, 115; Jewish difference and, 219n9; Jews and military service and, 131; League for the Rights of Man and, 152, 220n32; Léon Blum and, 117; pardoning of Dreyfus and, 106; public opinion about, 110, 117; right-wing politics and, 107–8; separation of churches and state (Combes Law) and, 96, 116; universalism and, 95, 187; Zionism and, 114, 183, 215n27, 226n53
Drieu la Rochelle, Pierre, 142
Drumont, Édouard: admirers of, 221n45; as antiuniversalist antisemite, 137; economic and cultural antisemitism and, 61, 99–100, 107–8; Émile Zola and, 99–101, 102, 104, 214n14; *La France juive* by, 99, 107–8, 126, 214nn13–14; homegrown French fascism and, 142; on Pétrus Borel's review of Rachel Félix, 209n43; Union Générale Bank scandal and, 100–101
Dumas, Roland, 227n13
Duport, Adrien, 44, 205n62, 205n65

Eliot, George, 114
emancipation of blacks, 76, 200n47
emancipation of Jews: abstract principles of justice and, 41; aftermath of, 40–46; assimilation and, 17–18, 23, 29; Crémieux Decree and, 74; debate over as context for new idea of nation, 38, 39–40; France as first site of, 192; as incitement to violence, 41–42, 43–44; Jewish nationalist critiques of, 11, 201n2; as necessary for reorganization of the state, 44–45; nonassimilation and, 8, 198–99n21; opponents of, 33; regeneration and, 39, 42, 45, 46; Revolutionary preoccupation with, 30, 34, 44, 203–4n29; Sephardim versus Ashkenazim and, 43–44; terms of, 8, 45, 92
Endelman, Todd M., 208n23
Enlightenment: description of Jews' physical qualities and, 25; French language and, 193; Jews as test case for principles of, 13–14, 29–30; Sartre's critique of rationalism and, 140, 144, 145, 147–48; theories of black difference and, 201n49

INDEX 233

equality for Jews: 1775 lawsuit of the Jews of Metz and, 19–22; *Declaration of the Rights of Man* and, 33, 34; equal application of laws and, 34, 38; equal treatment of France's religions and, 213n51; as path to social improvement, 24; Revolutionary shift toward, 33
Estates General, 204n33
Esther (play), 50–51, 54–55, 57–59, 64, 69, 207n3, 207n7

Falcon, Cornélie, 53, 207–8n16
fascism, 142, 166, 180, 184
Fayard, Jean, 216n8
Féher, Ferenc, 201n2
Feldman, David, 11, 198n18, 198–99n21
Félix, Rachel: Adolphe Crémieux and, 71, 210n62; Anglo-American commentators on, 209n50; antisemitic criticisms of, 51, 55–61, 63, 69, 70–72, 209n43; assimilationist-pluralist continuum and, 140; in *Bérénice* (play), 207n6; caricature of, 210n52; death and funeral of, 54–55, 71; as enthusiastically performing her Jewishness, 54, 63, 65–66, 71, 93, 208n20, 208n24; *Esther* (play) and, 50, 54, 55, 57–59, 64; fame of, 53–54; family and childhood of, 54, 63–64, 65, 208n22; golden age of Franco-Judaism and, 53; legitimist critics of, 210n58; "Marseillaise" and, 69, 70, 210n61; museum exhibit on, 207n8; name of, 54, 208n22; in *Phèdre* (play), 60–61; philosemitism and, 63–65, 66–68, 72, 209nn49–50; pluralism and, 63–68, 193; praise for, 62–63, 64–65, 68, 69, 71; as quintessentially French, 210n61; Revolution and, 68–69, 71–72; romantic liaisons of, 54, 71, 210n65; scholars on Jewishness of, 207n8; training of, 64, 65; universalism and, 62–63, 68–72, 137
Félix, Raphaël, 60, 208n22
Félix, Rébecca, 60, 208n22
Fernando, Mayanthi, 197n3, 198n10, 200n39
Feuerbach, Ludwig von, 98
Feuillant party, 205n62
Fichte, Johann Gottlieb, 59–60
film: antisemitism in, 137–38; Jewish-themed works of the 1980s and 1990s and, 161; Jews in, 121–23, 216n18; police use of, 218n49. *See also specific films*
Finkielkraut, Alain: versus Alain Badiou, 181; on anti-French sentiment, 168; anti-Zionist far left and, 166–68, 172–73; banning of the veil and, 168–69, 170–71; *communautarisme* for Arabs versus Jews and, 166; as critic of postmodernism, 178; *Haaretz* interview and, 165–66; Holocaust and, 166, 188; *L'identité malheureuse* by, 10, 168–71; on ideology justifying antisemitic violence, 166, 170, 172; on Jews' victim status, 226n6; *Le juif imaginaire* by, 160, 166; on *laïcité*, 168–69, 200n31; on liberal versus republican secularism, 171; neorepublicanism and, 165–72, 179–80; "Nous sommes tous des juifs allemands" and, 188, 226n6; on oikophobia, 169–70; Sartre and, 160–61, 222n57; Strauss-Kahn affair and, 171; Tariq Ramadan on, 224n29; on terrorist attacks, 164–65; universalism and, 10, 163, 167–68, 169, 171–72, 223n9
Flandrin, Louis-Hugues, 92
Foa, Eugénie, 84, 90, 213n35
Fould, Achille, 52, 207n12
Fourier, Charles, 98
France: anti-French sentiment and, 168; as capital of the new antisemitism, 164; equality of opportunity in, 11; French language and, 193, 227n12; as fundamentally Catholic, 59; homegrown fascism in, 142; as inherently antisemitic, 6–7; Jewish suffering as paradigm in, 161; Jews as essential to, 192, 195; Jews' insecurity in, 192; largest populations of Muslims and Jews in Europe and, 2, 197n2; minority problems of, 2, 4, 10, 171, 180; nation defined by ideology not blood and, 37–39. *See also* French culture; French Revolution; Vichy period
Frankel, Jonathan, 201n2, 204n44, 209n41
Freedman, Jonathan, 59–60, 209n50
French culture: changing meaning of culture and, 59–60; as closed to Jews and other foreigners, 62, 63; fears of Jewish cultural takeover and, 60–61; Franco-French war and, 69; Jews' access to, 58, 67, 68; Jews as uniquely capable of contributing to, 63–64; Jews in the arts and, 53, 57–59, 60–61, 65–66, 207–8n16; neoclassicism and, 68, 69, 210n58; Romanticism and, 60, 62, 65; theater and, 51
French Revolution: aesthetic legacy of, 67–69; bicentennial of, 162; definition of nation and, 68, 205n49; French language and spread of ideals of, 193; Jewish emancipation and, 17, 30–46, 198n15; July Monarchy battle over, 71; nation defined by ideology not blood and, 37–39, 45; neoclassicism and, 68, 69; opposition to king's execution and, 205n62, 205n65; political versus religious persecution of Jews in, 205n55; redefinition of the nature of Jewishness and, 40; regeneration unnecessary for citizenship and, 130; rights for blacks and, 75; universalism and, 3, 14, 137, 154, 179, 183–84, 187, 193, 197n6; values of, 189–90. *See also* Jacobins
Freud, Sigmund, 177
Friedlander, Judith, 159
Furet, François, 17

Gallois, Léonard, 205n51
Galster, Ingrid, 218nn3–4, 219n17
Garb, Tamar, 218n3

234 INDEX

Garçon, François, 217n41
Gauchet, Marcel, 31, 62–63
Gautier, Théophile, 62, 82–91, 212n27, 212n32, 213n40, 213nn47–48
Genet, Jean, 181
Gerson, Stéphane, 200n37
Gilman, Sander, 127–28, 129, 217n36
Glucksmann, André, 174
Gobineau, Arthur de, 66, 99
Goudchaux, Michel, 71
Goldmann, Annie, 216n21, 217n42
Goldstein, Jan, 132, 216n24
Gouges, Olympe de, 201n48
Grand illusion, La (film): 1958 version with restored scenes and, 121, 216n16; affirmation of Jewish soldier in, 130–31; as antifascist statement, 118, 137; antisemitism and, 118–21, 124–28, 132, 133–37; antiuniversalism and, 124–26, 127; assimilationist-pluralist continuum and, 140; belonging defined by blood and soil and, 124–26; critical reception of, 118–21; cuts in 1946 version of film and, 119, 216n11; image of the Jews in minds of French public and, 138; the "Jewish Question" and, 120–21, 124, 134, 137; the name Rosenthal in, 124; non-Jewish stereotypes in, 130–31, 217n37; philosemitism and, 120; positive connotations of Jewishness and, 137; producers of, 216n12; pseudo-scientific racial categorization and, 136; representations of Jews in, 118–19, 122, 123–30, 137–38, 140, 216n12, 217nn26–27; Rosenthal as stand-in for Jean Renoir in, 135; story line of, 118; symbolic inclusion of Jews in, 130–36, 137, 138, 154; sympathetic treatment of Germans in, 119; universalism and, 130, 134, 137; the word *Jew* in, 124–26, 133, 134–35
Grand Sanhedrin: civil versus religious law and, 40; creation of, 47; divorce and, 206n75; Judaism as universalist religion and, 48, 94; membership of, 206n74; Napoleon's questions for, 206n78; new definition of Jewish identity and, 47, 48–49; precedent for colonial assimilation and, 92–93; redefinition of Jewishness and, 94; resistance to Napoleon on intermarriage and, 48
Grant, Richard B., 100–101, 214nn13–14
Grégoire (Abbé): on allowable occupations for Jews, 26; antisemitic description of Jews and, 25–26, 32, 42; assimilation and regeneration and, 20, 32, 80, 134; as assimilationist universalist, 137, 151; call for renunciation of the Talmud and, 26; Christian instruction for Jews and, 27; Christian mistreatment as cause of Jewish degradation and, 151; civic improvement of the Jews and, 24–25; elimination of Yiddish and, 27, 203n20; equality before the law and, 35;

Essay on the . . . Regeneration of the Jews and, 25–27, 32, 42; exculpating Jews by blaming Christians and, 26, 35; influences on, 21, 23; Jewish communalism and, 26–27, 28; Jewish difference and, 14, 32, 33, 40; on Jewish vices, 79; *Motion in Favor of the Jews* (1789) and, 31–32, 35; report on Jews of the east and, 204n32
Gunning, Tom, 218n49

Ha'Am, Ahad, 201n2
Haitian Revolution, 200n47
Halévy, Fromental, 53, 54, 90, 207n15, 212n32
Halimi, Ilan, 164, 192
Hammerschlag, Sarah, 188, 198n16, 219nn8–9, 225n43, 226nn5–6
Hargreaves, Alec G., 197n2
Harris, Ruth, 214n1
Hazan, Éric, 173–75, 176, 225nn33–34
Hegel, G. W. F., 59–60, 148
Hell, François, 21, 41
Hennebelle, Guy, 216n21, 217n42
Herder, Johann Gottfried von, 59–60
Hermon-Belot, Rita, 20, 202n9
Hertzberg, Arthur, 201n2
Herzl, Theodore, 114, 215n27
Hess, Jonathan, 22–23, 202n13
Higonnet, Patrice, 198n13, 204n38, 205n55
Hillel, 48
Hitler, Adolf, 176, 180, 182
Hollande, François, 2, 189, 192, 227n11
Holliday, Judy, 54
Hollier, Denis, 220n26, 221n40
Holocaust: American imperialism and, 225n40; changing attitude toward Jews after, 158; commemoration of, 163; cultural relativism and, 169; denial of, 221n46; "excessive" memory of, 176–78, 223n12; *La grande illusion* (film) and, 119; Holocaust fatigue and, 166, 223n12; ideology of victimization and, 178, 188; Jewish identity and, 160–61, 179; mandated education about, 192–93; meaning of term, 193; origins of Zionism and, 183; as Shoah, 192–93, 195; silence about, 143, 220nn19–20
Hoog, Anne Hélène, 207n8, 209n49
Horkheimer, Max, 218n5
Hourwitz, Zalkind, 24–25, 28–29
Hugo, Victor, 60, 68–69
Hugon, André, 216n18
human rights: discourse of, 179, 220n32; hypocrisy of French commitment to, 9; postwar advocacy for, 152. See also *Declaration of the Rights of Man and the Citizen*
Humboldt, Wilhelm von, 59–60
Hyman, Paula, 47, 216–17n25
Hypercacher supermarket attack, 1–2, 164, 186–95, 197n1, 226n2

INDEX 235

Iffla, Mme Auguste, 53
immigration and immigration restrictions, 4, 162, 164, 180, 223n1
Ingres, Jean-Dominique, 66
intermarriage: between Christians and Jews, 32, 36, 47; conversion and, 91; dissolution of Jews as a people and, 48, 105, 112–13, 115, 154; as forbidden for Jews, 87, 90, 213n40; Napoleon and, 48
Isidor (Grand Rabbi), 54–55
Islamic State, 1
Israel: Alain Badiou and 173–77, 180, 181, 184; analogy with Nazi Germany and, 167; Éric Marty and, 181–84; immigration to, 2, 195; Jewish solidarity with, 155, 159, 166–67, 188; Palestinian conflict and, 164, 168; Sartre and, 221n40

Jacob, François, 157
Jacobins: abolition of slavery and, 200n47; assimilation and, 7; centralization and secularization and, 198n13; dissolution of Jews as a people and, 112; historical Jacobins and, 198n13; Jews as, 205n55; meaning of *Jacobin* and, 204n38; mediating bodies between state and individual and, 47; nature of republicanism and, 198n14; totalitarian tendencies of, 17, 162; two lines of thinking about Jews and, 205n55
Jaher, Frederic Cople, 39, 205n50
James, Henry, 209n50
Janin, Jules: criticisms of Rachel Félix by, 58–59, 62, 63, 64, 69, 71; praise for Rachel Félix by, 50–51, 64–65, 69, 71, 209n49; on Rachel Félix's death, 54–55, 71
Jewish identity: after the Holocaust, 158–59, 222n61; Alain Badiou and, 176–83; civil versus religious law and, 47, 92–93; clothing and, 4, 198n10, 206n79, 227n9; common history and, 148, 151, 158, 220n26, 221n40; communalism and, 26–28, 36–38, 45, 79, 148, 204n44; *communautarisme* and, 165, 173, 178, 179–80, 181; cosmopolitanism and, 166–67, 188, 226n6; diet and, 14, 26, 32, 204n37; difference and, 94, 96, 141, 157–59, 187, 194, 222n49; ethical versus ethnic, 176–77, 188, 226n53; ethnicity and, 147–48; evasion versus abjection and, 151–52, 160; in France versus Algeria; 74; French identity politics and, 223n7; Holocaust and, 160–61, 179; inauthentic and authentic Jews and, 144, 151, 155–56, 158–59, 161, 221n36; Jacques Derrida and, 159, 221n54; "Je suis juif" and, 186–89; Jewish "race" and, 135–36; language and, 27, 29, 192–93, 195, 203n20, 206n79; loyalty to France and Judaism and, 45–46, 206n78; mercantilist defense of Jews and, 40; name changes and, 54; Nazi-era Star of David and, 141; necessitated by antisemitism, 115; nomadism and, 166–67, 177, 223n13; "Nous sommes tous des juifs allemands" and, 188, 189, 226n3, 226nn5–6; positive connotations of Jewishness and, 137; preservation of, 8, 199n22, 199n26; religious practice and, 29, 36, 148, 151, 158; universalism and, 17, 94, 139–40, 144, 148, 153, 159, 162, 180–81, 185, 198n12, 213n52; *See also* Israel; Jews and Judaism; Zionism
Jewish Museum of Brussels, 164
"Jewish Question," the: assimilationist-pluralist continuum and, 18–19; Émile Zola and, 96, 97–98, 105, 114–16; Enlightenment-era debates over, 18, 22, 24; French republicanism and, 115; *La grande illusion* (film) and, 120–21, 124, 134, 137; Jean Renoir and, 118; Marx and, 98; Napoleon and, 46; Nazis final solution to, 142; Sartre and, 143–44, 147–48, 153–54, 155–56; socialist revolution and, 144, 155–56
Jews' alleged physical qualities: associated with alleged moral failings, 25, 66; feet and, 128; in film, 126–27; illness and, 127–28; Jewish difference and, 14; male Jews as castrated and, 129, 217n36; Marcel Dalio's image on posters and, 138; nose and, 129–30, 137, 138, 150; philosemitic and antisemitic descriptions in literature and, 84–85; positive connotations of, 65–67; pseudo-scientific racial theorizing and, 66, 99; psychiatry and, 128, 217n35; Sartre's portrait of the Jew and, 149–50, 220n29
Jews and Judaism: 1775 lawsuit of the Jews of Metz and, 19–22, 24, 26; 1777 defense of Alsatian Jews and, 21–23, 26; in Algeria versus France, 77–82, 92–94, 211–12n15; blood libel and, 60, 209n41; Christians' historical oppression of, 20, 22–24, 26, 28, 32, 41, 151, 202n8; citizenship and, 7, 8, 17, 36–37, 38–39, 43–44, 52; civic improvement of, 24–25, 27–28; civilizing mission and, 76–77, 79, 81–82, 91, 93, 211n4; civil versus religious law and, 47; conversion to Christianity and, 21, 27, 54, 87, 208n23; definition of nationality and, 45, 201n50; dissolution of Jews as a people and, 96, 103, 105, 112–15, 154, 156, 193; divorce and, 73, 206n75; election and salvation and, 182–83; as essential to France, 192, 195; in film, 121–23, 216n18; French national imaginary and, 12, 198n15; in French politics, 7, 42–43, 204n33; George Washington's letter to, 34, 204n39; in ghettos, 71; golden age of Franco-Judaism and, 52–53, 57–59, 67–68, 71, 93, 207n10, 207n12, 207–8n16; as "good to think," 13, 18, 29–30, 200n46; insecurity of in France, 192, 195; international solidarity among, 8, 199n24; as Israelites versus Jews, 56; Jewish consistories and, 40, 78, 81, 88, 110, 206n79; Jewish refugees in France and, 122,

236 INDEX

Jews and Judaism (*continued*)
216n19; Jews as Jacobins and, 205n55; meaning of *le juif* and, 208n30; mercantilist defense of, 19, 22, 202n8; messianic tradition and, 148, 220n28; military service and, 128, 130–31, 206n76, 217n42; as model minority, 194; *Motion in Favor of the Jews* (1789) and, 31–32; non-assimilation or particularism of, 8, 46, 167, 179, 181, 191, 198–99n21, 202–3n15; as *persona non grata* in France, 201–2n4; population of, 12, 18–19, 29, 50, 52, 94, 104, 117, 158, 197n2, 211n7, 222n51; pre- and post-Revolutionary models of including, 30, 32–33, 39–40; as proxy for debates about democracy, 203–4n29; religious versus secular regeneration of, 20, 202n9; Sartre's portrait of, 147–52; supersessionism and, 181, 182, 184, 226n51; as symbols for work of national reconstruction and, 42; as test case for Enlightenment principles, 13–14, 29–30; as test case for powers of regeneration and, 39–40; as test case for values of the French Revolution, 198n15; universalism and, 4–6, 10, 14, 48–49, 93–94, 167, 176–77, 179, 181, 184, 187, 193; utilitarian defenses of, 19–20; various groups of in France, 19, 31; World War I patriotism of, 218n46. *See also* Algerian Jews; antisemitism; emancipation of Jews; equality for Jews; Israel; Jewish identity; Jews' alleged physical qualities; moneylending; philosemitism; Zionism
Joskowicz, Ari, 208n23
Journal des Débats (newspaper), 58, 209n35
Judaken, Jonathan, 157, 220n18, 220n25, 220n28, 221nn43–44, 226n3
Judith, Mlle (Julie Bernat), 53, 208n18, 208n22
Judt, Tony, 221n35
Juive de Constantine, La (Gautier and Parfait), 82–91, 212n27, 212n32, 213n38, 213n40, 213nn47–48
Julian, Mlle, 53
July Monarchy: cultural and economic antisemitism during, 55; equal treatment for Jews under, 94; French Revolution's legacy and, 71; positive connotations of Jewishness during, 65, 68; rabbis on state payroll under, 94; rights for blacks and, 75; universalist discourse during, 137

Kalman, Julie, 207n11
Kant, Immanuel, 220n22
Kantor Center for the Study of Contemporary European Jewry, 164
Kaplan, Alice, 142, 216n13, 219n11
Kaplan, Zvi Jonathan, 201n51
Karp, Jonathan, 202n11
Kates, Gary, 45–46, 203–4n29
Katz, Jacob, 214n11, 215n23
Katznelson, Ira, 198–99n21

Kauffmann, Uri R., 211–12n15
Kennedy, John F., 187
Kleeblatt, Norman L., 217n39
Koren, Roselyne, 214n4
Kritzman, Lawrence, 159, 223n4
Kselman, Thomas, 208n23

Lacorne, Denis, 223n3
Lacoste-Veysseyre, Claudine, 212n28
Lacretelle, Pierre-Louis, 19–22, 24, 26, 35, 202n9
laïcité: banning of the veil and, 168–69, 170–71, 190–91, 194; changing meanings of, 172, 190; Combes Law and, 11, 115–17; versus *communautarisme*, 163, 170, 171; equal treatment of France's religions and, 52–53, 93–94; erasure of difference and, 3, 4, 10, 168–69, 197n9; freedom from Catholic Church, 10; freedom of and from religion and, 190, 193; hard-line form of, 96, 200n35; hostility to minority difference and, 96, 171; Islamist opposition to, 190; as juridical concept, 11; Muslims and, 162–63, 180, 186-87, 190; national identity and, 170; new versus historical, 11, 200n39; pluralist universalism and, 187; supersessionism and, 182; tolerance and, 200n31; universal value of, 168; violations of, 224n23
Lang, Fritz, 122
Lanzmann, Claude, 139, 157, 161, 174, 193
Lassner, Phyllis, 218n5
Lavater, Johann Kaspar, 25
Lavaud, Martine, 62
Lazare, Bernard, 109, 114, 215n26, 219n9
League for the Rights of Man, 152, 220n32
Le Chapelier, Isaac-René-Guy, 43
Leff, Lisa Moses: 35, 48, 93, 204n30, 211n4, 213nn51–52, 206n71
Le Pen, Jean-Marie, 158, 221n46
Le Pen, Marine, 2, 197n9
Lerner, L. Scott, 202n5, 202–3n15, 202n5, 203n23, 207n5, 210n61
Leroux, Pierre, 99
Levinas, Emmanuel: Derrida on, 222n54; difficult universal and, 185, 226n56; Jewish identity and, 159; Judaism as antidote to Nazism and, 225n36; on Sartre's approach to antisemitism, 140, 147, 219n6
Lévi-Strauss, Claude, 200n46
Lévy, Benny, 148, 157–58, 220n28, 225n44
Lévy, Bernard-Henri, 174
Lévy, Georges, 101
liberalism, 140–41, 154, 156–57, 193, 201n49, 211n2
liberty, 30, 35, 179
Lipstadt, Deborah, 226n2, 227n10
Lisle, Claude Joseph Rouget de, 69
Louis-Philippe, 52, 73
Louis XIV, 69
Lovenjoul, Charles, 212nn27–28, 213n40

INDEX   237

Lyonnet, Henry, 208n22
Lyotard, Jean-François, 166

Magnan, Henry, 120
Malesherbes, Guillaume-Chrétien de Lamoignon de, 204n32
Malino, Frances, 29, 203n23
Malinovich, Nadia, 199n26
Mandel, Maud S., 223n7
Mann, Thomas, 225n36
Maoism, 185
Marcellin, Émile, 210n55
Marcus, Laura, 198n18, 202n5
Marrus, Michael, 219n12
Martineau, Louis-Simon, 43–44
Marty, Éric, 173, 174, 180–84, 225nn49–50
Marx, Karl, and Marxism: Alain Badiou and, 179; anticapitalism and, 13; antisemitism and, 155; easy universalism and, 185; the "Jewish Question" and, 98; supersessionism and, 181; as universal Jew, 177; Young Hegelians and, 98
Matras, Christian, 129
Maulnier, Thierry, 142
Maurice, Charles, 55–58, 62–63, 68–69, 72, 208n27
Maurras, Charles, 140, 142, 145–46, 152–53, 221n45
Maury (Abbé), 41
Maury, Jean-Sifrein, 205n57
Mavidal, M. J., 205n56
McDonald, Christie, 214n5
Meige, Henri, 217n35
Memmi, Albert, 159–60, 161, 222n57
Mendelsohn, Ezra, 212n19
Mendelssohn, Moses, 21–22, 23, 202n14
mercantilism, 19, 22, 29, 40, 202n8
methodology, 14–16
Meyerbeer, Giacomo, 53, 54, 209n38
Michman, Dan, 214n4
Millker, Christopher L., 211n8
Milner, Jean-Claude, 173, 174, 184–85, 226n54
Mirabeau, Honoré-Gabriel de Riqueti, comte de, 23, 24, 38, 202–3n15
Misrahi, Robert, 139, 157
Mitterand, François, 227n13
Mitterand, Henri, 214n6
Modiano, Patrick, 160, 161, 222nn60–61
Moine, Raphaëlle, 216n24
moneylending: Affair of the False Receipts and, 21, 41; Christians leaving Jews no other choice and, 20, 26, 35–36, 41, 104, 150–51; civil versus religious law and, 47; decree of 1808 and, 29; economic vices and, 20–21, 25–26, 28–29, 31–36, 41; Émile Zola and, 95, 96–105, 108–11, 114, 214n14; fears of Jewish financial takeover and, 60-61; in *La grand illusion* (film), 123–26, 129, 136, 137, 217n42; literature depicting, 62; meaning of *le juif* and, 208n30; restrictions on, 29, 33, 41–42, 206n76; Sartre's portrait of the Jew and, 149–51; Union Générale Bank scandal and, 100–101; Young Hegelians and, 98
Morihien, Paul, 218n2
Morin, Edgar, 157
Moyn, Samuel, 220n32
multiculturalism, 157, 163, 165, 223n3, 223n9
Muslims and Islam: in Algeria, 75–78, 80–82, 83, 86–91, 194; antisemitism and, 162, 165–66, 170, 173–76, 187, 197n2, 200n35; banning of the veil and, 4, 10, 168–71, 179–80, 190–91, 193–94, 200n31, 224n23; civil law versus religious law and, 88–89; *communautarisme* and, 163, 172; dhimmis and, 74; divorce and polygamy and, 73, 76, 80, 89, 92; in *La juive de Constantine* (Gautier and Parfait), 82–91; *laïcité* and, 11, 116, 162–63, 190; Muslim women's confinement and, 80, 89–90; population of, 197n2, 213n44; radical Islamism, 166; terrorism and, 164, 192; Valls and, 194; violations of French secularism and, 224n23

Napoleon: Assembly of Jewish Notables and, 47, 48, 92; civil law versus religious law and, 40; Grand Sanhedrin and, 47, 92–93, 206n74, 206n78; Infamous Decree of 1808, 206n76; intermarriage and, 48, 112; Jewish consistories and, 47–48; Napoleonic code and, 46–47; neoclassicism and, 210n59; restrictions on moneylending and, 29; rights for blacks and, 75
Nathan-Treilhet, Mme, 53
National Front party, 2
nation and nationalism: debate over Jews during Revolution and, 38, 39–40; defined by blood and soil, 96, 99, 117, 124–26, 142, 145–46, 169–70; defined by ideology not blood, 37–39, 45, 68, 146, 169–70; definition of nation and, 45, 205n49; equal application of laws and, 38; Jewish forms of, 167; Jews as nation within a nation and, 46; universalism and, 179, 183–84, 205n55. *See also* Zionism
Nazism: analogy of Jews to Nazis, 176, 188; final solution of, 142; *La grande illusion* (film) and, 118; image of Marcel Dalio and, 138; Judaism as antidote to, 225n36; metaphors of antisemitism and, 72; republican universalism and, 184; Vichy state and, 178–79; the word *Jew* and, 225n37; yellow star and, 222n60
Netanyahu, Benjamin, 2
Nirenberg, David, 13, 30, 203–4n29, 226n51
Nochlin, Linda, 129
Noiriel, Gérard, 197n2
Nord, Philip, 215n22
Nougayrède, Natalie, 226n1

oikophobia, 169
On the Riviera (film), 216n20

Ophuls, Max, 122
Ottoman Empire, 74–75
Ozouf, Mona, 11

Pagès, Alain, 214n4
Palestine and Palestinians, 167, 173–74, 183
Parfait, Noël, 82–83, 212n27
Parinet, Elisabeth, 214n13
Parlement of Metz, 204n32
Pasta, Giuditta, 53, 207–8n16
Paul (Saint): Alain Badiou's universalism and, 167, 176–83, 225n44; anti-Judaism and, 224n18; easy versus difficult universalism and, 184; election and salvation and, 182–83; Judaism's role in Christian theology and, 13, 48; supersessionism and, 184, 226n51
Paxton, Robert O., 142
Péguy, Charles, 109, 215n26, 219n9
Pépé le Moko (film), 122
Péreire, Émile, 52, 207n10
Péreire, Isaac, 52, 207n10
Pétainism, 184
Petit, Philippe, 226n54
philosemitism: Alain Badiou and, 180; anti-semitism and, 7; Émile Zola and, 95–96, 107–9, 113; *La grande illusion* (film) and, 120; *La juive de Constantine* (Gautier and Parfait) and, 84–86; late-twentieth-century cultural philosemitism and, 161; mercantilist, 29; Rachel Félix and, 63–65, 66–67, 72; in speech versus policies, 195; in theater, 51; without Jews, 113
Piette, Christine, 207n9, 211n7
Pinkevitch, Albert, 216n12
Pinto, Isaac de, 20, 202n8
Pissarro, Camille, 129
Pithon, Rémy, 121–23, 137, 216n19, 217n40
pluralism: in Anglo-American context, 3, 6; antipluralist universalism and, 96, 223n12; versus French republican model of citizenship, 10; pluralist model of universalism and, 68, 169; Rachel Félix and, 63–68. *See also* assimilationist-pluralist continuum
Poliakov, Léon, 208n26, 214n9, 214n12
Popular Front party, 117, 120
Portalis, Jean-Étienne-Marie, 48
postcolonialism. *See* decolonization
postmodernism, 11, 178, 223n9
Proudhon, Pierre-Joseph, 99

Rachel (Jewish actress). *See* Félix, Rachel
Racine, Jean: *Bérénice* (play) by, 207n6; *Esther* (play) by, 50–51, 54–55, 57–59, 64, 69, 207n3, 207n7; *Phèdre* (play) by, 60–61; Rachel Félix as incarnation of, 71; Rachel Félix's particular talent and, 64–68; republican ideal and, 69; in tears, 63, 69, 72

Ramadan, Tariq, 224n29
Rancière, Jacques, 188, 226n5
Rapport, Michael, 197n6, 205n55
Raynaud, Philippe, 225n44
Rebatet, Luicen, 142
Réflexions sur la question juive (Sartre): anti-antisemitism and, 144–47, 219n6; antisemitism in, 140–41, 149–50; changes in French intellectual landscape and, 157; context of writing of, 143; inauthentic and authentic Jews and, 144, 151, 155–56, 221n36; the "Jewish Question" and, 147–48; Jews as individuals and members of a group and, 153; portrait of the antisemite in, 144–47, 220n25; portrait of the Jew in, 147–52, 159, 220n26; portrait of the "democrat" in, 152–56; publication history of, 218n2; reactions of first Jewish readers of, 139–40, 218n3; roots of antisemitism in French philosophy and, 218n5; Sartre's influence and, 221n42; Sartre's targets in, 142; universalism and, 144, 150–52, 154–56, 161, 221n38
regeneration: Algerian Jews and, 74, 77–82; assimilation and, 20–22, 26–29, 33, 41–42, 80, 201n1, 202n8; of decreasing importance to Abbé Grégoire, 32; forced, 24; Jews as incapable of, 41; Jews as test case for powers of, 39–40; of Jews versus Christians, 28; pre-Revolution approach to including Jews and, 30, 39–40; religious versus secular, 20, 202n9; to reverse degeneration, 67; as side effect of versus prerequisite for equality, 34; as test case for Enlightenment principles, 29–30; universalism and, 39, 96, 134, 203n19; as unnecessary, 28, 39–41, 45–46, 130, 134
Regnault de Saint-Jean D'Angély, Michel, 44, 205n65
Reign of Terror (1793–1794), 198n13
Reinharz, Jehuda, 205n53
religion: communalism and, 4, 198n12; freedom of versus freedom from, 3, 171, 190, 193; official state religions and, 52–53; prohibitions against religious dress and, 4, 168–71, 179–80, 190–91, 194, 198n10, 224n23, 227n9; relegated to private sphere, 47; religious liberty and, 35; as threat to imperial authority, 47. *See also* Catholics and Catholicism; Christians and Christianity; Jews and Judaism; Muslims and Islam; separation of churches and state
Renan, Ernest, 99
Renoir, Jean: antisemitism and, 121, 138, 217n41; the "Jewish Question" and, 118; Jewish refugees in cinema and, 216n19; as leftist director, 118; philosemitism of, 120; Popular Front and, 120; *La règle du jeu* by, 126–27, 138; scenes of eating in films of, 216n24; universalism and, 130, 134, 137, 193; vertical versus horizontal divisions

among people and, 121, 131–32. See also *Grand illusion, La* (film)
republicanism: antifascism and, 137; antisemitism as threat to, 95, 194; colonialism and, 73; Jacobins and, 198n14; the "Jewish Question" and, 115; neorepublicanism and, 165–72, 179; right of difference and, 10; secularism versus liberal secularism and, 171; subversion of, 172; terrorist attacks and, 190; universalism as underlying ideology of, 2, 3, 197n5, 197n8; values of, 69, 171, 172. See also republican universalism
republican universalism: Alain Badiou and, 178–79, 184; Alain Finkielkraut and, 168–72; allowing for minority difference, 186, 199n26; Émile Zola and, 108, 115, 116, 139, 140, 156; decline of, 161, 162, 169; hypocrisy of, 9, 179; Julien Benda and, 117; requiring assimilation, 40, 96, 144, 154, 159; Sartre and, 140, 144, 154, 156, 161; as solution to France's minority problem, 162, 168, 189, 194, 197n8. See also *laïcité*; universalism
Revolution of 1848, 69, 71, 75
Rewbell, Jean-François, 43, 44, 205n64
right to difference: French republic imperiled by, 10; versus hard-line universalism, 187; limits of, 194; as watchword of the 1990s, 162
Riqueti, Honoré-Gabriel de. *See* Mirabeau, Honoré-Gabriel de Riqueti, comte de
Robespierre, Maximilien: acceptance of Jewish difference and, 18, 41, 42, 67; assimilationist universalism and, 154; dissolution of Jews as a people and, 112; equality before the law and, 34; Jacobins and, 198n13; Jews as citizens and, 37; universal rights versus exclusionary nationalism and, 205n55
Robinson, Edward G., 54
Rodrigue, Aron, 77, 211–12n15, 212n23
Rollmer, Frank, 216n12
Romanticism, 60, 62, 65, 68–69
Rose, Jacqueline, 226n53
Rosenfeld, Alovin, 224n14
Rothschild, James de, 52, 100–101, 109
Rothschild family, 98–99, 110
Rousso, Henry, 142
rue Copernic bombing, 191, 222n56
Rybalka, Michel, 218n2

Saada, Emmanuelle, 76, 199n27, 201n1, 201n50
Sabrina (film), 216n20
Saint-Domingue, 200n47
Samuels, Maurice, 205n54, 213n35, 213n38, 215n1, 219n17, 220n26
Sartre, Jean-Paul: actions of during World War II, 142–43, 220n18; affirmation of difference and, 157, 161; anti-antisemitism and, 7, 144; antisemitism and, 155, 221n35; assimilation and, 140–41, 156, 221n40; concrete liberalism and,

140–41, 154, 156, 157, 193; Émile Zola and, 156; erasure of Jewish difference and, 156, 187, 193; *L'être et le néant* (Being and Nothingness) by, 147, 220n25; family of, 222n59; general philosophy of, 219n6; homegrown French fascism and, 142; influence of, 159–61, 221n42; Jewish messianic tradition and, 148, 158, 220n28; the "Jewish Question" and, 143, 144, 147, 153–54, 155–56; Jewish readers' gratitude to, 139, 143, 157; Jews as individuals and members of a group and, 162; negative view of Jewishness and, 157–58; right to difference and, 158–59; rootless Jew and, 219n9; Six-Day War and, 159; source of identity and, 152–53; universalism and, 140, 144, 147, 180, 221n38. See also *Réflexions sur la question juive* (Sartre)
Savy, Nicole, 213n48
Schechter, Ronald, 13, 18, 29–30, 45, 200n46, 203–4n29
Schnapper, Dominique, 205n49
Schor, Naomi, 156, 193, 197n7
Schreier, Joshua, 76, 78, 81, 87–90, 92, 212n21
Schwartz, Vanessa, 218n49
Schwarzfuchs, Simon, 206n73, 206n78
Schweitzer, Albert, 222n59
Scott, Joan Wallach, 9, 170–71, 198n14, 199n28, 200n32
Scott, Walter, 84
Scribe, Eugène, 90, 212n32
Scruton, Roger, 169
Segré, Ivan, 176, 225n40
separation of churches and state, 11, 36, 52–53, 96, 116–17, 204n41. See also Combes Law
Sepinwall, Alyssa Goldstein, 20, 25–26, 201n49, 202n9, 203n19, 203n20
Serceau, Daniel, 136, 217n42
Sesonske, Alexander, 216n12
Shakespeare, William, 85, 98, 212n32
Shepard, Todd, 210–11n1
Shoah. *See* Holocaust
Shoah (film), 161, 193
Shohat, Ella, 224n22
Shurkin, Michael, 211n2
Silverman, Max, 218n5, 221n36, 221n38
slavery, 75–76, 200n47, 201n2, 201n49
Sloschtsch, Nahum, 215n29
socialism, 99, 155–56
Sorkin, David, 36
Spaak, Charles, 216n16
Spinoza, Baruch, 177
Stam, Robert, 224n22
Stavisky Scandal, 122
Stein, Sarah, 82
Stern, Kenneth, 207–8n16
Sternhell, Zeev, 214n2, 219n15, 220n24
Strauss-Kahn affair, 171

Sturken, Marita, 218n48
Sue, Eugène, 207n15
Suleiman, Susan, 140, 149, 150, 220n29
Surkis, Judith, 211n13
Swetschinski, Daniel, 205n53

Taguieff, Pierre-André, 174, 223n2
Talmud, 23, 26, 28
terrorism: immigration and, 164; new antisemitism and, 164; responses to, 164–65, 186, 188–95; shootings at Jewish school in Toulouse and, 164, 192. *See also Charlie Hebdo* attack; Hypercacher supermarket attack; rue Copernic bombing
theater: Jews in, 51, 53, 57–59, 60–63, 207–8n16; representations of Jews in, 85. *See also* Félix, Rachel; *and specific playwrights and plays*
Thiéry, Claude-Antoine, 24–25, 27–28, 203n22
Third Republic, 95
Toussenel, Alphonse, 98–99, 104, 179
Trarieux, Ludovic, 220n32
Traverso, Enzo, 166, 226n53
Trigano, Shmuel, 7, 179, 201–2n4, 222n56, 224n23
Trubowitz, Lara, 218n5
Truffaut, François, 216n11, 216n17

Union Générale Bank scandal, 100–101, 214n15
United States, 10–11, 30–31, 37, 174–75, 225n34, 225n40
universalism: 1775 lawsuit of the Jews of Metz and, 19–22; Alain Badiou and, 163, 165, 172–85; Alain Finkielkraut, 10, 163, 165, 167–72; Algerian colonization and, 73–74, 76, 80–83, 87, 92, 94; American, 3, 10–11; antiuniversalism, 118, 124, 137, 156, 171; anti-Zionism and, 167; assimilation and, 4, 7–9, 19, 40, 63, 74, 80, 83, 92, 94, 96, 105, 114, 118, 148, 151–52, 155, 162, 187; benefits of, 4, 6, capitalism and, 179; Catholic, 2–3; challenges to, 2, 4, 162; civilizing mission and, 76, 91; definition of, 2; Dreyfus Affair and, 95–96, 154; easy versus difficult, 185; Émile Zola and, 96–97, 105–8, 113–16, 156; Frenchness of, 167, 168; *La grande illusion* (film) and, 118, 124, 130, 134, 137; historicizing, 5–6; intellectuals and, 118; Jew as symbol of, 13–14, 68–9, 71; Jewish emancipation and, 31, 34, 40–42; Judaism as universalist religion and, 48, 93–94, 182–84; *laïcité* and, 3–4, 11, 96, 115–16, 170, 171, 172, 187, 190; language and, 193; Marxism and, 156, 163, 193; Napoleon and, 47–49, 92; philosophical, 179; pluralist form of, 9–10, 41, 67–68, 72, 74, 94, 118, 121, 130, 134, 137, 140, 154, 172, 193–95; political equality and, 2–3, 7, 67, 95, 117, 162; Rachel Félix and, 62, 63, 68; racism and, 9; Saint Paul and, 167, 177–79, 181; Sartre and, 139–40, 152–54, 161–62. *See also* republican universalism; universal versus particular

universal versus particular: Algeria and, 80, 94; Christianity versus Judaism and, 167, 179, 181; Combes Law and, 116; French opposition to minority difference (*communautarisme*) and, 3–4, 5–6, 162, 171–72, 186–87, 191; French Revolution and, 40, 51; *La grande illusion* (film) and, 130, 133–34; Jewish difference and, 14, 18, 175, 183–84; Napoleon and, 48; theater and, 57, 63–68, 72; welcoming difference and, 72, 193–94, 195. *See also communautarisme*; republican universalism; universalism

Valabrègue, Bernard de, 20
Valls, Manuel, 189–95, 227n8, 227n13
Veil, Simone, 157
Vichy period: anti-Jewish legislation and, 141; cultural relativism and, 169; French universalism and, 178–79; League for the Rights of Man and, 152, 220n32; participation in Nazis' final solution and, 142; revenge of the anti-Dreyfusards during, 115; Vichy Syndrome and, 142
Vidal-Naquet, Pierre, 218n3
Voltaire, 202n8
voting rights, 201n48

Wagner, Richard, 60
Wallerstein, Immanuel, 199n29
Washington, George, 34, 204n39
Watts, Philip, 219n11
Weil, Patrick, 76, 197n8, 198n12, 209n47, 223n1
Weill, Michel-Aaron, 212n19
Weill, Nicolas, 171, 200n35
Wellington, Arthur Wellesley, Duke of, 208n24
Wiesel, Elie, 225n36
Wieviorka, Michel, 164, 221–22nn47–48
Wilder, Gary, 199–200n30, 210–11n1
Wilson (film), 216n20
Wilson, Nelly, 215nn28–29
Winter, Cécile, 175, 176, 225n39, 225n41
Winter, Jay, 220n32
Wistrich, Robert, 214n7
Wolitz, Seth L., 218n5, 221n42, 222n58
women: divorce and polygamy and, 89; excluded from citizenship, 38, 76; French male behavior toward, 169; Jewish versus Muslim attitudes toward, 89–90; right to vote for, 201n48; as unassimilable, 14, 33, 201n49; veil and, 168–71, 179–80, 190–91, 194, 224n23, 227n9
World War II, 141, 142, 143, 188. *See also* Holocaust
Wurmser, André, 214n15

Yerushalmi, Yosef, 220n26
Young Hegelians, 98

Zanuck, Darryl, 216n20
Zard, Philippe, 225n36, 225n37
Zionism: anti-Zionism and, 166–68, 172–73, 174–75, 181–82; Dreyfus Affair and, 215n27, 226n53; Émile Zola and, 114; foundations of, 114; inspiration for, 215n27; Jewish nomadism versus, 167; Judeophobia and, 223n2; origins of, 183. *See also* Israel
Zipperstein, Steven J., 201n2, 204n44
Zola, Émile: antisemitism and, 7, 95–96, 101–4, 107–9, 111–12, 115, 156, 215n25; *L'argent* by, 95–103, 107–12, 114, 214n5, 214–15nn15–16; assimilationist universalism and, 118, 137, 139–40, 151–52, 154; Combes Law and, 116; death of, 106; dissolution of Jews as a people and, 96, 103, 112–16, 134, 154; Édouard Drumont's *La France Juive* and, 99–100, 214n14; as hero of Dreyfus Affair, 95, 96, 103, 106, 115; influences on, 98; intermarriage and, 48; "J'accuse" by, 103, 106, 219n8; the "Jewish Question" and, 96, 97–98, 105, 114–16; libel trial and conviction of, 106; philosemitism and, 95–96, 107, 108, 109, 113; "Pour les juifs" by, 103, 104–5, 108, 111–15; republican universalism and, 143–44, 183; Rougon-Macquart series of, 215n16; Sartre and, 156; universalist utopia of, 147–48; *Vérité* by, 96, 106–15, 147–48, 154, 156; Zionism and, 114

www.ingramcontent.com/pod-product-compliance
Lightning Source LLC
Chambersburg PA
CBHW021941290426

44108CB00012B/925